THE NEW CATHEDRALS

Sports and Entertainment
Steven A. Riess, *Series Editor*

Other titles in Sports and Entertainment

Anything for a T-Shirt: Fred Lebow and the New York City Marathon, the World's Greatest Footrace
Ron Rubin

Black Baseball Entrepreneurs, 1860–1901: Operating by Any Means Necessary
Michael E. Lomax

Blacks at the Net: Black Achievement in the History of Tennis, Vol. 1.
Sundiata Djata

Catching Dreams: My Life in the Negro Baseball Leagues
Frazier Robinson with Paul Bauer

Diamond Mines: Baseball and Labor
Paul D. Staudohar, ed.

Glory Bound: Black Athletes in a White America
David K. Wiggins

Muscle and Manliness: The Rise of Sport in American Boarding Schools
Axel Bundgaard

Playing Nice and Losing: The Struggle for Control of Women's Intercollegiate Athletics, 1960–2000
Ying Wushanley

Running with Pheidippides: Stylianos Kyriakides, The Miracle Marathoner
Nick Tsiotos and Andy Dabilis

Sports and the American Jew
Steven A. Riess, ed.

THE NEW CATHEDRALS

Politics and Media in the History of Stadium Construction

ROBERT C. TRUMPBOUR

Syracuse University Press

Syracuse, New York, 13244-5160

First Edition 2007
07 08 09 10 11 12 6 5 4 3 2 1

The paper used in this publication meets the minimum requirements of American National Standard for Information Sciences—Permanence of Paper for Printed Library Materials, ANSI Z39.48–1984.∞™

For a listing of books published and distributed by Syracuse University Press, visit our Web site at SyracuseUniversityPress.syr.edu.

ISBN-13: 978-0-8156-3132-3
ISBN-10: 0-8156-3132-4

Library of Congress Cataloging-in-Publication Data

Trumpbour, Robert C.
The new cathedrals : politics and media in the history of stadium construction / Robert C. Trumpbour.—1st ed.
p. cm.
Includes bibliographical references and index.
ISBN 0–8156–3132–4 (cloth : alk. paper)
1. Stadiums—Design and construction. I. Title.
GV413.T78 2006
725'.8043—dc22 2006027531

Manufactured in the United States of America

CONTENTS

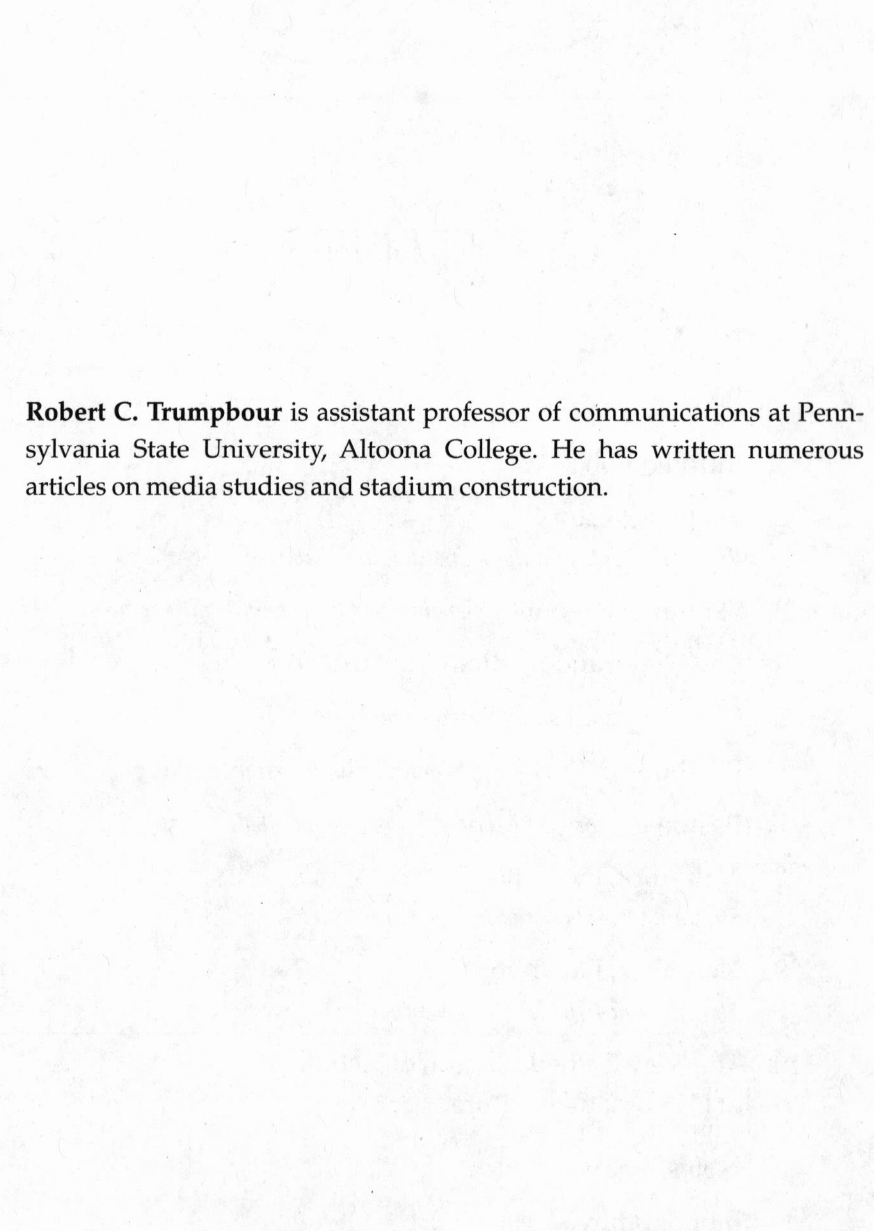

Robert C. Trumpbour is assistant professor of communications at Pennsylvania State University, Altoona College. He has written numerous articles on media studies and stadium construction.

PREFACE

STADIUM CONSTRUCTION has moved forward at an unprecedented rate in the United States in the past 20 years. Some would classify it as an epidemic. Virtually every major American city has either replaced a sports facility or has contemplated taking such action. Even smaller cities have jumped into the game, building or renovating minor league ballparks, college arenas, or high school stadiums. Many grade school and Little League facilities have become more lavish, with door-to-door fund-raisers, higher tuition, and enhancement of taxpayer subsidies making these athletic projects possible. This construction is taking place as economic uncertainties face education, health care, and other segments of society.

This text is an effort to examine the issue from a broad cultural perspective. The goal is to offer a longitudinal overview of the issue to better understand why sports stadiums are a priority for communities throughout the nation. Isolating a single cause would be unwise because so many issues come into play. But economic imperatives, the desire for media attention, and perceived community status are all forces that compel cities to consider stadium construction even when local schools, for example, may be struggling for resources.

The decision-making process for stadium policy varies widely. In some communities a voter referendum provides the mechanism for construction or rejection of construction. In other communities, funding decisions are made by elected bodies or nonelected committees. Some decisions are made through a combined referendum-legislative process that is a difficult-to-explain hybrid of policy outcomes. Because of this challenge, the case study has been employed. Roger Wimmer and Joseph Dominick assert that a key advantage of the case study is the "ability to deal with a wide spectrum of evidence."[1] The complex nature of political maneuvering during stadium-related negotiations cannot be captured in a highly structured research design that puts a premium on statistical rigor. Charles Ragin argues that "flexibility, a hallmark of the case-oriented approach, enriches the dialogue between ideas and evidence."[2]

Many scholars have examined the issue from an economic perspective. Others have examined the stadium by focusing on the city, applying urban scholarship. Some have written about the stadium in a celebratory fashion, looking nostalgically at old facilities, many of which are no longer in use, or providing a largely positive analysis of recently constructed venues. Fewer researchers have closely examined media coverage and the politics of stadium construction.

Because the major league sports stadium serves as today's model for communities, it is the central focus in this effort. However, I offer some focus on ancient and past models from ancient Greece to college football construction. This is so that the recent past, the present, and the future can be better understood as a part of a larger progression of human history. Ideally, such analysis will help to contextualize the current policy landscape with construction in previous generations.

I examine political institutions, sports franchises, and media coverage because these three are among the most important factors in determining the outcome of the stadium issue. The complexity of this issue requires more than a single research strategy. The stadium debate intersects with cultural studies, economics, law, urban studies, civic planning, sports administration, mass communications, and sociology. As a result, this project will be interdisciplinary in scope. I have been influenced by James Carey, Jane Jacobs, C. Wright Mills, Lewis Mumford, Robert Park, and Steven Riess. My focus has been sharpened by authors whose stadium research has preceded mine. As such, I am indebted to Joanna Cagan, Michael Danielson, Kevin Delaney, Neil deMause, Rick Eckstein, Rodney Fort, Philip Lowry, Roger Noll, James Quirk, Mark Rosentraub, Richard Sheehan, Neil Sullivan, and Andrew Zimbalist, among others.

The first chapter offers a general introduction to stadium construction as part of the larger framework of the American urban landscape. The second chapter examines the history of stadium construction on a broad scale, looking at the development of these structures from ancient civilizations to the emergence of capitalism, team sports, and present-day construction. Taxpayer subsidy of stadium construction is a recent phenomenon, and the urban "growth model" is one ideology that has been used to justify construction. Although recent economic scholarship overwhelmingly refutes the growth potential of such construction, the linkage of stadium construction to the growth model persists. This occurs, in large part, because public relations efforts often tout projected benefits as part of highly partisan sponsor-funded feasibility studies.

In this vein, the third chapter focuses on economic arguments because such arguments are often employed to justify starting such projects. This chapter attempts to explain complex arguments in a manner that renders it useful to those without economic or stadium-related expertise.

The fourth chapter explores the role of media. Practitioners and stadium researchers make conflicting claims about the fairness of stadium coverage. Former *Pittsburgh Post-Gazette* editor John Craig argues that despite adopting an editorial position that supported stadium construction, "We did not compromise one inch on fair news coverage and gave equal prominence in our reporting to people on the other side of the argument."[3] I try to evaluate whether media institutions achieve their frequent pledges of fair and balanced coverage.

Subsequent chapters contain case studies on selected cities. Any reader familiar with the stadium issue should be able to recognize patterns and tendencies that are consistent across other regions not covered in this analysis. Pittsburgh and Cincinnati anchor the examination of smaller market major league cities, and Boston and New York are larger market examples. Specific attention is given to other regions to avoid an exclusively northeastern focus.

The final chapter closes with a broad overview of the stadium issue and an examination of how this issue has shifted over time. The present-day actions of media practitioners, political leaders, and the broad public are connected to potential future policy directions.

A project this extensive could not have been completed without the support of many individuals. First, I would like to thank my wife, Jill, for her steadfast support and love. I am thankful to all in the Trumpbour and Zary families. Their patience with me as deadlines approached was often saintlike. My two sons, Luke and David, provided many infectious smiles that offered inspiration to complete the project. My parents, Robert Trumpbour Sr. and Virginia Droesch Trumpbour, and my eleven brothers and sisters all helped in some way. My brother, Jack, was particularly generous with his time. My mother and father-in-law, Gene and Audrey Zary, provided support that often went above and beyond the call of duty. Gene unfortunately passed away before the project was finished. I am grateful for the inspiration of my niece, Mary, and my friends Bruce Barlow and Kurt Knee. They may be in a better place now, but their brief lives on earth continue to inspire me.

I am extremely thankful for the help of Steven Riess. His work with the many professionals at Syracuse University Press, particularly Ellen Goodman, has been appreciated every step of the way. I am deeply appreciative of the editing suggestions and outstanding support offered by Julie DuSablon, and I am thankful for behind-the-scenes efforts from Lynn Hoppel, Lisa Kuerbis, Kay Steinmetz, and Therese Walsh as the project neared completion. I am also indebted to friends and colleagues who have patiently tolerated my lack of availability as I assembled this project. Special thanks also to Richard Barton, Bruce Berenson, Bob Bluthardt, Suzanna DeBoef, Mark Dyreson, Gerald Gems, Kevin Grace, Rodrigue Labrie, Michael Lomax, Patrick Parsons, Beth Robinson, Neil Rudel, Subir Sengupta, Helen Sheehy, Ronald Smith, Susan Smith, Mila Su, Rick Trimble, and Larry White as well as countless others at Pennsylvania State University, Saint Francis University, Southern Illinois University, Western Illinois University, and Manasquan High School. The Cincinnati Public Library, the University of Cincinnati Library system, the Carnegie Library in Pittsburgh, the University of Pittsburgh's Hillman Library, the Boston Public Library, and the New York Public Library also helped to make this a better project, as did colleagues in the Association for Education in Journalism and Mass Communication, the North American Society for Sport History, and the Society for American Baseball Research.

I am also indebted to the Harvard Law School and their Labor and Worklife Program for inviting me to present my research as the manuscript was nearing completion. Thanks are also in order for the many residents of the cities I visited. I cannot thank you enough for opening up to my inquiries. The warmth and hospitality that I encountered were deeply appreciated. Each of the places that I examined has unique strengths, but none seem more important than the commitment of so many enthusiastic citizens to the vitality of their proud cities.

The current cycle of professional stadium building may be coming to a close soon because only a few teams have failed to complete new stadium deals, but a call to build a new generation of sports facilities will begin in a few years, possibly when some innovative individual concocts an idea that changes the power structure in stadium construction policy. When this happens, I hope the involved communities consider a full range of budgetary priorities before committing significant funding to a new stadium and that political leaders, media practitioners, and team officials act with courage. The emergence of professional team sports is a relatively recent development when compared to many other institutions that are part of our civilization. With this in mind, there are no assurances that communities will continue to look at professional sports as a symbolic indication that a city has achieved "major league" status.

THE NEW CATHEDRALS

1

INTRODUCTION

FROM THE MIDDLE AGES to the advent of the Industrial Revolution, many great cities of Europe were best known for their ornate and inspiring cathedrals. By the nineteenth century, American cities worked to build a more modern identity through construction of luxuriously appointed railroad stations. As the twentieth century unfolded, urban pride took a more blatantly commercial direction with the skyscraper serving as a tangible display of urban progress. As architects mastered construction techniques, the pervasiveness of these grand structures seemed to diminish a single building's capacity to serve as a defining landmark for a given community.

Instead, these tall buildings served as part of a larger skyline that seemed similar from city to city. Most of these grand buildings were intended for commerce; hence, their doors were largely closed to the general public. For a brief period, the shopping mall, a decidedly suburban concept, may have captured the imagination of some citizens, but the ubiquitous nature of mall architecture and its transparent commercial goals have dimmed its luster in the eyes of many.

As the twenty-first century unfolds, many cities struggle to maintain a unique identity that might capture the imagination of its citizenry and those beyond. Construction of one new building may help to improve the overall image of a community, but only in a small, incremental way unless the facility somehow becomes a recognizable symbol of community pride. Public officials struggle to encourage major development of urban infrastructure through tax abatements for corporate construction and direct funding for other building projects.

Subsidized airports and convention centers have served as a gateway for commerce and tourism, but these projects do not seem to have the same inspiring power once held by the beautiful cathedral, the ornate train station, or the huge skyscraper proudly built in years past. A number of civic leaders have turned to stadium construction as a visible way to enhance their city's image. Central to this visibility is the enthusiasm of media institutions regarding coverage of professional sports. Such enthusiasm, made apparent through multibillion-dollar broadcast agreements, provides potentially positive national exposure to a community that might otherwise be overlooked or covered in a negative manner in typical news reporting.[1]

In recent years, the stadium has supplanted the ancient cathedral as the most visible and recognizable structure in many communities. More Americans are likely to readily identify Yankee Stadium than nearby St. Patrick's Cathedral. Further, local newscasts are more likely to choose the city's stadium as a scenic backdrop for weather updates than a cathedral or a skyscraper. Yet some of this nation's most recognizable sports structures have a limited future. Tiger Stadium and Yankee Stadium, two of America's oldest major league facilities, may be on line for demolition. The former has been replaced by Comerica Park, and the latter is perilously close to being replaced by a new facility to produce greater revenues for the team owner.

Fenway Park's status as a baseball landmark has significantly improved with new team ownership, and Chicago's Wrigley Field remains another historic facility that appears to have a secure future. But all bets are off in other cities. Taxpayer subsidy of new sports facilities has made this reshaping of the sports landscape a hotly contested political issue. Citizens have questioned whether the sports palaces of yesteryear should be replaced. Team owners and civic leaders frequently ignore or marginalize the relevance of such questions.

Civic leaders, at the urging of sports franchise owners, are engaged in a nationwide stadium construction boom unlike any other in American history. In 1976, James Michener suggested that the Age of the Stadium had emerged.[2] Michener was correct in noting that stadium construction in the late 1960s and early 1970s helped to create a sports-oriented identity for a number of cities, but the urban commitment to stadium construction during these decades pales in comparison to the dramatic mobilization of similar resources in American cities in the past twenty years. Furthermore, the current construction boom has expanded beyond the major city. Minor league ballparks, university stadiums, spring training sites, and even youth-oriented ballparks have been upgraded or completely rebuilt in a multitude of small towns in recent years.

To demonstrate how stadium construction has expanded considerably since Michener's assertion, one need look no further than the recent record of construction in professional sports. As the twentieth century was ending, 83 percent of North America's major professional sports franchises (baseball, basketball, football, and hockey) were either playing in new facilities, constructing new facilities, or pushing the public to fund the construction of new facilities. As the century was closing, Fitch IBCA, an international financial rating organization, stated that of the 120 major professional sports franchises in North America "41 teams are playing in the 33 new stadiums or arenas . . . constructed since 1990, [and] 49 are seeking new facilities or have new facilities currently under construction."[3]

The luxurious nature of these new facilities is also a defining characteristic of this new "age of the stadium." At one time, the Louisiana Superdome, opened to the public in 1976, was regarded as the most lavish example of stadium expenditure in the United States. By 1997, economists Roger Noll and Andrew Zimbalist concluded that the Superdome was no longer a unique example of spending extravagance. They report that its cost, "about $163 million, approximately $450 million in today's dollar, . . .[once] stood out as a wild anomaly. Today it would fit nicely in the upper range of the standard experience."[4]

The opening of Seattle's Safeco Field in July 1999 at a cost of $517 million is an example of this new generation of "upper range" stadiums. Despite considerable controversy and $100 million of construction overruns, Washington State Representative Steve Van Luven confidently argued that "baseball, we found out, brings people together in this state. . . . When the legislators put this piece of [stadium] legislation together, they did it for the kids and for the future of baseball in the state of Washington."[5]

Many argue that despite the grandeur of these new palaces, sports has been anything but unifying in recent years. Although the Mariners made early overtures to cover cost overruns, their initial strategy after construction completion was to renege on that commitment.[6] As the team took this path, Van Luven subsequently argued that "the Mariners will lose in the court of public opinion and the court of law." Public outrage and threatened legal action pushed the Mariners to rethink their cost overrun policy. The result was a team agreement to commit $60 million more for the cost of the new ballpark.[7] Since then, Seattle Seahawks owner and billionaire Paul Allen has refused to release his team's financial report, despite agreeing to do so before moving his team into a $430 million stadium. State Treasurer Mike Murphy has stated with embarrassment that Allen "has basically thumbed his nose, or another digit, at us for a long time."[8]

In cities throughout North America, vigorous debates have persisted about whether public subsidy of stadium construction is a prudent expenditure for taxpayers. That debate has been extremely contentious. The rising price of game tickets, the haughtiness of athletes and owners, and the increasing level of spectator stratification that has intensified with the creation of new luxury skyboxes have made modern sports contested terrain. Frank Deford argued that in an earlier era the stadium was a "twentieth century village green where we could all come together in common excitement. . . , but now that the stadiums have become, in effect, incidental attachments to royal suites, it is even more difficult to justify publicly financed stadiums."[9]

Deford's analysis of the village green may reflect sports values frequently trumpeted in post–World War II America, but a tradition of economic segregation can be uncovered in earlier generations as well.[10] Construction of the first enclosed professional ballparks was undertaken, in part, to exclude what was perceived to be unsavory elements of the community. The father of professional baseball, Harry Wright, frequently insisted on higher ticket prices, in one case equating the entertainment value of high-quality baseball to the offerings of an upscale downtown theater.[11] During the Progressive Era, as concrete and steel ballparks emerged, some team owners offered ticket pricing schemes to ensure that the most affluent baseball fans might be rewarded and presumably separated from the riffraff according to seat location.

Steven Riess traces the political and social dimensions of baseball during the first major period of stadium construction in the United States.[12] He exposes the link between political forces and those involved in creation of the physical infrastructure of professional sport in the early years of the twentieth century. Riess argues that Progressive Era stadium construction was politicized in many ways, with graft and political favor evident as a residual by-product. Nevertheless, sport, particularly baseball, was viewed ideologically as something that "stood for fair play, individualism, and community pride."[13]

Riess uncovers the subtle cultural landscape of commercialized sport's early years, offering a point of comparison with today's environment. In the Progressive Era, politicians had much greater control over team owners, often dictating the terms necessary for a franchise to locate within the city limits. His work also explains how today's often accepted ideology of sport as a positive force in community development was formed. These insights are critical to understanding the origins of arguments that shape the current sports landscape. Ronald Smith's examination of collegiate sports in the years predating much of Riess's work serves to illuminate the emergence of a "commercialized, professionalized, and rationalized" system of athletics that has helped to shape the current sports landscape today.[14] Early Ivy League football helped, in many ways, to provide a foundation for the symbolic institutional importance of sport within a community. Many institutions' emulation of the Harvard-Yale sports management model led to a wider acceptance of an ideology that emphasized the somewhat illogical correlation between winning on the field and winning in a significantly broader communal sense.[15]

In the same vein, the athletic achievements of professional sports teams often overshadow the civic accomplishments of America's great cities in national press coverage. Nationally distributed photos and video images of sports teams' parades after winning a championship are one such example. The coverage of these celebrations on CNN and ESPN and in local news outlets throughout the nation can be sharply contrasted to the relative lack of coverage afforded to programs that might successfully combat a particular city's poverty or crime. Political leaders are tempted by the same pressures as college presidents when priorities of athletic subsidy and more traditional institutional expenditures are debated.

At a time when instant communication technologies blur the concepts of time and place, such examinations of how we define and shape our communities are important. Civic leaders throughout the globe fight a difficult daily battle to create an environment that sets their communities apart from other places. These efforts are undertaken to avoid being classified as irrelevant or easily interchangeable with other cities. Ironically, many civic leaders have turned to the same strategy, investment in modern entertainment venues, as a means of creating a civic identity that extends beyond an immediate metropolitan area. This project will examine this strategy. Doing so might benefit future generations. After all, as the luster of new sports facilities begins to wear off, as it surely will, the call for new construction will commence in cities throughout North America and, for that matter, throughout the world.

2

STADIUM HISTORY

Religious Roots and the Transition to Secularism

AS THE CROWD ROARED in anticipation for the opening play of the first regular season game in brand new Gillette Stadium, President George W. Bush stood by to flip a coin that would start the contest. The president's agenda was filled with meetings that focused on national security, the 2002 midterm elections, and a struggling domestic economy. On September 9, 2002, two days before the first anniversary of America's worst terrorist attack, the nation appeared to be on the verge of war with Iraq. Troops were already deployed in Afghanistan in search of Osama bin Laden and other members of the Al-Qaeda terror network. But the president took time from this hectic schedule to offer the 2002 Super Bowl Champion New England Patriots a symbolic imprimatur, helping to christen this sparkling new facility.

Many of the screaming fans may not have known it, but Bush owed much to the sports world. Without professional sports, his ascent to the most powerful position in the world may have ended without success. He gained political experience by assisting his father's campaigns, but it was not until he took an ownership role in the Texas Rangers, a professional baseball club, that his involvement in the political arena began to take on a more personal dimension.

This indirect route to power began with a stadium referendum that required a carefully crafted media campaign to convince the public to provide heavy subsidies for a new ballpark. Failure might have pushed him back into the private sector or substantially limited his political options. His ability to convince Arlington's taxpayers to provide millions of dollars to construct a new ballpark brought him a tidy profit that exceeded $14 million, but more importantly, it gave him statewide credibility that made him a viable candidate for the Texas gubernatorial race. After a surprising defeat of incumbent Texas Governor Ann Richards, Bush emerged as a Republican front-runner for the 2000 presidential election.

After winning a presidential contest that had all the dramatic elements of a major sporting event, Bush confronted an international crisis that unexpectedly pushed him more profoundly into the limelight. In spite of the gravity of these events, he was still seen on C-SPAN promoting youth baseball with the legendary Cal Ripken Jr. Bush also traveled to various cities to visit new ballparks, presumably to demonstrate that, even in this time of crisis, he understood the interests and passions of the typical American. Some of these visits received media attention at a time when the nation struggled to make sense of an international landscape that offered dramatic evidence of virulent hostility to the American way of life.

The terrorist attacks of September 11, 2001, had a profound impact on many institutions in the United States, and sports was among them. Entering a major league sports venue in many cities brought more restrictions for fans. Most stadiums tightened security policies. Some no longer allowed portable coolers or small backpacks, and the working press were now expected to open their satchels and equipment bags for security inspections. Service trucks that were once routinely allowed to park along side a stadium were now carefully monitored and scrutinized before gaining permission to come near the facility.

The security checkpoints at sporting events were necessitated because of an anti-Western ideology that was formulated by a terribly misguided group of religious fanatics. Ironically, the stadium, both as a concept and as a form of architecture, emerged from ancient religious origins in a place not far from the region where this terrorist ideology took shape. As Middle Eastern terrorists were making secret plans in remote international outposts to destroy major landmarks that represented modern capitalism and Western culture, many communities in the United States unveiled strategies to invest heavily in stadium construction. Most of these projects involved large taxpayer subsidies and included great controversy. Stadium construction had become so widespread that almost every major American city was affected by the issue in some manner.

To understand how we have arrived at this current status in stadium construction, it is helpful to trace the history of stadium construction itself.

The stadium in both ancient and modern cultures had humble roots, but over time, facilities in both eras have grown in stature and complexity. The political dynamic associated with sports infrastructure has also shifted dramatically over time, indicating that the past is not necessarily a prelude to future stadium-related policy formation.

Most individuals would correctly regard the stadium as an ancient concept. Closer examination of the stadium's history reveals that its emergence as a commercial entity is a rather recent development. Public funding of stadium construction is even more recent. With less than a handful of exceptions in major league sports, public subsidy of stadium construction on a large scale did not emerge in North America until after World War II.

The significance of myth in sport and literature serves to heighten the importance of sport's ancient heritage. The perpetuation of unsubstantiated myths about major professional sports leads many citizens to believe that the institutions, individuals, and organizations that currently control the sports landscape will remain unchanged in years to come. Stadium history is important because it reveals both the invention of tradition and the stark likelihood of change. The eventual direction of this change, however, is less certain and will be determined largely by the nature of political activism, citizen involvement, and consumer preferences. The history of sports can offer insights and clues as to where future stadium-related policy might move.

Development of the Athletic Facility: Ancient Greece and Rome

Historians cannot speak with unanimity regarding the early origins of the term "stadium," yet most will acknowledge that the original Greek *stadion* was built with reverential and religious intentions. The earliest stadiums contained only enough seats for judges and a few dignitaries, so remaining patrons stood along the embankment of the facility. As such, David Gilman Romano indicates that the origins of the term stadium may be derived from the Greek verb meaning "to stand" and that the term *stadion* literally meant "the standing place." Romano further suggests the origins of the stadium could have evolved as a result of Greek ambassadors visiting Egypt in the sixth century BCE.[1] Religious construction, including temples and stone columns, served as an initial architectural link to the earliest stadium designs. The connections between Egyptian and Greek cultures are echoed by other historians. Oswyn Murray observes that early

Greeks "were enormously impressed by Egypt, its great antiquity, its highly stratified society, its powerful religion and massive monuments."[2]

The literature of epic poet Homer refers to a "running place" or "racetrack" in the ninth century BCE.[3] Evidence of the term *stadion,* the precursor to the modern name *stadium,* does not emerge until the fifth century BCE in the literature of Herodotus, Simonides, Pindar, and Bacchylides. The Greek *stadion* was originally a simple track surface. The *stadion* was built in close proximity to an altar and might contain a grandstand that was built into an earthen embankment. The term *dromos* was used to describe a stadium-like facility with no spectator space. Footraces were among the most common competitions held in these structures, but field events such as javelin, discus, long jump, wrestling, and boxing were also prevalent. Herodotus was the first to describe the term *stadion* as a unit of measurement.[4] A *stadion* was one full length of the track, approximately 600 feet. After this unit of measurement gained acceptance, a race of this length was commonly referred to as a *stadion* or *stade* by fellow Greeks.

Although many of these ancient edifices may have been forever lost because of physical decay or replacement, archeologists have uncovered a number of these ancient facilities. Panathenaic Stadium in Athens, originally built in the second century, was utilized for the 1896 and 2004 Olympics.[5] Evidence unearthed by modern archeologists demonstrates the religious basis of the original Greek *stadion.* One bronze statue from approximately 490 BCE depicts a runner with the words "I belong to Zeus" inscribed on the athlete's right leg.[6]

Roman athletics was a more secular experience. Adapted from the circular shape of the theater rather than the rectangular dimensions of the Greek running track, the coliseum gives testimony to the way Roman sport evolved; a higher priority was ascribed to entertainment and spectatorship. The gratuitous violence and homage paid to high-ranking Roman leaders rather than a deity pushed a visit to the coliseum further into the realm of the secular.

Comparing the Greek and Roman experience, Lewis Mumford argues that in Roman sport "one finds . . . greater concentration of varied activities, a higher degree of formal order, [and] an expansion of the themes already found elsewhere in the Hellenistic town."[7] The secular shift could be seen in decorative accessories in these structures. The Greek statuary, with a focus on mythic gods, were supplanted by a Roman focus on civic leaders. Mechanisms for funding the construction and the events themselves reflected a secular shift in sports.

Funding the "bread and circuses" of Rome was largely a private undertaking. Paul Veyne writes that the great architectural masterpieces of Rome "were built by notables who bore the expenses out of their own pocket. These same men paid for the public spectacles staged each year to the delight of the populace."[8] Before the construction of permanent arenas such as the Roman Coliseum, events took place in hastily constructed wooden structures that appear to have been dismantled after a performance or after a series of performances. The first century is regarded by several historians as a time when construction of "edifices of spectacle" was most profound.[9] A manifestation of a highly competitive political order, the spending of private money on public facilities became a channel for conspicuous consumption that allowed Roman leaders to display their individual power and achievement.

Historians are divided on whether construction of the great Roman Coliseum marked a respect for laboring citizens or a contempt for the lower class. Rudolfo Laciani argues that site selection and construction strategies reflect utter disdain for the Roman worker. The locale was described as "marshy, damp, and unsteady" with "an abundance of local springs."[10] In addition, Vespian's architects planned the project without resorting to the use of machines. Paul Veyne counters that Vespian's construction strategy had a worthwhile civic intent. According to Veyne, the refusal to use machines was "for fear of reducing the lower orders of Rome to famine. . . . The emperor treated much if not all of Rome as though he were its curator or guardian."[11] In short, Veyne believed that construction choices were made to ensure jobs for poor citizens.

Lewis Mumford suggests that the decadence of Rome is ever present in today's urban America, manifested in the violent spectacles of the gridiron. According to Mumford, violent modern-day football contests, with their array of sensory-bombarding, consumption-oriented thrills, are evidence that "though not a stone has yet crumbled, . . .the barbarian has already captured the [American] city from within."[12] Anthropologists in centuries ahead may regard American sport, particularly football and ice hockey, as excessively violent, but the Roman sporting experience, with its intense focus on death, was brutal beyond comparison.[13] Nevertheless, the audience's role in the sporting experience is somewhat similar in Rome as in today's modern stadium. The Roman model of sport marked a shift from a Greek ideal of citizen participation to full acceptance of passive spectatorship.[14]

Rome's secular model of sport and the evolution of stadium construction from temporary wooden facilities to grandiose permanent structures parallels the development of sport in America. Once Roman sport evolved to a perverse festival of consumption, the stratification and ordering of the fan experience was decidedly similar to the seating arrangements accorded the modern American fan. One historian observes that the coliseum's "entrances, staircases, [and] passages . . . were designed with such skill that each person, whether of the senatorial, of the equestrian, or of the plebeian order, could gain his seat without trouble or confusion."[15]

The Stadium and Its Modern Evolution: The U.S. Ideology of Commercialism

The architecture of professional sport in the United States evolved, as in Rome, from temporary wooden structures to more permanent structures of the same material. After fire jeopardized the safety and profitability of an emerging enterprise, concrete structures were devised. As was the case in Rome, the initial structures were privately financed. Although some exceptions existed (the opening of the Los Angeles Memorial Coliseum in 1923, Chicago's Soldier Field in 1924, and Cleveland Municipal Stadium in 1931), public financing of sports facilities did not emerge as a widespread funding mechanism until later in the twentieth century.

In its earliest years American sports seemed to be patterned after the British model that put a premium on amateurism. Disdain for professional athletics in Britain was a defensive mechanism used by the upper class. Those pushing for amateurism often used moral arguments to defend their position, but one goal of amateurism was exclusionary. Insistence on amateur status in early sport prevented common citizens, many with decidedly more athletic prowess, from participating in organized athletics. The same disdain for professional athletics is visible in the rhetoric of century-old American sports, but the competitive excesses of the American sports enthusiast led to bending rules of amateurism to gain an upper hand on the field of play.[16] The competitive American temperament fueled the emergence of professional sports and quasi-professional collegiate athletics. James Walvin aptly summarized the trajectory of American sport in the nineteenth and twentieth centuries, stating, "even when the Americans copied a European form of leisure, they invariably made it bigger, more spectacular, and often as not, more lucrative."[17] The emergence of the modern stadium was an extension of this philosophy.

Professional baseball's viability as a commercial product became evident after the famed undefeated season of the 1869 Cincinnati Red Stockings. Before their well-publicized tour, phony amateurism was rampant and savvy baseball fans knew this. Players were often given full-time jobs that required little or no effort. In one extreme case, George Wright, the premier shortstop for the Washington Nationals, was "employed" as a government clerk in 1867, but his work address, 238 Pennsylvania Avenue, was a public park close to the White House.[18] In another example, the New York Mutuals, entrenched in William "Boss" Tweed's political patronage, were routinely assigned to do-nothing jobs in the city's coroner's office.[19] Stephen Guschov argues that a good ballplayer lived a charmed life because he "literally would have no real expenses to meet. Everything was handed to him by business leaders who were happy to see him playing for the home team."[20] Professionalism was tacitly incorporated into the fabric of baseball before 1869, but the Red Stockings of 1869 served to legitimize professionalism by virtue of their unparalleled record of 56 victories and a single tie. Civic pride influenced the attempt to corral the finest athletes, and civic pride later led to more ornate ballpark construction.

However, the enclosed ballpark of the Gilded Age was a temporary wooden structure. It was not generally a symbol of civic pride, but, rather, a spartan, utilitarian setting. In the 1860s and 1870s a fenced-in ballpark typically meant "a split rail fence had been erected . . . behind the outfielders and around the perimeter of the entire grounds . . . [to keep boisterous fans] from crashing the gate and or storming the field while a game was occurring."[21] In these early years, baseball entrepreneurs might even position overflow crowds on the sidelines and deep in the outfield. More elaborate construction strategies were eventually employed as the number of baseball fans increased and the ideology of professionalism began to take hold. Better fences were installed to ensure more efficient collection of game revenues. Until the 1890s, when public transportation changed the dynamic of urban life, these facilities remained largely temporary structures. Historian Michael Benson indicates that with the early ballpark: "Players often assisted in construction. . . . [Major League] teams . . . would change home grounds routinely. Sometimes they just changed sides of town. Sometimes they changed states. . . . If a franchise did outlive its ballpark. . . , a new ballpark was sometimes constructed in its place in a matter of days, maybe during a road trip."[22]

As the nineteenth century closed, more permanent structures were built. The popularity of baseball led many team owners to conclude that the sport was sufficiently mature to support greater infrastructure investment. Developments in other areas of urban technology provided further incentive. The electric trolley, popular by the turn of the century, offered fans, or "cranks" as they were known then, convenient transportation to games.

The allure of baseball appeared to be so popular for independent streetcar operators of the time that Steven Riess notes "some companies even supported franchises at a loss because of anticipated profits from increased use of their streetcars." Financial backing from streetcar companies was common even at the minor league level, with a variety of southern cities benefitting from this construction. In New Orleans, a streetcar line went so far as to build a new ballpark in 1898 while providing direct financial backing for the city's minor league team, the Pelicans.[23]

Politicians and well-connected prominent citizens worked together to control ballparks in the Progressive Era. An owner unwilling to let political leaders share in profits might find zoning regulations altered in ways that made ownership useless or severely devalued. John Brush, owner of a Cincinnati baseball team, reportedly sold his interest in the franchise after alleged disclosure of "municipal improvements" on his ballpark land by Republican power brokers. In 1901, Ban Johnson, a powerful figure in baseball history, was thwarted in his efforts to establish an American League foothold in New York because of political machinations of the ruthless Andrew Freedman, then owner of the Giants. Even after Freedman's political coalition lost political clout, Johnson's effort was stymied until 1903 when he caved in to demands for shared ownership by a former police chief, a well-connected professional gambler, and a former city superintendent of buildings.[24]

Ballparks were privately owned and privately maintained primarily because profits were high and the ideology of the era was less receptive to subsidy of private enterprise. Local government maintained a powerful regulatory position, however. In many cases, regulations were devised to extract wealth, prestige, or a combination of both in a manner that benefitted well-connected officials. Despite baseball's positive and wholesome image, below-the-surface political opportunism was the order of the day.

Even when predatory actions were taken to eliminate competition, politicians and their friends did not regard their machinations as reprehensible. George W. Plunkitt, a legendary Tammany Hall boss, made the distinction between "honest" graft and "dishonest" graft, proudly stating in 1905 that "I got rich from honest graft." According to Plunkitt, politicians practicing "honest" graft "didn't steal a dollar from the city treasury. They just seen their opportunities and took them."[25] Civic leaders could ruthlessly cut a road or a trolley line through a team owner's property if he was unwilling to deal with political leaders on their terms.[26] The message of such action was clear to any emerging entrepreneur: cooperate or face severe consequences.

In *From Ritual to Record* Allen Guttmann isolates secularism, equality (among competitors), specialization, rationalization, bureaucracy, quantification, and establishment of records as elements of modern sports.[27] This shift in sports from religious to the secular also fueled an ideology that could be found in the corporate board room and in the blue collar workplace. These ideas contributed to stadium construction.

The movement of sport into a secular and rationalized direction accelerated its prominence in Progressive Era newspapers. Sport helped build newspaper circulation in the penny press era. Nevertheless, a tension existed in such publications between high and low culture. Major urban newspapers often catered to low culture, of which sport was a part, but they also included a variety of features that exposed cultural tensions among classes. Society pages and stories about museums and the city orchestra often competed with coverage of tawdry crimes and blood sports such as boxing. Even within the sports page, such values were contested. Ivy League football was often highlighted, but some citizens regarded sports as low-class entertainment that should be avoided. To counter this resistance, sports entrepreneurs portrayed professional ballplayers as wholesome and heroic figures. Eventually, such an image appeared to take hold in the American psyche, setting the stage for greater expenditure on sports infrastructure.

If an ideological trend existed in American society at the time, it appears to have been an acceptance of commercialism and a tacit agreement that many parts of society could benefit from rationalized bureaucracy. These ideological tendencies were extended to sports infrastructure and management. As an example, the emergence of Taylorism, a management strategy, ushered in an era of specialized, rationalized, and bureaucratized assembly-line production on a grand scale.[28] A day in the automotive plant was not conceptually different to the type of specialization of Progressive Era sports. Players were assigned specific positions, given new and specialized equipment (e.g., baseball gloves) to improve their performance, and fans were ushered to predetermined ballpark seating that tended to divide individuals along class lines. Records were kept on the field of play, paralleling the routine performance audits that were part of a new industrial society.

Record keeping extended to the financial ledger, where team owners became increasingly concerned with maximizing revenues and minimizing liabilities. Increased seating capacity in the early years of sports meant simply adding rows of wooden seats. As Americans displayed a greater willingness to pay admission, owners contemplated the benefits of larger, more permanent facilities while weighing the apparent liabilities of wood construction. The emerging popularity of tobacco products presented fire hazards, and the potential for collapse further endangered fans and exposed owners to unwanted liability and negative publicity.

Philadelphia's cozy Baker Bowl, destroyed by fire in 1894, reopened with a brick and concrete grandstand in 1895, a departure from the tradition of wooden ballparks.[29] The park served as home to the Phillies until 1938. Philadelphia's Athletics were more popular than the Phillies during most of this period, so the innovative construction by team owner William Baker was largely unappreciated by baseball fans and fellow team owners. Poor maintenance because of limited revenues further clouded the reputation of this unique facility.[30]

Regardless, reinforced concrete and steel were making inroads in the construction industry, so it was only a matter of time before a sports facility would be built with these elements. The Cincinnati Reds included concrete and steel in prominent portions of their Palace of the Fans, completed in 1902, a move that influenced construction elsewhere in that city. But America's first fully concrete and steel stadium was not built by a sports entrepreneur. Instead, Harvard University built a steel-reinforced concrete football facility in 1903. It remains a national landmark and is still used to this day.

The facility was inspired by the enthusiasm of selected Harvard faculty and wealthy alumni from the class of 1879 shortly after fire destroyed a section of the university's wooden bleachers in 1902. Its cost was $310,000, or about $69 million in today's dollars. At the time some believed that the concrete structure could not survive New England's rugged winters. Others had doubts that the concrete could accommodate large crowds. Robert Campbell, a Harvard alumnus and architecture critic for the *Boston Globe,* described the landmark as "the biggest single chunk of concrete in the world up to that time."[31] Built in a mere four and a half months, the facility featured a construction process accelerated by an on-site minifoundry. This allowed the transport of slabs to their needed destination via rails that were also temporarily installed on the construction site. Although the stadium was an architectural wonder at the time, media coverage was initially sparse by today's standards. The public became familiar with the stadium through numerous mentions of the structure in game-related coverage, but the edifice itself was not the basis for extensive reporting as is the case today.

Yale and Princeton, Harvard's biggest rivals on the gridiron, did not construct similarly large facilities until 1914. Before that, several professional baseball teams built new ballparks with private funds. Professional football, in its infancy, could not build its own stadiums, in part because the product was strictly blue collar, struggled with funding, and was barely recognized by major newspapers.[32] Some would argue that media emphasis of college football accelerated stadium construction and changed institutional priorities. In the early 1900s, some college presidents feared termination if unable to field a winning team, despite a commitment to academic excellence, in part because of the rising importance of sports in American culture.[33] Ohio State University's administrators regarded stadium construction as a positive means of community outreach, launching its first-ever capital campaign in 1919 with the sole purpose of raising money for football stadium construction.[34]

The University of Illinois constructed another impressive facility in 1923. University officials regarded it as a public relations vehicle and an engine of regional economic growth. An article aimed at the institution's alumni argued that the stadium served as "an advertisement for the university" and also "hastened the development of real estate in south and southeast Champaign." Although the facility never brought the sort of development that would make Champaign a major urban area, it served as a national landmark where the legendary Red Grange christened the stadium with heroics that garnered weekly media attention.

Grange's subsequent move to professional football was one of the most important moments in the early years of professional football. It took place at a time when most sports enthusiasts regarded professional football with disdain. The emergence of an automobile culture and the proximity of Champaign to Chicago resulted in coverage of Grange's college-level exploits in a manner that would not have occurred a generation earlier.[35] Grange's jump to the professional game did not bring immediate popularity to the product, but it allowed many football fans to justify following the less-prestigious professional game.

The strategy of "community outreach" that was pursued by Ohio State, Illinois, and other public land grant institutions had an exceedingly rational basis. Media publicity was partially responsible for the sport historian Ronald Smith's recent assertion that despite Harvard's nation-leading commitment to endowed professorships, it was better known for constructing "the first concrete stadium in America."[36] In such an environment, it is hardly surprising that a number of rival university football programs eventually committed resources to new facilities.

It is unclear whether Princeton and Yale's decade-long delay in stadium construction was partly the result of initially unenthusiastic media coverage of Harvard Stadium's 1903 construction. The *Harvard Crimson,* a publication generally limited to student and faculty circulation, often gave this unique facility front page coverage, but commercial newspapers did much less to publicize this new edifice. Early media coverage of the first all concrete and steel sports facility would be perceived as inadequate today. The *Boston Herald* focused primarily on game coverage, making a fleeting front-page mention of the new stadium but showing considerably greater concern for Harvard's inability to defeat Dartmouth. The *Boston Herald*'s front-page photo positioned closest to the Harvard gridiron story was of the Yale versus Princeton game rather than the new stadium. The *New York Times,* a generally reliable source for Ivy League football coverage, quickly noted the opening of Harvard Stadium in a single sentence and then moved to game coverage.

Before the next round of big-time collegiate stadium construction in 1914, professional baseball began its first major era of modern construction. This era began in 1909 with the completion of two projects on opposite sides of Pennsylvania. Pennsylvania's role as a national leader in steel production and energy resources, in the form of coal and steel, made it an appropriate region for such innovations. The state's blue-collar industrial mentality was tempered by a civic desire to demonstrate that communities were cultivating an emerging upscale citizenry. This civic desire contributed to the push to build these unique landmarks. Shibe Park opened in Philadelphia on April 12, 1909, and Forbes Field opened in Pittsburgh about two and one-half months later on June 30, 1909.

Benjamin Shibe, a sports equipment manufacturer, was majority owner of the Philadelphia Athletics.[37] His ability to obtain positive press was the result of minority ownership by Sam "Butch" Jones, an Associated Press sports reporter, and Frank Hough, the *Philadelphia Inquirer*'s sports editor. Both actively promoted the team. In 1905, during the Athletics first World Series appearance, the *Philadelphia Inquirer* heavily covered the championship, featuring not only traditional reporting but a newspaper-sponsored promotion promising "to give the team $1,000 in gold if they win the World Series."[38] Jones and Hough helped in the site selection for the ballpark that preceded Shibe Park and made sure that positive coverage continued during and after Shibe Park construction.

Both Forbes Field and Shibe Park represented large capital outlays, but the economics of the Progressive Era helped make such projects feasible. Low overhead for players' salaries meant that owners could retain the bulk of ticket revenues, which could be plowed back into schemes that would deliver future profits. Labor was also relatively cheap, in part because of an influx of immigrants from Europe. Furthermore, if a franchise owner could adroitly use connections to steer clear of political land mines that were so prevalent in urban America, restrictions on new construction and commerce were limited. Pittsburgh's recognized status as the "smoky city" reflected this tolerant acceptance of mercenary endeavors.

The 1909 media coverage of Philadelphia's and Pittsburgh's new ballparks was more extensive than previous sports facility coverage. Discounting articles from the student-run *Harvard Crimson,* Boston-area coverage of the 1903 Harvard Stadium and Cincinnati's debut of the Palace of the Fans were both less profound. Opening day for each Pennsylvania facility serves as a compelling barometer for this assertion.

Boston newspapers covered the Harvard football story on the front page, but focused more on the game itself than the new stadium.[39] The coverage was not even accompanied by a photograph of the new sports facility. The *Cincinnati Enquirer* did not offer front-page coverage as the Palace of the Fans was inaugurated, instead choosing to push inaugural coverage to page 4. However, the *Cincinnati Post* did offer front-page artistic renderings of this day's action, likely to be the first use of front-page visual images for a ballpark's inauguration in a big-city newspaper. But the reporting offered below these illustrations revealed exceedingly superficial coverage of the game itself rather than a focus on the new ballpark.[40]

In contrast, both Pennsylvania markets offered more generous focus on the new ballparks and displayed front-page photos of the new facilities. Pittsburgh's inaugural coverage provided a five-photograph collage with a more technically advanced layout than a typical 1909 *Pittsburgh Post* front page.[41] The popularity of the new cement and steel ballparks gave rise to duplication of the concept far beyond Pennsylvania's borders. As with many sporting and commercial trends during the Progressive Era, success inspired widespread imitation.

In 1910 Cleveland dismantled the wooden grandstands of League Park, replacing them with a concrete and steel double-deck structure. Chicago's Charles Comiskey broke ground for a palatial new ballpark on February 10, 1910, opening to the public less than six months later. New York's famed Polo Grounds, a site of sporting activity since the 1870s, was renovated in 1911 with new concrete and steel sections after a raging fire destroyed most of the ballpark in April. Cincinnati, proud home of the first fully professional team, opened a concrete and steel ballpark on April 11, 1912. Nine days later Detroit flexed its industrial muscle, opening Navin Field, later renamed Tiger Stadium. On the same day, the Boston Red Sox christened Fenway Park. This construction boom included some minor league parks, but the most impressive were major league ballparks in the northeast and urban Midwest.

Serious football construction was limited to the college game during the Progressive Era. Early professional teams used whatever facilities might be available. In one example, the Providence Steam Rollers, an early NFL franchise, played home games on the interior of a bicycle-racing track.[42] It was not until the advent of television that professional football began to challenge professional baseball's preeminence. Not surprisingly, the 1960s featured the explosive growth of multipurpose facilities frequently designed to give the viewing needs of professional football significant consideration, often at the expense of baseball.

Before design of multipurpose and football-specific facilities, professional sports construction clearly favored baseball. Nevertheless, collegiate football stadium construction gave rise to taxpayer-funded stadium construction in the 1920s. During this period of heavy university-based construction, several cities determined that such construction might help to enhance their community's national profile. Pasadena built the Rose

Bowl in 1922 as a monument to its annual bowl game. Los Angeles and Cleveland constructed large multipurpose facilities in 1923 and 1931, respectively, with the intention of attracting the Olympic Games for their cities. Chicago erected Soldier Field in 1924 as a monument to military veterans. Most significant to the future of stadium-building policy, these facilities marked a new commitment to public financing of sports-related construction.

Construction after World War II: The Stadium as a Reflection of Civic Pride

Despite introduction of public subsidies in the 1920s, professional sports owners did not generally perceive the potential of public financing as a means of increasing profits until the 1950s. While superficial historic analyses regard Walter O'Malley's move to Los Angeles as a defining moment in changing the dynamic between community and the sports franchise, more incisive analysis recognizes Milwaukee's construction of publicly financed County Stadium as a precursor to the westward movement of professional baseball and to an ideology that legitimized stadium subsidies.

As O'Malley was negotiating the Dodgers's fate, he intermittently referred to "a 'Milwaukee formula,' whereby in return for playing in a publicly owned stadium, the city could recoup revenue from tax receipts and concessions."[43] The Braves's move from Boston to Milwaukee in 1953, four years before the Dodgers's westward shift, demonstrated to baseball executives that public funding of baseball facilities was feasible and could improve profitability. In the early 1950s the Braves were derided by one Boston sportswriter as "a $600,000 bouncing check." They managed to attract a mere 281,000 New England fans for the entire 1952 season.[44] After moving to Milwaukee, the Braves attracted 67,714 fans in their first two games. By the end of the season, team attendance had increased more than 750 percent above 1952 levels; 2,131,388 fans visited the new publicly financed ballpark in 1953.[45]

After Milwaukee's dramatic financial success, teams began to see the value of a new publicly funded stadium. Momentum for a construction boom was created. During the 1950s, media coverage in several cities linked civic pride with stadium building. Team owners, journalists, and politicians appeared to be intent on selling an ideology that community support for a new stadium was an expected part of the duties of a city that had earned "major league" status.

The New York metropolitan area did not follow these trends, however. Walter O'Malley, owner of the Brooklyn Dodgers, hoped to build a new ballpark with his own funds to replace aging Ebbets Field, but was consistently rebuffed in his attempts to gain help for the project by city politicians. Robert Moses, the legendary power broker and city park commissioner, repeatedly stonewalled O'Malley's desire to privately purchase land through use of eminent domain procedures.

The Dodgers case is significant in that it demonstrated that a profitable team owner could be coaxed into leaving an already lucrative market if political leaders were insensitive to team owner demands. The team's West Coast move introduced baseball to both Los Angeles and San Francisco, by virtue of Horace Stoneham's simultaneous shift of his Giants from New York to California. The Dodgers initially played in the less than optimal Los Angeles Coliseum, a facility that was ill-suited for baseball. Walter O'Malley then pushed forward plans to construct Dodgers Stadium, a privately funded enterprise that was made possible by land subsidies provided by Los Angeles city leaders. On the other end of the state, the Giants moved into Candlestick Park, a taxpayer-subsidized facility, perpetuating the arrangement that had been established in the 1953 Boston to Milwaukee franchise shift.

Shortly after the Dodgers and Giants moved to the West Coast, the Continental League, a failed attempt to challenge baseball's existing power, pinned its hopes on convincing cities such as Minneapolis to construct new ballparks. Major League Baseball accelerated league expansion to some of these metropolitan areas. This expansion's purpose, although not explicitly stated, was to fend off the Continental League's challenge to baseball hegemony.[46] Baseball executives used public financing as a carrot for cities interested in achieving major league status. The odds of attracting a team diminished without a tangible plan to build a publicly financed ballpark.

Press coverage often became a major factor in the push to attract a major league team in the late 1950s and early 1960s. Jay Weiner's account of Minnesota's press coverage during this era suggests that public funding of a stadium was at the core of the Minneapolis/St. Paul strategy to attract a major league franchise. According to Weiner, newspaper stories that might educate the public about the financial liabilities of public funding faced editorial censorship.[47] The Minnesota ballpark, Metropolitan Stadium, opened on April 21, 1961. It reflected the sports architecture of that era.

The stadium of this period was built for baseball. The sight lines and overall configuration of these parks were typically better suited for baseball than football. That would change in the mid-1960s with the advent of circular stadiums, a design that combined characteristics of both modern and ancient architecture. These facilities were not ideal for football spectatorship, but in general they were even less accommodating for baseball viewing. The soft circular design of these facilities made for easier crowd-related camera panning, a media strategy popularized by ABC's sports production guru, Roone Arledge, than the quirky ballparks with sudden angles and a less geometric configuration.

They also became a visible symbol of civic pride as many individuals regarded these facilities as futuristic. Such was the desire of the time. The emerging space program and the arms race fostered a culture that privileged innovation. To enhance the focus on modernity many of these ballparks featured artificial turf and electronic scoreboards. However, the circular stadium had its roots and inspiration in the ancient architecture of Rome.

Robert Moses's design philosophy in constructing New York's Shea Stadium was to emulate the architectural grandeur of the Roman Coliseum in a setting that offered such modern amenities as easy highway access. Moses's biographer Robert Caro argued that "Shea Stadium . . . was his answer to Caesar's Coliseum. And the Park was surrounded by his great roads, the cloverleafs and broad ribbons of concrete that to him represented beauty."[48] Moses regarded Shea Stadium and the park surrounding it as a monument to his greatness as a city planner.

Construction began not long after baseball-friendly Dodger Stadium's opening in Los Angeles, an event that may have prompted the egotistical Moses to respond in kind. He did more than simply build the municipal stadium at the site that he previously tried to push onto Walter O'Malley. Moses took steps to publicize this monumental project, integrating this facility into the 1964 and 1965 New York World's Fair, a massive public display that attracted millions to the Queens site. The circular design of Shea Stadium, both ancient and futuristic, caught on beyond Gotham's borders.

Perhaps the most celebrated use of circular design took place with the construction of Houston's Astrodome, a facility that opened to the public in 1965. If Robert Moses perceived New York's circular stadium design as a reflection of the past, the designers of Houston's facility were firmly committed to creating a stadium that reflected the future. Judge Roy Hofheinz cajoled politicians, the press, and anyone else who would listen into building the Astrodome with the purpose of creating a facility that was so lavish that it would raise the national stature of Houston.

After the Astrodome opened, Hofheinz remarked that "nobody can ever see this and go back to Kalamazoo, Chicago, New York, you name it, and still think this town is bush league." Stephen Klineberg, a sociologist at the University of Houston, called the Astrodome's completion "the most exciting thing that has ever happened to Houston."[49] Before the construction of this huge indoor edifice, ballparks and stadiums were designed first and foremost to showcase sports. The Astrodome became a place that many people visited primarily to see the facility itself. The game, while entertaining, was secondary to the experience created by this new building's unique design.

This focus on indoor entertainment inspired political leaders in New Orleans to construct a similar facility that was even more massive. The Louisiana Superdome opened to the public in 1975. Its circular dimensions are so large that the entire Astrodome could be physically contained within its interior.[50] Despite the Superdome's vastness, the Astrodome was the most talked about sports venue in the United States for a full decade after its construction.

If the typical ballpark reflected a Progressive Era desire to master and shape nature, the Astrodome took this notion to its most absurd extreme. When initial attempts to grow grass inside this enclosed building failed, the Astrodome's architects used science to resolve the dilemma. Natural grass was replaced by a space-aged plastic grass produced by a multinational chemical and fiber manufacturer. Houston's oppressively humid summers were held in check by an air conditioning system that cooled the stadium to a comfortable 72 degrees. Spectators were kept entertained by the most elaborate scoreboard ever built.[51] Years before the advent of the Jumbotron or DiamondVision, the Astrodome featured a massive $2 million scoreboard that entertained fans with animated electronic programming.

The Astrodome attracted national media attention that overshadowed Houston's teams. This coverage often suggested that Houston was emerging as a high-tech city. So many regarded the Astrodome as such a technological marvel that it was commonly referred to as "the eighth wonder of the world." A *Sports Illustrated* article in 1965 referred to the Astrodome's high-tech scoreboard as "an electronic accomplice . . . which can lead cheers, sass umpires, and do everything but pinch hit."[52] Houston gained substantial media exposure when President Lyndon Johnson visited the Astrodome's newly created "Presidential Suite," a luxurious precursor to today's sumptuous skybox. The Astrodome also contained several less opulent suites that were leased to local corporations. It also featured an on-site bowling alley, a barber shop, a circus room, and a number of other amenities never before included in a stadium.

As much a theme park as a stadium, the Astrodome became a high-tech destination that attracted out-of-town visitors. In the early years, visitors and television viewers were treated to images of groundskeepers, concessionaires, and ushers wearing silver space suits. For a city previously regarded as low tech and backwater, Houston received a welcome image change. Involvement with NASA's space program contributed further to this image upgrade, but the Astrodome became a place where American citizens' perceptions about a newly emerging high-tech Houston were reinforced.

As Houston gained attention for this architectural creation, other cities looked to build new facilities with the same "modern" circular design. Stadium construction on the West Coast, followed by projects in New York and Houston, prompted a "keep up with the Joneses" desire to build new taxpayer-funded facilities. The rise of televised network sports programming in the 1960s helped bring vivid visuals of these new stadiums to a broader national audience, intensifying the incentive to build. Several of the cozy old Progressive Era ballparks were replaced in the 1960s and early 1970s by much larger facilities with the hope that these structures would portray a thoroughly modern image. The stadium had become a symbol of community pride, and taxpayer funding was expected.

St. Louis opened Busch Stadium in 1966. Oakland unveiled Alameda County Stadium, and Anaheim opened a new ballpark in the same year. Although none of these stadiums were domed, the St. Louis facility copied Houston's construction of fifty-five private stadium boxes, building thirty-nine private suites into its facility. Interestingly, the luxury suite was not integrated into most other facilities. Owners appeared to be satisfied to pack as many fans as possible into the new ballparks. With the notable exception of Kansas City's Lamar Hunt, typical team owners would not revisit the skybox or luxury suite concept for at least another decade.

In 1970 Busch Stadium was converted from grass to artificial turf. As St. Louis made the transition to artificial turf, other facilities were opening with modern plastic grass integrated into their ballpark construction plans. Cincinnati's Riverfront Stadium and Pittsburgh's Three Rivers Stadium both opened in 1970. A year later, another multisport facility, Veterans Stadium, opened in Philadelphia. As these sports palaces were completed, national coverage often focused on the integration of modern turf into the stadium design, giving communities extra publicity for investing in a unique new product.

Older "rust-belt" cities enjoyed this association with modernity. Working hard to shed an image as a run-down mill town, Pittsburgh, in particular, hoped to show itself capable of adapting to change. The transition of Pittsburgh's sports culture from traditional Forbes Field, constructed in 1909, to a modern circular stadium with artificial turf suggested that the Steel City was willing to move forward despite stereotypes to the contrary.

With the construction of Three Rivers Stadium, Pittsburgh also helped to usher in another new concept: the stadium club. Although other cities may have had on-site club facilities, Pittsburgh's Allegheny Club was formed with a primary mission of helping to defray stadium-related costs in an attempt to make finance, construction, and maintenance of the new stadium feasible. The club offered members a restaurant facility that overlooked the action, a precursor to the club and skybox seating that is part of today's design.

The ballparks in New York, St. Louis, Cincinnati, Pittsburgh, and Philadelphia were essentially similar. Kansas City's construction of two sports-specific facilities marked an important departure from this multipurpose architecture. The Kansas City model contained a baseball park and football stadium in close proximity to each other. This created a new paradigm in sports facility construction. This two-stadium facility, now known as the Truman Sports Complex, was built on the outskirts of Kansas City. The complex offered convenient highway access and sport-specific spectator sight lines that represented an improvement over what was available in the multipurpose parks constructed just a few years earlier.

The Kansas City project proved to be a harbinger for the stadium construction arrangements that took place in the 1990s and beyond. The

Kansas City project began with a countywide citizen's referendum vote in 1967. Both were publicly funded despite the considerable wealth of Chiefs owner Lamar Hunt and Royals owner Ewing Kauffman. The two ballparks were carefully tailored to each particular sport, but the projects would not have taken this shape if Chiefs executives did not push for a separate football-only facility. As such, this project marked a transition to a dynamic that gave football teams greater negotiating leverage. Before this construction, taxpayer funding for a football-only facility was unlikely, particularly in light of a mere eight to ten home games scheduled annually.

Kansas City dedicated millions of taxpayers' dollars to build the football stadium first, an indication that football was overtaking baseball as America's most popular spectator sport. The Royals opened their baseball stadium after the Chiefs' first season in the new facility was completed. The Chiefs were able to move ahead of the baseball team in construction priority because they were a championship caliber team, whereas the Royals were an expansion team that had yet to make its mark.

The Jackson County, Missouri, referendum that paved the way for Kansas City construction required two-thirds citizen approval, a seemingly insurmountable goal. Further complicating this process was the manner in which the referendum was constructed. Instead of combining highly desirable construction projects with the stadium, a common tactic in modern stadium referenda, citizens had the ability to separately vote for only those items that they wished to fund from a total $102 million package. Forty-two million dollars was dedicated to stadium construction alone. The remainder was allocated to schools, roads, and other infrastructure needs.

Media coverage may have helped some citizens to determine how to vote, but the campaign was much less focused on direct media influence than more recent stadium referenda. Community elites, most in favor of stadium construction, focused their resources on careful interpersonal contact with voters rather than on direct contact with local media. Chiefs President Ray Evans set up a phone bank at his downtown Traders National Bank office to facilitate the interpersonal contact. Workers systematically called every voter in Jackson County, often working twelve-hour days to accomplish the task. Football team employees recruited supporters to hand out flyers at busy public locations. On election day, team representatives utilized the thorough records obtained during phone contacts. They dispatched cars to the homes of people who would have otherwise missed the vote. The strategy was based on a formula established by a strategist who had helped to elect the brother of a Chiefs' board member to the office of governor of Kansas. When the votes were counted, the stadium referendum passed with a 68.1 percent majority.[53]

The Kansas City project was ahead of its time in its overall dedication to opulent stadium amenities that became, in and of itself, a media story. Team owners Lamar Hunt and Ewing Kauffman dedicated $17.5 million of their own funds to furnish luxury skyboxes, team offices, and stadium clubs. Lamar Hunt appointed his personal skybox with seventeenth-century art, furniture, and unique treasures gathered from France and Spain.[54] Hunt had taken stadium standards one step beyond the luxurious digs created by Houston's Roy Hofheinz. The skybox was now more than a place to comfortably watch a football game. It was a tangible way for the wealthy to consume conspicuously in a manner that might even shock Thorstein Veblen.

Wealthy team owners might not have the capacity to perform heroic deeds on the field, but a subsidized stadium offered a new venue where owners could flex their competitive muscle through well-publicized consumption. This competitive impulse extended further, with civic pride as a goal. Political leaders in various locales jockeyed to top the opulence of previous stadium projects. The result was completion of several massive indoor structures in New Orleans, Seattle, Montreal, and the Detroit suburb of Pontiac in the mid-1970s.

After listening to years of haughty derision from New Yorkers, New Jersey politicians successfully brought a New York cultural treasure, the Giants, to its borders. The New Jersey Sports and Exhibition Authority opened the doors to Giants Stadium in 1976. To the dismay of New Yorkers, the football Giants abandoned their long-time Yankee Stadium home to play in a football-only facility at East Rutherford, New Jersey.

New York responded with a dramatic renovation of Yankee Stadium to ensure that its coveted Yankees would not be swayed to cross the Hudson River. Before Giants Stadium was completed, city officials showed their extreme displeasure by locking the Giants out of both Yankee and Shea Stadiums. The team scrambled for a temporary home. Ironically, they settled in for a season of football at one of the only regional facilities large enough to handle large NFL crowds, the ancient Yale Bowl in New Haven.

The heavy construction of indoor stadiums in the 1970s was followed by a slowdown in the late 1970s and early 1980s. Double-digit interest rates and an economic recession contributed to the pullback. The cost of financing construction rose dramatically during this period, making stadium-related funding a luxury that most communities were unwilling to consider. Dramatic cost overruns in New Orleans and Montreal further scared leaders away from new construction. Montreal's cavernous Olympic Stadium left the city with a $1 billion debt.

Instead of new stadium construction, sports owners and stadium authorities looked to less expensive renovation to maintain profitability. Denver, Atlanta, Detroit, Anaheim, San Diego, and San Francisco completed renovations that were substantially cheaper than the new initiatives undertaken several years earlier. Minneapolis's Metrodome and Indianapolis's Hoosierdome, built in 1982 and 1984, respectively, were construction anomalies during this period. The Hoosierdome was constructed to lure the Colts, an NFL franchise, away from their Baltimore home. The Metrodome's construction occurred because it meshed with the desires of several key leaders in the Twin Cities. Minneapolis newspaper executives emerged as the most vigorous proponents of this construction.[55]

In the 1980s, stadium renovation outpaced new construction. The limits of public subsidy compelled Miami Dolphins owner Joe Robbie to finance his own new stadium in south Florida. He opened the facility's doors in 1987. The 1990s ushered in a new era of stadium construction, however. This period was punctuated by relocation threats; the introduction of "old style" architecture; increased demands for subsidized ballparks; transfer of teams to a new, more aggressive generation of entrepreneurs; and a grassroots backlash against team demands for taxpayer-funded sports palaces.

Politicians of the past readily aligned themselves with the local team when trawling for votes, but this strategy no longer ensured elected officials a safe harbor as sport and politics became uncomfortably intertwined. If a franchise left town, a politician might be made a scapegoat. But if political leaders voted to provide multimillion dollar subsidies to wealthy team owners, they might face the wrath of an angry electorate. To insulate themselves, many politicians pushed for public votes on stadium proposals. As owner demands for new stadium construction intensified, media coverage became an increasingly important dimension of this next era of stadium construction.

The Current Era of Stadium Construction: A Changing Sports Landscape

As the bonds for many civic stadium projects of the 1960s were due to expire in the 1990s, team owners were confronted with the knowledge that competing owners were pushing their host cities to construct new stadiums. They wanted facilities that could exploit new economic opportunities. Skyboxes commanded high prices from corporate clients, and this revenue was fully shielded from league revenue sharing schemes. In addition, novelty seemed to attract larger crowds, and the technology integrated into these facilities provided the capacity for larger profit margins. Wider concourses offered greater potential for in-stadium retailing and improved concession revenues. New electronic devices and seats with built-in cupholders helped to entice casual fans to consume more prodigiously. Visible and attractive concession areas provided desired convenience and encouraged even higher levels of food and drink purchases during games.

Increasing player salaries, the result of limited owner discipline as free agency permeated the sports marketplace, pushed many team owners to seek new revenue streams. These revenues were used as a means of enlarging profit margins and, if winning was a priority, to attract top-tier free agent ballplayers. New publicly subsidized facilities seemed to be the easiest avenue for owners to take in order to remain competitive with other sports franchises. Baseball salaries strike many fans as excessive, but ballpark subsidies make many of these hefty paychecks possible. Alex Rodriguez's ten-year, $250 million contract averages out to about $45,000 per at-bat, a figure that exceeds the annual earnings of a typical worker.

A shift in the composition of team ownership further added pressure to new stadium construction. The transition of management from the local family to the big-time corporate leader ratchetted up competition for greater revenues. With few exceptions, owners were no longer a select club of insiders. They were now a cross-section of the nation's most aggressive capitalists, a core of individuals used to bending rules for their own benefit. Seattle Seahawks owner Paul Allen, North America's fourth richest person, is an example of this trend. Although he has earned enough to finance several stadium projects on his own, his competitive impulse prompted team sale and potential franchise relocation threats if his team did not receive a new taxpayer-subsidized stadium. These tactics ultimately led to construction of a new stadium and implosion of the Kingdome after the structure provided Seattle residents with a mere twenty-four years of service.

The NFL has been more successful at controlling players' salaries than Major League Baseball has, in part because of a negotiated salary cap with the NFL Players Association. But the influx of NFL executives with financial success in other endeavors has helped to push stadium construction to the forefront in several communities. For this new breed of owners, gaining a competitive edge through subsidy is an expected way of doing business. For such individuals, maximizing profits, regardless of the strategic consequences for competing owners, is a routine managerial response. Sharing of broadcast revenues, an NFL practice, may make stadium subsidies less necessary than in baseball, but such subsidies have become widespread because they can be easily obtained. For entrenched owners who make up the "old guard," calls for stadium subsidies reflect a desire to keep pace with this new breed of NFL entrepreneur. In some cases, the owners of a previous generation, such as former Ravens's owner Art Modell, with limited money management skills, demanded a lavish new stadium to offset personal financial inefficiencies.

It is probable that some of the old guard owners fear the vast resources and potential ruthlessness of new ownership. The NFL's old guard may be significantly more affluent than a typical American, but compared to software tycoons and pharmaceutical company heirs who have more recently purchased franchises, old guard resources are much more limited. Although team owners collectively determine future policy at annual owners' meetings, the wealth disparity is a likely source of uneasiness for less-affluent owners. If owners with extremely deep pockets collectively decide to raise salary cap limitations to openly compete for free-agent talent, it has the potential to challenge the financial solvency of some long-time owners. For these individuals, new stadium construction has become an avenue for ensuring long-term financial stability.

When the Broncos and Falcons faced each other in Super Bowl XXXIII, the total gross revenues for television broadcasting the 1999 event were approximately $150 million.[56] The Super Bowl is clearly the most watched sporting event in America, but the broadcast profits paled in comparison to the revenues sought by many team owners for stadium construction. A 1996 report indicated that "$7 billion has been spent over the past three years to build or renovate 30 major sports facilities in America," an average of over $230 million per facility.[57] Franchise owners have put up some of the construction funds, but in recent years, taxpayers have taken on a substantial burden of skyrocketing stadium construction costs.

A $60 million public commitment in 1995 to renovate the San Diego Chargers's facility helped to pave the way for its role as host of the 1998 Super Bowl.[58] In today's economic environment, many owners would regard $60 million as seed money for minor cosmetic improvements. For some owners, new stadium construction has become the real "Super Bowl." The structural integrity of most older buildings was sound, but in the eyes of team owners those huge ballparks were financially obsolete.

The Changing Landscape: Today's New Ballparks

In a sense, the rules of sports management have shifted from the field of play to the field of high finance. As a result, professional teams often contribute significant amounts to organizations that attempt to shape public opinion. In 1997, Michael Armacost, Brookings Institution president, indicated that the funding discrepancy between stadium advocates and stadium critics is typically "more than twenty to one."[59] More recent stadium initiatives have featured campaign funding disparities of double and triple that number. Because most of this money is aimed at media-related expenditures, pro-stadium forces have a decided edge unless news coverage vigilantly pushes to maintain balance.

Such balance is hard to achieve, however, because opposition tends to be dispersed among the general populace, whereas stadium proponents are generally cohesive and easily organized by self-interest. This is a common pattern within the American political system, but the stadium issue differs from other special project subsidies in the level of media attention afforded to sports teams. As a result, an unorganized public is much more aware of stadium-related subsidies than they might be for other types of business subsidies. Despite this awareness, the public may not receive full disclosure on stadium issues in media coverage. As an example, subsidy coverage on televised baseball broadcasts is likely to be heavily skewed by how broadcasters are selected for these events. Game-day broadcasters are generally approved by team owners, making it less likely that they would reveal information that might call stadium subsidies into question.

Owners can control some elements of media coverage. But the public is not easily sold on the idea of ballpark subsidy, so the issue has polarized sports fans. Claims that new facilities can rejuvenate the economic condition of large cities are often vastly exaggerated. Feasibility studies and impact reports often contain flawed assumptions that overestimate the long-term benefits of stadium construction to the economic vitality of a community. These assumptions are so consistently flawed that Kevin Delaney and Rick Eckstein, authors of significant stadium-based research, appropriately refer to these community-specific reports as "fantasy documents."[60]

Scholars often underestimate the potential for stadium construction to lift the collective spirit of an area that has recently acquired a team or the collective shock experienced by a city victimized by a sudden departure. From an economic standpoint, one might argue that Cleveland's expenditure of approximately $231,000 per job in the Gateway Project was a poor investment in the city's infrastructure.[61] But the project lifted community pride, and it reversed the decline of a blighted inner-city neighborhood. The raw economics of Cleveland's construction are questionable, but the emotional lift experienced by citizens helped to offset some of the sting that came when Art Modell moved his NFL team from Cleveland to Baltimore after the 1995 season.

The new franchise "free agency" in sports, spurred by Al Davis's court victory against the NFL in 1984, has profoundly changed the ground rules for stadium construction in major metropolitan areas across the country.[62] Davis's court challenge opened the floodgates for team relocation and stadium subsidy. He knew the financial stakes when doing this. In a 1985 NFL owners' meeting, Davis argued that because of his move, "franchises' leverage in the superstadium game had made a quantum leap, and that [transgression from a traditionally cohesive NFL policy] made everyone more money than they could have otherwise hoped for."[63]

The departure of the Browns from Cleveland after many years of sell-out crowds hammered home how dramatically these ground rules had changed for NFL cities. The change was so profound that shortly after Art Modell moved his team to Baltimore, the House Judiciary Committee orchestrated hearings in 1996 that investigated the nature of franchise free agency. Before Al Davis's shift of his Raiders franchise, the NFL was a paragon of unity and stability.

Randy Roberts and James Olsen trace much of this cooperative management style to the immigrant, Catholic heritage that was part of the cultural upbringing of some early NFL owners whose operations were managed through behind-the-scenes handshake agreements. In these early years, owners were less likely to make stadium requirements and relocation a concern.[64] Once expansion resulted in a more diverse ownership profile, it was only a matter of time before individualism challenged the league's cooperative management structure. Bottom-line economics, including limited broadcast revenues, had an impact on the NFL's geographic stability in these early years. Before 1960, the NFL was much less prestigious and less able to dictate key economic decisions. Its audience was primarily blue collar, not today's demographic mix that includes a more upscale clientele. In its early years, the NFL often played second fiddle to baseball and, on occasion, college football. Television contracts were so insignificant that through part of the 1950s, NFL games were carried on the now-defunct DuMont Television Network. In the early 1970s, former CBS Sports Chief Bill MacPhail admitted that although the NFL was perceived to be a better package by some executives, in the mid-1950s he "would have preferred the network to have college football."[65]

The NFL's policy of revenue sharing both television income and gate receipts worked to create parity, allowing small market teams such as Green Bay to compete with New York and Chicago; more recently a new breed of owner, seeking individual rather than collective success, has looked to concession sales, parking fees, and skybox revenues to gain an edge over competing owners. Major League Baseball's heavy reliance on local broadcast revenues has cultivated a higher level of individualism among team owners, making the geographic stability of franchises less than certain. Despite this, baseball owners have been less inclined to succumb to franchise free agency in recent decades, but they continue to use the threat of movement as an effective method of obtaining new stadium financing.

The ability of some owners to generate vast revenues from stadium sources has inspired many owners to look at new construction as a panacea for lower than desired revenues. In 1994, Dallas Cowboys owner Jerry Jones was able to extract over $37 million in stadium-related revenues, in part, by adding sixty-eight luxury suites. That year, Jones more than doubled the stadium revenue of any other NFL franchise and generated a 25 percent increase in the value of his team.[66] Although his strategy was a renovation, not new construction, Jones set a standard that other NFL owners looked to as they devised independent strategies to manage their respective franchises. The Cleveland Browns, a relatively new NFL franchise that began play in 1999, crafted a stadium package that yielded the team $49 million in annual revenues before the team ever played a single down.[67] By their fourth year of play, the team pulled in more stadium-related revenue than was grossed by the television network for broadcasting the Super Bowl in 1999.

The result is a system that is more entrepreneurial than cooperative, particularly in dealing with the regional stadium authorities. Now that the genie is out of the bottle, team owners are willing to carefully shape media campaigns in an attempt to obtain new deals that maximize stadium-related revenues. What must be examined is whether the vast subsidy required to keep up with this "stadium game" is worthwhile to those communities considering such an investment.

Without doubt, the prominent media coverage that professional sports has received increases the desirability of retaining or acquiring a major league franchise. The publicity of nationally televised broadcasts on major networks gives host cities abundant publicity, which may include numerous aerial views of the city skyline. Routine coverage of the city's team on evening newscasts and in morning newspapers throughout the nation is another attractive benefit. This generally benign coverage can be contrasted to typical news stories that often focus on crime, natural disasters, or bizarre events. Such news stories do little to enhance the reputation of a city and are likely harmful to their reputation.

For a city with a positive cultural heritage and a clear identity, the need to offer brand-new facilities might be a luxury that can be avoided. Metropolitan New York, for example, can afford to share a single stadium between two NFL franchises, simply because New York's national stature is unquestioned and its economic vitality is secure. Despite this, the recent push to dedicate more than $2 billion for a stadium on Manhattan's West Side shows that even the most secure metropolitan areas can fall prey to civic one-upmanship. New York's foray into the 2012 Olympic bidding process offers further evidence that even the most secure metropolitan areas are likely to be pushed into stadium construction by internal and external interests. Such interests offer an array of compelling arguments for a city to consider construction of new sports facilities.

For many cities, particularly those in the Northeast "rust belt," declining stature is a real concern that tempts city leaders to ante up hundreds of millions of taxpayer dollars to avoid being classified as "second class." As Charles Euchner asserts, it is often the cities struggling most with image and infrastructure concerns that must bid the highest to remain in the high-stakes stadium game. Franchise free agency has allowed more cities to make a legitimate bid for a professional team, raising the stakes of franchise relocation considerably.[68] With a limited supply of teams available, the virtual monopoly status of the NFL and Major League Baseball can be leveraged by an owner to obtain the best stadium deal possible.

In cities without a team, the payoff for attracting a major league franchise is national publicity as a "big league" player and any economic, cultural, and psychological benefits that the region might accrue. Such a scenario encourages cities to raise their level of subsidy to a point beyond what may be prudent for a city with a major league team. Leaders with franchises in place must then make the difficult choice to provide an excessive stadium subsidy or risk the loss of a team. It is literally a civic "keep up with the Joneses" game.

The stadium game showed signs of slowing after the September 11, 2001, terrorist attacks, but it has intensified more recently. Attempts to regulate team movement with federal legislative measures have been fruitless. House Judiciary Committee hearings in 1996 shed light on the issue, but this led to no change whatsoever in federal policy. At best, the congressional inquiry pushed the NFL to develop a plan to appease Ohio's citizens after the loss of their team. At worst, the outcome, no specific legislative action, let owners know that the most powerful national political forces would do little or nothing to stand in the way of future franchise shifts.

The symbolic value of sport to a community can be seen in the high level of community subsidies that are offered to team owners when they threaten to leave a community. Whether "keeping up with the Joneses" is economically rational merits more detailed examination.

3

STADIUM ECONOMICS

Separating Myth from Reality

LOS ANGELES, the nation's second largest media market, with Hollywood's influence, has challenged New York as the nation's most significant media center. It does not have an NFL team, so various smaller cities have been threatened by franchise relocation if a new stadium is not built for their local team. Team owners might cry poverty or argue that they cannot compete if a new stadium is not built. But several factors serve to minimize the real-world impact of owner-reported accounting losses. One is the capital appreciation of a team owner's outlays. This increased value often makes sports investment prudent, even if a reported operating loss is legitimate. Another is tax laws that allow owners to take advantage of unorthodox strategies such as depreciation of their player roster. These factors put owners in a position to offset short-term losses or limited profits over a longer time horizon.

Nevertheless, the threat of NFL franchise relocation to Los Angeles has pushed some cities to build a stadium at heavy taxpayer expense. Los Angeles, confident of its world-class status, has resisted calls for substantial stadium subsidies, a move that has cost them chances to obtain an NFL team. In 1999 Robert McNair committed $700 million to the league, outbidding Los Angeles investors. McNair chose Houston as his NFL home and started play in 2002.

Minneapolis and Indianapolis have long engaged in stadium battles that have pitted them against Los Angeles. Team owners might not mention relocation in their strategy. They do not have to make the relocation threat explicit; media sources and an engaged public readily connect the dots for them. In such a scenario, owners can deny any intent of moving while gaining the type of leverage that might prompt support for their goals.

Seattle Seahawks owner Paul Allen indicated that he would not purchase the team if it could not remain local. The alternative would have been sale of the team to an out-of-towner, presumably with less loyalty to the community. Allen then stated that a precondition for taking over was a new stadium, which voters narrowly approved, despite his multibillionaire stature. This strategy allowed Allen to position himself as someone concerned about Seattle while gaining millions in stadium subsidies.

When ESPN's Chris Mortensen reported that the Indianapolis Colts were "on a faster track to Los Angeles than people realize," Jim Irsay, principal owner of the team, was portrayed in the press as someone who was "trying to douse those rumors."[1] But the owner appeared to be dousing those rumors with gasoline. Irsay publicly indicated he would like to remain in Indianapolis. This was juxtaposed with periodic trips to Los Angeles. Shortly after the Mortensen story, *USA Today Sports Weekly* reported that Irsay "has been spotted on golf courses, in fancy cigar bars, and he reportedly has spoken with some of the power brokers associated with trying to bring football back to Los Angeles."[2] Irsay was doing nothing illegal, yet without saying a word, his travel itinerary sent a strong message that was understood by the citizens of Indianapolis.

Taxpayers have directly subsidized the Colts since a 1998 stadium lease renewal that included a $20 million renovation. The 1998 lease did not expire until 2014, but it had an escape clause that allowed the team to leave by 2006 if they did not earn median NFL revenues or better. To make up for earnings shortfalls, local leaders budgeted a $12 million subsidy for the Colts in 2003.[3] Some speculated that without larger subsidies and a new stadium, Irsay would remove his team in 2006. Irsay's father moved his team from Baltimore to Indianapolis in a 1984 middle-of-the-night exodus. Even with a departure threat, 71 percent of Marion County, Indiana, residents opposed financing a new stadium in 2002. Sixty-seven percent of those polled expressed opposition to "using over $10 million in metro-area tax revenues to keep the Colts from leaving."[4] Despite opposition, officials continued the subsidies and quietly purchased $7.2 million worth of land as a future stadium site.[5]

Indianapolis Star columnist Bob Kravitz argued that "if the commissioner could see fit to move franchises out of Los Angeles (twice), Houston, and football-mad Cleveland, what is to make anybody think the league is losing sleep over the welfare of a market our size?"[6] Area citizens grew used to talk of a new stadium as rumors of a move to Los Angeles percolated. Colts fans routinely sold out the RCA Dome, but fewer skyboxes and its rank as the smallest NFL facility doomed its future. Political leaders, afraid that inaction would cost them an NFL team, voted in 2005 to allocate more than half a billion dollars to build a new venue for the Colts. The facility would also serve as part of a convention center, prompting assertions it would offer added economic benefits.

Former Minnesota Vikings owner Red McCombs periodically denied plans to sell his NFL team before putting the team up for sale in 2004. In 2002 McCombs vehemently argued that "there is no truth to any of the rumors. . . . There are no talks taking place regarding the sale of the team."[7] As he was making such claims, he was organizing a "garage sale," an effort to dump assets of marginal value such as file cabinets and old tackling dummies. Many interpreted this as an attempt to "clean house" before selling the team to a new owner who might shift the franchise to Los Angeles. Because a similar move occurred decades earlier when the NBA's Minneapolis Lakers headed to Los Angeles, some residents' fears about such a move were understandable.

McCombs's "garage sale" appeared to be a failure, but enough people concluded that an out-of-town sale was possible. The owner then admitted a team relocation might occur, suggesting that a lease with the Metrodome might be legally circumvented.[8] The lease, which many citizens believed would protect the Vikings from moving, was not set to expire until 2011. Sale rumors were fortified by coverage that labeled McCombs as a man with "a history of impulsive decision-making" and "a hog-wild, unpredictable Texan with no Midwest ties." Reporters reminded the public of his unexpected sale of an NBA team, the Denver Nuggets, after a single phone call.[9] He hoped to turn this impulsiveness into profit.

McCombs was not shy about bringing up relocation and his desire to move away from his lease with the Metrodome.[10] But citizens reacted coldly to taxpayer support for a new stadium, so McCombs was forced to sell without a deal in place. McCombs more than doubled his initial $245 million investment, selling the team to Zygi Wilf for $600 million. One of Wilf's first ownership moves was to appoint Lester Bagley vice president of public affairs and stadium development. Wilf is not from Minnesota, but he resisted initial threats to move the team. He hopes to build a stadium in

Anoka County.[11] These plans, initiated by McCombs, have been well received by the NFL.[12]

Economic Claims, Sports Franchises, and the Community

Team ownership brings with it profound revenue generating capacity, even if losses are entered in the books on occasion. But do such revenue generating opportunities extend to the broader communities from which the teams reside? The goal of this chapter is to explore the economic merits of stadium construction for those who live in the cities that host teams.

When veiled threats are made to leave a community, cities must either ante up or live with the possibility of being painted as an area in decline. The negative attention of such an outcome compels many civic leaders to extend lavish subsidies to stadium projects. Do such subsidies make sense? From a symbolic standpoint they might, but from an economic standpoint, the answer is less positive.

The emergence of Baltimore's Camden Yards as a popular tourist destination spurred stadium construction in a number of cities. Claims of economic growth were commonplace as this new venue attracted fans during the 1990s. The dramatic increase in stadium building in the wake of such claims pushed urban scholars and policy analysts to carefully examine this building trend. Most of this scholarship focuses on the economic prudence of such construction. Does a new stadium mean economic growth for a community? Various factors must be considered to fully understand the answer to this question.

When a franchise threatens to leave a community, regional financial analysts often paint a rosy picture of the economic contributions made by the team. Local studies are often commissioned by well-intentioned leaders who are convinced that a positive outcome is needed to build a new ballpark. A report might be prepared by a large accounting firm or a professor at a local university. The study's author may be reluctant to upset the desires of a community's elites since these people, if satisfied with the outcome, could benefit the author's institution in a variety of ways. The goal is often retention or attraction of a team, not necessarily preparation of an objective document. As such, city-specific economic analyses should be approached with skepticism. Such documents are typically so skewed in their assumptions that stadium researchers Kevin Delaney and Rick Eckstein refer to such reports as "fantasy documents."[13]

An independent analysis should bring forward the full range of factors that determine whether a metropolitan area can improve its economic standing with a stadium subsidy. Such analyses must look beyond temporary construction jobs. After all, these positions will disappear once a stadium is completed. When a city threatened by team relocation succeeds in retaining a franchise, the number of new jobs created are typically limited to those temporary positions dedicated to construction unless a long-term strategy is devised that reinvigorates the neighborhood surrounding the stadium. Even with such reinvigoration, the result may be a simple reshifting of local spending priorities, rather than a true long-term economic renaissance. The key to achieving real economic growth is a venue's ability to attract out of region dollars. Unless a community is so culturally barren that a vast percentage of people routinely leave the area to seek outside entertainment options, the impact of sports-oriented local expenditures on a region's vitality is limited.

Increases in regional entertainment revenue might occur, if a new stadium is sufficiently unique that it attracts a great deal of visitor interest from sports fans far outside of the area. The key to real economic growth is attracting *new* revenues, not drawing from existing regional resources. Bringing in dollars from the metropolitan area itself is not typically sufficient to bring substantial growth because such dollars, if not spent on sports, would be spent in other ways within the community. In short, an evening at the local stadium can be substituted by a decision to attend a movie theater, a concert, or a local mall; all these alternatives bring economic benefits to some local entrepreneur.

Increases in outside revenue are presently limited by the ubiquity of new stadium construction throughout the nation. Simply put, if people will not travel long distances to visit a sports facility, its economic benefit is hurt. As more and more cities complete new facilities, opportunities for unique architecture that do not border on the absurd are limited. Furthermore, attracting new external revenue could be hurt by the likelihood that enthusiastic local ticket purchases would restrict ticket availability to those living outside a metropolitan area's boundaries. Policies that prevent ticket resale, such as a threat to remove a reselling patron from a season ticket list or limited walk-up sales caused by a personal seat license requirements, hinder the attraction of outside revenue. Because of these factors, a new venue is more likely to recycle entertainment dollars within an area rather than create substantial new economic growth.

The typical fan looks at the vast commercial activity that occurs during a ballgame and assumes that the economic impact is dramatic. What that person fails to consider is that the majority of this activity takes place during a compressed five- to eight-hour period on a limited number of dates. Unlike a busy retail facility or an office complex that may be opened for twelve or more hours almost every day each year, a ballpark provides a more intensely frenetic environment, but the activity is compressed into a very short time.

What is less examined is the tendency of many high-paid professional athletes to spend large portions of their salary outside of a host community in areas that they consider "home." This outflow of fan-generated revenue may provide a negative drain on the regional economy. Scholarship examining stadium construction, unless funded by an organization that specifically benefits from new construction, almost universally supports the assessment that claims of economic growth are marginal and in some instances the economic impact may be negative.

Putting Stadium Subsidies into Perspective: Analysis of Experts

The Brookings Institution examination of this issue, edited by Roger Noll and Andrew Zimbalist, provides one of the most comprehensive overviews of the economic complexities of the stadium construction issue. A variety of economists, each with different areas of expertise, offer a range of theories about why construction continues in light of a poor return on investment.

Robert Baade and Allen Sanderson argue that the impact of new sports facilities to spur job creation is highly exaggerated and largely skewed by a number of questionable assumptions that are often part of economic feasibility studies that are generally conducted by individuals lobbying for stadium construction.[14] They argue that the economic impact of a team is significantly less impressive than feasibility studies suggest because sports-related spending tends to "realign economic activity within a city's leisure industry rather than adding to it."[15]

Baade and Sanderson compare Alabama's subsidy to Mercedes Benz in 1993 at about $200,000 per job to the taxpayer cost for stadium subsidies. The authors cite employment projections provided by an Arizona Office of Sports and Development study, which estimated the average subsidy for a Phoenix baseball stadium as exceeding $705,000 per full-time job.[16] These projections were prepared by Deloitte and Touche for the pro-sports agency. There is little reason to believe this accounting firm would underestimate such figures because it was in their client's interest to establish the most appealing job creation numbers possible.

Dennis Zimmerman suggests that the current system of stadium finance has been "made worse" by existing federal legislation aimed at stemming the tide of subsidies. These subsidies can take many forms but are primarily the result of federal policy that allows tax-free funding of municipal projects. He suggests that a greater percentage of stadium construction costs should be shifted to those enjoying stadium-related activities in the form of personal seat licenses, higher ticket prices, and taxes on broadcasting fees.[17]

Rodney Fort offers the "setter" model as a tool for understanding how owners can obtain more lavish facilities than might be reasonable in a more competitive marketplace. Instead of regarding the decision as a simple "voter preference" issue, Fort's model creates a scale of various policy options ranging from a worst-case scenario of "no team" to the franchise's desired outcome, construction of a "Taj Mahal" at taxpayer's expense.[18] According to Fort, teams often have the ability to "obtain more spending than the median voter prefers by making the reversion outcome highly undesirable."[19] Fort describes the "no team" scenario as the "reversion outcome."

James Quirk and Rodney Fort offer two detailed analyses of the stadium issue unrelated to the Brookings Institution research. The first effort, published in 1992, provides comprehensive economic and historic analyses of stadium construction.[20] Their second work, published in 1999, contains fewer data but is much more critical of stadium subsidies. The harsh tone of the more recent effort, aimed primarily at team owners, league officials, and political leaders, suggests that these authors believe that the current direction of professional sports management has worsened.

In their initial effort, Quirk and Fort examine historical trends in stadium construction, isolating three eras of stadium construction. The first begins in 1909 with the construction of concrete ballparks such as Philadelphia's Shibe Park and Pittsburgh's Forbes Field. The second can be traced to the 1950s when direct municipal funding in the construction of Milwaukee County Stadium was used to entice a team to abandon an existing market. Although the Boston Braves were not generally missed in New England, team knowledge that franchise free agency was a profitable option served to fuel subsidy expectations, leading to highly publicized franchise shifts elsewhere. They delineate the third era as the current period, in which cities, counties, and states often combine resources either to entice franchise movement or to retain an existing team.

Quirk and Fort admit that some of their figures are based on educated speculation. They state that "financial data on stadium operations are scattered, even for those stadiums that are publicly owned, and for a number of publicly owned stadiums and arenas, no published data are available." They attempted to fill in gaps with a survey that had a response rate of about half. Of those responding, "half refused to divulge information on the grounds of confidentiality."[21] Despite this deficiency, the data offer researchers a basis for comparative analysis.

Their most recent effort recognizes the dramatic increases in stadium subsidy between 1992, when their first book was released, and 1999.[22] As such, they emotionally argue against taxpayer-subsidized construction. They offer Seattle as a case study. In this example, voter rejection was overturned by legislative maneuvering in order to construct a lavish new ballpark for the Mariners to replace the Kingdome, a facility that was barely twenty years old as the vote was set. Despite considerable taxpayer subsidy, Mariner ticket prices more than doubled when the new ballpark opened. Quirk and Fort argue that Seattle's long-range agreement to give taxpayers 10 percent of the team's operating profits is absurdly misguided, though it may reduce some taxpayer objections.[23] They assert the state has no control over the team's accounting practices, and a franchise can easily eliminate profits through perfectly legal tactics, such as provision of selected benefits or through direct payment of bonuses to owners, players, or major executives.

The authors provide another example of misguided government policy as they demonstrate the foolishness of an agreement that subsidized the San Diego Chargers for unsold tickets. This agreement made it more profitable to leave seats empty than to sell them. Not surprisingly, the franchise failed to post a winning record from 1997 until the agreement expired. In 2000 the team posted the worst record of any NFL franchise, but unless capital appreciation was desired, the team had no financial incentive to improve its on-field performance. The possibility of a franchise shift to Los Angeles is one factor not mentioned by the authors that may increase the desire to improve the team's on-field performance. Such a move could lead to dramatic capital appreciation. After the possibility of an expansion franchise for Los Angeles fell through in 1999, the NFL would not want to shift a weak team to Los Angeles because such a move could cause a fan backlash and siphon off television ratings in the nation's second-largest media market. In 2002, the Chargers improved their record to 8-8. Since then, the team has pushed for a new stadium, with rumors of a Los Angeles departure circulating at times.

The House Judiciary's testimony on February 6, 1996, focused on sports franchise relocation and included a thorough analysis of the economic and emotional impact of stadium construction that is often prompted by efforts to fend off team relocation. Included is testimony from major league sports executives, political officials, lawyers, scholars, and, believe it or not, a single rabid sports fan who garnered national attention for wearing a dog costume on game days.[24] Judiciary Committee testimony by scholars typically cited the "monopoly" status of sports leagues as a rationale for legislative action. The University of Illinois's Stephen Ross concluded that "for many years now the principal difference between the most profitable and least profitable franchises was not the quality of the organization or the team but the success of the team owner in negotiating a lucrative stadium deal."[25] The NFL argued that possible legislation could "have the effect of locking a team into its current facility with the threat of potentially ruinous financial penalties."[26] The league further argued that claims of monopoly status are specious since the NFL "competes in a broad sports and entertainment market."[27] They asserted that one purpose of its managerial structure "of separately owned and managed teams is to enhance public confidence in the integrity of the athletic competition within the league."[28]

Many individuals have suggested that community-based ownership might achieve the same objective while limiting threats of team movement, which has served as a key stimulus for subsidized stadium construction. Whether other forms of taxpayer subsidies would follow a community ownership model, such as overt subsidies to attract coveted free agent players, is less clear, however. The tenuous position of communities has sparked several scholarly efforts aimed at educating the public about the range of issues related to modern sports management tactics. Michael Danielson argues that owners' attempts to play community against community to maximize revenues has resulted in a weakening of ties between the team and its host community.[29] While he does not directly argue that such weakening might diminish long-range support for sports, it is logical to assume that such a scenario is possible. Danielson concludes that the problem of community-based stadium subsidy has worsened in recent years. He asserts that communities "will remain very limited partners of professional sports, building most of the arenas and stadiums, paying more and more of the capital costs, and being frozen out of decisions, profits and equity shares."[30]

Charles Euchner argues that cities have been weakened by demographic shifts to the suburbs, making them more vulnerable to team owner threats to move outside city limits. Despite the negotiating strength of team owners, he states that "imaginative and skilled politicians with public support are able to strike better deals than more ordinary politicians."[31] He concludes that a national approach to urban policy would improve matters because "the cannibalistic struggles for sports franchises undermine the prospects for nationwide prosperity and security."[32]

One recent study has uncovered a possible incentive for stadium building. Gerald Carlino and N. Edward Coulson examine fifty-three of the nation's largest cities and offer data that residents pay 8 percent higher rents in central cities of areas with NFL teams. Such an outcome suggests that higher property tax revenues might accompany a team's presence. For political leaders this might be a large enough benefit "to perhaps justify the provision of subsidies to NFL teams." However, they also offer data suggesting that residents in NFL cities make on average 2 percent less than those in non-NFL cities, suggesting that on an individual level, having a team might cost more in taxes while less income is earned. Because NFL teams tended to be in the largest markets, with Los Angeles as a glaring exception, the possibility that other big-city amenities contributed to the differential is uncertain, but they offer comparative information on six somewhat comparable cities that have varying situations with team relocation to fortify their overarching argument. The study ultimately suggests that the symbolic value of sports prompts some people to pay more and earn less to reside in a given city.[33] They assert that the team, not the stadium, may prompt this outcome, yet this offers an incentive for teams to push self-interested political leaders and real estate investors for subsidy.

Stadium Construction: The Intersection of Economic and Legal Issues

Although financial records are not available for most professional sports franchises, several economists have successfully estimated team balance sheets using publicly available figures related to television income, ticket revenue, and tax policy.[34] These economic estimates can demystify claims made by team officials regarding profit and loss. Richard

Sheehan, a sports economist, looks beyond season-to-season payroll issues and considers the total investment landscape, including capital appreciation and tax benefits, to determine whether sports teams are a prudent investment. Although he compiled his research in 1996, a time of dramatic prosperity on Wall Street, he concludes that "given the choice between putting your money in stocks or bonds, on average over the last twenty years you would have been better off putting your money in a sports franchise in any major league."[35] As such, cries of economic hardship may be overstated attempts to gain stadium subsidy leverage. That some of America's most successful entrepreneurs have gravitated to this industry strongly suggests that profitability is typically achieved in sports.

Legal issues also affect the economics of stadium construction. Legal precedents that have fostered franchise mobility also have the capacity to constrain league sanctions against team movement. These legal rulings hurt cities' negotiating base while empowering individual owners to aggressively play one city's bid for a team against another. When NFL franchise owner Al Davis legally challenged the league in his attempt to move his Raiders from Oakland to Los Angeles in 1982, the courts were asked to determine whether teams were individual, competing entities, much like independently owned gas stations, or whether they were constrained by the strategic control of a larger organization (the league office), much in the manner that a corporate branch office was compelled to follow the directives of a larger parent company.

In franchise relocation decisions the courts have ruled that individual sports teams act as individual competitors rather than as a unified organization. The result of this interpretation has undermined league stability, and team owners have been given greater latitude to shop for better financial incentives from any city. League commissioners have adjusted to these political realities. As such, leagues have stepped back from restrictive attempts to limit franchise movement. Such laissez-faire policies may be welcomed by league officials, but unless serious legislative proposals addressing the stadium subsidy trend gain traction, pinpointing the motives of league officials is problematic. Federal legislation could be crafted to overturn the current legal status of sports franchises, but Congress has demonstrated little desire to act, leaving cities to fight among themselves for coveted sports teams.

City officials, on the other hand, have taken considerable action. They have competed among one another, offering lavish incentives either as a way to retain their home team or to entice an outside franchise to move. This competitive bidding has become so prevalent that small towns occasionally jump on this bandwagon. When Al Davis was contemplating a move from Los Angeles, Irwindale, California, aggressively attempted to lure the Raiders to their community. When tiny Green Bay planned a subsidy vote for its NFL team, even smaller New Berlin, Wisconsin, drafted a resolution "inviting the Packers to relocate to Waukesha County if Brown County residents vote[d] down a sales tax to help renovate Lambeau Field."[36]

In recent decades urban scholars have struggled with the declining influence of cities as more affluent residents and corporations establish residence in outlying suburbs. In *City Limits,* Paul Peterson argues that cities are systematically weakened in competition for jobs, taxpayers, and resources. He indicates that such intercity competition creates an unhealthy "growth machine" model that systematically encourages projects aimed at growth while diverting resources from social services. His solution is counterintuitive; he calls for greater federal subsidy of social programs that would improve the quality of life in a city, with a reduction in funding as a region's economy improves. His logic is that the reduction of such subsidies would limit incentives to heavily subsidize businesses as a means of attracting outside firms. He never mentions stadium building, but his contention that intercity competition can frequently inspire counterproductive local-level policy invites deeper analysis of sports teams.[37]

Big-Time College Football and the Economics of Nonsubsidy

The decision to construct a new stadium is often driven by fear of team relocation rather than a real need for new facilities. Increasingly, incentives aimed at team owners have moved beyond a game of what economists call diminishing marginal returns to become a game of negative economic returns. When the fear of departure is eliminated, cities can make more rational economic decisions. In such cases, renovation may be a better policy decision than new construction. Big-time college football offers a comparative model that supports such an assertion. The emergence of professional sports has guided much of the recent sports construction policy, but, historically, big-time collegiate sports was responsible for much of the commercialization and rationalization that has helped professional sports to emerge.

Long before the NFL was a major entertainment option for Americans, the collegiate game was considered an outstanding commercial product. Pondering the football landscape in the late 1950s, Bill MacPhail, vice president of CBS Sports, argued, "Back then I would have preferred to have college football. . . . I thought the color and the rah-rah . . . school spirit thing had it all over the pros." MacPhail admitted that he was wrong as the 1960s unfolded and the NFL emerged, yet college football still has a wide following and is an important element of current network sports programming.[38]

With the exception of player salaries, big-time collegiate athletics are managed in a manner similar to the professional model. In some of the most popular university venues, if student sections are factored out, ticket prices often correlate with prices paid at professional football games, although perennial losers must understandably set lower prices to attract fans. The University of Michigan's single game ticket prices for the 2001 season were $51, $47, and $43, with season ticket packages established at $47, $43, and $39, depending on the location of the seats.[39] These reported prices do not include annual booster club donations that are often required to obtain premium section seating. After such expenses, Pennsylvania State University's relatively new end zone club seats averaged $257.50 per game.[40] The cost is in the same range as that for some NFL patrons who purchase a personal seat license and spread such a payment over a multi-year period. NFL ticket averages in 2000 were $47.69 and had risen to $54.75 by 2005. Major League Baseball, with many more games scheduled, averaged $21.17 in 2005.[41]

Major college conferences and the National Collegiate Athletic Association work diligently to maximize television revenues in a manner that parallels professional sports. If brand-new stadium construction led to substantially enhanced broadcast rights fees or greater game-day concession revenues, it would be unwise to forgo such possibilities without careful cost-benefit analysis, something that is routinely taught at business schools in every major university. Limited evidence suggests that championship teams at big-time universities may improve an institution's enrollment goals.[42] The link between institutional fund-raising and athletic success is less clear; more favorable studies suggest a modest correlation between donations and on-field success, but others suggest no correlation or a negative outcome. In some instances such research concludes that athletic expenses may be so substantial as to offset or outpace any fund-raising gains.[43]

Economist Andrew Zimbalist argues that "the main contributors who appear to respond to athletic prominence are boosters, not the typical alumnus or academic philanthropist" who might benefit the broader goals of an institution.[44] Despite uncertain evidence of athletics as a revenue generator, the boosters cited by Zimbalist might coax some administrators to invest in sports infrastructure. Anecdotal evidence of fund-raising success, ranging from private gifts, licensing revenue, broadcast rights, and bowl receipts, might further convince such individuals to believe the link between sports and financial success is tangible and worth pursuing.[45]

Such factors might be regarded as incentives to push even harder for new stadium construction. After all, if people believe that a new stadium might contribute to better talent recruitment, a better game-day experience for donors, and new revenue streams through nationwide merchandise sales, broadcasting rights, and bowl revenues, why would big universities not push harder to construct new sports palaces for their respective schools?

The most significant difference between collegiate sports and the professional model is that a university does not have the capacity to threaten franchise relocation. A secondary issue is a competitive landscape that forces competition among conferences for broadcast revenue, a consideration that is less of a factor in major professional sports. Such interconference competition should make slight qualitative differences (such as newer sports facilities) more important, particularly because networks are inclined to pay substantially more for a top conference's broadcasting rights than for a second-tier conference. In short, with all issues on the table, university administrators must determine what action is most prudent based on *all* economic factors rather than from a weak negotiating position with an unpredictable team owner.

In most cases, major universities chose to renovate rather than build an entirely new facility. New construction is held in check because the threat of team relocation is eliminated. In examining five of college football's most successful conferences (Atlantic Coast Conference, Big 10, Big 12, Pac 10, Southeastern Conference), the average stadium was more than sixty-five years old.

Universities throughout the nation have not abandoned stadium construction entirely. Many universities have made renovation plans. New football stadium construction is not widespread, however. The University of Pittsburgh (Big East) moved into a new facility in 2001, as did Stanford (Pac 10) in September 2006, offering evidence that a new stadium may be

Ages of Stadiums by Conference

Conference	*Number of teams*	*Oldest*	*Newest*	*Average*
Atlantic Coast Conference	12	1913	1968	1944
Big Ten	11	1917	1982	1940
Big Twelve	12	1920	1975	1936
Pac Ten	10	1921	1972	1939
Southeastern Conference	12	1914	1973	1931
Total Average				1938

Source: Munsey and Suppes Web site (http://www.ballparks.com), July 2006.

desirable to a major university sports program. However, if the entire Pac 10 decided to fund new construction for every member institution, the average for all institutions in the five major conferences would still be about fifty-five years old, ancient by professional football standards.

Some urban universities may be constrained by site availability, but big-time college football is composed of a high number of land grant and rural institutions that could maneuver new land with much less restriction and cost than a typical professional team. In such an environment, new stadium construction would be selected if such a path were more economically beneficial. Even the most expensive university-level renovations are cheaper than new construction at the professional level. Most university stadium renovation projects cost less than $100 million, approximately one-third the cost of a low-priced professional sports project. Even the most lavish university renovations are cheaper than the least expensive newly constructed professional venues. Ohio State University's $187 million renovation was one of the most expensive university-owned projects in North America, yet this extensive stadium work was at least $25 million cheaper than the least expensive professional football stadium of a similar period. The University of Michigan eclipsed Ohio State University's dramatic project in 2006 with a planned $226 million renovation of their 107,501-seat stadium, but with increases in construction costs, that project will be at least $100 million cheaper than any professional football stadium that has been proposed or was under construction from 2005 onward. In fairness, many college facilities get by with cheaper bench seating and more narrow concourses. This may suppress construction costs somewhat, but university administrators would move to more lavish construction if adding new comfort amenities made economic sense. Simply put, without major taxpayer subsidy, new construction is generally less prudent even when athlete salaries fail to depress bottom-line profits.

League officials in professional sports have struggled with public resistance to maximize subsidies, fighting hard to keep calls for renovation off the policy agenda. After all, if teams could simply renovate at a lower cost and remain competitive, it would hurt the overall capacity of a league to extract windfall subsidies that primarily benefit team owners. Additionally, new construction often affords a newly renegotiated lease agreement, providing owners with a convenient means of escape from less than desirable long-term agreement. Newer leases tend to give owners a greater percentage of concessions, skybox revenues, in-stadium advertising, and other revenue streams.

Green Bay's public ownership of the Packer franchise was problematic for some of the NFL's most powerful executives for years. Because the Packers are owned by a limited number of citizens who serve as "shareholders," the possibility of relocation could not be used as leverage. This ownership structure has been prohibited by the league in subsequent NFL franchise agreements, in part to prevent community-owned teams from limiting profitability for individual owners. The founders of the Packer franchise were immensely prudent in their ability to prevent relocation or team sale by profit-thirsty shareholders. To prevent departure from Wisconsin, the team bylaws stipulate that any proceeds generated from a team sale would become property of the local American Legion post. In essence, team shareholders would receive no direct benefits in any attempt to liquidate the franchise. When the bylaws were drawn up in the 1920s, however, no one ever conceived that an NFL team might be worth more than $700 million.

In recent years, NFL owners have had to deal with the uncomfortable knowledge that Green Bay's public ownership formula could be raised each time an owner threatened to move unless a new stadium was built. A 1998 policy analysis by Joseph Bast of the Heartland Institute offered one reason why this public ownership formula might be a dramatic concern to owners. According to Bast, "The franchise is the least subsidized sports team in the country because its ownership by fans makes it unable to credibly threaten to relocate. The results have been good for the host city, the fans, and the team."[46]

If such analysis was restricted to think tank reports with limited circulation, NFL owners might not be concerned about the Green Bay model.

But the public turned to this community-based model as an example of how sports might be restructured. Sportswriters and fans frequently cited Green Bay as an example of how professional sports should be managed. Best-selling author Mike Lupica waxed poetic about the beauty of Green Bay's ownership model, suggesting that "when an owner does put a team up for sale in this country, in any sport, the first thing he must do is make a public offering."[47] Presumably, such an offering would allow community ownership, circumventing a messy relocation battle. Sportswriter Bob Glauber demonstrated similar enthusiasm about the Packers's model, ranking the team's fans absolute best in the NFL. Glauber gushes that the enthusiastic support of this "city of less than 100,000 [for the Packers] . . . remains one of the most compelling stories in pro sports."[48]

Green Bay's stadium, built in 1957, is ancient by NFL standards. Yet it was still considered serviceable before renovations. Paul Attner, a writer for the *Sporting News,* argued that "for a real football fan, this [Green Bay's Lambeau Field] is Mecca."[49] *Sports Illustrated*'s Richard Hoffer placed Lambeau Field ahead of all other NFL venues in a ranking of twentieth-century sports facilities before renovations were made.[50] It is not surprising that the marketing success of the Packers in the relatively spartan Lambeau Field might be an irritant to NFL owners seeking fancier venues. After all, the Packers might be regarded as evidence that massive stadium subsidies are not necessary for teams to survive. Furthermore, moving forward on a $50 to $100 million college-type renovation might send the wrong message for future stadium projects.

As a result, after debating the need for a new stadium, the Packers president Bob Harlan, with the support and backing of the NFL, spearheaded a campaign to obtain public financing for a $295 million renovation of Lambeau Field. The total amount of this proposed project exceeded the most extravagant college renovation project by almost $70 million and was more expensive than at least three brand-new NFL projects. The Packers proposed a $160 million taxpayer subsidy, with $92.5 million of the remaining funds to come from a one-time $1,400 assessment on season ticket holders and $20.4 million to be acquired through the sale of nonvoting stock in the football franchise. In brief, $272.9 million, or over 92.5 percent of the total cost, was directly paid by the public in one way or another.

Better locker room and training facilities could benefit the franchise in luring free-agent players, but a number of renovations had little to do with football operations. The project included an expansive, five-level atrium, an expanded Packer Hall of Fame, additional rest room facilities, 12,000 feet of space for retail shops, expanded skyboxes, new indoor club seating, and an addition of 8,000 to the overall seating capacity of the stadium. Although impossible to determine how much influence the NFL exerted, evidence suggests that the NFL was elated to see the project move ahead. The project was prominently displayed on the NFL's Web site, including a May 10, 2000, news release inviting the public to a Lambeau Field ceremony where former Wisconsin Governor Tommy Thompson signed a bill authorizing a referendum vote to fund $160 million in construction costs through a 0.5 percent Brown County sales tax. According to this release, a "family-day atmosphere" would "celebrate" the event, with free parking, free admission, and full access to the Packer Hall of Fame.

Another indicator of strong league support could be found in the relative silence of NFL officials as veiled threats were published regarding the future of the team if extensive renovation was rejected. Even though the team's bylaws prevented a move out of Wisconsin, rumors that the NFL might eventually close down the franchise began circulating in early 2000. At the end of February, such talk earned the imprimatur of Packer management. According to Bob Harlan, if the voters failed to ante up for major renovation, bankruptcy of the Packers might ensue and "the board of directors could decide to liquidate the franchise." Harlan further argued that after completion of this "liquidation," the league could step forward and grant a new franchise to the significantly larger and presumably more profitable Los Angeles market.[51] Although the NFL's generous revenue-sharing formula made such a series of events unlikely, league officials failed to comment on Harlan's doomsday scenario. Understandably, because a positive taxpayer vote would eliminate the argument that a community model limited stadium subsidies, it was not in the interest of the league to comment or clarify.

With NFL backing and veiled threats, the Packers were able to obtain public approval for a half-cent sales tax levy to fund their stadium project. Despite the consistent loyalty of Packer fans before the 2000 vote, the measure passed with only 53 percent support. On the Sunday before the referendum, a number of people campaigned against the measure, bringing "Vote No" signs into Lambeau Field on game day.[52] The political action committee fighting for the referendum reported spending more than $420,000 through late August to ensure passage.[53]

After the Packers's project took shape, the City of Chicago and the

Bears moved forward in 2001 and 2002 to renovate historic Soldier Field, a facility that was initially constructed in 1924. The total cost of the Chicago project was $587 million, with $365 million devoted to the stadium work. Underground parking costs of $75 million would directly benefit the team. The remaining $147 million was split among outdoor parking, site work, and surrounding infrastructure. The new facility bears little resemblance to its original architectural form; a brand new stadium was actually built within the exterior shell of this historic structure.

The McCaskey family, principal owners of the team, committed $200 million of team resources, a bit more than a third of the total cost. The team's allocation has been touted as "one of the largest such contributions made by an NFL team for a publicly owned facility."[54] A portion of this amount was funded through an NFL loan and the sale of personal seat licenses (PSLs), a fee that fans must pay to be eligible to buy season tickets. The PSL revenue is counted as a part of the team's contribution, but that portion has been paid for entirely by fans.

The $295 million Packer and subsequent $587 million Bears renovation models are less a reflection of the type of cost savings that can be achieved in renovation and more an artifact of generous subsidies that are readily available to professional teams. Executives in both organizations have capitalized on rabid emotional support to acquire extravagant amenities that would not be normally integrated into a university renovation. Unless a stadium has severe structural deficiencies, renovation is likely a more cost-effective option, particularly in football, where usage is generally limited to fewer than a dozen games a year. Taxpayer and fan subsidies (in the form of PSLs) skew free-market economics so that owners are encouraged to build new facilities rather than to renovate existing venues.

If such an assertion is true, why have selected owners chosen to build their own new facilities when heavy subsidies are largely unavailable? With lucrative taxpayer subsidy, such private financing schemes are much less common today. Nevertheless, the decision to privately build is partly driven by ego but is also influenced by capital appreciation of team value and generous infrastructure and land subsidies that might be extended to team owners by political leaders. These subsidies can include public resources for road construction, land, parking lot paving, and site preparation.

Jack Kent Cooke privately financed a new stadium that was opened for the Washington Redskins in 1997. Cooke passed away as construction neared completion. Although he did not enjoy the new stadium during his lifetime, the value of his estate increased immensely, revealing why some owners might self-fund a higher percentage of new construction if subsidies were otherwise unavailable. Cooke acquired sole ownership of the team for approximately $15 million, purchasing 25 percent in 1960 for $350,000 and the balance through a series of purchases that were completed by 1979. In 1999 the team was sold to settle Cooke's estate for $800 million. In an ironic testimony to the transitory nature of sports industry "empire building," after the team was sold, Jack Kent Cooke Stadium was renamed FedEx Field in a multimillion dollar naming rights agreement. The official press release announcing the deal with FedEx failed to even mention Cooke's name.[55] Nevertheless, Cooke did not entirely bankroll the project. The State of Maryland provided a $70 million subsidy, skirting the direct subsidy issue by allocating these funds for infrastructure and surrounding road work.

Robert Kraft, the New England Patriots owner, also received a $70 million infrastructure subsidy from Massachusetts in his privately funded project, which opened in 2002. San Francisco offers yet another example of private financing for a new sports facility. A clear lack of public support for a new ballpark, as voiced in four failed referenda, was partially offset by political maneuvering that resulted in land subsidies and tax abatements for new construction.[56] A vibrant regional economy and creative management approaches helped pay for a variety of costs with limited public subsidy. Twenty million dollars was raised simply by placing an eighty-foot-tall Coke bottle in a prominent ballpark location; $50 million was raised through a naming rights agreement with Pacific Bell, a prominent West Coast phone service provider; and $60 million was raised by selling personal seat licenses for the best seats in the ballpark.

In one difficult-to-foresee misstep, the management of the Giants negotiated a long-term energy deal with Enron, a now-defunct company that hoped to raise its corporate profile in the wake of energy deregulation. Nevertheless, the Giants made many astute moves that limited the need for taxpayer funding. They were successful in extracting fees from Chevron, a petroleum company, for the rights to sell ballpark tickets at its Bay Area gas stations. Chevron hoped to profit from more customer traffic. Although unable to fully fund the ballpark, Peter Magowan, owner of the Giants, demonstrated that even in high-cost urban areas, taxpayer subsidy can be limited dramatically.[57]

Stadium Spending in Perspective: Comparisons to Other Areas of the Economy

On a broad sociological level, the sum total of stadium construction expenditures are not significant. The $27.85 billion (inflation adjusted to 2005) that has been allocated for major league stadium and arena construction of venues opened during the twentieth century pales in comparison to the $497 billion allocated by the federal government to cover a single year of Social Security benefits in 2004 or the more than $300 billion projected for the military occupation of Iraq.[58] A one-week economic downturn in April 2000 cost investors a total of $2.1 trillion in stock equity losses. This total could have built over 75 times more major league facilities than were constructed in the entire twentieth century.[59] The $34 billion paid to support family dogs or the $42.4 billion spent nationally on weddings in a single year might provide sufficient funding to rebuild every major league football and baseball stadium currently in use.[60] In short, if measured as a portion of the larger national or global economy, such construction expenditures are relatively minor.

Nevertheless, at the microeconomic level, stadium costs are substantial and cannot be overlooked. If these funds were diverted to other programs, they would profoundly affect many people. As a result, it is no accident that demands for new stadium construction meet with considerable grassroots resistance, particularly when so many professional athletes' salaries exceed $1 million per season. When local service organizations are forced to conduct bake sales, raffles, and other nickle-and-dime fund-raisers to survive, it should not surprise anyone that stadium subsidies are less than well received by many citizens.

One hundred million dollars would finance only about one-third of a low-cost professional sports construction project, but it could also provide enough funds to double the nationwide capacity for the Boys and Girls Clubs of America.[61] One hundred million dollars could also provide 400 quarter-million dollar block grants to various community organizations for a multitude of worthwhile projects, many that would have greater economic benefit than a stadium.[62] As inner-city citizens look at decaying community assets and meager social service budgets, it is not unreasonable to understand why some citizens regard stadium subsidies with extreme anger.

However, some in the community may believe that the prestige of maintaining major league status is worth the subsidy. Such arguments have been bolstered by creative tax schemes contrived by pro-sports politicians to shield local taxpayers from stadium-related expenditures. The careful crafting of "visitor fees" on rental cars, hotel rooms, and other tourist services have virtually ensured that a large portion of subsidies will be paid for by out-of-town visitors, many with no desire to visit the ballpark.[63]

New construction has become more lavish than projects that were considered top quality during the 1960s and 1970s. The rising cost of construction in major cities as the twenty-first century opens should raise deep concerns that stadium-related spending, if unchecked, could quickly eclipse total expenditures of the past century. If spending continues at its recent pace, more could be spent on stadium and arenas during this century's first fifteen years than in the entire twentieth century.[64] Amenities have grown more important with each new building cycle. Until that trend changes, there is little reason to believe future stadium expenditures will decline.

Of similar concern are recent trends that minimize the stated cost of stadium construction. Deals often involve free land and tax breaks, and cleverly burying other costs might cause the public and even experts to undervalue the amount devoted to sports-related construction. Judith Grant Long has researched the potential cost of such undervaluation. Her findings suggest that traditional reporting methods have underestimated the cost of stadium and arena building to taxpayers by approximately 40 percent.[65]

Extensive media coverage of sports has been one reason why some citizens believe that stadium expenditures are worthwhile despite overwhelming scholarly evidence that such construction has little or no direct effect on the overall long-term economic growth of a region. The nationwide exposure of a community in daily sports coverage is perceived to have an intangible public relations value that is difficult, if not impossible, to quantify. The perception of "major league" status is as important to mayors of cities in decline as almost any other factor. In this vein, frequent national exposure of a major league home team is a compelling psychic benefit for citizens of a given metropolitan area. When the Rams moved from Los Angeles to St. Louis, numerous voices articulated the move's cultural significance. A far from elegant, yet heartfelt, citizen's remark that without an NFL team, "we're a cowtown," probably best summarized the gut-level value of such media exposure to some citizens.[66] Determining the merits of such public funding is problematic since symbolism and image are difficult to measure, but one thing is clear: Local economic claims regarding stadium subsidies are almost universally flawed.

An NFL pact that required broadcasters to pay $17.6 billion over eight years for transmission rights for this once-a-week sports product provided clear testimony to the premium that many citizens place on major league professional sports. Owners are highly aware of the coveted status that sports holds within a metropolitan culture. They often have the capacity to utilize this highly desirable cultural capital to bargain for the best possible stadium arrangement. The potential threat of franchise movement becomes a "wild card" that gives owners bargaining leverage that is difficult for political leaders to counter. Whether media coverage skews this bargaining process in a manner that provides an unfair negotiating edge for team owners merits further examination.

4

THE MEDIA AND STADIUM CONSTRUCTION

THE URBAN SCHOLAR Peter Eisinger argues that with today's current focus on stadium and convention center construction we have made a philosophic transition from a policy dedicated to residential services to a visitor-oriented, entertainment-based policy. Such policy is predicated on a desire to lure suburban outsiders and distant visitors to the city. Eisinger argues that such reliance on middle- and upper-class "bread and circuses" marks a fundamental policy transition away from the philosophic direction of nineteenth- and early twentieth-century infrastructure.

Eisinger suggests that projects of this earlier era served city residents in a more democratic manner; in short, the libraries, parks, and public health facilities constructed during this period benefitted a broader array of citizens. Recent stadium construction tends to have a less democratic benefit to the citizenry.[1] It is predicated on provision of upscale services as a means of maintaining an image outside the borders of a community. Eisinger does not emphasize some elite-driven construction of the past such as opera houses, orchestra halls, and museums, but overall, his optimistic argument about the past has merit.

A pervasive media landscape facilitates such "image-based" decisions. But as political decisions are made that cater to well-heeled suburban visitors, have local media institutions provided coverage that maintains a democratic process? Roger Noll and Andrew Zimbalist's research on behalf of the Brookings Institution provides a compelling argument that funding discrepancies for stadium campaigns offer considerable advantages to pro-construction voices.[2]

Mark Rosentraub suggests that the interlocking commercial interests of media organizations and sports franchises create a natural tendency to favor stadium construction.[3] Rosentraub further argues that stadium coverage tends to favor team owners because sports reporting brings a desired demographic to a given medium. As a result, he suggests that politicians "may be very receptive to supporting sports issues if it means favorable exposure [for them] in the media."[4] George Sage combines arguments of the Brookings Institution effort and Rosentraub. Because of momentum established by community boosterism, Sage argues the deck is stacked against those who oppose new stadium construction.[5] Charles Euchner offers another hypothesis, arguing that "the local media tend to be 'boosterish' toward the local team because of the glow of major league status that they receive from their association with the team."[6]

Yet other evidence suggests that pro-construction slanting is not inevitable, nor is the validity of a pro-construction hypothesis certain. Joanna Cagan and Neil deMause argue that the press informs the public about "the stadium swindle" with articles that expose the subsidies given to team owners.[7] Jay Cross, former head of business development for the Miami Heat basketball team, vociferously argued that even though his team spent over a million dollars on a carefully designed media campaign to construct a new arena, "the press didn't cut us any breaks."[8] Cross is current president of the New York Jets. Jose Francisco Marichal examined early 1990s press coverage of fourteen cities and suggests the outcome of pro-stadium boosterism is less than certain. He asserts that "community actors tended to raise questions about the stadium development issue. . . , the project-related actors tended to support this issue. . . , [whereas] government actors tended to act as something of a 'swing vote,' with divergent camps on either side."[9]

Peter Richmond's exploration of Baltimore's Camden Yards offers an overview of the immense task of constructing a new sports facility. The concept of a ballpark that was intended to echo the past succeeded primarily because of media exposure of the idea. The original plan to integrate an aging railroad warehouse into an old-fashioned stadium design was launched by Eric Moss, an architecture student at Syracuse University. Positive press coverage of Moss's design resulted in revised architectural plans from construction firms bidding on the Camden Yards project. If left to professional architects, the overall design of this trendsetting ballpark might have been substantially different.[10]

Overall, the scholarship of stadium construction tends to suggest that a media bias occurs that favors new stadium construction. Such coverage is more commonplace than a balanced coverage that offers a full range of points of views on this issue. A publisher's tendency to act as a community booster in many instances may contribute to this tendency.

The Booster Spirit, Media Routines, Public Relations, and the Public

Although the American press highlights a commitment to balance and fairness, often using the term "objectivity" to reflect this desired goal, many practitioners would agree that news reporting devoid of bias is problematic. Many variables confound a reporter's ability to report *any* event with full accuracy. Personal bias, media routines, managerial bias, and numerous external influences can cause coverage to stray from an objective ideal. The ideology of boosterism may further complicate a reporter's ability to provide accuracy in news coverage, particularly with issues related to sporting institutions.

Even without consideration of stadium-related coverage bias, it is difficult to deny that the booster spirit has contributed mightily to stadium building. It is hard to find scholarship that defines boosterism, but it can be separated from generic calls for economic development by an individual's positive emotional bond to his or her community. Boosters want to promote their city because they are enthusiastic supporters of a given locale.

Sports-related coverage, with its focus on highly emotional competitive comparisons to other cities, is more inclined to reflect boosterism than dispassionate economic rhetoric. Individuals want their region to be regarded as "major league," and professional sports franchises have become a convenient and recognizable yardstick of this "major league" status. During national telecasts of sporting events, stadiums are routinely shown and cities are often talked about, prompting civic boosters to support stadium construction even when economic logic might suggest that alternative action would yield greater returns.

The booster mentality is deeply ingrained in the American psyche and, despite denials by some media practitioners, it is an inherent part of modern journalism. It has been part of America for centuries; hence, it is an ideology that may be less likely to shift with time. Daniel Boorstin traces boosterism to the booster press that facilitated nineteenth-century westward expansion.[11] However, evidence of boosterism can be traced to colonial settlement.[12] As such, it is important to recognize that knee-jerk boosterism is a part of the fabric of many communities, making opposition to the political demands of the home team a potentially risky practice.

Further complicating this civic boosterism is a layer of sports industry boosterism that has permeated media coverage since the emergence of professional athletics in America. The boosterism that came with big-time collegiate athletics in the late nineteenth and early twentieth centuries served to cultivate a jingoistic reporting model that stressed localism. During the earliest years of college football, newspapers throughout the country dutifully reported top-rated Harvard and Yale scores, the most important football powers of the time, but more coverage was often afforded to local successes. As an example, the *Atlanta Constitution* often featured banner headlines of John Heisman's Georgia Tech football squad.

With the emergence of professional baseball as a commercial product, the linkage to positive coverage was more often directly influenced by the self-interest of newspaper management. Joseph Pulitzer and many of his contemporaries often regarded positive coverage of the home team as a circulation booster. Team owners were equally enthusiastic about obtaining positive publicity. Aaron Champion, the primary financier of the famed 1869 Cincinnati Red Stockings, was described as "delighted with the arrangement" that permitted Harry Millar, a newspaper writer, to join the team on road trips. Stephen Guschov describes Millar's role as "more of a publicity flack for the club than . . . a hard nosed reporter."[13] Some early reporters were directly linked to team ownership. In 1901, Frank Hough, sports editor for the *Philadelphia Inquirer,* and Sam Jones, an Associated Press writer, teamed up with Connie Mack and Benjamin Shibe to buy the Philadelphia Athletics baseball team. Shibe owned half the team, Mack owned twenty-five percent, and Hough and Jones each held twelve and one-half percent. Not surprisingly, boosterism permeated the *Inquirer*'s coverage. Historian Bruce Kuklick states that "Hough's column 'Don't Knock—But Boost' greatly helped the franchise."[14]

Although boosterism is an important element in the push for construction, the ability of team owners to leverage their monopoly status contributes to the dramatic increase in stadium building across the nation. In short, the popularity of a team within a community gives franchise owners an opportunity to extract substantial subsidies at a time when political leaders are limiting funding in many other areas. As city after city turns to stadium construction to enhance, create, or preserve "major league" status, a divided public struggles with the various issues surrounding public subsidy of the profit-generating sports industry.

The role of mass media in this stadium construction boom is considerable. The certainty that a professional team receives continuous national media attention intensifies the desire of city leaders to maintain "major-league" status at almost any cost. Team owners, aware of the symbolic value of their product, have pushed hard recently to achieve vast government subsidies. The level of this funding is so profound that city leaders often turn to county and state sources. Unlike Progressive Era politics where the city leaders had the upper hand in negotiations, the power has shifted to team owners.

The public relations prowess of sports leagues has contributed to this power shift. Former Houston Mayor Bob Lanier contends that "these sports teams have the best PR machines in the world." According to Lanier, "They really do a marvelous job of couching issues in ways favorable to themselves. The NFL PR machine undertakes to personalize the issue—between the team and the mayor. That's big-time pressure."[15] Not surprisingly, in response to this "big-time pressure," the mayor often becomes a most spirited advocate for stadium construction.

That football and baseball franchises are adept at public relations is significant to their success. After all, the public relations market has become saturated with special interests, so teams have to push hard to cut through competing clutter. The importance of public relations cannot be underestimated as a force in the democratic process. Ray Eldon Hiebert and Sheila Jean Gibbons assert that "the amount of news that originates in public relations offices . . . has been estimated to be as little as 30 percent and as much as 80 percent."[16] Even if the lower figure is accurate, such influence is considerable.

Media scholar Stuart Ewen cautions that public relations has a clear potential to diminish political participation while undermining the democratic process. According to Ewen, "Publicity becomes an impediment to democracy . . . when the circulation of ideas is governed by enormous concentrations of wealth that have as their underlying purpose, the perpetuation of their own power. When this is the case—as is too often true today—the idea of civic participation gives way to a continual sideshow, a masquerade of democracy calculated to pique the public's emotions."[17]

Whether media coverage of stadium construction reflects a shift from "civic participation" to what Ewen calls "a continual sideshow" merits careful examination, particularly when the self-interest of media institutions have the potential to cloud construction-related coverage decisions. A number of media companies own professional franchises.[18] Rupert Murdoch's News Corporation owned the Los Angeles Dodgers for several years and for a period maintained a minority interest in the New York Knicks and New York Rangers. Time Warner, by virtue of Ted Turner's involvement with the company, owns the Atlanta Braves, the NBA's Atlanta Hawks, and the NHL's Atlanta Thrashers. The Tribune Company owns the Chicago Cubs, and Disney, parent company to ABC and ESPN, for a time owned the Anaheim Angels and the Anaheim Mighty Ducks. The latter, an NHL franchise, was named after a popular movie marketed by Disney, further blurring the line between media product and sports marketing. Smaller media corporations, including newspapers and television stations, often maintain a minority ownership position in teams within their community. The *St. Louis Post-Dispatch*'s parent company maintains minority ownership in the St. Louis Cardinals baseball franchise.

Minnesota Metrodome construction offers mixed messages regarding media ownership's involvement in stadium building. Jay Weiner's detailed background of the Metrodome's construction shows that press influence played a part in the subsidy process but that reporters did not appreciate attempts to influence their reporting. John Cowles Jr. was an active supporter of the decision to build this indoor facility. He also served as chairman of the Minneapolis Star and Tribune Company, described by Weiner as "the region's most powerful media outlet and opinion maker."[19] Cowles presided over editorial positions supporting new construction, but certain vagaries of the market challenged the credibility of such endorsements. First, a grassroots "Green Fan" movement led by Philadelphia transplant Julian Empson Loscalzo prompted citizen opposition to an indoor stadium.[20] Second, an independent core of media practitioners may have attempted to offset the boosterism of *Star Tribune* management.

Weiner cites an act of journalistic muscle flexing on March 1, 1979, when forty-five writers and editors collectively paid to run an advertisement expressing uneasiness with their boss's active support of this issue. Cowles allowed the advertisement to run, but this decision may have been colored by approval of construction days earlier. The advertisement assured readers that "our professional principles have not been undermined by Cowles' involvement in the stadium issue. . . . But to prevent even the appearance of such a conflict of interest, we believe management should avoid a leadership role in sensitive political and economic issues."[21]

The linkage of higher circulation to sports coverage creates a powerful incentive to favor booster-oriented policies that ensure continued success of the home team. Mark Rosentraub offers evidence of newspaper circulation declines when labor disputes prevent games from taking place. He further argues that the *Dallas Morning News* reported its highest circulation during the Cowboys's Super Bowl coverage. Rosentraub concludes that "the media has discovered a 'golden goose' in sports and that goose is rarely analyzed for officials who must decide whether or not a [stadium construction] subsidy is needed."[22]

The intermingling of commerce and reporting is evident after stadium construction is completed. In many cities, the giant scoreboard, which has become an increasingly successful revenue generator, features the local media companies as highly prominent sponsors. When Bank One Ballpark was completed in 1998, for example, the most visible scoreboard advertiser was the *Arizona Republic* with a large placement below an old-fashioned circular clock. The ballpark was renamed Chase Field in September 2005, but the newspaper's prominent scoreboard visibility has not changed.

The fees paid by television stations and major networks for sports broadcasting rights further complicate the ability of reporters to provide comprehensive coverage of all issues surrounding stadium construction policy. The NFL's multibillion dollar agreements with television networks reflect a capital outlay so substantial that broadcasters are compelled to take dramatic steps to ensure an adequate return on this huge expense. According to Lawrence Strauss, such contractual largess may diminish critical coverage of sports teams because "big money can tempt the networks into viewing the sports organizations they cover as marketing partners."[23]

Whether slanting of local news coverage would result because of these substantial financial commitments is problematic, but the television and radio stations that broadcast these games have made it abundantly clear that live coverage of the local team is highly desirable. Some stations have even changed network affiliations after league contracts were lost by a network.[24] Such desirability presents a potential for slanting news because stations are often measured by their commercial success.

The *Los Angeles Times* coverage of the city's newly constructed Staples Center offers a noteworthy example of how commerce and media self-interest can affect news reporting of sports-related projects. On October 10,

1999, the newspaper created a 162-page magazine special that centered on the opening of a new $400 million facility that was the new home for the NBA's Lakers and Clippers and the NHL's Kings. Articles were universally supportive of the new arena. One article, entitled "What the Staples Center Could Do for L.A.," provided an array of reasons why the new structure would lead to a revitalization of downtown Los Angeles. Unknown to the public, the editorial staff, and even editor-in-chief Michael Parks was publisher Kathryn Downing's agreement to share revenues from this publication with Staples Center management.

The publication generated $2 million in revenues but was castigated by the public and much of the newspaper's staff once this revenue-sharing agreement was uncovered by *New Times,* a smaller weekly publication. Kathryn Downing indicated that her attempted reconciliation meeting with the staff "was the angriest, most confrontational meeting I've ever seen at the paper." Although most of the national focus of this story evaluated the morally questionable decision to shield the public and the newspaper's reporting staff from knowledge of this cross-promotional effort, a deeper ethical question should be addressed. Was the news staff so willing to comply with cues given by management that the quality of news coverage was jeopardized? Of particular concern is the news staff's complicity in assembling 162 pages of puffery. Although it is possible that stories critical of the Staples Center may have been edited or killed by individuals who knew of the profit-sharing arrangement, evidence of such tampering has not surfaced. If one of America's finest newspapers was content to produce an uncritical celebration of a subsidized arena, should readers question the credibility of subsequent news coverage produced by this award-winning newspaper? It was only after this agreement with the Staples Center was exposed that more critical coverage was provided.[25]

The construction of sports cathedrals has contributed to a vigorous national debate about the role of sports in American society. Many argue that stadium construction contributes to the economic vitality of American cities, inspiring others to invest in the future development of a community. This argument is frequently advanced by the pro-stadium lobby. Despite significant evidence challenging this argument, it is often the most compelling and powerful claim advanced by pro-stadium advocates. The "quality of life" argument, while potentially more credible, appears to be a less vociferous argument. The ability of an entire metropolitan area to enjoy the home team is difficult to quantify, yet the benefits are palpable for anyone exposed to a game-day atmosphere or lively debates on the day after an exciting hometown victory.

Nevertheless, dramatic public opposition has followed stadium construction efforts. This opposition takes many trajectories. Some argue that a subsidy is welfare for the rich. Others state that such monies would be better spent in other areas. Several have suggested that team owners and athletes, the primary beneficiaries in new construction, have not earned the privilege of subsides. Multimillion dollar contracts for athletes and multibillion dollar television packages for owners are often cited as reasons for funding opposition. Headlines received by athletes for troubles ranging from drug abuse, drunk driving, criminal assault, and rape have further eroded the desire of many citizens to support any attempt to subsidize the sports industry.[26]

Arguments on both sides of the stadium debate reveal much about the politics and culture of a community. Exclusion and privilege, both driving forces in the earliest decisions regarding ballpark construction, permeate today's dialogue. Media coverage of the stadium construction debate tends to reflect reporting trends found in other types of news coverage. Michael Schudson argues that "to understand news as a culture requires what categories of person count as 'who,' what kinds of things pass for facts, or 'whats,' what geography and sense of time count as 'where' and 'when,' and what counts as an explanation of 'why.' "[27] News coverage does not take place in a vacuum. Media routines reflect conscious and unconscious choices that combine to shape news coverage. The actors chosen, the prioritization of arguments, and placement decisions are made as part of a dynamic process that includes input from both internal and external sources. Reporters must frequently navigate a diverse assortment of issues while struggling to determine which voices merit prominence.

Charles Bantz, Suzanne McCorkle, and Roberta Baade assert that managerial desires to shape the news-gathering processes to achieve assembly line efficiencies foster a "lack of flexibility, lack of personal investment in the product, an evaluation of newswork in productivity terms, and a mismatch between the newsworkers expectations and the factory in which they work."[28] These scholars firmly argue that productivity, measured in terms of total news output, is often more valued than concern for product quality. This recent tendency to regard institutional productivity and profitability as paramount concerns may shape news coverage in both intentional and unintentional ways.

Reporters may not consider the public policy ramifications of reliance on familiar Rolodexed sources, but they may intuitively understand that reporting quality suffers when factory-style reporting prevents comprehensive analysis of issues. A study by the Pew Research Center for the People and the Press concluded that at all levels, "majorities of working journalists say that increasing bottom-line pressure is hurting the quality of [news] coverage."[29]

A number of scholars have focused more specifically on ownership issues. Ben Bagdikian argues that corporate media concentration has hampered the ability of local reporters to cover news. Bagdikian states that "in a world of multiple problems, where the diversity of ideas is essential for decent solutions, controlled information inhibited by uniform self-interest is the first and fatal enemy."[30] Theodore Glasser suggests that restrictions against reporter involvement in political issues are more than offset by routine management participation in community institutions such as corporate boards, think tanks, and charities. He argues that the detached objectivity that drives contemporary reporting strategies are "largely a matter of efficiency—efficiency that serves . . . the needs and interests of the owners of the press, not the needs and interests of talented writers, and certainly not the needs and interests of the larger society."[31]

Harvey Molotch, an urban scholar, indicates that local interests provide a potential source of news bias because of an editorial deference toward coverage that is perceived to bring regional economic growth.[32] He also argues that such bias is not restricted to the newsroom; it permeates virtually all levels of society because a "growth machine" model has been adopted as part of a larger core ideology.[33] The focus on economic growth as opposed to more neutral reporting has implications in what is covered, but it may also determine what is not covered.

Media-reporting biases of both inclusion and omission must be regarded in approaching stadium-related issues. Much of the negotiation related to construction policy takes place behind closed doors, making after-the-fact analysis increasingly important to understanding this issue. Team owners often insist on low-profile negotiating tactics, despite the significant role of public funding in policy proposals. Civic leaders are reluctant to resist team owner's desires, in part due to an increased willingness of teams to abandon a region for a better stadium arrangement elsewhere. In recent years, deterioration of personal relationships between team owners and key civic leaders has accelerated franchise relocation, leaving politicians vulnerable to criticism.[34]

Because of the "closed-door" nature of stadium negotiations, media coverage of this issue is important. It represents the public's primary access to information and has the potential to shape how this issue is perceived by citizens. This coverage is one element of a broad set of variables that ultimately determine the shape of stadium construction policy. It is only one factor, but it is an important variable in every case study that involves stadium construction.

5

CINCINNATI

Let's Build Two

CINCINNATI IS A CITY of contrasts. The lazy paddlewheel riverboats on the banks of the Ohio River offer a stark contrast to a more contemporary city that operates at a faster pace than these relics of yesteryear might suggest. It is a polite city that mixes Southern and Midwestern cultures, but it has also been a lightning rod for uncivil controversy. Riots and unrest permeated the city in 2001 after a police officer shot an unarmed civilian. The Mapplethorpe Exhibit and Ku Klux Klan rallies have also brought heated controversy.

These confrontations can be contrasted with an accommodating cultural heritage that was reluctant to choose sides in the Civil War and was so reflexively generous to nineteenth-century beggars that the *Cincinnati Daily Enquirer* claimed that "adjoining cities and towns [were] shipping their paupers here."[1] More recently, the region's reputation for civility was cited in the *USA Today's Four Sport Stadium Guide* when explaining Cinergy Field's dimensions. According to this book's authors, "the field's perfectly fair, symmetrical, average dimensions. . . , reflect the city's reputation as a polite town."[2] Cinergy Field was demolished in 2002 to make way for Great American Ballpark, which opened in 2003.

The city received national attention for racial unrest and allegations of police brutality in 2001. What was not covered were popular city block parties in the same Over-the-Rhine neighborhood that was the site of unrest and acrimony. Although anger over racial issues may be palpable in some neighborhoods, Cincinnati has not erupted into chaos, as has happened in some cities dealing with dramatic racial tension.

A population that is politely conservative on social issues can be contrasted to abrasive popular culture icons who have emerged from the area. Pornography magnate Larry Flynt and popular talk show host Jerry Springer seem to reflect everything that a typical Cincinnati resident abhors, yet Flynt's empire emerged from his Cincinnati base, and Springer first gained a spotlight, not as a Cincinnati talk show host, but as a politician who was eventually elected Cincinnati's mayor.[3] The less-than-clean reputations developed by Springer and Flynt as well as the baseball legend Pete Rose are also an ironic contrast to Cincinnati's largest employer, Procter and Gamble, the nation's largest producer of cleaning products.

It is a parsimonious culture with a population that wants to maintain necessary city services but is reluctant to part with tax dollars unless a program can be justified as necessary. This thrift may have deep roots, evolving from a manufacturing culture that derived its resources for soap production from animal fat by-products obtained at the many slaughterhouses that shaped the early years of Cincinnati's shift from agriculture to industrial production.

Determining why Cincinnati citizens might willfully spend dollars on stadium subsidies might seem like a mystery, but this might be understood as part of a long-standing desire to be identified as a major league city. Stephen Guschov's history of Cincinnati baseball traces the formation of the nation's first fully professional baseball team in 1869 to a desire for civic pride that was cultivated, in part, by the derisive moniker "Porkopolis," which was often attached to Cincinnati by the haughty citizens of Chicago.[4] The term "Porkopolis" was so pervasive that in 1876, Cincinnati's baseball team was nicknamed the "Porkopolitans" to the dismay of many, but with the approval of Josiah Keck, the team owner who derived his profits from meat packing.[5]

The historian Carl Abbott argues that Cincinnati's wealthy classes of the nineteenth century allowed the Cincinnati economy to languish while Chicago and St. Louis moved forward through a more aggressive boosterism that attracted industry and investment.[6] If Cincinnati proved to be a laggard in boosterism, it was ahead of its time in identifying professional athletics as a means of achieving prominence. Robert Harris Walker, a professor of American Studies, argues that "residents of this city not only enjoy their baseball, but feel that the city is judged by its baseball."[7] Cincinnati's heritage of sports-oriented boosterism created a fertile terrain for stadium construction as the 1990s unfolded. It should be of little surprise that the Queen City was the first urban center east of the Mississippi River to approve plans that would simultaneously subsidize construction of two major league ballparks.[8]

Cincinnati: An Overview of Stadium Construction History

Cincinnati has a high level of enthusiasm for sports, and this enthusiasm is reflected throughout the city's cultural fabric. Despite many losing football seasons, former Bengal players are often featured in local advertisements. Billboards for food products endorsed by the retired quarterback Boomer Esiason might be found on Vine Street, as are radio advertisements and public service pitches featuring the Hall of Fame lineman Anthony Munoz.[9] The Cincinnati Public Library features sports-related displays and has even published thousands of copies of a staff-produced baseball-related bibliography for free distribution to citizens to encourage use of their sizable collection of sports-related materials.[10] The University of Cincinnati offers an abundance of sports-related resources including a large collection of dissertations and theses acquired from colleges and universities throughout the United States. Cincinnati hosted the 2004 Society for American Baseball Research's national convention.

Further evidence of the regions's passion for sports abounds. Cincinnati Reds legend Johnny Bench has been featured on the cover of *Cincinnati Magazine* several times. The Cincinnati Pops Orchestra has tailored its performances to include baseball themes.[11] A Cincinnati road was named in honor of Pete Rose. Despite Rose's banishment from baseball for gambling infractions, many Cincinnati residents continue to look favorably upon this sports icon, often calling talk shows to argue that he has been treated unfairly by baseball's executives. The city council was even featured in *Sports Illustrated*'s feature "Sign the Apocalypse Is Upon Us" in 2000 for considering a proposal of "a citywide Bud Selig Exclusion Zone" after the commissioner said he would continue to prohibit Pete Rose from involvement with Major League Baseball.[12]

A recent *Cincinnati Magazine* issue called the Reds Cincinnati's "most precious institution."[13] During Marge Schott's tenure as Reds owner, she capitalized on this local passion, adorning local buses with billboards that prominently featured Reds logos in advertisements for her car dealership. This commercial use of sport has deep roots. The first fully professional baseball team, the Red Stockings, was initially formed in 1866 by attorney Aaron Champion, "an enormous civic booster . . . [who] believed that if the city of Cincinnati prospered, so would he."[14] Champion believed that a winning baseball team could instill civic pride, and as the son of a prosperous merchant, he was familiar with the world of commerce. He hired Harry Wright, a handsome, athletically gifted English native with New York roots, to lead the new team.

Initially, the Red Stockings were outclassed by teams from New York and Washington, but by 1869, the all-professional formula established by Wright became the future model for baseball in America. The 1869 Red Stockings stunned the baseball community with a remarkable record of 56-0-1. Baseball historian Steven Guschov remarked that "Harry Wright's men were not just hired gun professionals, but also were pioneers and teachers of the burgeoning game."[15] Children attempted to emulate the fielding and hitting techniques of these athletes. Similarly, baseball teams elsewhere would try to copy Harry Wright's managerial tactics.

The impact of Cincinnati's undefeated season on the future of baseball was profound. Professionalism, a concept often regarded as undesirable in sports during the Gilded Age, gained currency and credibility and was fully entrenched by the Progressive Era. Wright reinforced the credibility of professionalism with a regimen of tough practices and an insistence on healthy diet that excluded excessive drinking. The uniform style, adapted from English cricket outerwear but offset with unique bright colored hosiery, was also a hallmark of the Cincinnati squad. Mixing a unique style with a focus on winning, Wright's team furthered the credibility of sports as paid, commercial entertainment. The commercial model stood in contrast to the previously established English model of sports, one that was predicated on genteel, aristocratic amateurism.

This process was evolutionary, not revolutionary, however. The refusal of some teams to play less-affluent professional squads offers evidence that the English model based on elitism had not entirely disappeared in 1869. However, baseball that was predicated on commercial values was emerging, and that model would eventually displace the old world's amateur model. Albert Spalding, a sporting industry legend and organizer of rival teams, made the linkage between sports and entertainment clear. In a question that reflects the current-day ethos of sport, Spalding rhetorically asked, "How could it be right to pay an actor, or a singer . . . for entertaining the public, and wrong to pay a ballplayer for doing exactly the same thing?"[16]

Acceptance of this new ideology in sports eventually led to the need for ballparks and stadiums that were more elaborate, and over time, these structures became a reflection of civic pride. Cincinnati was a leader in this ideological process, but the ballpark as a revenue-generating venue developed in New York, not Cincinnati. Cincinnati's first ballpark was less of a profit center and more of a necessary locale to retain a ball club that, through success, became a symbol of community pride. Cincinnati's first professional ballparks offer modest philosophic parallels to the subsidy model of today.

The Cincinnati Base Ball Club, as it was then known, initially paid $2,000 to rent the Live Oak Base Ball Grounds in 1866, moving to the Union Cricket Club Grounds by 1867. The club president Aaron Champion allocated $10,000 to refurbish the Union Grounds, presumably utilizing the club dues of its 380 members to fund the improvements that included field grading, sodding, and the construction of stands and a clubhouse. An early artist illustration suggests this was a more elaborate facility than other ballparks of the era. Canvas canopies provided some players and scorers with protection from the hot sun, and a shaded wooden grandstand, topped with an American flag, offered a more special environment for Cincinnati's more affluent fans.[17]

As baseball's popularity increased, membership in the cricket club declined. By 1868, the baseball club had assumed all Union Ground debts, an indication that baseball had overtaken cricket in Cincinnati. This indebtedness complicated Champion and Wright's goal of fielding an "all professional" team. To solve the problem, Champion offered an $11,000 stock issue in 1868 and a $15,000 stock issue in 1869.[18] With total team payroll at $9,300 for the 1869 season, a portion of these funds were likely allocated to ballpark improvements.[19] Ticket sales further enhanced the club's income as it embarked on its first fully professional season.

The team was less stable in the 1870s and 1880s, however. After declaring bankruptcy the team's ballpark was auctioned off, piece by piece, in 1872, with much of the structure used as firewood. Cincinnati baseball moved to the Avenue Grounds in the 1870s and then to Bank Street and Finley Street Grounds in the early 1880s.[20] Early attempts to fence in ballparks, including the Union Grounds, had an exclusionary dimension, but one of Cincinnati's first large major league ballparks was more egalitarian. League Park, erected in 1884 for the Reds, reflected the blue collar environs of an abandoned brickyard surrounded by factories. Early on, the ballpark was not a source of community pride. Its stands collapsed on opening day, the first time they ever held spectators, reportedly killing one person and injuring others.[21] The park was destroyed by fire in 1900. A wooden facility was quickly built to replace it.[22]

The team's owner John Brush began to construct a more permanent facility in 1901, opening it in 1902. Despite limited capacity (approximately 5,000 fans attended its first day), this park, still formally identified as League Park, was most often called the "Palace of the Fans." The Palace was unique in its use of classical architecture, giving fans a touch of elegance not seen elsewhere. With Corinthian columns and arches built into the structure, parts of it had the look of a federal building with a curving, theater-like, balcony-style upper deck. Mostly concrete, the peripheral sections also contained wooden remnants of the earlier ballpark.[23]

The *Cincinnati Enquirer* chose not to include the inaugural coverage on its front page, but it did offer a five-column photograph on page 4, likely the first ever newspaper photograph of a major league ballpark's opening ceremonies. The May 17, 1902, coverage offered evidence of civic pride. Judge Howard Ferris was headlined stating, "I now turn over to you forever the Palace of the Fans." A May 16, 1902, sports section article preceded the inauguration festivities.

Cincinnati's reporting reflected an increase in prominence for ballpark construction. The team's decision to hold the dedication ceremonies when the New York Giants were in town may have been a strategic move to let those beyond Cincinnati's borders know that the city derided as "Porkopolis" was committed to an upscale sporting experience as extravagant as any ballpark in the nation. However, the New York press did not cooperate. The *New York Times* failed to mention the new ballpark at all, focusing exclusively on the game's outcome.

In 1912, after other cities had constructed higher capacity fully concrete and steel facilities, Cincinnati replaced this classical structure with a less-ornate 20,000 capacity ballpark that was then called Redland Field. In 1934, when the Reds were purchased by manufacturing magnate Powel Crosley, the ballpark was renamed Crosley Field. After a winning team captured the city's enthusiasm, Crosley Field was expanded in 1939 to accommodate 30,000 fans.

Following the construction of several municipal ballparks elsewhere during the late 1950s and early 1960s, the tradition-rich Crosley Field began to be regarded as an archaic community eyesore. In an age that glorified cutting-edge technology, it was difficult to defend an old-fashioned ballpark that reflected the quaint values of yesteryear. The unique upward-sloping outfield, a feature that challenged luminaries such as Babe Ruth in the twilight of his career, was no longer a desirable quirk for a game that was seeking to modernize its image. Leveling the outfield was not possible because of an underground stream. At the same time, the Crosley Field neighborhood was becoming more commercial and less residential.

Riverfront Stadium's construction was encouraged by local media in numerous articles over a number of years. In July 1959, the *Cincinnati Enquirer* appealed to civic pride and a cultural emphasis on modernity in an in-depth series that chronicled stadium construction in other cities. A front-page introduction to the series asked: "Can the Cincinnati Reds be lured away? Would the availability of a fancy, modern stadium in another city do it?"[24] The series featured many photographs and included strategies used by civic leaders elsewhere to lure away baseball teams from other cities. The most emphasized strategy was the construction of a new ballpark. The first article offered a subheading that cautioned "if we dilly-dally, we'll lose the team." It indicated that Powel Crosley threatened to move the team if better parking facilities and better overall facilities were not forthcoming. The need for a new stadium was strongly suggested, but renovation of Crosley Field in exchange for a long term city pact was also discussed. Stadium proponents argued "an industry that brings prestige plus several million dollars a year to the city is too valuable to risk."[25]

Subsequent coverage focused on modern amenities and prestige. Attracting the Braves by constructing Milwaukee's County Stadium was described by "most citizens" as "the city's biggest step forward in years."[26] San Francisco's Candlestick Park was described as "the newest and most modern in the nation." The article did more than generate envy for this taxpayer-funded West Coast ballpark, it provided justification for direct media involvement in the campaign to construct a stadium. According to the author, "The four daily newspapers spearheaded the drive. As soon as business leaders and merchants figured out what a major league team would mean for the city in terms of spending, they got on the bandwagon. . . . It was an easy sell."[27]

A day after the San Francisco article, a front-page model of an $8 million stadium intended for Cincinnati's Carthage Fairgrounds was featured, presumably to excite readers. A same-day article about the Twin Cities simultaneously constructing two ballparks offered an example of a community willing to take bold action to acquire a team. Minnesota did not yet have a major league franchise, so the veiled threat of a Reds departure might have been intended. A Los Angeles story rounded out the series, but this series did not bring a new stadium closer to fruition.

The campaign to replace Crosley Field eventually moved to the riverfront. If examined through the prism of today, it is possible that construction would have taken place away from that location because Reds owner William DeWitt was never enthusiastic about that location. Instead, he preferred construction in Blue Ash, a place that, at the time, offered greater access to highways. With no guarantees of a football franchise when construction decisions were being made, it is likely that current policy and press coverage would have given greater attention to DeWitt's desires than occurred in the 1960s as he was lobbying for a stadium.

The development of Riverfront Stadium was a drawn-out evolutionary process. Establishing credibility for a riverfront site may have been sparked by one individual's modest attempt to install a statue in a visible public location. One of the earliest proposals, released in 1948, considered a riverfront stadium as part of a larger plan to improve the entire downtown area. The City Planning Commission did not focus on the stadium as an essential part of this redevelopment, but indicated it would be an important feature that might improve the economy if approved. According to their report, "The Cincinnati Convention and Visitors Bureau estimates Cincinnati has lost $1 million a year for lack of facilities for major sports events."[28]

The Planning Commission strategy did not focus on a new riverfront stadium, and citizens did not appear to believe this was a problem. Furthermore, riverfront development did not seem to attract a multitude of supporters, so proposed construction here had limited political currency. In the 1950s and the early 1960s much of the citizenry considered the dilapidated riverfront beyond hope. The lack of prime development during this time suggested that many government officials and the business community were in fundamental agreement. The poor condition of the riverfront clouded the ability of citizens and leaders to see this land as a potential resource. Louis Leonard Tucker described the riverfront as "dismal and dirty. [It was] the city's depository for sand, gravel, coal, and junk; filled with decaying buildings and the accumulated filth. . . , hardly a visually exciting front yard for the Queen City."[29]

An initial push for symbolic development of the riverfront was made in 1959 by Robert Acomb, president of the Queen City Printing Company.

After a conversation with his daughter, Jill, revealed that she had no knowledge of the historic origins of the city's name, he decided that a statue of Quinctius Cincinnatus, the legendary Roman military leader and farmer, would serve to educate youth about the city's classical origins. Acomb convinced a number of his colleagues at the Cincinnatus Association, an exclusive civic club, that the idea had merit, only to have the idea turned down by the city's museum director. The director considered the notion of a Roman statue in front of the museum low-brow and tacky. Nevertheless, the idea gained some traction. In July, a *Cincinnati Enquirer* article focusing on the future of Crosley Field quoted John Lloyd, chairman of the Civic Stadium Development Committee, touting a riverfront location as the place "where almost everyone believes the [new] stadium should be." Although Lloyd's remarks appear to reflect public sentiment, evidence suggests that other sites may have been more attractive to the public and to Reds management.[30]

After months of riverfront development inactivity, the Cincinnatus Association approached the City Planning and Park Board with an idea that would expand the development of Cincinnati's riverfront beyond what was initially proposed. At this meeting Acomb and his colleagues received a green light to investigate the notion of a riverfront park that would include installation of a statue. The desire to expand riverfront development beyond the statue may have been accelerated by a legislative maneuver in 1959 to raise the city's bonding authority by $30 million. After one failed attempt to place a $4 million bond issue on the ballot in 1961, architects were solicited as part of a well-publicized contest to develop plans for this park. Although the contest failed to produce a winning entry, it garnered considerable coverage and sparked enthusiasm for proposals to develop the riverfront. Tucker described this process as "the key to riverfront renewal [with] the first move in a domino game . . . [passage of] the $6,600,000 bond referendum of 1962."[31] Although a large park area was not constructed, part of the bond issue included convention center funding. The subsequent construction helped to make stadium construction at the riverfront more viable.

By the mid-1960s the dialogue had shifted to almost full acceptance of the notion that, if approved, ballpark construction would take place at the riverfront. In 1965 attorney Judson Allgood, representing bonding consultants to the Hamilton County Commissioners, confidently reported that a stadium "could be financed, constructed, and paid for without new taxes."

Media coverage suggested that revenues from team rent, ticket fees, concession sales, and parking were sufficient to pay for what was reported to be a $20 million project.[32] Less than a month later, a front-page story estimated the total cost at $35 million. An accompanying story suggested adding a dome, and an adjacent photo of Ohio Governor James Rhodes in football formation with five local politicians fostered public enthusiasm for political efforts to lobby for an expansion NFL team. The six photographed politicians were reportedly set to travel to the NFL Pro Bowl to examine "the city's chances for a grid franchise."[33] Former Cincinnati Mayor Gene Ruehlmann asserted that Governor Rhodes's visible involvement at this Chamber of Commerce luncheon "really lit a spark" for the project.[34]

By the middle of 1966 the riverfront location was solidified. A government-commissioned feasibility study isolated the riverfront as the best stadium site. A publicly circulated bulletin from the Hamilton County Good Government League in May 1966 further emphasized riverfront development momentum. This document stated that the Reds's first choice was a site in Blue Ash, but "after several days of negotiating, [Reds owner] DeWitt gave approval to the steering committee's number one choice, the riverfront."[35]

By June the stadium issue shifted to a debate about aesthetics, construction, and financing. An eighteen-member Stadium Selection Committee, formed in 1966 and chaired by *Cincinnati Enquirer* Vice President Charlie Staab, met to determine a design approach. Utilizing St. Louis' new circular stadium (Busch Stadium) as a model of modernity, civic leaders and stadium engineers overruled William DeWitt's desire for a horseshoe-shaped stadium that would have left a part of the stadium open for a view of the Ohio River.[36] Despite a number of known construction impediments, on July 7, 1965, the *Cincinnati Enquirer*'s lead story enthusiastically announced that "Cincinnati's new riverfront stadium would cost $34,379,000 and be open by August 15, 1968."

Media coverage during the remainder of 1966 and in 1967 followed two trajectories. The first focused on overcoming construction obstacles. The second touted specific aspects of the stadium that would better serve fans and the community. On July 9, 1966, the *Cincinnati Post*'s highly visual front page touted the new design, trumpeting how it would bring the fans closer to the action than at Crosley Field. The article's second sentence quoted James Finch, a project architect, stating that fans would be so close to the field that "any closer and they'd be in the game."[37] An April 2, 1967,

Cincinnati Enquirer article focused on the press amenities and their capacity to attract televised network coverage of Cincinnati events.[38] Two days later the focus was on the diverse events that could come to Cincinnati if construction was completed. Soccer, pageants, circuses, art shows, concerts, rodeos, and even road races were all listed as possibilities that might enrich the lives of area residents. According to the author, "There is no limit to what Cincinnatians will be able to do with their new riverfront stadium."[39] Shortly after many positive articles appeared, an agreement was finalized between city and county officials to underwrite $42,250,000 in construction bonds.

In 1968 and 1969, reporters suggested that construction was most threatened by financial constraints. By 1970, community pride began to emerge more prominently. As the stadium neared its June 1970 opening, media focused on civic achievement and "world-class" elements that were integrated into the stadium. Among the initial obstacles complicating construction were land acquisition, rerouting railroad traffic around the site, political bickering, funding complications, and surrounding street redesign. Public input and grassroots objections went largely unreported. Two rare exceptions were an unsuccessful petition drive by Walter Kelly, president of the Hamilton County Democratic Club, to place the issue on the November ballot and intermittent coverage of a lawsuit to block construction because the "structure [was] designed peculiarly to benefit an individual rather than the taxpayers in general."[40] The suit was unsuccessful and opportunities for appeal were exhausted after a 1968 verdict from the Ohio Supreme Court.

The legendary football coach Paul Brown pushed hard in the early stages to convince the city that quick stadium construction action was required to gain an NFL expansion team. The NFL's response from Cincinnati representatives was reserved distance. Network representatives were similarly noncommittal about Cincinnati's chances. After rumors circulated that Seattle and New Orleans were network favorites, a CBS representative told Paul Brown that "they don't care where the new franchise goes." Brown tried to rush construction in 1966, but Republican city council leaders could not be convinced that Cincinnati was a front runner for an NFL team. This point of view, coupled with a desire to hammer out a long-term lease with the Reds, delayed the decision to dedicate funds to produce detailed stadium construction plans.[41]

After legislative foot-dragging seemed to ensure at least a one-year delay on the project, news reports gradually shifted coverage of obtaining an NFL franchise to a more likely scenario of obtaining a less prestigious AFL team.[42] In one case, coverage focused on the Reds as an attractive prize for Milwaukee civic leaders, with William DeWitt reassuring local fans that "they're not going to get Cincinnati." This statement came two days after city officials postponed funding of architectural planning for the proposed stadium. Instead of making relocation threats, DeWitt worked with Council Majority Leader Eugene Ruehlmann, local business leaders, and others to attract private funding for the desired architectural reports.[43]

At the urging of Cincinnati's mayor, Charlie Staab utilized his clout as vice president of the *Cincinnati Enquirer* and as Chamber of Commerce head to raise funds for these architectural plans. According to journalist Dennis Breen, "Staab's newspaper began churning out articles that appeared more like press releases, cheerleading and listing daily campaign contributions." The polarization that Breen argues was caused by this overt boosterism was either downplayed or fully omitted from newspapers during this period.[44]

Architects and city officials used periodic threats of price increases as a rationale to move forward.[45] Most leaders regarded such construction as inevitable, but for those opposing the project, price increases served as a compelling argument to avoid construction entirely.[46] A 1967 front-page article focused on rising costs as construction was still uncertain. It used bold type to highlight only two paragraphs. The first bold-faced paragraph summarized the expert analysis of the stadium's architect from Atlanta, George Heery, before the city's Capital Improvements Committee. The bold copy indicated that "the underlying significance of Mr. Heery's report was that the longer the city delays the award of the contract the higher the cost will be."[47] Cost concerns did not appear to provoke comparison shopping among architects or construction firms, however. Officials regarded George Heery and co-designer James Finch to be sufficiently expert in all facets of stadium design that seeking other firms appeared to be unnecessary. The primary contractor, Huber, Hunt, and Nichols, seemed to be chosen with a similar lack of controversy.

A number of politicians regarded a signed long-term agreement between the city, the Reds, and the new football team as a necessity before moving forward.[48] A particular concern to council members was the potential for an operating stadium deficit that would have to be absorbed by taxpayers. Although the stadium debt was funded through Hamilton

County's bonding authority, the city would be in charge of the maintenance, operation, and presumably expenses not covered by rent, concessions, and parking revenues. When an agreement was reached on financing and facility maintenance, the deficit issue was not resolved, but city and county officials seemed to tacitly agree that a 3 percent hotel tax might be enacted if deficits became an issue.[49] Such a tax was approved by city officials in 1969.

DeWitt's battle with city officials over a long-term contract and his general dislike for the riverfront location eventually prompted him to sell the team to a coalition of local leaders led by Francis Dale, *Cincinnati Enquirer* president. The investment might have provided incentive for media bias, but this is problematic because before and after construction, news coverage in the *Cincinnati Enquirer* and the rival *Cincinnati Post and Times Star* was typically positive. Most of the reporting focused on ensuring project completion rather than whether the project deserved taxpayer support. Citizen input was limited to political and business leaders. William DeWitt's input was also pushed to the margins for a variety of reasons, the most notable of which were a consensus among politicians, business leaders, and stadium experts. His input may have been limited by his civic mindedness, too, a factor that prevented him from using relocation threats to gain an upper hand. Instead of acquiescing on elements of construction with which he disagreed, he sold the team, insisting that the Reds remain in Cincinnati before finalizing the transaction.

The overall tone of construction coverage in the years before the *Cincinnati Enquirer*'s top executive actively involved himself in a coalition to purchase the Reds suggests pro-construction coverage was inevitable regardless of whether Francis Dale's activist investment took place. Nevertheless, Dennis Breen concludes that "political orchestrations, newsprint manipulation, hard-nosed pragmatics, and big money gave birth to Riverfront Stadium."[50] Whether the generally positive *Cincinnati Enquirer* press coverage represented self-interest or a natural honeymoon period is uncertain. However, throughout the process the *Enquirer* appeared slightly more aggressive than the *Cincinnati Post and Times Star* in pushing for construction.

As the stadium opened, media coverage featured glowing praise of this new civic monument. Although the stadium was not fully completed when opened on June 30, 1970, it was proudly showcased by the local media and appeared to create street-level excitement. The *Cincinnati En-*

quirer created a special "Souvenir Edition" with text and pictures that heralded the greatness of the new facility and congratulated those whose efforts made Riverfront Stadium possible. The cover contained a commentary by Bob Harrod, *Cincinnati Enquirer* city editor, who called the circular facility "a crown for the Queen City." Harrod argued that the stadium, constructed where "warehouses, bawdy houses, [and] produce houses once stood, . . .has changed our skyline, our pulse, our very lives. It looms over the city today as a monument . . . to the people of Cincinnati and their faith and pride in themselves and their community."[51] Some of Cincinnati's residents regard the 1970 All Star Game as the stadium's true opening because it showcased the stadium and the city in a way that had not been done before.

Marge Schott, Mike Brown: Cultural Capital, Civic Pride, and the Push for New Facilities

By the 1990s professional sports had moved into a more overtly mercenary direction. American sports had always been commercial. Even in 1869, George Wright's baseball team maintained an intense eye on bottom-line profitability. But by the 1990s, television revenues for team owners had grown substantially, and the amount of revenue that could be derived from stadium agreements also increased. Players also complicated the process, using intricate collective bargaining pacts to grab a larger slice of the pie than was possible in preceding decades. With an increasingly competitive entertainment landscape that included many leisure options, team owners were more willing to leverage their ownership status against civic pride early in the negotiating process, rather than as a last resort. As new satellite and aviation technologies erased the significance of time and space, cities were less likely to call the shots when dealing with team owners. Franchise relocation had become easier than ever to arrange.

Major league executives knew that in a multichannel television environment, their product offered a valuable entertainment option to emerging communities looking for symbolic recognition of their metropolitan growth. In the 1990s, the Northeast, the industrial Midwest, and large California cities no longer held hegemonic power over franchise location decisions. The burgeoning Sun Belt now offered teams new choices. Negotiating power shifted to team owners, and they used this leverage more profoundly than ever before. Many owners knew that departure threats would be treated with trepidation, particularly by political and business leaders who could push stadium construction forward.

Cincinnati's team owners were aware that their product had enormous value as a regional cultural asset. When it became clear that both the Reds and Bengals could improve their bottom line with separate new stadium agreements, it was only a matter of time before owners would begin to portray Riverfront Stadium as a regional liability despite its structural soundness. As these pronouncements were made, journalists no longer relegated team owners to less-prominent coverage. Marge Schott, owner of the Reds, and Mike Brown, owner of the Bengals, jockeyed to establish positions that could maximize their revenues in ways that were not possible a generation earlier.

Political leaders, citizens, and business leaders looked on in frustration as coverage focused on the owners' desires for new ballparks for their respective teams. Marge Schott tended to adopt a reclusive posture through much of the process, likely driven by a belief that the Reds were a more profound source of civic pride, and Mike Brown, recognizing his team's shorter tenure in Cincinnati, was initially more approachable but was also difficult to work with as lobbying efforts unfolded.

Part of the problem in dealing with these owners was the contractual relationship between the stadium authority and the teams. The Riverfront Stadium lease stipulated that both parties would be treated as "equals." In response, each party churlishly complained when one franchise seemed to gain any benefit not obtained by the other. The lease further compounded acrimony between the teams, because facility renovations and structural changes required the agreement of both parties before construction could begin. When revamping the stadium created a perceived disadvantage for one party, little effort was made to determine whether the proposed renovation might be undertaken in a manner that could be creatively beneficial to both teams.

One such example involved the opening of a "stadium club." Instead of working out a compromise that would create lucrative opportunities for both clubs, years of bickering left this section of the stadium unused and largely unfinished. The stadium club, currently a coveted revenue stream for teams, was proposed in the 1970s, but Cincinnati team owners avoided such plans because it might mean less seating for regular patrons. A large portion of stadium revenues were retained by the city to minimize stadium deficits, so team owners seemed to react protectively to known revenue streams instead of seeking out creative new opportunities.

In 1974 the notion of a stadium club was advocated by the Reds. The Bengals dragged their feet, citing a disparity in free memberships that favored the Reds and the potential loss of regular seating.[52] Months earlier, the city advertised the availability of "private loge boxes" as an amenity that would be available for a newly proposed indoor sports arena. But the potential for expanding such a concept for Riverfront Stadium to utilize this vacant area for "club" seating never appeared to garner significant media coverage.[53]

In 1988, almost two decades after initial discussions for a stadium club began, the Reds and the Bengals pushed the city to complete construction of the project, but both parties strenuously objected to paying for any of the costs.[54] By 1994, the city expressed a desire to commit $16 million to create luxury boxes and a stadium club, regarding this expenditure as a means to improve stadium-related revenues. The plan was vetoed by Marge Schott, in part because some construction would jeopardize the status of areas that were popular with Reds season-ticket holders. City leaders responded to this setback by shelving plans despite an agreement with the Bengals that promised improvements in the team's revenue picture.

Similar bickering and infighting was exerted during a scoreboard controversy in the late 1970s, providing further evidence of a tendency for contentiousness on almost anything related to stadium management.[55] Despite acrimony, all parties demonstrated a capacity for cooperation when concession revenues were jeopardized by concession and souvenir sales on Riverfront Stadium's plaza. On April 2, 1976, Judge Thomas Heekin upheld the right of city officials to allow the Reds to exclusively contract with Cincinnati Sportservice, Inc., for vending rights on stadium property, banishing independent licensed vendors to the less-desirable property perimeter.[56]

Periodic problems between the teams and stadium management were evident to observant citizens, but arguments that Riverfront Stadium was an archaic relic did not begin to surface until it became apparent that teams in other cities substantially improved their financial position through new construction. A 1990 economic study touted the tremendous benefits of Riverfront Stadium to the local economy. The study, released by the Greater Cincinnati Chamber of Commerce, was prepared using data provided by George Vredeveld, an economist at the University of Cincinnati. The study concluded that Riverfront Stadium's economic impact from 1970 to 1990 was $2.6 billion. Vredeveld's very generous inflation-adjusted figures estimated a $4 billion economic impact in 1990 dollars, or almost $6 billion in 2005. The study attempted to capture all direct and indirect revenues related to events held at Riverfront Stadium. Included were revenues from such diverse sources as stadium concessions, local restaurants, and area hotel bookings. A *Cincinnati Enquirer* article summarizing the study led with a quote from Michael J. Comisar, a restaurateur, praising the wisdom of city leaders for the stadium's downtown proximity. He concluded, "Thank God it was built downtown. It has been a home run for business here."[57]

As this highly optimistic report was released, new stadium projects were under way elsewhere. Camden Yards, opened in 1992, served as a powerful and nationally recognized symbol for Baltimore's highly touted waterfront entertainment complex. By 1994, the Baltimore Orioles ranked second in stadium revenue, eclipsed only by the Chicago White Sox, which also benefitted from a taxpayer-subsidized facility that opened in 1991. Baltimore's and Chicago's 1994 stadium revenues totaled $19.7 million and $22.4 million, respectively. With less fanfare, the Dallas Cowboys added sixty-eight luxury suites in 1994. The renovation generated over $37 million in stadium revenue and a whopping 25 percent increase in the team's market value in just one year.[58]

Once these stadium-generated revenues became public knowledge, it was clear that a new or heavily renovated stadium could increase a team owner's revenue picture substantially. If a significant taxpayer subsidy could be arranged, the lion's share of these revenues could be retained by the team owner. Particularly attractive to owners was the fact that stadium-generated revenues, exclusive of ticket sales, were exempt from league revenue sharing agreements. If teams worked harder to attract more traditional fans in regular seating, they would have to share a portion of such ticket revenue with colleagues, but with the new reliance on upscale clubs and skyboxes, they could pocket 100 percent of many forms of newly generated stadium revenues.

As a result, the 1990s were a period of great tension for stadium management, particularly in Cincinnati. In 1993, Mike Brown "threatened to leave town with the team if there wasn't a breakthrough on a renovated stadium or a new stadium for the pro football franchise." At the same time, the Reds's management invoked their contractual right to "equal treatment," complaining that a number of renovations were needed to satisfy them. To avoid further stadium-related deficits, officials contemplated managerial changes, including private sector management and peddling stadium naming rights to a willing corporate suitor.[59]

Even though Cincinnati had retired only about half of the original Riverfront Stadium debt, the Reds and Bengals began to make increasingly difficult demands for new amenities or entirely new facilities by the early 1990s. What was particularly difficult was that the team owners acted in a highly competitive manner. Temporary cooperation was rare and was generally followed by acrimonious demands for "equity." If Mike Brown negotiated a benefit that was previously unavailable to both parties, Marge Schott would soon complain of unfair favoritism. If negotiations shifted to pacifying the Reds, Mike Brown would offer less than subtle suggestions that the Bengals might take drastic action.[60] Citizens and political leaders had no doubt that Brown was suggesting possible negotiation with other cities, even if this outcome was not fully articulated. Owner claims that virtually any stadium renovation violated a lease agreement that called for "equal treatment" complicated management decisions. Almost any action might be used as evidence of a contractual breech that could trigger a franchise move.

A most difficult part of this entire process was a lack of consistency and clarity on the part of team owners. Marge Schott made occasional demands for a new stadium. Shortly after articulating such a demand, she frequently withdrew from stadium-related discussions. Although Schott was often unreasonable and cantankerous, city council members hurt their negotiating position with Schott in several ways. In March 1994 the seeds for future acrimony were sown when Schott refused to sign off on Riverfront Stadium improvements that would benefit the Bengals. Some city council leaders, frustrated with Schott's intransigence, "criticized her, questioned her loyalty, and even laughed at her demands."[61]

In attempting to shame Schott into signing a short-term agreement without making modest attempts to confront her demands, bitterness and suspicion were cultivated. Less than two months later, the city readjusted the stadium's market value upward from a depreciated value of $19.8 million to a book value of $47 million in response to a controversy involving the school board and the county. The move may have seemed harmless to a typical citizen, but this readjustment widened the rift between Schott and the city. This financial decision took place just days after Schott made overtures to purchase Riverfront Stadium, a maneuver that would have avoided the heavy-handed request for two brand-new facilities by both owners.[62] Although impossible to determine precisely how Schott perceived this action, it is likely that she regarded it as hardball posturing to extract a maximum sale price from her. Not surprisingly, she backed off plans to purchase Riverfront Stadium shortly after this reassessment issue surfaced.

Mike Brown was initially more amiable but was also difficult to pin down. Brown alternated his demands periodically, although openly admitting that failure to meet his deadlines could result in franchise relocation. In November 1993, Brown framed his demand for a new stadium as a civic-minded attempt to remain in Cincinnati. In a front-page story featuring a panoramic photograph of Brown standing inside Riverfront Stadium, he indicated that a new stadium was essential to securing the Bengals's future in Cincinnati. But Brown said he would be willing to accept a less-generous subsidy to remain in Cincinnati than might be offered elsewhere. He cited Baltimore specifically as a city that might be courting NFL franchises if they failed to receive an NFL expansion franchise in the months ahead. Brown argued that the possible level of subsidy offered by Baltimore could make any team the NFL's "number one money producer." Brown was firm in a demand for a subsidy, yet he presented the case in a manner that projected him as civic minded. The article concluded with Brown's assertion that "rising player costs and decreasing TV revenues could put his club in the red as early as 1994."[63]

Public opinion data revealed that Brown's veiled threats to move were an essential ingredient in obtaining taxpayer funding. Without such threats, the public was united in opposition. Early in the process, opposition was so clear that even franchise relocation threats were limited in their ability to gain public support. An April 1995 *Cincinnati Post*/WCPO poll of 531 area residents revealed that 81 percent opposed increased property taxes, and 72 percent opposed higher sales taxes to build a new stadium. Fifty-eight percent believed that a single new stadium should be built to retain the Bengals, but 65 percent opposed taxpayer funds for such a facility.[64]

Despite public opposition, civic leaders, feeling backed into a corner by team owners, voted to increase sales tax by 1 percent without consideration of a referendum.[65] Civic leaders tried various strategies to make this tax hike palatable. The most emphasized argument was that half of the increase would be paid by visitors or businesses rather than Hamilton County residents because out-of-town shoppers tended to frequent the county malls.[66] These claims did not appear to assuage the citizenry. Tim Sullivan, a popular sports columnist, stated that "the man in the street is in a foul mood. He doesn't much like the idea of subsidizing millionaire owners, and he despises politicians who would commandeer his cash for that purpose . . . It is a difficult proposition to court people after you have told them their opinion doesn't count."[67]

Tim Mara, a local attorney, emerged as an opposition leader, threatening a petition drive that eventually succeeded in forcing this issue to a public referendum. The certainty of defeat prompted modifications; the sales tax increase was cut from a penny to a half cent and prison construction was eliminated from the legislation. A 4.3 percent property tax reduction was added to make the overall package more appealing.[68] With these adjustments, the proposal was set for a March 1996 vote. Both sides fought hard for positive media coverage as election day approached. Public support was tepid, but political concessions gave the proposal a chance for passage.

Issue One: The Media, Public Input, and the Result

Issue One, as the Cincinnati area stadium referendum was called, was intensely debated. In the months before the referendum, street-level conversations about the issue were commonplace. Media coverage also confronted the issue in a direct manner. News coverage was extensive, with a variety of televised stories, newspaper articles, editorials, and citizen letters providing further information that could be used by voters.

Approval of Issue One was pushed forward by a carefully crafted media campaign that was largely coordinated by Columbus-based HMS Partners, Ohio's largest advertising agency.[69] They had worked with high-profile national clients and had vast experience in political advertising. Polling evidence suggested that voters were likely to defeat the measure without a dramatic push. The situation was so bleak that David Milenthal, the chief executive officer of HMS Partners, confessed that he thought "the task was impossible" in the early stages of the campaign. His first order to key leaders on the pro-stadium side was a stern warning to "shut up" until a firm plan was in place.

The aggressive advertising and public relations blitz offered the public a variety of reasons to support Issue One. The plan was predicated on establishing the perception of "grassroots" support that was not entirely controlled by community elites. Money was borrowed early to buy advertising. The strategy created a perception that the campaign was not run by big money interests, despite subsequent financial support from power brokers.

The economic benefits of stadium construction were highlighted repeatedly. One television ad featuring Cincinnati Mayor Roxanne Qualls briefly flashed the prominent graphics "6,800 permanent jobs" and "$296 million per year," suggesting immense economic benefits if the tax passed. Other ads were created, but Qualls remained the most popular spokesperson because of behind-the-scenes evidence that women's support was essential for Issue One passage. Routine public opinion research allowed advocates to fine tune their message as the vote neared.

As the campaign moved forward, economic claims were overshadowed by assertions that new stadiums were essential to maintain a major league image. The notion that loss of Cincinnati's professional football team would diminish the quality of life for area citizens was also pushed. Another key argument was that much of the tax would be paid for by others because the sales tax was often paid by outsiders who happened to work or shop in Hamilton County.

The threat of the football team's departure was made much more ominous by the loss of Cleveland's football team to Baltimore, rumors of the Seattle Seahawks moving to Los Angeles, and speculation that the Tampa Bay Buccaneers might be planning relocation. The timing of the Browns move was the single most important factor that made a seemingly impossible campaign goal achievable. Many stadium advocates asserted that defeat could mean transfer of the Bengals to Cleveland or possibly Los Angeles. Citizens were reminded that Cincinnati was smaller than both cities, so they were bargaining from a position of weakness unless new stadium revenues somehow equalized the economic benefit of remaining in the region.

Mike Brown reminded citizens of other cities' desire to host an NFL team and suggested that it would be more profitable to move his franchise to Cleveland.[70] Nine days before the vote Brown announced that he would contribute a minimum of $25 million for the football stadium. The move was likely prompted by internal research that indicated support for the stadium issue was weak. Marge Schott made no similar overture, instead making moves that jeopardized the referendum's success. Schott continued to battle city officials on Riverfront Stadium lease terms, arguing twelve days before the election that the city owed her $3.1 million. She stated that despite disagreements with political leaders, "a new stadium with increased streams of revenue is essential" for the team to continue its winning record.[71] Schott may have believed that, in the long-run, a Bengals departure, a likely outcome without a football stadium subsidy, could result in a more lavish facility for the Reds.

Television coverage was often driven by sound bites and superficial arguments, in part the result of a medium that relies on visual images and drama. Overall, stadium construction advocates tended to receive more favorable coverage than subsidy opponents. An optimistic study prepared by the University of Cincinnati's Center for Economic Education tended to serve as the basis for economic claims. Even when opponents were given air time, it was often in a defensive posture, with quick, superficial sound bites that refuted rosy economic projections.

Radio coverage may have been even more supportive of the referendum. WLW, Cincinnati's most powerful AM station, was firmly supportive of Issue One. *Cincinnati Magazine*'s Linda Vaccareiello described their pre-vote air strategy as a "relentless [pro-stadium] drumbeating by WLW radio personalities."[72] Stadium opponents were unorganized and dispersed unevenly throughout the community. Issue One supporters were motivated by self-interest and more willing to fund an organized campaign that would achieve victory.

Story placement in the *Cincinnati Enquirer,* the region's most successful newspaper, provided one indicator that the issue was deemed critically important by local media as the referendum neared.[73] Sixty-five percent of the Issue One news stories from December to the referendum date received some form of front-page placement. Forty percent were on the front page, and 25 percent were on the front page of an internal section. Only 35 percent of the coverage from December 1, 1995, through March 19, 1996, was relegated to the newspaper's inside pages.

The *Cincinnati Enquirer* was not reluctant to lead with an anti-stadium quote in some of its news coverage. Nevertheless, pro-construction voices were favored in the weeks leading up to the referendum. As the election neared, pro-stadium voices were allowed significantly greater placement in the more visible first and second positions, and appeals in the third position were somewhat evenly distributed. During March 1996 news coverage, pro-stadium voices were over four times more likely to be used as the first quotation, with a higher than two-to-one ratio favoring the pro-tax position in second quotes. The third quote position offered 54 percent reflecting pro-tax sentiment and 46 percent taking an anti-tax position.

Close scrutiny of public opinion data reveals that vigorous opposition to the stadium tax weakened as the election neared, but then shifted back to greater balance in the month of the vote. By mid-January, evidence of a shift from opposition to majority support emerged. A Cincinnati Post/WCPO-TV poll, completed on January 11, 1996, reported that 49 percent of the respondents supported the sales tax and 40 percent were in opposition. The emergence of a pro-construction position made intense vocal opposition by well-established political leaders less likely.

This weakening of opposition is also reflected in news coverage tendencies that consistently favored the stadium tax. The *Cincinnati Enquirer*'s staff-generated opinion columns were skewed to favor the stadium construction initiative more than was reflected in available public opinion data. This opinion bias provided significant evidence of editorial boosterism. Staff-generated opinion includes editorials, staff opinion columns offered in news, business, and sports sections, and op-ed page "guest columns." Letters to the editor were not included in this analysis because letters are not generated through solicitation or direct action of *Cincinnati Enquirer* employees. A mix of citizen points of views in the letters to the editor section offers evidence that the *Cincinnati Enquirer* did not censor critical opinions that might have undermined their editorial position. Not all letters are published in major city dailies, but competent editors try to ensure that letter submissions accurately reflect the varied thoughts and values of their community.

Although it is possible for elites to use the letters section to further their objectives, it is also reasonable to conclude that some of these elites are more likely to be afforded a "guest opinion" column than typical citizens. Staff columns, guest opinions, and editorials are generally afforded more prominent placement, larger headlines, and in some cases include artwork, photos, or layout features that set them apart from letters to the editor.

A pro-construction slant should not be surprising. A February 11, 1996, article outlining the *Cincinnati Enquirer*'s "agenda" for the year argued that "opinions have their greatest impact at close range, so most of our arsenal . . . will be targeted locally." The first priority listed in this effort to mobilize opinion was to "continue our series of editorials focusing on the importance of keeping both of Cincinnati's pro sports franchises." According to the staff, maintaining such a posture was important because "keeping both teams is essential to tourism, economic development, jobs, riverfront renewal, downtown renewal, and community pride."[74]

It should be of little surprise that the opinion content of the *Cincinnati Enquirer* was not particularly accommodating to individuals wishing to offer alternatives to new stadium construction. In an analysis of opinion-based content from February 1, 1996, through the day before the vote, March 19, 1996, only one solicited opinion column expressed full opposition to Issue One. A blend of nineteen editorials and staff or guest columns expressed pro-construction sentiment. Six columns were sufficiently ambivalent in their posture to be labeled "neutral." In short, 73 percent of Issue One–solicited opinion content was clearly pro-stadium, 23 percent was neutral, and a single article, a mere 4 percent, opposed taxpayer subsidized construction. If neutral opinion columns were pulled from this analysis, pro-construction voices outpaced anti-construction voices by a 19-1 ratio, a lopsided percentage differential of 95 percent to 5 percent.

Some opinion content that does not directly address stadium construction as a primary theme could have had an impact on the issue. Two examples are the focus on Marge Schott and her management of the Reds and articles that identified cities that might take steps to obtain an NFL franchise. The latter is significant in that a strong undercurrent of innuendo suggested that Cincinnati's NFL franchise could be relocated if stadium subsidies were not approved.

Opinion slanting had a likely impact on referendum support, yet verification of potential effects is problematic. Because of the comfortable margin of victory, it is unlikely that opinion content change would have altered the outcome of the Issue One vote. Nevertheless, the presence of such opinion column bias should concern citizens, community leaders, and journalism practitioners. After all, if public opinion data on this issue were extremely close, such profound pro-subsidy biases could have a number of meaningful ramifications on policy outcomes.

A traditional argument is that such bias would inspire individuals to follow the leadership exhibited on the opinion pages. An alternative outcome might be reflexive citizen rejection of overt media bias, inspiring citizens to vote against a stadium subsidy in greater numbers, particularly if citizens believed media practitioners were simply mouthpieces for powerful interests. On a journalistic level, a profound imbalance could affect the credibility of the messenger, ultimately diminishing the credibility of the medium in future policy debates.

The *Cincinnati Enquirer* pro-subsidy opinion content may not have had a negative mobilizing effect largely because the subtle and complex nature of opinion-related content. This subsidy support meshed closely with citizen ambivalence in a variety of ways. Even when opinion columns actively supported the stadium tax, the columnists frequently reflected a general distaste for the subsidy issue itself. Peter Bronson, the editorial page editor, aptly captured citizen ambivalence in a February 11, 1996, op-ed piece. Bronson argued, "I'd vote for the stadium tax in spite of the owners. . . , but it would be nice if they would quit dickering around like Mr. Haney on Green Acres and pry open their checkbooks in time to help voters choke down the tax. . . . Without the Reds and the Bengals, Cincinnati is Hooterville with soap salesmen."[75]

On the Sunday before the referendum, Bronson offered another pro-subsidy op-ed piece that was openly critical of regional leadership. Although enthusiastically endorsing the subsidy, he admitted that the "voters have a right to be steamed" because "the downtown 'in-crowd' can be excruciatingly arrogant, like some student council planning a dance without asking anyone but the cheerleaders and football players."[76] The business editor, Jon Talton, maintained a similar tone as he argued that a pro-subsidy vote was necessary to maintain a healthy regional economy. Talton tempered his subsidy enthusiasm stating that "it might not be fair. It might not be right. But it is the economics of sports in the 1990s." Nevertheless, according to Talton, support for the tax was prudent because "1996 will be the year when Cincinnati decides whether it will remain a major city, or accelerate a decades-long decline into second-rate status."[77]

Cartoons and graphics provided by the *Cincinnati Enquirer* also favored stadium subsidy. Jim Borgman, a Pulitzer Prize–winning cartoonist, offered two very powerful subsidy-focused cartoons before the referendum. On the day of the stadium vote, Borgman's cartoon featured an overhead illustration of the downtown area, with several of the streets leading into a sink drain. Underneath a visual intended to suggest that Cincinnati might be headed "down the drain" if the referendum failed was the simple caption "Plan B."[78] A week before the vote, Borgman offered a cartoon with a caption "how they should have pitched it" suggesting that residents outside Hamilton county would pay a sizable portion of any sales tax increase. The cartoon showed a well-dressed man holding a document headlined

"Sales Tax Plan." Three conversation balloons appeared next to this individual to reflect him whispering "Psst. . . . We found a way to make outsiders pay part of your property taxes, fund our schools, and build two new stadiums. . . . And they can't even vote on it."[79]

The single example of stadium subsidy opposition before the referendum was brutally overwhelmed by pro-construction voices. As a result, Tim Mara's anti-tax op-ed piece on Sunday, March 17, 1996, probably fell short of its desired goal. In this edition, Mara had his opinion vociferously juxtaposed by Jeff Berding, the campaign manager of the pro-stadium campaign.[80] Both pieces received similar headlines and equal column space. Nevertheless, directly above these two opinion pieces was a pro-subsidy editorial featuring a headline that was more than twice the size of the op-ed headlines.[81] Furthermore, the editorial was fortified by a large graphic intended to discredit Mara's stadium tax position. The graphic displayed downtown Cincinnati, featuring a huge entrance sign similar to those occasionally posted at city or state borders. The simple sign read "Welcome to Nowhereville, Ohio, Tim Mara, Mayor."[82]

Below this anti-Mara illustration, readers were invited to turn to the inside pages of this opinion section where the Bengals owner Mike Brown was given space to make his case, which predictably favored the stadium tax.[83] Above Brown's column readers were further reminded that the next day's newspaper, published one day before the election, would include stories on "how a half cent tax can boost our economy, create jobs, and spread stadium costs regionally." If Mara's positioning in the lower right corner of the opinion page did not substantially marginalize his message, the pro-stadium editorial, the bold pro-referendum headlines, the negative anti-Mara graphic, and Berding's opposition column certainly conveyed second-class stature for this lone anti-tax voice.

Mara may have been the only well-known tax opponent willing to go on record in op-ed commentary, but the opinion-page deck was so heavily stacked against subsidy opposition that it transgressed journalistic norms of fairness. If another well-known opposition voice could not be found, the *Cincinnati Enquirer* staff could have, at a minimum, sought out articulate average citizens and accorded those individuals more prominent op-ed space to offer some level of balance. With citizens voting for the stadium initiative at 61 percent levels, a three-to-one pro-tax slant might be expected, particularly when the publication was on record as highly supportive of Issue One. But pro-construction voices outpaced anti-construction voices by a lopsided 19-to-1 ratio. With the one op-ed exception, which was overwhelmed by pro-tax voices, the letter to the editor was the only refuge for anti-tax sentiment on the newspaper's opinion pages.

Ironically, the first letter to the editor on the Sunday before the vote was authored by George Vredeveld, an economics professor at the University of Cincinnati. He accused media coverage of irresponsibly pandering to the anti-stadium position "in its zeal to cover 'all sides of the story.' " He further contended that the press allowed anti-stadium voices to repeatedly launch "politically motivated criticism" against an economic report that he was instrumental in preparing. Vredeveld appeared to be stung by skepticism that did not emerge in his prior stadium-related analysis, including his 1990 Riverfront Stadium study that was not tied to calls for new construction subsidies. Overall, his arguments may have had validity in isolated news coverage, but reporting bias often favored stadium construction more than was reflected in measured public opinion on the issue.[84] If his accusations were extended to the opinion page slant, Vredeveld's claims were decidedly off-base. The 1996 stadium referendum gained support of slightly more than 61 percent of Hamilton County voters, reflecting the outcome desired by the University of Cincinnati economist. His economic projections might have been suspect, but his advocacy was supported by voters. The threat of team relocation and the claims of economic growth convinced the public to ante up for stadium construction.

The Election Aftermath: Overruns, Citizen Frustration, and Soul Searching

After voters approved stadium funding, editorial criticism of stadium issues took on a more critical edge. When the Bengals announced their personal seat license campaign, informing season ticket holders they would have to pay hundreds or thousands of dollars for the privilege of purchasing their tickets, *Cincinnati Enquirer* sports columnist Paul Daugherty referred to the Bengals claims of "exciting new amenities" in return for this fee as "a crock." He stated that this was "the cost of doing business in the era of rampant greed."[85] In 1997 the *Enquirer* included several highly critical columns and editorials. Nevertheless, this more hard-edged tone took place *after* stadium taxpayer funding was assured. Regardless, the tone adopted after the Issue One referendum contributed to a debate about ballpark location, which, in turn, led to another important stadium policy decision that again involved Hamilton County residents.

Passage of Issue One may have satisfied team owners, but citizen response was not universally enthusiastic. Although some citizens expressed relief, even elation, that the local teams would remain in Cincinnati, others stoically braced themselves for the uncertainties of the construction process. Initial coverage was optimistic about public participation in the process. An April 4, 1996, guest opinion featured Hamilton County Commissioner Bob Bedinghaus, the chief architect of Issue One. Bedinghaus told citizens that "over the next several months, we will be working to get the best deal for the taxpayers," and the county commission planned to host "a public forum seeking input on the design of the stadiums . . . to involve as many community members as possible to allow everyone a say in the future of the community."[86]

Two days later, sports columnist Tim Sullivan presented his stadium "wish list." He encouraged people to submit their proposals to the *Enquirer* offices, which would then "be passed on to the appropriate parties." Sullivan assured readers that "the will of the people will be heard even if it means giving Gilbert Gottfried a microphone."[87] Citizens offered similar enthusiasm. The "Readers' Views" section featured a number of pro-construction letters, with an occasional dissenting opinion, and six positive letters appearing on March 26, 1996. After several months, a public meeting was set up as "the first and only opportunity for public input before the stadium sites are chosen."[88] Predictably, the riverfront was recommended by experts.

The call for public input contributed to a second unexpected, citizen-generated referendum, one that focused on the site location for the Reds's ballpark. The unusual referendum was pushed forward by a popular city council member and his allies in an attempt to move baseball construction away from the riverfront and into a neighborhood in which he had a vested interest. Before the baseball site referendum occurred, however, disputes between team owners and political leaders unfolded.

Mike Brown continued to make demands that were intended to push his stadium project ahead, focusing primarily on land acquisition issues. Brown's successful use of veiled threats in the referendum campaign cultivated repetition of this tactic when preconstruction negotiations became difficult.[89] One controversy centered on control of future land development processes and ancillary road funding, pitting city and county officials against each other.[90] Brown sided with county officials, in part because this position would provide him with greater leverage in future development, with his immediate goal to situate ample parking closest to the stadium. The city objected to the agreement between Brown and county officials because it could jeopardize long-term plans to develop the riverfront as a larger entertainment district. Their goal was to attract more than just football spectators to the city.

A variety of compromises were made, helping city and county officials to reach an agreement one hour and fifteen minutes after Mike Brown's artificially imposed deadline.[91] The deal appeared to limit Bengals's control of the riverfront property that was not directly situated on the football stadium site. Nevertheless, subsequent wording in a spring 1997 agreement between the county commissioners and Mike Brown appeared to enhance the Bengals's power over riverfront development beyond what was acceptable to city officials.[92] Although site preparation had been under way for months, formal groundbreaking ceremonies for the Bengals's new stadium finally took place amid much fanfare on Saturday, April 25, 1998.[93]

The stadium situation was initially more complex for the Reds than for the Bengals. City and county leaders held their breath as negotiations took place with an unpredictable Marge Schott. Schott, still irritated by what she perceived as preferential treatment for the Bengals, vacillated positions to such an extent that one county leader proclaimed that dealing with the Reds is "like negotiating with Jekyll and Hyde—you don't know what to expect from one day to the next."[94] As the rocky negotiations unfolded, citizen activists worked to control both political and media agendas, eventually forcing an unprecedented referendum on ballpark location.

Before the 1996 referendum, Schott tinkered with the idea of purchasing Riverfront Stadium, possibly believing that outright ownership would eliminate irritating controversies with the city and the county. After the referendum passed, Schott abandoned the ownership proposal. She toyed with the notion of moving the team to northern Kentucky, but she could not attract sufficient funds to push such a plan forward. She also made several failed demands to step ahead of the Bengals, despite frequently opting out of the referendum campaigning process.[95]

As it became clear that the Bengals positioned themselves better with political and civic leaders, momentum increased for ballpark construction in a less-affluent inner-city neighborhood. By April 1997, four options emerged for the Reds. The team preferred new construction on a riverfront site west of the Roebling Bridge, but city officials had hoped to use this site for nonsports development. The second location was a site nicknamed "the Wedge," which would tightly squeeze a stadium between the Riverfront Coliseum and the old stadium. A third option was relocation at a site called Broadway Commons, an area located in Over-the-Rhine, a section of the city in need of infrastructure improvement between the northern fringe of downtown and a rugged inner-city residential area. A final option was refurbishing Cinergy Field.[96]

Schott, unwilling to accept construction at the Broadway Commons site, briefly backed off demands for a new stadium and considered a fourth option, accepting a major renovation of Riverfront Stadium, renamed Cinergy Field after a $6 million naming rights agreement was reached to help defray stadium expenses.[97] Several political leaders were excited about the prospect of financial savings. Nevertheless, after numerous meetings with city and county officials, she decided to endorse new construction at the Wedge site. This location was later renamed "Baseball on the Main" after some riverfront proponents determined that the "Wedge" moniker may have pejorative connotations that could be exploited by site opponents.

Schott's desires were supported by most business and county-level elites. City leaders were less certain about the Broadway Commons choice, but it gained some populist appeal and was the alternative offered to citizens in an odd ballpark location referendum. An energetic group of citizens, led by Cincinnati Councilman Jim Tarbell, attempted to redirect the stadium construction issue to Broadway Commons. The seeds for grassroots support were first planted in 1994 when Tarbell teamed up with Peter Guggenheim, a marketing and special-events specialist, to launch a media campaign for this cause. A first step was formation of a group called the Committee to Restore Intimacy in Baseball. They followed with advertising, a direct-mail campaign, and attempts to lobby both city leaders and Marge Schott.[98]

Unlike typical movements that quit after being steamrolled by elites, the Over-the-Rhine advocates continued to push forward, refusing to surrender. The Broadway Commons backers may have lacked political and economic clout, but they had an infectious enthusiasm. They cleverly obtained media publicity and eventually gained the endorsement of Cincinnati's mayor and several media practitioners. Tarbell's supporters built a large facade of an old-fashioned ballpark on the Broadway Commons property.[99] This display provided opportunities for highly visual media coverage. A large photo of the facade appeared in an article about site selection as the 1997 baseball season opened.[100] Jim Tarbell combined his city council election campaign with promotion of the Broadway Commons, handing out Jim Tarbell baseball cards instead of traditional campaign literature. He also obtained publicity by seeking trademark approval for "Broadway Commons" days before the referendum.[101] Tarbell was so effective at obtaining publicity that Jim Borgman presented a humorous cartoon with a tuxedoed Tarbell lifting a top hat to expose baseball-like stitch marks in his bald head.[102]

Broadway Commons advocates created a very sophisticated Web site that included various graphic representations of a new stadium situated in the neighborhood so that citizens could see what the final product might look like. To offset complaints that this proposal would be inconvenient or hurt downtown development, photographs were carefully crafted to show the site's proximity to Route 71, a major interstate, and downtown Cincinnati, with one photo taken from the Cincinnati Public Library, located in the heart of downtown. The Web site quoted experts, recruited volunteers, listed endorsements, provided distribution sites for yard signs, and even solicited on-line credit card donations.[103]

The campaign to build a ballpark at Broadway Commons appeared to be doomed on July 1, 1998, as Marge Schott and county officials entered an agreement to build on "the Wedge" site.[104] However, Tarbell and his supporters pushed ahead, working feverishly both to ensure that the referendum was procedurally sound and to obtain the required 26,800 valid signatures needed to get the site location issue on the November ballot. On Sunday, July 27, 1998, Cincinnati Councilman Todd Portune and Jim Tarbell delivered 44,562 petition signatures to the Hamilton County Administration Building. This forced a second sports referendum, one that was a simple thumbs-up or thumbs-down on the Broadway Commons location.

Both sides waged a strong campaign, and each side was closely matched on financial resources.[105] The pro-riverfront campaign organized a political action committee that it named "Move Greater Cincinnati Forward." Not surprisingly, the largest contributors to the riverfront campaign were the Cincinnati Reds and the Greater Cincinnati Chamber of Commerce; their donations were $50,000 and $25,000 respectively. Both sides appeared to garner adequate media coverage, and opinion content was not as one-dimensional as the funding referendum. The *Cincinnati Enquirer* endorsed the riverfront option although some staffers, including the sports columnist Paul Daugherty and the political columnist Cliff Radel, endorsed Broadway Commons.[106]

The Broadway Commons plan had several advantages, including lower overall cost for construction and site preparation. An unscientific *Cincinnati Enquirer* poll revealed that 425 favored the Broadway Commons site and only 151 favored the riverfront proposal, but the self-selection of the polling process clearly skewed the results. On election day, 65 percent voted for the riverfront site, and only 35 percent endorsed the Broadway Commons location.

The backing by key elites may have helped the riverfront option, but a number of other factors probably hurt the alternative. First, to get on the ballot required framing the issue as a revision of the county charter. Some voters may have viewed amending the county charter for a ballpark's location as a dangerous precedent. Some may have believed that the charter would evolve into an unwieldy smorgasbord of special interest amendments rather than an overarching governing document.

A second concern involved the unpredictability of Reds management. Marge Schott was often a loose cannon, but before the referendum, she announced intentions to sell some of her shares to take a minority role in the team. This created uncertainty regarding the Reds's future in Cincinnati. Although some voters may have liked the Broadway Commons idea, it was clear that the Reds were committed to a riverfront location. In February 1997 the team threatened a lawsuit if a riverfront site was not approved.[107] In an era of franchise free agency, some citizens may have believed that failure to pacify Schott and her eventual successor, hard-nosed businessman Carl Linder, could trigger a team move or a protracted lawsuit. Even though such a scenario may have been unlikely, after months of veiled and overt threats from the Bengals, citizens were repeatedly conditioned to regard sports teams as highly mobile.

Racial and class division may have been more subtle and less visible contributors to the failure of Broadway Commons. As Tarbell sought early publicity for his campaign in 1994, news coverage indicated that some citizens were "worried about criminal activity in the surrounding neighborhoods and interstate accessibility."[108] Whispers about safety in the Broadway Commons area may have triggered fears from white suburban voters, many of whom regularly commuted to more affluent downtown areas within walking distance of the riverfront. Finally, citizens knew that the most powerful members of the community supported riverfront construction. Many were tired of the stadium debate and may have believed that any decision challenging elites might result in negative complications.

Citizens who simply wanted order, harmony, and progress may have feared the potential for future acrimony. Some citizens may have become victims of "stadium fatigue" and simply wanted the entire issue to be resolved in the most expedient manner possible.

As construction plans moved forward on the football stadium, citizen disgust became increasingly apparent.[109] Projected cost overruns left many people disenchanted. Even *Cincinnati Enquirer* columnists and editorial writers who were initially supportive of the stadium subsidy grew tired of frequent cost overruns and team owner demands. A 1997 editorial accused Brown and Schott of "arrogant, rude, and greedy" behavior, further stating that instead of thanking the public for millions of generous subsidies, they have "threatened and bullied our elected officials, whipsawed the public, and exploited every opportunity to grab everything in sight."[110] Two and a half years later, sports columnist Tim Sullivan described the football project as one "that is destined to be remembered as the most feckless use of public funds since the $400 toilet seat."[111]

The long, drawn-out process did little to foster public support for stadium construction. During the Issue One campaign, many officials frequently told the public that no "Plan B" existed. After the vote, however, Cincinnati Councilman Todd Portune said that he had been asked to hold back plans for an indoor multiuse facility that would be home to the Bengals until after the referendum result was determined.[112] Although some discussion surfaced regarding a domed stadium before the vote, the idea never received a thorough public airing even though some citizens may have regarded this as a way to attract more nonfootball events to the region.

Equally frustrating was the uncertainty of the entire stadium construction process. The public was often presented with figures that appeared to be calculated with decimal-point precision, but as plans moved forward, each subsequent estimate seemed higher. Explanations for the increased costs suggested that early planning was superficial and haphazard. In the opening stages, a renovation option appeared to hold promise for cost containment. In 1994, estimates of $44.4 million and $48.3 million were advanced to convert the twenty-four-year-old facility to baseball or football only operation, potentially saving millions on the need to provide two brand-new ballparks.[113] In 1995, Cincinnati mayor Roxanne Qualls announced a $540 million plan to build two new stadiums, with taxpayers shouldering "$410 million of the cost, about 75 percent."[114] Estimates for the Bengals's stadium were set at $270 million before the referendum. By

March 6, 1996, just days prior to the referendum, residents were told that basic renovation to keep Riverfront Stadium operational would require "a backlog of deferred maintenance totaling $54 million," at least $5 million more than either 1994 renovation proposal.[115]

Two years after Issue One referendum approval, newspapers reported that the "guaranteed maximum price" for football stadium construction would be $290 million, with the real cost for land acquisition, site preparation, and construction set at $403 million. As Paul Brown Stadium prepared to open in 2000, total construction costs were listed at $453.2 million, over $52 million more than the initial estimated subsidy for both projects.[116] If baseball costs were not contained, the total construction bill could exceed three-quarters of a billion dollars. The *Cincinnati Post* estimated that "the actual cost could exceed $967 million. . . , [a figure that] represents $1,141 for every [Hamilton] county resident, not including interest."[117]

Many citizens were so befuddled by ever-changing economic projections that many simply regarded the stadium issue as an absurd farce that was beyond public control. General fatigue was intensified by the long debate about ballpark location that resulted in selection of a riverfront site, the desired choice of community elites. An undercurrent of hostility was evident in casual conversations in restaurants and grocery store checkout lines. A local artist, Amy Gallagher, and friend, Keith Baker, designed a "Shoot Me, I Voted for the Stadium Tax" T-shirt. The design proved so popular that in November 1997, *Cincinnati Magazine* indicated that "people call day and night wanting shirts. Retail stores want to stock them. Production had to be turned over to a silk-screen shop in order to meet demand." Many citizens believed they were manipulated into voting for new construction by leaders who were further accused of suppressing more reasonable construction estimates.[118] Political leaders responded to such allegations with claims that the 1996 figures reflected a "best guess" in light of limited planning funds before the Issue One referendum.[119]

The urban affairs scholar David Swindell has argued that keeping estimates "as low as possible" can be politically rational during a referendum campaign, but it can "backlash" if costs differ dramatically from what was initially sold to the voters.[120] Such a reaction was evident in Hamilton County. As early as December 1997 a group calling themselves "Citizens for Major League Sanity" handed out leaflets before sporting events that advocated spending limits and cost containment on stadium construction.[121] By October 2000, citizen resentment for the stadium issue was so entrenched in the regional culture that one columnist stated that an attempt to host the 2012 Olympic games "may be compromised by Bengals' backlash."[122]

Individuals outside the region would be puzzled by the football reference since football has no place in Olympic competition, but local citizens had no problem quickly connecting the Olympic bidding process (and its linkage in 2000 to a Salt Lake City hosting scandal) to the drawn-out stadium issue. Understandably, residents, fatigued with budget overruns and seemingly endless political dialogue, had less enthusiasm for sports-related expenditure than ever. A 2000 Internet poll revealed that 80 percent were opposed to Cincinnati hosting the 2012 Olympics.[123] Cincinnati was eliminated from hosting contention in the first round of cuts. Although the reasons for elimination are unclear, street-level research from U.S. Olympic Committee visits may have revealed a deep-seated public resistance to future sports-related construction.

Many residents remained comforted by Cincinnati's ability to retain its identity as "major league," but an uneasy feeling persisted that citizens had been hoodwinked by elites and team owners during the stadium construction process. As Paul Brown Stadium opened, the sense of communal triumph, similar to the 1970 Riverfront Stadium opening, was tempered by citizen uneasiness about the dramatic financial and psychological costs of this project.

Cost overruns were not the only concern. A fan-instigated class-action lawsuit kept the stadium in the news in 2001 after team officials failed to place season ticket holders in locations of their choosing, charging those patrons for more premium placement. In response, county and team officials were compelled to readjust some fans' seating or provide personal seat license refunds.[124] To take some sting out of the stadium issue, the county allocated $1 million in legal fees to an effort intended to recoup $45 million in cost overruns from Los Angeles–based NBBJ Architecture.[125] A $14.25 million settlement was reached in October 2004.[126]

Completed construction might provide long-term benefits to some downtown interests, but football stadium construction may have limited, or at least delayed, city development of residential properties in the downtown area.[127] Some businesses considered leaving the downtown area after years of parking and construction-related problems.[128] What began as a simple defensive effort to prevent team relocation turned into an extended series of unexpected lessons on the relationship of professional sports with special interest politics. Despite that, some recent construction has brought new housing stock to the downtown area.

Media coverage of the new stadium's first events revealed both positive and negative reaction even though the citizens quoted in each article were almost universally Bengals's fans. Positive coverage tended to focus on community pride or the state-of-art qualities of the stadium itself. Adrienne Hundemer, a construction worker from Dayton, Ohio, summarized this view stating "I am proud to be a part of this. . . . They say this is the best facility in the NFL."[129]

The *Cincinnati Enquirer* indicated that it received about 900 fax and e-mail reactions after the Bengals's opening exhibition game in Paul Brown Stadium. Many citizens gushed about the modern facilities and the image boost the stadium might provide. One citizen argued that it dispelled Mark Twain's notion that "Cincinnati is 10 years behind everywhere else . . . [since Paul Brown Stadium] puts us 20 years ahead." But overall, the *Enquirer* indicated that response was tepid as "most of you came down in an area about as gray as the stadium's concrete concourses." A typical response argued that "the city can be proud to have a fine stadium . . . [,but] I would be more proud if I didn't have such a sense of outrage over the high price tag." Ken Bauman, a long-time Bengals season ticket holder, was irritated over both the location of his new seats and the $4,800 seat license that was required for eligibility to buy season tickets. He asserted that if offered a full refund for his seat license, you could "color me gone."[130]

The novelty of a new stadium had inspired first-season sellouts for all other nonexpansion franchises to build new facilities since 1997, but in Cincinnati sellouts were the exception, not the rule.[131] In 2000, the team had only two sellouts. As the season unfolded, it became clear that a new stadium would do little to help improve the Bengals's on-field performance. With an 0-4 start, Bengals fans were treated to the indignity of network television blackouts for each unsold home game. This long-standing league policy prevented locals from watching the home team if the game did not sell out 72 hours before kickoff. Many Cincinnati fans determined that a mediocre on-field product was not worth further investment of their hard-earned dollars.

Unfortunately, because the new stadium's capacity was about 5,000 more than the old facility, sellouts were harder to achieve. Almost 7,000 seats were vacant for a typical Bengals game in their first season at the new field.[132] During home games, Bengals fans' options were often limited to radio broadcasts or buying a ticket to attend the game. Only eight of the first twenty-two games in the new stadium were sellouts.[133] Nevertheless, in 2003 the Bengals showed signs of improvement, more the result of a new head coach, finishing a respectable 8-8. Fans responded with improved attendance. Marvin Lewis, one of the few minority coaches in the NFL, worked tirelessly to turn around a franchise that had become a national symbol of on-field futility. With his guidance, local excitement is returning. In 2005, the team posted its first winning season in fifteen years, made the playoffs, and home field attendance continued to rise.

Mike Brown took some action to limit public backlash against construction after repeated public outcry, dropping an unpopular clause in his lease calling for public subsidies if ticket sales fell below 50,000 seats.[134] In 2000, construction officials were quick to publicize that the county would not incur financial penalties, payable to the Bengals as outlined in the team's lease agreement, if for some reason stadium construction did not finish on schedule.[135] But there were limits to what Mike Brown would do to satisfy the public. In the first season, fans questioned the franchise's commitment to player acquisition, and on-field maintenance was so poor that visiting quarterback Mark Brunell described game conditions as "by far the worst I've played on in my whole career." The team was responsible for on-field maintenance, but assessing blame in this instance was as convoluted as other stadium issues.[136] In the heat of construction, the chosen sod farm lost its lot of bluegrass turf to drought. Instead of lining up a new supplier, project supervisors substituted a Bermuda-based sod from the same vendor. Team officials told the public that a weekend of Pee Wee football contributed to the poor conditions.[137] Despite a poor field, a sluggish economy, and a losing team, Brown raised ticket prices by $4 for the 2002 season.[138]

When the Bengals finished 2002 with the worst record in the NFL, with only one of their two victories at home, Hamilton County Commissioners explored the possibility of filing a lawsuit against the Bengals for "breach of contract." Such a suit had populist appeal because of frequent claims that the team would be more "competitive" once the new stadium was in place.[139] In 2004 county officials pushed forward a more compelling claim that the Bengals used the NFL's monopoly position to extract an unfair negotiating advantage.[140]

This lawsuit appears to have a slim chance of victory, but the odds are heavily stacked against the county because such a victory would be a landmark ruling. Despite team warnings that moving forward could have serious consequences, the county filed the lawsuit hoping to possibly revise lease terms and recover millions in damages. The county is in a precarious position. Should they win the suit, the ruling could terminate the lease, potentially allowing for a more taxpayer-friendly agreement. But without specific court-directed remedies, such a "victory" might free the team to move elsewhere, a move that might put the Bengals in another city just as the team is shedding its "loser" image. The Bengals have countersued the county, seeking $30 million in damages, with about $16 million sought for "construction related complaints" and $14 million to resolve an Internal Revenue Service judgment on seat license fees that cost the team $13,326,355 in 2002.[141]

Despite the legal action, enthusiasm for a team that is finally shedding its doormat status sparked heavy sales for Bengals merchandise and skyboxes in 2004.[142] Although the team did not post a winning season until 2005, they were among the NFL's most profitable franchises.[143] Yet savvy citizens could see beyond the glitter of a fancy new stadium, recognizing that insider self-interest and elite appeals for community enhancement were curiously intertwined.

Less than two months after the 1996 stadium-tax referendum, Jeff Berding, the stadium tax campaign coordinator, signed a three-year contract with the Cincinnati Bengals. His new job focused on community relations and marketing, with a key responsibility to "sell suites at the planned stadium to major corporations—most of which contributed money to the $1 million pro-tax campaign." Not surprisingly, the Bengals, a primary referendum beneficiary, contributed $300,000 to Berding's carefully orchestrated 1996 media campaign.[144]

Targeted campaign contributions continued after construction began. Four years after the 1996 vote, Mike Brown and his attorney donated $13,500 to County Commissioner Bob Bedinghaus's reelection campaign. Bedinghaus was the most vocal county-level spokesman for the stadium.[145] He may have appreciated the donation, but his involvement in the stadium issue was politically costly. His association with construction overruns contributed to his defeat at the hands of Democrat Todd Portune who was more skeptical throughout the stadium debate. Without the stadium issue, a Bedinghaus defeat was not likely. It was the first time in more than three decades that a Democratic challenger was able to unseat an incumbent Republican commissioner.

Bedinghaus landed on his feet, however, obtaining a job with the Bengals, as a consultant in 2001, then as Director of Development for Paul Brown Stadium in 2004. One of his first tasks in this newly created position was to take a "lead role" in installation of new artificial turf, a move that was expected to lower maintenance costs and make the venue more useful for other purposes.[146] Ironically, during the referendum debate, replacing the old stadium's artificial turf with natural grass was seen as a benefit. Although the team picked up the initial tab for the turf installation, a clause in the lease makes it likely that the cost will be paid by taxpayers once seven publicly funded stadiums have a similar product installed.[147]

Another individual gained a new career opportunity. In the months before the stadium opening, reporter Geoff Hobson was placed on the team's payroll. Hobson covered stadium issues while at the *Cincinnati Enquirer.* His referendum coverage was particularly effective in explaining the potential for franchise relocation if the tax vote failed.[148] Hobson's new role was to provide team-related stories for the Bengals's newly designed Web site. The team described Hobson as an independent reporter, but fellow journalists questioned the extent of his independence. Cincinnati sports-talk host Andy Furman suggested that Hobson's reporting would be curtailed by Mike Brown if it turned negative; Furman cited his personal banishment from Bengals-related talk-show coverage on game days as evidence.[149] Hobson's coverage of stadium construction issues diminished when he left his *Cincinnati Enquirer* reporting job. In 2000 a *USA Today* report, Hobson indicated "he doesn't have time to write about the stadium issue but will do so if team officials have anything new to say about the topic."[150]

Public enthusiasm, anger, pride, and ambivalence were visible as Paul Brown Stadium opened. Citizens held similar views as construction plans unfolded at the new Cincinnati Reds ballpark. Corporate leaders, aware of public sensitivity regarding sports construction, took some steps in 2000 that might not have been offered under normal circumstances. After Cincinnati's beloved Reds fell short of a postseason playoff spot in 2000, a Cincinnati demolition company offered to remove the artificial turf at the old stadium so that the 2001 Reds could play on a more desired natural grass surface. The move would presumably help the team make a smoother transition to their new ballpark in 2003 and help the Reds to win in 2001 and 2002.[151]

Unfortunately, the Reds did not make the playoffs in either season, and once ownership was far enough along in the construction process, focus on the bottom line eclipsed an earlier commitment to pacify fans. In 2003, Reds management cut back on acquisition of new free-agent ballplayers, despite earlier suggestions that a new ballpark was a key ingredient in fielding a winning team. Ironically, on-field successes of low payroll, old stadium teams in Oakland and Minnesota may have inspired this more economical strategy. The 2003 Reds introduced fans to their sparkling new stadium with a 69-93 record, finishing just one game away from last place in their division. Before the 2003 season began, *Sporting News* columnist Ken Rosenthal, recognizing earlier claims by Reds management, wrote, "If there is any justice, the [new] place will be empty enough for the Reds to qualify for their precious revenue-sharing funds."[152]

Cincinnati had gained national attention, but much of it was not the kind of publicity that was anticipated when citizens voted to put tax dollars into sports facilities. Nevertheless, area residents seemed happier with the Reds construction effort. The facility was initially occupied by a new Reds owner, Carl Linder, a shrewd and aggressive businessman. It was named "Great American Ballpark" in a thirty-year, $75 million naming rights deal that was struck with one of his entities, the Great American Insurance Company. In 2006, Linder sold his principal interest in the team to a group headed by Bob Castellini, a lifelong Reds fan who appears more committed to winning than did the previous ownership. Fans appear happy with the change, and after five straight losing seasons, improvements in team performance are likely to bring more fans to the new ballpark.

The ballpark included nostalgic touches along with shiny futuristic amenities. The dugout seats from Crosley Field and Riverfront Stadium were transferred to the concourse areas, a move that allows fans to briefly relax in seating used by the stars of previous generations. Bronze statues of Crosley Field legends Joe Nuxhall and Ernie Lombardi greeted fans on their way into the ballpark. Gleaming tabletops and multiple television monitors now line the posh club areas. Even though the taxpayers were responsible for $279.3 million of the stadium's $290.5 million price, approximately 96 percent of the total construction cost, the process was less stressful than the nearby football field's construction.[153]

Special newspaper sections and enthusiastic television and radio reports offered evidence that the new ballpark was more warmly received than the Bengals's new home. Street-level conversations appeared to confirm such an outcome. Brisk sales of a hardbound book, prepared to recapture the pride of opening day, offered another slice of evidence that area residents seemed generally satisfied with the Reds's final product.[154] Reds management did pay a price for poor on-field performance, however. They were forced to cut ticket prices in 2004 and must hope that after the novelty of a new ballpark wears off, fans do not stay away because the team bears little resemblance to the championship caliber teams that inhabited the old stadium. A 2004 decision to close the ballpark's Machine Room Grille during the off season offered further evidence that the novelty of the new ballpark may be an insufficient lure for fans. The restaurant offers a nostalgic theme of the Big Red Machine's championship days. It was touted as a year-round attraction before construction, but limited foot traffic prompted the closure decision.[155]

Riverfront Stadium was imploded on December 29, 2002. Few local media voices expressed regret at the demise of a facility that was aggressively touted as world-class three decades earlier. *Cincinnati Enquirer*'s Paul Daugherty argued that "it has the ambience of a coal mine: plastic grass, soulless concrete, medieval restrooms."[156] The emphasis on stadium-related economics had become so pervasive that some coverage even focused on the economic benefits that resulted from implosion of Riverfront Stadium.[157] Although many citizens believed a new skyline with two ballparks was an improvement, some were nostalgic about the old facility and the teams that had played there. Todd Sledge of Anderson Township recalled attending games with his father and grandfather, suggesting the aftermath felt "like the death of the Big Red Machine."[158] Reaction to crumbling concrete varied widely. An individual hosting an implosion party casually joked that "no one should have to watch a building blow up without a bloody Mary."[159]

In looking at the Issue One vote, a 1997 Brookings Institution analysis concluded that the citizens of the Cincinnati metropolitan area, "desperately afraid of being perceived as another Louisville, Lexington, Dayton, or Columbus, . . .bought a lot of image . . . at a pretty high price."[160] This price may include some service-related sacrifices. Revenue projections indicate that Hamilton County's formula for stadium funding will fall short and that additional county revenue streams could be needed to underwrite these projects. Hamilton County Commissioner Phil Heimlich described the situation as a "ticking time-bomb" and suggested social service cuts may occur if the revenue picture does not improve.[161] In 2005, the cost of the ticking time bomb was known. Analysts projected the total sales tax deficit would escalate to $191.5 million in 2032 even with optimistic regional growth assumptions.[162] The rosy economic stadium projections did not come to fruition. United States census figures revealed that Cincinnati led all Ohio cities in population loss. Once the new football stadium was finished, the number of jobs in the downtown area did not increase; some downtown stores closed in 2002 despite the new construction.

The residents of southwest Ohio were not alone in their desire to maintain a "major league" image. In Pittsburgh, Seattle, Boston, Milwaukee, Green Bay, Houston, and other metropolitan areas, the allure of major league status prompted new calls for stadium subsidies. Local politicians, media organizations, and citizens supported such subsidies because of the powerful symbolism tied to major league sports. America's most powerful leaders gave Cincinnati positive reinforcement. In a 1996 visit to Cincinnati, President Bill Clinton opened his remarks offering "congratulations on the recent success of your stadium and education referendum," calling this citizen choice for subsidy "an impressive thing."[163] Former President George H. W. Bush, Clinton's predecessor, threw out the opening pitch in the inaugural ceremonies at Great American Ballpark. His involvement helped put Cincinnati on the map, if only temporarily.

Media coverage has been a critical force in fostering "major league" aspirations in cities throughout the nation. Although cost overruns in Cincinnati tempered enthusiasm for major league sports regionally, it did little to curtail the national subsidy trend. In 1996, before much of the anti-stadium backlash hit the region, Rick Horrow, an NFL consultant, argued that Cincinnati was "going to be a case study that gets presented to owners and city officials around the country."[164] The successful media campaign in Cincinnati had broad implications for other team owners clamoring for new facilities. As 1997 approached, the citizens of Pittsburgh were among those who would be exposed to some of the lessons that were unearthed in Cincinnati.

6

PITTSBURGH

Power Politics and Steely Persistence

PITTSBURGH IS A CITY with a unique topography. A visitor is likely to get lost in a complex landscape of hills and surrounding waterways. This topography provides a multitude of barriers for roads, bridges, and neighborhoods. In a similar manner, the political landscape is often an insular system of hierarchical leadership with the capacity to confound even the most agile analyst. Important policy decisions are as likely to be mulled over in an unassuming North Side sandwich shop as in a nicely appointed boardroom.[1]

Allegheny County's waterways and lush green hills provide boundaries that make land navigation difficult, but these features also offered a fertile environment for heavy industry. As the twentieth century unfolded, industry leaders established a hierarchical managerial style that often excluded input. Although political leaders were popularly elected, they often struggled to pacify captains of industry, cognizant that luminaries such as Charles Schwab and Andrew Carnegie could determine their future. The result of this early twentieth-century landscape was a polluted and blighted city that was highly profitable for business elites.

After World War II, steel industry successes made change seem unlikely, but as the nation shifted away from manufacturing and automation increased leisure opportunities, people became less tolerant of pollution and blight. Within this context decisions were made regarding Pittsburgh's future. Mayor David Lawrence convinced business leaders, most notably Richard King Mellon, to reduce air pollution. This made Pittsburgh a cleaner city as downtown construction reshaped the city's commercial center. This environmentally friendly transformation faced grassroots and corporate opposition, but the mayor was able to prevail by carefully selecting allies while using the media to sway the public.

In 1955, Lawrence and Mellon again teamed up, not to address pollution, but to discuss a municipal stadium that would presumably enhance the national stature of Pittsburgh.[2] It was the first time that the notion of a publicly funded sports palace was entertained by Pittsburgh's elites, but before it could be built, other city projects were undertaken. This building boom, focused primarily on downtown Pittsburgh, is commonly called "Renaissance II."

This transformation of Pittsburgh brought pride to a city on the verge of economic decline. Nevertheless, Pittsburgh's reputation as a dirty steel town persisted, and this negative reputation hurt nonindustrial growth. The region's population increased during the Progressive Era but was now shrinking. Mill workers' children looked elsewhere for opportunities as steel mills closed. Lawrence and others worked hard to shed Pittsburgh's image as a "rust-belt" city incapable of change. Three Rivers Stadium was built at the end of the Lawrence-inspired construction boom.[3] It was completed in 1970, a time when a thoroughly modern stadium brought community pride. Joseph Barr was mayor during much of the planning and construction, and Peter Flaherty was at the helm when the stadium was completed.

Early History: Pittsburgh Leisure and Forbes Field Construction

In Allegheny County, the ultimate shape of public policy is often determined by selected community elites with access to political leaders. As a result, leisure has often served as a hegemonic barometer for public resistance to leadership. In the Progressive Era, Pittsburgh's citizens flocked to commercial leisure options as a means of resisting the moralistic direction of elite-inspired public parks and libraries. In the 1960s picketing and labor strife during stadium construction served as an indicator of public distaste for corporate restructuring that cost many citizens their livelihood. At the end of the twentieth century, opposition to stadium construction became a means of resistance for citizens who believed that community elites, team owners, and athletes were exploiting their popular cultural institutions for personal gain.

Pittsburgh was at the center of a technological revolution in the nineteenth century, and area steel and coal were at the core of shaping the first half of twentieth-century America. Technology was a big part of the culture as the twentieth century unfolded. The telegraph made it easier for captains of industry to manage their vast resources from a distance, and an emerging film industry created cheap entertainment that helped Pittsburgh's blue collar employees forget the intense rigors of the workplace.[4]

Technology was also woven into the sports institutions of the region. Forbes Field was a technological marvel when unveiled in 1909. This ballpark was one of the first fully steel reinforced concrete ballparks in the nation. It included automated laundry machines in the clubhouse, on-site telephones, rest rooms for ladies (not a 1909 ballpark standard), and an underground parking garage. Press coverage during Forbes Field construction revealed a level of community pride that exceeded previous stadium projects throughout the country. Nevertheless, boosterism was a gradual process. Until it was clear that Forbes Field would be a unique source of pride, local media were reluctant to categorize its construction as a success.

Various factors encouraged downplaying the initial construction of Forbes Field. A most pragmatic concern was the practical politics of ballpark construction in 1909. Open competition between rival sports leagues gave politicians the upper hand in negotiations. If the more established National League wanted to place a team in a market, Ban Johnson's upstart American League might be enticed to host a competing franchise. Politicians could serve as gatekeepers with the ability to delay or block the entry of competing franchises.[5]

Understandably, team owners treaded reluctantly on political turf. Some owners kept a relatively low profile, while pushing behind the scenes to obtain positive publicity. Such a strategy might have been encouraged by public reluctance to accept professionalism in athletic endeavors. Until the success of the legendary 1869 Cincinnati Red Stockings, most sports fans regarded professional athletes with disdain. Even during the Progressive Era, distaste for professionalism in athletics could be uncovered. Only after prolonged marketing of baseball as a quintessential American sport did broader acceptance of athletic professionalism gain currency. Steven Riess suggests that coverage of professional baseball was skewed to position owners as "public-spirited citizens whose primary concern was the welfare of the community."[6] In reality, owners were guided by self-interest more than any other factor. Regardless, this positive image helped ticket sales and could minimize unreasonable demands from local politicians.

Other owners faced political complications when constructing less-elaborate ballparks, so the Pirates's owner Barney Dreyfuss's relative quiet before a Forbes Field groundbreaking was not surprising.[7] On October 26, 1908, Dreyfuss was reported to have purchased land in Pittsburgh's Oakland neighborhood. Newspapers erroneously reported that this land would be the future site of a University of Pittsburgh and Carnegie Tech football field.[8] Although subsequent news coverage suggests that Dreyfuss disclosed his intent, this was curiously omitted. At the time, both universities were in the process of situating their campuses nearby. In 1895 Andrew Carnegie chose Oakland to build his own cultural facilities, including a library, a music hall, and an art institute. These cultural assets made such a move attractive to local universities and to Dreyfuss. The ballpark also served Carnegie's interests, bringing traffic to his new cultural monuments.[9]

Cognizant of an eastward migration of an upwardly mobile middle class, Dreyfuss regarded Oakland as a potentially profitable location. Installation of a nearby streetcar system provided a flexible transportation network. It allowed the ballpark to draw from a broad audience, but could probably attract a more affluent clientele. This would better position Dreyfuss to maximize profit. However, Dreyfuss suggested democratic motives, calling the transportation facilities "in Oakland . . . [better] than in any other part of the city."[10]

Unlike more recent stadium-related publicity, typically punctuated by years of planning-related stories, media coverage of Forbes Field construction began on December 15, 1908, a mere seventeen days before groundbreaking. Two days before, the newly formed Pittsburgh Athletic Association announced unfulfilled plans to build a stadium in nearby Schenley Park. They were confident the site would serve as a venue for the 1912 Olympics.[11] The first reports of ballpark construction were low-key but often received large headlines. Two stories on surveying and grading the land received coverage as prominent as the actual groundbreaking. The initial story boasted that "Pittsburgh's new park will likely eclipse all other major league plants in the land."[12]

Four days before groundbreaking, the *Pittsburgh Post* reported new ballpark plans in Boston, Chicago, and St. Louis. They proudly repeated that "after next July the Smoky City will be able to boast the best baseball plant in the world." This article explained that, despite Dreyfuss's disclosure of intent, "many refused to credit the story."[13] In short, until the team moved heavy equipment into Oakland, reporters did not believe that Dreyfuss's plans would come to fruition.

The evolution of ballpark construction during the Gilded Age and the Progressive Era might explain such coverage tendencies. The first professional teams were a bit more than a generation removed from Dreyfuss's team. Some of these pioneers played a limited home schedule, deriving more revenue from barnstorming tours in hastily constructed wooden ballparks.[14] Michael Benson's ballpark encyclopedia is scattered with "name of park unknown" entries for Gilded Age and Progressive Era venues.[15] Before Dreyfuss took over the Pirates, many teams erected unimpressive wooden structures that did nothing to contribute to community pride. Owners were also dependent on the vagaries of local politicians. A team might have to abandon a politically desirable site for another location in mid-season. In a number of instances owners expected players to assist in both ballpark construction and field maintenance, further diminishing the shrine-like qualities that we have come to associate with ballparks.

As electric streetcars permeated the urban landscape, more intricate wooden structures emerged, giving a level of permanence to professional teams. The popularity of tobacco products eventually conspired to make masonry structures more appealing for safety-related reasons. Four separate fires in 1894 caused Baltimore's team to build some cement and steel stands after insurance coverage became prohibitive.[16] At approximately the same time, sections of Philadelphia's Baker Bowl were also victimized by fire. A large brick, steel, and concrete grandstand was subsequently built.[17] Philadelphia and Boston preceded Pittsburgh in opening large concrete and steel ballparks, the former in April 1909 for the Philadelphia Athletics, the latter in 1903 for the Harvard University's football team.

Reporting tendencies in Boston and Philadelphia were not as aggressive as in Pittsburgh when Forbes Field prepared to open in June 1909. Initially, the Forbes Field project was covered with a similar low-key approach. The Pirates owner Barney Dreyfuss received positive press coverage of groundbreaking on January 1, 1909, but he was not even on hand for the event. He chose to vacation in Louisville, Kentucky, where his family initially settled as German immigrants. No formal ceremonies marked the movement of heavy machinery into Oakland. The *Pittsburg Press* gave more prominence to the city marathon, but did include the groundbreaking's coverage on the first page of the "sporting section." Boosterism increased as the park began to take shape. The coverage by the *Press* and the

Post of the groundbreaking mentioned field drainage and highlighted the Chief Engineer C. E. Marshall's experience with Panama Canal construction, important because of the frequent drainage problems at the Pirates's current home, Exposition Park.[18]

Progressive Era newspapers straddled the line between catering to wealthy elites and appealing to the less-predictable masses. A generation earlier, newspapers maintained a clear ideological posture, but journalism was shifting to a fact-based "objective" style that allowed a newspaper to sell to a broader public while minimizing alienation of individuals responsible for highly coveted advertising revenue. Because eye-grabbing headlines helped spur sales, far-fetched medical news or sizzling murder plots often competed with political stories.[19] The *Pittsburg Press* and *Pittsburgh Post* were still considered Democratic partisans, but nonpartisan boosterism, a less-risky substitute for political ideology, gradually took root.

Pittsburgh's uncertainties were complicated by an expanding population. The population increase offered profitable opportunities for newspapers but created a difficult-to-determine readership profile. From 1870 to 1910 the city's population ballooned from 139,256 to 533,905.[20] An influx of immigrants from eastern Europe created unhealthy, tightly clustered housing. New citizens were not too familiar with American culture. These newcomers rapidly diluted the old guard mix of English, Irish, Scots, and German citizenry.

Sports helped to increase newspaper circulation, but it also served as a subtle class-related battleground.[21] Affluent citizens pursued two different paths in this clash. Some shut out the unwashed rabble, retreating to hunt clubs and exclusive resorts. More progressive citizens tried to improve leisure options for all, with the hope that the uplifting inspiration of such endeavors would result in a more productive citizenry. Some were inspired by idealism. However, industrialists, including Pittsburgh's Andrew Carnegie and Detroit's Henry Ford, were motivated by a desire to foster a more productive and less cantankerous workforce.[22] Francis Couvares argued that Carnegie's construction of a museum, music hall, and library in Pittsburgh had "an explicit social agenda: to define, create, and disseminate 'the highest culture' and thereby to civilize the inhabitants of the industrial city."[23] Similarly, Roy Lubove suggested that "public recreation posed no threat to private economic prerogatives, and had positive advantages as social control mechanisms."[24] Many of Pittsburgh's workers resisted the moralistic intentions of the wealthy, including Mary Schenley's donation of 300 acres for a city park in 1899. The city's dedication of acreage for elite activities such as golf and bridle paths discouraged some workers from partaking in more wholesome recreation.

Newspapers often gave more space to park development and high culture than ballpark construction. The park movement was spurred in part by a belief that such cultural assets could tame and civilize unruly children and provide an uplifting recreational experience to individuals challenged by the rigors of work. A *Pittsburgh Post* editorial championed this cause by arguing that open play spaces provided a child with an outlet "to train himself and be trained for future health and usefulness."[25] Frederick Law Olmstead's park design successes in other cities prompted an outpouring of support for pastoral recreation throughout the nation.[26]

In Pittsburgh, working-class skepticism about elite intentions drove many workers to consumer-driven recreation. These entertainment options were gritty and blue collar: the corner bar, the pool hall, the prize-fighting ring, and the nickelodeon. Others offered a slice of rural greenery and an upscale veneer with greater freedom and less threat of well-intentioned upper-class moralizing. Kennywood, an area amusement park, featured mechanical rides and a pastoral backdrop. It opened in 1898 and quickly became a popular recreational choice.[27] Baseball was another attractive commercial product, so media coverage gained momentum as ballpark construction neared completion. Such coverage was relatively safe. Forbes Field's combination of architectural innovation and pastoral green appealed to various segments of the population.

For the elites, baseball might be a back-door opportunity to introduce their values to less-privileged visitors. Baseball cultivated acceptance of a meritocracy and production standards, in the form of player statistics. Baseball's system of managerial hierarchy and specialized position play taught bureaucratic efficiency and skill specialization. Construction technology and ballpark management cultivated passive acceptance of elite-inspired innovation. Baseball's pastoral setting may not have been as uplifting as an elite country club, but a well-manicured diamond may have inculcated workers with the industrialist's notion of man's ability to master nature.

Blue-collar mill workers may have seen the new ballpark as a way to escape their rickety ethnic tenements. It was an upscale experience in a well-heeled neighborhood. Recent immigrants probably regarded it as an opportunity to partake in a thoroughly American community-binding experience. For veterans of the modernized steel mills, watching skillful ballplayers may have evoked memories of an earlier era when craftsmanship was more respected in industrial production.[28] By the 1900s, skilled workers and artisans were a dying breed, replaced largely by interchangeable semiskilled labor that improved output and better served management. More efficient steel- and glass-making techniques distanced many workers from their craft and shifted power from the worker to a Tayloresque supervisor.

Pittsburgh's working class was often suspicious of free leisure offered by elites, correctly determining that the same individuals responsible for oppressive working conditions had ulterior motives in their philanthropy. Skepticism of the philanthropic intent of a cadre of upper-class moralists prompted regional historian Francis Couvares to argue that "leisure reform only accelerated the rush of [Pittsburgh's] working people into the arms of merchants of leisure who were fashioning a new mass culture."[29] In response, sports sections catered to a broad range of recreational interests. College football, particularly the Ivy League variety, appealed to an upper-class audience fearful that technology and new riches were softening youthful offspring.[30] Hunt club events and yacht racing appealed to the conspicuously consuming elite.[31] Boxing held appeal for the bachelor subculture that grew with mass immigration.[32]

In this matrix of choices, professional baseball was a safe haven for all classes. Not surprisingly, baseball received extensive coverage even when a newspaper's self-interest was not directly tied to the home team's financial success.[33] Barney Dreyfuss was not personally invested in local media, yet coverage of Forbes Field construction was universally favorable. Editorials and articles praised baseball for its positive influence on the populace.[34] Coverage took three other trajectories. The first centered on innovation and technology, the second exhorted community pride, and the third praised the owner for civic mindedness or business acumen.

These recurrent themes were often intertwined. Dreyfuss, a shrewd entrepreneur, intuitively understood technology's significance in shaping the urban landscape. He was not afraid to employ technological solutions. When Exposition Park's drainage problems threatened attendance revenues, Dreyfuss was the first owner to use an infield tarpaulin. He also installed special "box" seats and public telephones, used special turf from an Ohio sod farm, designed an underground automobile parking garage, and added crowd control devices such as turnstiles and exit ramps.[35] Such innovations were turned into positive coverage. G. H. Gillespie, a *Pittsburg Press* reporter, called the project "the acme of modern skill and science."[36]

Ballpark construction was frequently touted as evidence of world-class status as Forbes Field neared completion. One report, replete with pictures, used the phrase "finest athletic field in the world" three times in opening paragraphs. If the repetition was not convincing, comparative arguments explained that construction was superior to other cities, including Philadelphia's new venue. One story boasted that "nothing advertises a city like a good baseball team."[37] A St. Louis sportswriter asserted that "there is nothing in the United States that even approaches Forbes Field in size, accessibility, cost, or location."[38] A Harper's Weekly ran a story that praised Pittsburgh's "million dollar baseball park" as the city prepared for its unveiling.[39]

The excitement surrounding the ballpark's opening was palpable. Ticket requests from distant locations were reported. A month before completion, President William Howard Taft increased interest in the Pirates, sitting with fans in the old ballpark as the Cubs defeated the Pirates.[40] Spectators and celebrities visited the site as completion neared. On June 13, an estimated 10,000 fans visited the ballpark area, many so excited that they were seen "climbing into the grandstand and sitting for some time." Opening ceremony plans included a concert with two bands and introduction of dignitaries, among them the league president and a parade of ex-players. The mayor threw the ceremonial first pitch to the city's director of public safety.[41]

Forbes Field's opening received lead story status with several front-page photos.[42] An editorial triumphantly asserted that "opening day certainly justifies the management's judgment in erecting so worthy a monument to America's most democratic pastime."[43] The first weekend featured record baseball crowds and a highly publicized evening fireworks show. The show offered the team additional Fourth of July revenue because games were over before sunset.[44] Dreyfuss later utilized the ballpark for a variety of nonbaseball events when the team was on the road, including "the Hippodrome," billed as "Pittsburgh's combination vaudeville and circus."[45]

Newspapers announced that a requirement of these nonbaseball events was that "scenery must be moveable so as not to interfere with pennant baseball."[46] Such precautions were prudent, as the Pirates season concluded with a World Series victory over the Detroit Tigers, offering a national showcase for Pittsburgh. The booster press cheerfully chronicled this historic event. One reporter argued that the series enhanced the city's stature because "in every city and town throughout the United States, an army of fans await[ed] the result of each contest."[47]

Barney Dreyfuss's plan to create a ballpark that would attract a more upscale audience was visionary. His success was so profound that the Giants's legend Christy Mathewson joked that players could easily "lose a fly ball in the glint of diamonds in the stands." By adding luxurious ballpark amenities, Dreyfuss helped change the baseball experience, attracting more women and families. A more civilized atmosphere evolved. Pirates shortstop Honus Wagner sheepishly confessed that players gradually decided to "stop cussin' " during games.[48]

Pittsburgh's Second Era of Stadium Construction History: Three Rivers Stadium

The unintended consequences of this cultural shift may have been greater support for professional sports. Sports evolved into a "quality of life" issue in many cities. With the drumbeat of the booster press, it was only a matter of time before the popularity of sports led to taxpayer subsidy for ballpark construction. Such subsidies led to a fundamental change in how owners and sports teams were covered in newspapers and on television.

In Pittsburgh, a more critical press emerged when new stadium projects were proposed. From 1968 to 1970 when Three Rivers Stadium was under construction, the media were generally supportive, but gone were the days of unquestioned positive press for team owners. As construction progressed, journalists covered issues such as minority hiring practices and controversy about political control of the stadium project.[49] However, construction coverage did not include recognition of public input to any appreciable degree.

After some discussion of a new stadium in the 1950s, Pittsburgh's planning began to gain momentum in 1963 but was brought to a standstill because of a legal challenge from the Civic Club of Allegheny County, which argued that the new stadium authority created an "illegal debt." The debt was challenged because the city would be responsible for expenditures that were in excess of revenues collected by the newly created stadium authority. The state Supreme Court rejected a taxpayer challenge of a Philadelphia stadium project a week earlier. Nevertheless, anti-stadium leaders believed that Pittsburgh could face a different outcome because Philadelphia's project was approved in a referendum, whereas the Pittsburgh project circumvented direct voter input.

The case was dismissed by the state Supreme Court on January 11, 1966.[50] Before the decision, Justice Herbert Cohen compared the financing plan to "a school district that has an authority build a school for it," and Justice Michael Musmanno pointedly asked the Civic Club's attorney, John Neely, "Do you think that today a city can hold its head up in the nation without an adequate stadium?" Neely responded that many citizens "who don't believe this . . . haven't had a chance to voice their objections," but Musmanno tersely countered that "I think it is just as important for a city to have a stadium as it is to have parks."[51] The court challenge slowed stadium progress and revealed some opposition. Nevertheless, most coverage portrayed the new stadium as a positive development. The stadium was touted as an engine for economic development and urban renewal. As specific plans were made in 1968, the proposed construction area was described as "a combination junkyard and industrial slum" that was badly in need of repair.[52]

Before Three Rivers Stadium was built, Forbes Field was a comfortable home for the Pirates, but the Steelers were in a much less-secure position. Initially, they played in Forbes Field but later shared Pitt Stadium with the University of Pittsburgh. Both arrangements relegated them to second-class status. In the Forbes Field arrangement, the Steelers were obligated to adhere to the whims of the Pirates, and the other facility was not controlled in any way by the professional team.

Public subsidy was not generally criticized as construction neared, largely because stadium advocates framed this as a profitable venture. Nevertheless, up-front taxpayer financing forced reporters to cover the project with greater scrutiny than if the project was entirely funded by team owners. As in Cincinnati, once the court decision eliminated any legal constraints, the public tended to be left out of the process. Civic leaders, elected officials, and experts were most featured in news coverage. As the bidding process was finalized, Stadium Authority officials and construction professionals moved to the forefront. A 1968 article focusing on the bidding timetable, heavily quoted Burrell Cohen, the Stadium Authority's project director. Cohen set April 20, 1968, as a tentative groundbreaking date with a caveat that an acceptable bid was needed.[53] Previous bidding that began in 1966 resulted in only three bids and estimates of at least $31.3 million, far in excess of the $28.5 million that the stadium authority had budgeted for this purpose.[54]

An acceptable bid arrived. Stadium groundbreaking involved a brief flurry of public participation, but once construction was under way, news coverage tended to give way to bureaucratic and technocratic control. After the groundbreaking, the public was frozen out of traditional news reporting, but concerned citizens utilized other methods to put their views on the table. Public opposition to the construction itself was marginal. Instead, public comment focused on construction procedures, what to name the stadium, and labor-related issues. Pickets, organized public marches, and letters to the editor were the most common forms of public expression. Articles did not include evidence of extreme opposition to the project itself, but limited evidence of distaste for stadium construction could be found.

One *Pittsburgh Post-Gazette* letter that preceded groundbreaking argued against "spending the money of future generations" after creating an autonomous "authority."[55] Another letter published five days after groundbreaking criticized political priorities, tersely wondering "how many sub standard slum-lord tenements . . . could be torn down and replaced by the $29 million that our splendid, shiny new stadium will cost."[56] Three weeks later, another citizen attacked neglect of education, stating this neglect stood in contrast to "the prime concern of our city [which] is allocation of nearly $30 million for a baseball field." In a move not generally practiced by the editorial staff, the letter was followed by an italicized "editor's note" explaining their editorial position and that the stadium debt "would be retired through contracts with the ballclubs who use the stadium. The city's only financial obligation in the stadium deal is to backstop to the bond issue. Hopefully, it will not cost the city a penny."[57]

Critical letters about the decision to build a stadium were rare. Instead, the public was much more captivated by the debate over a new stadium name. On the day before groundbreaking, the *Pittsburgh Post-Gazette* helped stir up interest in this endeavor with an editorial that vigorously argued that the stadium should be named after David L. Lawrence, the charismatic political figure who helped reshape Pittsburgh after World War II.[58]

Stadium groundbreaking coverage a day later focused heavily on momentum that was building to name the stadium in honor of Lawrence. The current mayor, the city council president, and several other politicians were listed among those supporting the notion of naming the stadium after David L. Lawrence.[59] Three days after groundbreaking coverage, a letter in support of the Lawrence naming was offset by two letters that advocated simply "Pittsburgh Stadium" and "Pittsburgh Memorial Stadium," respectively.[60] Approximately three weeks later, a letter from David L. Lawrence's son indicated that his family "would be honored" if the name of his deceased father was adopted.[61] A year later, after the Lawrence idea was moribund, an editorial lamented Pittsburgh's inability to recognize Lawrence's legacy in any civic structure.[62]

Most citizens seemed to hold little enthusiasm for naming the facility after a political leader. Many suggested that the name should reflect taxpayer desires because they would be funding the project. One citizen suggested naming the stadium after Jonas Salk, a local legend responsible for inventing the polio vaccine. Others focused on the Hall of Fame ballplayer Honus Wagner, the Pirates announcer Rosey Roswell, the former Pirates manager Bill McKechnie, and Martin Luther King.[63] Several suggested that it should be named in memory of American soldiers. Some argued for names with a civic orientation, and others questioned the prudence of naming the facility after any politician.[64]

Three Rivers Stadium, the name ultimately selected, emerged as a gradual process. On May 6, 1968, George Dorondo, a citizen from Butler, Pennsylvania, suggested the name "Mon-All-O," derived from the first syllable of each of the three rivers surrounding the site. He argued that "the three rivers were there long before our time and will be there long after."[65] Howard Burgwin of Pittsburgh appeared to be the first citizen to publicly suggest the "Three Rivers Stadium" name in a letter published on Wednesday, May 22, 1968. Burgwin argued that the "Three Rivers" name "couldn't offend anybody—alive or dead."[66] Because a few area businesses were named after the "three rivers," the name was already familiar to the public. Those in charge of the construction process did not let public prodding push them into a quick decision. Instead, the final name was announced months after public input on this issue had died down. Letters continued into the early summer of 1968, but the official naming announcement came in a relatively subdued fashion on February 12, 1969, after a long period of public silence.

In making the decision, the leaders appeared to recognize public opposition to the use of a specific politician's name, but they framed the choice in terms of broader national trends in order to avoid alienation of elites who may have lobbied for a specific dedication. Arthur Gratz, the chairman of the Stadium Authority, stated that the board "considered naming the stadium for an individual, such as a sports figure, a statesman, or a businessman who may have dominated the Pittsburgh scene," but "the trend in the big leagues to name new stadiums for identifying geographical figures . . . 'tipped the scales' " in favor of the Three Rivers Stadium name. Cincinnati's Riverfront Stadium was cited, as was Chavez Ravine (Dodgers Stadium), and Houston's Astrodome.[67] The low-key announcement may have been a strategic move to limit criticism. If so, it was an apparent success. Little objection was raised after the naming announcement.

In a small way the stadium naming issue may have given the public a sense that they were part of the process even though significant decisions were made by political appointees, construction professionals, and civic leaders. Team owners almost certainly had input on a number of important policy decisions, but their position in media coverage was downplayed considerably compared to more recent media coverage of stadium construction. Franchise relocation threats were absent from the dialogue.

Rather than making such demands, as is the case in current stadium negotiations, sports franchises tended to be pressured by leaders to act in a more civic minded manner. When it appeared that the stadium financing could not be completed without entering into a deficit, the Galbreath family, owners of the Pirates, agreed to increase their rental fees from $355,500 per year to $405,500 per year.[68] Owners were not generally quoted in stories about design or stadium construction matters. Instead, their role was largely to serve as tenant and to be present and visible for ceremonial functions such as groundbreaking festivities.

During the groundbreaking ceremonies for Three Rivers Stadium, the owners were presented in a manner that helped humanize them within the community. As part of the festivities, Art Rooney, owner of the Steelers, kicked a ceremonial first field goal, and John Galbreath, owner of the Pirates, caught ceremonial pitches tossed by Mayor Joseph Barr. Groundbreaking ceremonies on April 25, 1968, were orchestrated to achieve a variety of goals. First, they helped to celebrate the culmination of many years of planning. Second, they were an opportunity for politicians and local celebrities to publicly take the stage. Third, they served as a public relations vehicle for team owners who were less visible in media coverage than present-day owners. Finally, the ceremonies presented an opportunity for elites to symbolically reach out to the community in ways that may have been more sophisticated than the public would recognize.

Concerns about race relations serve as a cogent example. Instead of selecting the typical political figure or league executive, the Olympic hero Jesse Owens was chosen and heavily publicized to be the principal speaker.[69] In his remarks, he stated, "As long as men of all creeds and color can play football and baseball together here. . . , this hallowed ground is worthwhile under the eyes of God."[70] Racial tensions were a national concern as Pittsburgh prepared to break ground. Civil rights marches and concern over lack of equity in hiring practices were part of the national landscape in 1968. Blacks were often frozen out of high-paying construction jobs, but articles from as early as 1966 chronicled Pittsburgh's shortage of skilled construction labor.[71]

The murder of the civil rights activist Martin Luther King Jr. on April 4, 1968, brought racial tensions to a most ominous level as Pittsburgh moved ahead on stadium construction. The *Post-Gazette*'s front-page article announcing the stadium's formal bidding results was visually juxtaposed by photos of civil rights protests in Memphis a mere five days before King was killed by an assassin's bullet.[72] Riots broke out throughout the nation after King's death, and although Pittsburgh's situation was tame compared to some cities, a genuine fear persisted that race relations might divide and destroy the country.[73]

Inviting a prominent black man to be the keynote speaker at the groundbreaking ceremony may have helped alleviate racial tensions somewhat, but activist citizens were less than satisfied with mere symbolic representation. Instead, Pittsburgh's minority leaders attempted to make discrimination in the workplace a hot-button issue. Activists looked at the symbolic importance of the stadium in tailoring a strategy that would draw attention to their political agenda. Before construction, civic leaders took steps to address minority hiring issues, but some of these steps served to demonstrate the limits of minority progress. A 1966 accord between the Pittsburgh Baseball Employees Union and the United Negro Protest Committee to hire minority workers at Pirate games in Forbes Field highlighted the fact that minority workers were hired previously to serve as maids, porters, guards, and cooks but were unable to apply for more visible positions. Until the agreement, no blacks were ever hired as ushers or ticket takers.[74]

After being frozen out of many of low-skilled positions for decades, the minority community was ready to push for inclusion in higher paying skilled positions. An early agreement to hire minority heavy machinery workers provided some hope that protests might be unnecessary, but lack of immediate, tangible progress in this and other areas prompted more militant action.[75] The stadium job site became the protest venue of choice because of its symbolic importance to the community. The choice increased the chance of media coverage. Such stories often lacked the typical author's byline, perhaps an indication of the issue's volatility.

Progress on the minority hiring issue was constrained by bureaucratic inflexibility. Construction management and political leaders expressed a desire to help, but said their hands were tied because qualifications were set by the unions responsible for the various workplace tasks. Union leaders said they had to adhere to guidelines that required apprenticeships and training before individuals could advance to higher paid positions.[76] With a multitude of unions in a range of occupations, the ability to negotiate was an uphill battle despite efforts by political leaders to coordinate meetings that included all parties. When it seemed clear that progress would not be made, minority activists took to the streets, mobilizing stadium site protests.

These protests were blamed for "causing delays" according to Sam Casey, vice chairman of the Stadium Authority. Robert Collins, the project manager, estimated that a single-day shutdown caused a $20,000 to $25,000 loss as well as major problems with supply deliveries. To avert financial loss, an August 12, 1969, court order was rendered by Judge David Fawcett Jr. that required picketers "to keep moving, spaced 10 feet apart and . . . 'peaceably advertise their cause without injury or violence to any person or property.' "[77]

A subsequent court order from Judge Fawcett, rendered on August 15, 1969, further restricted the protests. The terms of this order restricted the Black Construction Coalition to twelve pickets on the stadium's West General Robinson Street entrance and eight pickets at the Manchester entrance. Michael Dismond, a spokesman for the coalition, argued that "all legal means have been exhausted," stating that the situation is so serious that there is "nothing but mass force left to stop it." He vowed to "stop the stadium job and all other construction jobs within the city" with a mass protest that was set for August 25, 1969.[78]

A day after the first court order, Broadway Maintenance Corporation, an electrical contractor, indicated that they would not send trucks through picket lines, slowing construction and giving the Black Construction Coalition a victory.[79] The picketers' cause was fortified by a story focusing on data compiled by the mayor's Commission on Human Relations. According to the report, "most of the unions listed . . . had a black membership of under two percent." Seven unions "refused to reply . . . to the commission's request for figures." Four of the unions reported all-white memberships; two of these had more than 1,000 members.[80] In the wake of such evidence, public opinion favored those pushing for greater minority representation.

Anticipating a highly volatile situation, the mayor closed down the construction site on August 25. Citing safety concerns, construction was also suspended for one day at the U.S. Steel, Pittsburgh National Bank, Bell Telephone, and Westinghouse buildings.[81] This action prompted construction workers to launch a protest outside the mayor's office. The massive volume of construction workers and minority picketers resulted in greater media coverage of these protests.

The protests on August 26, 1969, included a mix of minority and nonminority participants. In light of court-ordered restrictions around the stadium site and various violent incidents, numerous arrests were made. Thirty-two injuries resulted, including twelve police officers. According to reports, 180 arrests were made after police were pelted with rocks and protesters were attacked by club-wielding police. Three Catholic nuns were arrested, an indication that some of those arrested were nonviolent citizens marching for social justice.[82] On the opposite end of the spectrum some militant protesters were equipped with riot gear and chemical crowd-control agents reportedly more powerful than the police department's Mace. Other protesters brought German shepherds, presumably for protection or as a tool of intimidation. Because no laws prohibited dogs in public streets, some of these protesters escaped arrest.[83] Those who were arrested faced the wrath of David Fawcett Jr., the same judge who issued two prior rulings sternly limiting protests around the stadium site. He swiftly sent a dozen protesters accused of "indirectly blocking the stadium entrance" to the county jail.

The arrests and jailings served as an immediate deterrent. During the August 26 demonstrations, protesters moved from the stadium to the U.S. Steel Building, also under construction. After that, the stadium lost its place as the central protest site, but it served as a starting point for dramatic mass action. By September 15, 1969, one march, centered downtown and composed of a mix of white businessmen, housewives, hippies, and blacks, was estimated to include between 5,000 and 9,000 protesters. The crowd volume increased after officials called for further state-level study of the issue, something that infuriated black leaders. This was perceived as stonewalling and mobilized many participants to join the march.[84] One enthusiastic protester argued that the crowds exceeded the volume of civil rights marches in Selma, Alabama, and were "bigger even than the march after Martin Luther King was shot."[85]

Although public opinion polls were not a journalistic routine in the 1960s, letters to the editor, typically skewed to represent more affluent interests, were frequently highly sympathetic to discrimination faced by inner-city blacks. Supportive letters outpaced letters defending union or industry action by at least a two-to-one margin. A citizen from Mt. Lebanon, an affluent Pittsburgh suburb, touted an organization called Mt. Lebanon Citizens for Community Relations as "friends of the Black Construction Coalition and . . . solidly behind the coalition's efforts to open up more jobs for blacks in construction."[86] Appeals to social justice were also common, and the Vietnam War was used to defend minority hiring. One letter rhetorically asked, "Are we really going to tell the black fighting man returning from a distant war that he can't climb a steel girder or wear an electrician's badge?"[87] Another letter asked, "If black men can operate equipment in Vietnam, then why can't they operate construction equipment in Pittsburgh?"[88]

Some negative opinion followed the 1968 riots shortly after Martin Luther King's death, but by 1969, despite vocal protests by white construction workers, public opinion seemed to mobilize behind the minority position.[89] The limited support for union voices prompted a *Pittsburgh Post-Gazette* article that offered opinions from construction workers who had picketed City Hall while the stadium site was closed down due to protests. Despite public opinion momentum on the minority hiring issue, dramatic progress was not made. Instead, a few gradual victories slowly disengaged public anger. A few December articles suggested that progress had been made and an agreement was pending. A key feature of the agreement was federal backing for minority training in the construction trades.[90]

A number of stadium work stoppages and protests unrelated to the minority hiring issue may have diminished public intensity for this issue. One work stoppage was prompted by an effort to phase out ten-minute coffee breaks.[91] Days earlier a dispute between cement finishers and stone masons caused twenty cement laborers to briefly stop working.[92] Another work stoppage was caused by a union-based jurisdictional dispute over scoreboard installation.[93] Safety issues, union wage disputes, and demands for concession area upgrades also caused stadium construction delays.[94] A United Brewery Workers Union official added yet another distraction, threatening pickets if local beers were not placed on the concession menu.[95]

Despite all of these issues, minority representation required the attention of public officials. Sometimes officials acted in a delayed response to public opinion. Newly elected Mayor Pete Flaherty appointed John Henry Johnson, a black ex-Steeler running back, to serve as his representative on the Stadium Authority's board of directors.[96] Minority-related negotiations were still taking place in 1970, weeks before the stadium opened. Although it many have been too late to increase minority representation on that construction site, some agreements were reached to ensure that black applicants would receive consideration for new stadium-related positions.[97]

The actual decision to build Three Rivers Stadium was not generally questioned. Instead, construction procedures, stadium amenities, naming decisions, and hiring practices dominated many debates about the facility. In light of present-day controversy about stadium construction, this might seem odd, but can be explained by a variety of factors. The rhetoric of growth that surrounded the construction process may have led many citizens to believe that such construction would advance Pittsburgh's economy in a tangible way. Citizens also seemed to regard a new stadium as something that a community automatically did to assert its major league status. In 1976 James Michener wrote that he "would not want the building of great stadiums to be subjected to picayune supervision by the general public. Let the project be explained, justified and funded honestly; then let the men and women of vision proceed with the actual work."[98]

Explanations of how the project would be funded led many taxpayers to believe that the process was free of risk. On January 13, 1968, the stadium was described as "a self-amortizing, non-subsidized program." Burrell Cohen, Stadium Authority executive director, asserted that the stadium would produce "$1,670,000 in rental, parking revenues, and other income sources" while $1.6 million per year was required to amortize the stadium debt. Furthermore, as stadium financing plans were laid on the table, John Mauro, director of city planning, told reporters that "$500,000 a year in additional taxes will come in because of the stadium."[99] The self-funded stadium claim was repeated often. In addition, as the stadium was under construction, new opportunities for revenue were occasionally announced.

Some of these plans were ahead of their time, including "special boxes" and a lavish, upscale club within the stadium with windows overlooking the field of play. The upscale facility, to be called the Allegheny Club, would add at least $100,000 a year to stadium authority revenues. The cost of furnishing and maintaining the club would be drawn from club members dues, a move that would save $1.5 million dollars in construction costs.[100] The special boxes, a prelude to the commonly utilized skyboxes of today, were expected to add $277,500 to the stadium authority's coffers. Over a five-year period, this would help reduce the overall cost of the stadium by almost $1.4 million. Stadium-related advertising, including scoreboard revenue, was claimed to be a means of further enhancing the stadium's revenue-generating possibilities.[101] In each case, it appeared that the stadium authority, not the sports franchises, would be the principal beneficiaries of these new revenue streams. In light of this, construction appeared to be a win-win proposition for the entire metropolitan area.

As expenses increased, officials displayed sensitivity to public concerns about subsidy. In almost all cases, officials quickly offered rhetoric that assured taxpayers they would not be forced to subsidize overruns. In one exception, a city councilman charged on November 26, 1969, that overruns would result in dramatic subsidies for the Steelers and Pirates over the forty years of the lease.[102] Within a week of this claim, John Mauro, the city's planning director, forwarded a plan to city council that hiked ticket prices by ten to twenty-five cents to "eliminate the need for an annual city subsidy."[103] The plan was endorsed by the *Pittsburgh Post-Gazette* and was subsequently approved.[104] Both teams agreed to the additional fees. The total cost was now projected to be $35 million, $6.5 million more than the original $28.5 million estimate. As the stadium neared opening, demands from a New York concessionaire to substantially improve the facilities prompted further concern about subsidy. The public was quickly told that the estimated $1.3 million overrun "won't cost the public a dime." Instead, overruns in this area would be paid by the Pirates because their "failure to hire a concessionaire until only five months ago led to the problems they are now having." No comment from Pirates officials was offered.[105]

The Pirates and Steelers also signed forty-year leases that were expected to keep them in the facility until 2010. Citizens were left with the comfortable belief that professional sports would remain in Pittsburgh for an entire generation. A few isolated complaints about spending priorities could be found, but by and large, the public was given information that calmed them into a belief that the stadium project would never require taxpayer subsidy. A January 7, 1970, editorial argued that the new stadium would bring the city an annual tax windfall of $1.2 million.[106]

In this light, citizens may have regarded the stadium as a risk-free opportunity to achieve national recognition. Citizens were further enticed to support the project because various unique features would set the stadium apart from other venues. The Allegheny Club promised to deliver an upscale touch to a community that was nationally stereotyped as ruggedly blue-collar. Having a club-style restaurant overlooking the field of play offered a sports-crazy community an innovative amenity. Although the fees to join this club would probably limit membership to the wealthy, reports that the revenues from the endeavor would help build the stadium minimized objections from less-upscale citizens. Furthermore, the club might help offset the undesired "rust-belt" stereotype as corporate leaders visited and were entertained by Pittsburgh-based executives.

The stadium would also feature advanced lighting that was developed by engineers at Pittsburgh-based Westinghouse Corporation. These innovative mercury vapor floodlights might enhance the ability of television cameras to showcase Pittsburgh during national telecasts.[107] Tartan turf gave the stadium another high-tech feature. Although artificial turf became less desirable later, at this time such features were regarded as "cutting edge." A set of docking facilities would also be installed to allow boats to drop off passengers at the stadium entrance.[108] A new highway with ramps to the stadium would bring easy access, but stadium planners admitted that parking would be in short supply for at least a year.

Austerity measures reflecting the region's unstable economy caused cutbacks in projects intended to beautify the surrounding area, including a riverfront park. Despite this, as the stadium prepared to open, community pride was evident. Although some elements were unfinished, coverage offered nearly universal praise for the facility. In a front-page story on July 17, 1970, the *Pittsburgh Post-Gazette* indicated "it obviously made a big hit with the first nighters. Clearly they fell in love with it. They used adjectives such as terrific, great, and fantastic. But the most commonly heard word was: beautiful." Because construction was still in progress, officials posted a large sign welcoming fans while asking them to "Please excuse the temporary inconveniences. When it is finished YOU'LL LOVE IT."[109]

The Obsolete Ballpark: The Campaign to Replace Three Rivers Stadium

In the 1980s and 1990s Pittsburgh's media frequently suggested that the public's love affair with Three Rivers Stadium was short. Its circular design, a compromise to accommodate both football and baseball, limited the number of premium baseball seats to about 15,000. While a significantly better design for football, the circular configuration pushed upper deck fans on the coveted fifty-yard line slightly further away from the field than a more rectangular, football-only configuration. In 1990 sportswriter Bob Smizik argued that "almost from the day it was opened, Three Rivers was detested in Pittsburgh." According to Smizik, "It was more suited for football than baseball. . . , parking cost too much. . . , the concessions were too expensive. . . , and most of all, [it was not] a cozy little ballpark" like its predecessor, Forbes Field.[110]

As Three Rivers Stadium closed its doors on a rainy Saturday on December 16, 2000, many football fans offered indications that they would miss the thirty-year old structure, which was imploded two months later. Some fans stood on the pedestrian walkway sadly taking pictures. Vendors did a brisk business hawking disposable cameras and specially made Three Rivers Stadium T-shirts. Some spoke freely about how they would miss the place where Steeler history was made. Despite heavy rains, people came early and stayed late as the Steelers trounced the Washington Redskins, 24-3.

As people funneled out of the stadium, the frivolity and tailgating that usually followed a Steeler victory was tempered by a somber uncertainty regarding what would replace Three Rivers Stadium. The rain and chill of a Pittsburgh December and the intensity of an emotional postgame celebration may have put some damper on the final exodus. Area residents were cognizant that a local landmark faced the wrecking ball, and many fans seemed to understand the broader implications of this issue. The new football stadium, under construction just feet away from the old stadium, would likely include amenities unavailable at the old stadium, but some wondered whether it would have the same electrifying atmosphere.[111]

Although fan opinion regarding the old venue was often tinged with nostalgia, with few exceptions, the press continued its tendency to portray Three Rivers Stadium as a cold and impersonal building that inadequately served area fans.[112] Editorials following the stadium's closure seemed to hammer this message home. The *Pittsburgh Post-Gazette* described it as "a venue that many people found unsatisfactory," and the *Pittsburgh Tribune-Review* described it as "a vast, uncomfortable, public gathering space."[113]

The call to replace Three Rivers Stadium had little to do with the building's structural integrity which, despite labor controversies, could have remained useful for decades into the future. Instead, this stadium became economically obsolete for team owners. As other sports franchises around the country were signing heavily subsidized sweetheart deals that offered revenue streams from advertising, skyboxes, parking, and concessions, the terms offered to Pittsburgh's two professional teams looked woefully inadequate. A new stadium with a better lease became the quickest route to profitability. With a new contract team owners, not the stadium authority, would retain the lion's share of stadium revenues.

The campaign to build two new sports facilities took several twists and turns, including an overwhelming public rejection in a referendum to fund these facilities. The sales tax formula had proven successful elsewhere, but not in Pittsburgh. By September 1997 a carefully orchestrated media campaign unfolded. But before the campaign drew positive coverage, initial calls for a new stadium in the early 1990s were ridiculed and regarded as far-fetched and illogical. Media practitioners, civic leaders, and most citizens did not embrace the first attempts to build a new baseball-only ballpark.

Mayor Sophie Masloff's September 1991 proposal for a $100 million old-fashioned, natural grass stadium was warmly received by the Pirates, but the idea was portrayed as foolish by almost everyone else. Sportswriter Ron Cook called Masloff's stadium idea "ludicrous," citing respectable attendance as evidence that the Pirates did not need a new ballpark.[114] Political columnist Tom Hritz mocked her idea as financially unsound.[115] Associate Editor Tom Waseleski argued that a new ballpark would result in choking off important "financial capital. . . . for transportation."[116] Editor John Craig suggested that a new stadium might be acceptable, but teams should "figure out how to get government out of such involvements."[117]

Citizens offered similar analyses in letters and politicians were quick to criticize the idea.[118] Tom Foerster, Allegheny County commissioner, argued that the region had "some priorities that are way ahead of something like that." He stated that any attempt to build a new stadium should be the result of private funding.[119] Tom Murphy, then serving a term as a state representative, pointedly said the idea "doesn't seem to make any sense."[120] Masloff quickly withdrew her proposal. She received praise from the *Pittsburgh Post-Gazette* for recognizing the "widespread negative response" to her idea.[121] As her tenure came to a close, Masloff pushed through legislation for major renovations to Three Rivers Stadium.[122]

Ironically, Tom Murphy, a vociferous critic of Masloff's 1991 proposal, emerged as a prominent cheerleader for new construction. Before this happened, Murphy argued that city finances, job creation, and transportation infrastructure were more pressing community needs.[123] At the time, Murphy was Pittsburgh's leading candidate for mayor. He assumed that position in January 1994. Murphy continued to argue for measured caution until early into his first term.

An August 3, 1994, announcement that Pirates ownership would sell the team pushed Murphy to find a new owner.[124] Failure to attract a local investor could have placed Murphy in the unenviable position of being at the helm as the team moved to another city. The sale was triggered by owner attempts to renegotiate a more favorable stadium lease. Entrepreneurs in Charlotte, North Carolina, and Washington, D.C., were already expressing interest in bidding for the Pirates, prompting Murphy to quickly rearrange his political priorities.[125] Stadium building moved from a marginal concern to the top of his agenda.

The Pirates were owned by a consortium of local leaders who expressed dismay at their inability to maintain the club at break-even levels. The continued loss was caused, in part, by an unattractive stadium lease, the economic direction taken by competing team owners, and fans who were spoiled by the team's recent ability to produce winning teams. Owners in larger markets and small market owners with newer facilities could bid more aggressively for free agent talent, prompting several of the Pirates's best players to leave Pittsburgh. As the team's on-field success declined, so did public enthusiasm for the Pirates.[126]

With the loss of nationally known players, such as Barry Bonds, to larger market teams, the Pirates payroll declined from eighth to twenty-first from 1992 to 1993, yet Pirates management argued that they were still losing money.[127] Before putting the team up for sale, the team tried to improve their financial situation, but each move seemed to further alienate them from the city's blue-collar citizens. In 1993 the Pirates unsuccessfully took Pittsburgh to court, arguing that a 1985 verbal subsidy promise by former Mayor Richard Caliguiri legally entitled them to a $4.2 million payout.[128] The Pirates also placed restrictions on in-stadium catering, making outside food and beverages illegal in private lounge boxes. Some business owners argued this could double or triple the cost of stadium-related entertainment.[129] As these actions were taken, the team continued to say they needed a new ballpark. Steve Greenberg, the Pirates vice president for marketing and operations, argued that without one, the Pirates would lose attendance to nearby Cleveland, where there was a new taxpayer funded ballpark.

The quality of baseball suffered as Pirate veterans signed multimillion dollar contracts elsewhere. They evolved from a top-tier squad to a team struggling to stay out of last place. This created a fan backlash that further eroded ticket sales. Support was slammed again by a labor dispute shortly after the 1994 All Star Game, ironically hosted by Pittsburgh. This labor dispute terminated the 1994 baseball season and continued into 1995.

Pittsburgh's citizens, many one generation removed from the rigors of steel mill employment, were reminded that World Wars and a depression could not stop baseball, but this time, a fight over how to split up huge television and ticket revenues stopped play before a World Series could bring proper closure to the sport. Pittsburgh began to turn its back on baseball. Attendance in 1995 was the lowest of any Major League team, dropping from over two million in 1991 to a mere 905,517 in 1995.[130] The Pirates's last place finish in 1996 dimmed fan enthusiasm again, but overtures continued for a new stadium.

In this environment Mayor Tom Murphy asked area citizens to support new construction. Murphy's about-face was a gradual process. His initial opposition was softened by a trip with Pirates's management to Cleveland's Jacobs Field in 1994.[131] Murphy's personal struggle to secure an owner willing to keep the team in Pittsburgh may have influenced him most. After the team went up for sale in 1994, Murphy struggled with strategies intended to keep the Pirates from leaving. He developed greater empathy for Pirates's management after a national magazine's financial analysis indicated that the commercial value of the team was among the lowest in baseball, yet despite discount pricing, the city still struggled to find an owner.[132] After failed attempts to pin down bids from several prospects, Murphy worked to successfully convince Kevin McClatchy, heir to the Sacramento-based McClatchy Communications empire, to acquire the Pirates for $85 million. McClatchy's West Coast roots caused street-level speculation that the purchase was undertaken as a first step to moving the franchise elsewhere.

Ironically, the $85 million price paid for the team was less than half the cost of a new ballpark. Allegheny County could have purchased the team for less than it would cost to build a stadium, but league bylaws did not permit community ownership. Pittsburgh-area politicians were unwilling to confront this issue, presumably because such a challenge would almost certainly trigger a negative response from Major League Baseball's hierarchy. Part of the Pirates's sale agreement required politicians to move forward on funding plans for a baseball-only stadium within three years or risk another team sale. Major League Baseball pushed for a two-year window on the stadium issue, but backed down without explanation. Approximately two months later, the stadium authority altered the team's lease, offering the Pirates a bigger slice of concessions, luxury box revenue, and advertising income.[133] These new revenue streams were considered to be worth $6.5 to $7 million per year.[134]

As these transactions transpired, Pittsburgh's football team did not react passively. The team's president, Dan Rooney, began to jockey for subsidies that would enhance his team's profitability. Rooney was a tough, thick-skinned, parsimonious owner, much in the mold of the NFL founding fathers. Nevertheless, Rooney was much more focused on a long-term business strategy than his father, Art Rooney, the original Steelers's owner. Art Rooney and his contemporaries struggled to survive at a time when baseball was more popular. Many of these old guard owners were not particularly adept at management, but they benefitted from carefully cultivated community allegiances. Dan Rooney often urged cohesiveness among team owners, in a manner similar to his father, but as a new generation of owner emerged, he adapted to the new landscape, avoiding some of the managerial pitfalls of other old guard owners.

Rooney's initial response was pragmatic and civic minded. In February 1995, he questioned the need for construction, suggesting that Major League Baseball should address deeper economic problems instead of relying on a new ballpark as a panacea for revenue shortfalls. He pointedly asked "whether Pittsburgh can afford to finance a new ballpark when they are having trouble financing . . . [Three Rivers] stadium?"[135] As the Pirates obtained lease concessions and Rooney watched other NFL teams move into new facilities, he started to look for advantages for his franchise. He began this process with the subtlety of a sledgehammer. In an October 10, 1995, article, Rooney argued that "government officials needed to make a decision 'immediately' . . . on what he estimated would be, at minimum, a $75 million face lift for Three Rivers Stadium" to make it more football friendly. Rooney further asserted that "the Steelers needed control of the parking as an income producer," a revenue stream previously intended to defray stadium authority expenses. He cited economic competition with other NFL owners as the primary reason for making the demands.[136] Because the authority recently approved a multimillion dollar renovation, response to these demands were restrained and noncommittal.

A month later, Rooney used Art Modell's decision to move Cleveland's team to Baltimore to gain leverage. He argued that lucrative deals made by other NFL teams could hurt his team's ability to compete.[137] Once the Pirates's plans gained momentum, Rooney worked to influence the location decision so that it might cut to his advantage. He had been working to gain a foothold in retailing in the area surrounding the stadium. To ensure greater traffic, he recommended that the Pirates's ballpark be situated nearby to make the area "a destination site."[138]

Rooney conducted behind-the-scenes lobbying efforts, too. In June 1996, his family contributed $25,000 to Pennsylvania Governor Tom Ridge's reelection campaign, as part of a golf outing. Team participation in the select "Governor's Club" outing was not generally covered by Pittsburgh media, but this involvement offered the Rooney's access to Ridge, a supporter of state-level subsidies.[139] Team and league officials also visited the mayor's office in 1996. Neil Austrian, NFL president, told reporters that the Steelers ranked "among the NFL's bottom ten in local revenues." Austrian pointed to the stadium as a key factor in limiting Steelers's revenues. Mayor Tom Murphy agreed, stating that the Steelers "have to play in a competitive facility."[140] Rooney's son reminded the public about his father's earlier demand for a $75 million stadium renovation. While doing this he prepared the public for renovation cost increases, but continued to show a commitment to renovation rather than new construction. On November 21, 1996, Art Rooney Jr., Steelers's vice president and general counsel, announced that "the true costs are coming in somewhat higher than anybody anticipated." HOK Sports, a Kansas City–based stadium architect, offered a renovation estimate of $111 to $121 million. A new football stadium was estimated to cost between $160 and $180 million.[141]

Three weeks later, the $121 million became the cited estimate as the

HOK report was being assembled. The public was told that HOK's research would also determine costs for a new stadium.[142] The Steelers agreed to pay half the study costs, again performed by HOK Sports.[143] The final report, released in April 1997, did not deviate from the $121 million figure by a penny. They pegged the price of a new stadium at either $197 or $203 million, depending on the site location.[144] Reporters did not question the figures offered by HOK, trusting their architectural authority, despite a potential interest in advancing new construction. Two and one-half years before the report's release, HOK Sports presented Cincinnati with a renovation proposal for a facility somewhat similar to Three Rivers Stadium, estimating renovations at $48.1 million.[145] With the gap closing between renovation and new construction, a new stadium appeared inevitable.

Nevertheless, the Steelers held back on a call for a new stadium until September 19,1997, a mere two months before voters would go to the polls to decide whether to fund this project. As their request was made, new construction estimates were lowered to $185 million and renovation was rounded down to $120 million. The new construction option was chosen because the renovation figure "did not include infrastructure improvements or much work on the upper deck."[146] Presumably, the bulk of the renovation costs were aimed at cosmetic field and lower deck improvements. Reporters did not challenge these assertions. As the Pirates and Steelers jockeyed to obtain new facilities, others in the sports community worked to upgrade their physical plant. The Penguins, the city's hockey franchise, gained $10.5 million in taxpayer-funded improvements. Despite this investment, citizens were warned that "it could cost $75 million more to make the Civic Arena a financially attractive venue for another ten years or more."[147] Not to be outdone, the University of Pittsburgh requested $25 million in state aid for a $52 million convocation center that would serve university teams.[148]

The Media Push: Selling Two Stadiums to a Reluctant Public

As these actions were unfolding, the members of the public were being asked to dig deeper into their pockets to fund two brand-new stadiums. Some politicians hoped to circumvent voters, but offering a referendum may have been seen as a way to avoid the political fallout that might have occurred with unilateral action. Subsidy advocates hoped the process could offer the same outcome as Cincinnati's referendum. In that instance, public opinion was negative at the outset, but a well-orchestrated campaign set the stage for victory. Because Pittsburgh's team owners were generally liked and had a less confrontational past than Cincinnati's Marge Schott and Mike Brown, some leaders may have believed that the situation would move in their direction. A 1995 public opinion poll revealed 60 percent support for a new stadium "if it were the only way to keep the Pirates here."[149] This suggested that relocation threats might work.

In the early stages, organizers recognized the importance of a media campaign to achieve success. The Regional Renaissance Partnership, a coalition of business leaders willing to lead the battle, hired HMS Partners, an Ohio-based firm with a reputation for running successful stadium sales tax hike campaigns in Tampa and Cincinnati. The partnership was guided by community elites. It was chaired by Thomas Usher, chief of USX.[150] When public opinion did not move as hoped, primary responsibility for the campaign was shifted to the California-based firm Winner, Wagner, and Mandabach. This firm was chosen for their experience with referendum campaigns, but much of this experience was accumulated in California-style referenda that often focused on social issues, not the rough and tumble world of stadium subsidy.

Before the referendum, attempts were made to circumvent the ballot box. A Pittsburgh area legislator proposed a lottery aimed at sports facility funding. Because Pennsylvania had a lottery that funded senior citizen programs, Pennsylvania Governor Tom Ridge vigorously opposed that idea.[151] In its place, Ridge proposed privatizing Pennsylvania's state-owned liquor stores, auctioning them off to generate a one-time revenue windfall. Proceeds would be dedicated to improvement of cultural assets and included new ballpark construction. The state would provide a match to local investment in such facilities with these new funds. Presumably, this "match" would serve as an enticement to ante up money for sports facility construction. The proposal was met with heavy grassroots resistance. One poll revealed a 70 percent opposition.[152] The referendum process emerged as Ridge was still attempting to push a liquor store proposal though. After repeated attempts to sell the idea failed, the governor dropped the proposal, but pledged continued support for stadium construction.[153]

A June 10, 1997, Associated Press article suggested that the Pittsburgh vote was a particularly tough sell because, unlike Cincinnati, the state legislature had to formally approve the ballot initiative before it could be offered to voters.[154] Nevertheless, the proposal sailed through the state house and senate, making public opinion the most visible and difficult barrier for passage. Both Tampa and Cincinnati faced uphill battles and early polls were negative, so the likelihood of passage in Pittsburgh, although difficult, appeared achievable.

The Pittsburgh initiative faced an additional difficulty because it covered a much wider geographic range than Cincinnati or Tampa. Legislators and business leaders decided to offer the initiative in ten surrounding counties as a way to raise additional funds for Pittsburgh area projects. The legislation was made more palatable to outlying counties through creation of a formula that promised that 75 percent of all revenues to the tax collecting county and allowed some flexibility in how these monies were spent. An additional boost was given when the governor intermittently declared that $361 million in matching funds would be available for area projects even though such approval required formal legislative approval.

As with other stadium initiatives, the proposal was tailored to confront other local concerns. The referendum was expanded to include an array of projects aimed at economic revitalization. Convention center expansion, monies for the arts, and funding for construction programs in outlying counties were touted nonstadium benefits. In a move that later backfired, the partnership failed to consult surrounding county commissioners for legislative input. Such action might have strained the ability to craft a workable proposal. But it would have limited the perception that the initiative was driven by Allegheny county elites. Not surprisingly, county politicians opposed the proposal, undermining outlying support. Of the twenty-nine commissioners outside of Allegheny County, only three publicly supported the plan.

As election day closed in, advocates focused on media purchases and carefully targeted press releases with a war chest that had ballooned to more than $4 million.[155] One of the more compelling ads featured World War II–era factory footage, followed by a montage that suggested a more modern and optimistic future. The announcer compellingly stated, "We can continue to live in the shadow of the past and go downhill, or we can change and make our region strong again." The piece did not include a single stadium image, focusing instead on job, technology, and infrastructure footage. In another ad, Kevin McClatchy and Dan Rooney touted their $85 million commitment to the projects and their willingness to "sign a 25 year ironclad lease to show that we want to be here long-term."[156] These ads ran frequently as election day neared. The initiative gained further publicity when the popular Steelers's Coach Bill Cowher endorsed the plan in late

October. Paul Tagliabue, NFL commissioner, stressed the importance of a new stadium for the Steelers's future. On the evening before the vote, the Steelers appeared on ABC's Monday Night Football. Dan Rooney used this program as a platform for a last-minute appeal.

Opponents of the measure relied on door-to-door handbills, bumper sticker sales, T-shirts, yard signs, small personal donations, and an energetic but loosely organized effort that included letters to the editor and talk radio call-ins. Opposition recognized the significance of media access. Without adequate funding to produce television commercials, alternatives were sought by anyone passionate about blocking the proposal. Web site information was made available by the Allegheny Institute, a conservative regional think tank. Good Sports, a grassroots organization, also offered voters Web information. Both sites featured access to various resources that would further their cause. Opposition leadership used the Good Sports homepage to gain media exposure, asking supporters to make talk show call-ins and to submit letters to newspapers.[157]

Initiative supporters offered their own Web site, a rather simple-looking site that included detailed information in a format that had a more "grassroots" look than their underfunded counterparts.[158] Surprisingly, the page was pulled down on the day after election day, a move that limited postelection Web browsers to their opponents' sources. Such a move might be understandable if stadium funding had passed. Despite being outspent by a better than sixty-to-one margin, the November 4, 1997, measure was soundly defeated in all eleven counties. In some counties, the initiative was outvoted by nearly a four-to-one margin. Even in Allegheny County, the initiative's strongest base, the gap was a 16 percent margin.

The Limitations of Media Influence

If media are such a powerful mobilizing force for consumer products and political campaigns, why did the Regional Renaissance Initiative fail? After all, the pro-initiative lobby had a $4 million war chest and the tacit support of most local news organizations. Closer examination of media coverage may shed some light on this question.

News coverage in the months preceding the referendum was much more heavily skewed to favor pro-stadium voices than was reflective of public opinion. An analysis of the *Pittsburgh Post-Gazette* reflects the general coverage trends of Pittsburgh area media. If neutral voices were eliminated, two-thirds of the news quotes supported the initiative. Coverage of the anti-stadium viewpoint picked up slightly more representation as the referendum neared.[159] Quote selection reveals a sharp contrast between reporting and street-level community values. Fifty-eight percent in the *Pittsburgh Post-Gazette*'s home distribution area, Allegheny County, voted against the initiative. Opposition was even more intense elsewhere.

Local television coverage was typically more skewed in favor of stadium advocates, but this did little to sway the public. Average citizens and activist citizens on either side of the issue were almost three times less likely to be quoted as unelected sports industry representatives. A highly skeptical public was not sold by sports industry involvement. Repeated claims by leaders that this was "not a stadium tax" probably backfired because of heavy sports industry representation. Campaign organizers and team owners compounded this problem by maintaining high visibility in advertising and orchestrated campaign events. Public appeals from team owners and coaches served as a repetitive reminder that stadium construction was at the core of this legislation. Letters following the vote suggested some would have supported higher taxes for job-creating infrastructure if stadium construction was set aside.[160]

Economic arguments also undermined the campaign. Proponents argued most vociferously that a new stadium would provide economic benefits, arguing that growth would presumably follow stadium building. However, after opening a new stadium in 1970, sustained economic development surrounding the stadium's North Shore never took hold and the regional economy continued a downward spiral. Despite the presence of championship teams when this stadium was new, steel industry output was curtailed and in most cases shut down. The economy struggled in the 1970s and 1980s, with youthful population often moving to more prosperous locations.

Pennsylvania Governor Tom Ridge and Mayor Tom Murphy, strong advocates of the initiative, pushed the measure as a way to revitalize the region. At the same time, the governor's office was running radio advertisements stating that lower taxes were responsible for attracting new businesses. The logical consistency of conflicting pro-tax and anti-tax arguments left much of the public angry, confused, or distrustful. One letter to the editor cited this conflicting logic and argued that "the outspoken proponents of the stadium tax are their own worst enemies. Their threats and outlandish comparisons . . . are not only annoying . . . they also show the level of incompetence we have to deal with in Pennsylvania politics."[161]

In a similar example, proponents of the initiative often cited Cleveland as a clear example of a "regional renaissance," but failed to address that city's loss of their football team to Baltimore during the referendum period. When Allegheny County Coroner Cyril Wecht argued that Pittsburgh would be similar to a "jerkwater town in Mississippi" without the Steelers and Pirates, one citizen quipped "the last time I looked, the streets of Cleveland didn't fill with tumbleweeds and Mississippi hayseeds after the Browns' departure."[162] A byproduct of this public skepticism was a willingness to listen to initiative opponents who could offer a more ideologically rational explanation. This opened the door for the Allegheny Institute's campaign against higher taxes. The Allegheny Institute's anti-tax message was carried on the editorial pages of a smaller, secondary Pittsburgh area newspaper, the *Pittsburgh Tribune-Review.* The publication, headed by conservative ideologue Richard Mellon Scaife, offered an anti-stadium slant not offered in some cities that succeeded in stadium building.

Over the years, a consistent rejoinder of area businesses was that low taxes were needed to be competitive with other regions. The attempt to reverse this often-repeated argument fell on deaf ears when aimed at many residents on limited incomes. The initiative was also hampered by the imposition of a 1 percent sales tax hike in 1994 that was not offered as a voter referendum. Predictably, this Allegheny Regional Assets District tax (RAD) was unpopular when instituted, particularly because citizens were frozen out of the approval process. The request for a half-cent increase may have been too close chronologically to this sales tax hike.

Many Steeler fans considered the potential for a move in the style of Robert Irsay (Colts/Baltimore) or Art Modell (Browns/Cleveland) unlikely because of the long-standing commitment of the Rooney family to Pittsburgh. In essence, loyalty may have become a liability for them. Before the initiative's introduction, Rooney stated that "moving should be a last-ditch option when there's no other way to make a franchise work."[163] Many Pittsburghers were skeptical of the Steelers franchise mobility, despite the team's poor performance as NFL revenue generators.

Another factor was the blue-collar mentality of the electorate. Though passionate about sports, Pittsburghers can be more captivated by a lower payroll team of overachievers than a team of high payroll superstars. Unlike other cities, fans' complaints have been limited when the Steelers or Pirates release high payroll players. When quarterback Neil O'Donnell and outfielder Barry Bonds left Pittsburgh for lucrative contracts elsewhere, a common fan attitude was "don't let the door hit you on the way out." With such a parsimonious mind-set, the need for two new facilities when one was structurally sound seemed highly wasteful. Many fans suggested less extravagant options. Some suggested an overhaul of Three Rivers Stadium.[164] Others suggested that "millionaire ballplayers" pay the entire cost for new stadiums.[165] One individual foreshadowed a future alliance, suggesting a shared arrangement between the Steelers and University of Pittsburgh as a way to save money for both institutions.[166] Some voters might have been convinced to consider a compromise of a single new stadium, but two brand-new facilities seemed ostentatious for a population used to blue-collar teams and blue-collar amenities.

Despite a tendency to favor stadium construction, the *Pittsburgh Post-Gazette* itself may have contributed to the referendum's defeat. As an example, the news staff produced a thoroughly researched series that focused on various cities that made a stadium construction commitment, offering both positive and negative information. The articles typically put a positive spin on stadium construction but revealed alternatives that may not have been discussed by Pittsburgh's civic leaders. Citizens learned that Atlanta and San Francisco managed to build facilities through corporate funding. Even though Atlanta's Olympic model and San Francisco's relative affluence made implementation of similar ideas less feasible in Pittsburgh, the series may have inspired some to believe Pittsburgh could find a way to make creative alternatives work.

This series also alerted many about the public relations process in other cities. In some cases, once these techniques were out in the open, they were less effective tools for opinion manipulation. Explanation of the Cincinnati campaign on May 19, 1997, for example, unveiled strategies used by David Milenthal, the public relations consultant retained in Cincinnati and, later, Pittsburgh. This particular article also made reference to the high costs of construction. The story ominously closed with a quote from John Dowlin, the commissioner of Hamilton County, Ohio, lamenting that Cincinnati's stadiums "will never pay for themselves."[167] Finally, even though the *Pittsburgh Post-Gazette* strongly supported the referendum, they made a more profound effort to involve minority viewpoints in opinion-based content than did the *Cincinnati Enquirer.*

The choice of appeals by stadium proponents hurt their effort further. Despite use of sophisticated economic projections from experts, inflated long-term job creation claims were easily challenged by average citizens.

Moreover, opposition consistently made ethical appeals that seemed to resonate with the public. Cincinnati's pro-stadium forces tended to deflect this issue with a "just hold your nose and vote for it" attitude that emphasized retaining a "major league" image. Their opinion pieces frequently indicated that sports subsidies could not be justified on economic or ethical grounds, but should be made to achieve a greater regional good. Pittsburgh journalists were more reluctant to emulate that approach, leading some skeptical citizens to conclude that media representatives were acting as sports lobby shills.

Finally, too many people believed that an alternate plan would surface, and some hoped the alternative would give the public a better outcome than the single option offered in the referendum. Sports columnist Bob Smizik wrote, "Don't believe there's not a 'Plan B'. . . . Not to have an alternative course of action would be less than smart, and that's a phrase that can't be used to describe the people behind this proposal."[168] The public and Bob Smizik were right to make this assumption. Plans were undertaken shortly after the election to secure such funding.

The Election Aftermath: Bypassing Direct Democracy to Secure Taxpayer Funding

After the Regional Renaissance Initiative failed, stadium subsidy opponents celebrated, with some incorrectly thinking their victory was permanent. Team owners quietly withdrew from the spotlight and went to work. The battle was not over; key elites remained firmly committed to stadium building. A week after the election, Governor Ridge reintroduced another plan to auction state liquor stores and indicated he would push for state support of a single multiuse facility in Pittsburgh. Both of Ridge's ideas went nowhere. A *Pittsburgh Post-Gazette* editorial challenged the possibility of developing a facility that would satisfy team owners, stating, "If the governor has such a proposal in his pocket, we'd like to see it."[169]

Instead of scaling down funding expectations, stadium proponents worked on strategies to obtain similar levels of funding in ways that would bypass direct democracy. Eventually, stadium proponents succeeded, and the public, used to generations of hierarchical decision making, stoically watched as this process unfolded. Many citizens had tired of the bitter and protracted stadium funding odyssey. Letters to the editor about the issue slowed to a trickle, but an occasional angry volley could be found, particularly when legislative action was pending.

Leaders described the failed initiative as a message that the public wanted stadiums to be constructed with existing revenue streams, not as an outright rejection of new construction. They did not explore the possibility that the public may have wanted a less ambitious agenda. News coverage did not challenge leadership assumptions. In addition, media-based public opinion polls were not conducted to validate leadership assertions, and broad public input was not aggressively sought.[170] Despite that, periodic letters to the editor suggested that the public might be satisfied with one new stadium and a Three Rivers Stadium renovation.

Once the referendum failed, the shape of stadium construction policy was elite driven. What transpired was a meandering array of actions that took fifteen months to unfold. The outcome was a funding plan to construct two brand-new stadiums. The funding package involved a mix of local, state, and private funds. Before approval, Kevin McClatchy, owner of the Pirates, revealed plans for the team's new ballpark. His revelation was given lead coverage. Striking visuals were provided, presumably as a way to convince citizens that the project merited public support.[171]

The initial political step for stadium subsidies came from the RAD board on July 9, 1998.[172] This unelected board is responsible for oversight of regional asset funding, including stadium and recreational facilities. It is funded through Allegheny County sales tax revenues. Before RAD approval, agreements were reached with both sports teams to increase their contributions to the projects. The Steelers pushed their contribution from $50 million to $76.5 million, and the Pirates moved from $35 million to $40 million. Much of this extra funding would come from fans or taxpayers in the form of ticket surcharges, personal seat license fees, or naming rights. The latter would be retained by team owners rather than the stadium authority. To limit opposition and make this arrangement more attractive to citizens, team owners verbally agreed to cover all cost overruns and to remain in Pittsburgh until 2031.[173]

Once regional funding was in place, stadium advocates needed to acquire state resources. Without a state subsidy, the costs were too high to fund through Allegheny County's existing revenue structure. Although Governor Ridge frequently discussed providing a state match for such projects, this action required legislative approval. State-level approval ran into several difficulties. After failure to secure house support in November 1998, Pittsburgh Mayor Tom Murphy attempted to resurrect a piece of legislation that might allow back-door state funding.

The proposed legislation allegedly gave the governor authority to commit funds without legislative approval. Intense media publicity and subsequent outcry compelled Governor Ridge to decline support of the idea. Political analysts and legislators later offered evidence that the legislation could not have survived court challenges.[174] Murphy later apologized for his attempts to strong-arm the governor on what was frequently called "stealth legislation."

Without the votes for legislative approval, Pennsylvania's House and Senate adjourned in 1998 without moving forward. Subsidy opponents in the Pennsylvania House attempted to push a vote forward to cripple future state-level legislation. Those favoring stadium construction fought to prevent a vote so that they could continue their push in 1999. The pro-stadium legislators succeeded in pulling legislation off the floor before it could face a vote.[175]

To achieve state-level subsidy, behind the scenes meetings and mobilization of select publics became important. Courting minority support, as an example, became critical to gain borderline votes. Pittsburgh's African American newspaper, the *Pittsburgh Courier*, conveyed information that could conceivably mobilize public opinion to support stadium subsidies, so political leaders tailored their message to reach out to this constituency.[176]

After months of debate, maneuvering, and political horse-trading, Pennsylvania legislators approved a package on February 3, 1999, that had ballooned from $150 million in Pittsburgh stadium subsidies to $650 million in state projects, many entirely unrelated to stadium construction. The agreement allocated $320 million to finance four new stadiums. Pittsburgh would receive $75 million per stadium, about a third of the total costs, and Philadelphia would receive a total of $170 million for two new stadiums for their teams. Monies were also in place to assist Pittsburgh's convention center expansion, an item that was on the wish list in the 1997 initiative. The $330 million allocated for nonstadium projects gave supportive legislators in rural districts and smaller cities an opportunity to bring funding for pet projects home, minimizing fallout that might have occurred if asked to support a stadium subsidy alone.

Cincinnati's ballot initiative marked the first time in decades that a community simultaneously authorized funding for two professional sports stadiums. Pennsylvania had raised the stakes without direct voter action, agreeing to offer simultaneous taxpayer funding for a record-breaking four projects. The funding was introduced to the public not as a subsidy, but as a "loan" that would only require repayment if sufficient tax revenues were not generated to repay the funds. The terms of the loan were sufficiently generous so that even moderate levels of repayment by team owners would be unlikely. The plan was cleverly shaped for maximum public relations value.

If revenues fell short, payment would not be made until the end of ten-, twenty-, and thirty-year intervals. Inflation was not part of the calculus, meaning that owners would repay shortfalls in a highly discounted manner. In addition, higher ticket and concession prices and the "novelty effect" of a new stadium would minimize the chances of any initial payout. Dan Rooney took more dramatic steps to avoid future payout. His football franchise worked out an agreement with the University of Pittsburgh to share the new football facility. The university would phase out its aging stadium, giving the Steelers control over the city's only major football stadium.[177] Although new revenue streams would not be created because the university team previously generated economic activity in another section of the city, the Steelers would be credited with the revenues earned from these games as part of their commitment to the state's "loan" agreement.

Owners received further insulation from future stadium-related payouts. On May 28, 1999, long after funding was in place and construction preparations were in full swing, the Public Auditorium Authority raised the estimated total costs for both new ballparks by between 10.5 and 12.2 percent. Football stadium costs were listed at $261.6 million. The baseball facility estimates were raised to $252 million. Because team owners promised to pay for any "cost overruns," Stephen Leeper, Authority director, indicated that these new estimates were not cost overruns. As a result, taxpayers, not franchise owners, might absorb these increased expenses.[178]

Media coverage during the RAD board action in 1998 and state funding in 1999 favored the stadium construction position to a much greater degree than before the 1997 referendum. In the twenty days preceding the RAD Board vote, the pro-stadium position drew eleven times more quotations in *Pittsburgh Post-Gazette* coverage than opposition. Stories were less detailed and often received less prominent placement, too. Editorial and opinion columns with a pro-stadium position held a three-to-one margin over anti-stadium voices. Despite the disparity, more column space was offered to the anti-stadium position. Pro-stadium editorials were relatively short, whereas County Commissioner Larry Dunn, the only visible opponent showcased before the vote, offered a long piece on the Sunday preceding the RAD board vote.[179] The 1999 coverage of the state legislature's vote to allocate stadium funds followed a similar pattern. Pro-stadium voices continued to receive more prominent coverage, but an alternative to two stadiums finally emerged just days before final legislation was introduced. This eleventh hour reporting of an alternative to the elite-driven proposal made its adoption highly unlikely.

The alternate proposal offered evidence of how far the debate had shifted. This plan was similar to a proposal under consideration by the Allegheny Institute, the most vociferous opponent of stadium building in 1997. It suggested taxpayers should allocate $100 million to one new stadium, $65 million for a Three Rivers Stadium facelift, and $65 million to overhaul Pittsburgh's hockey arena. As the two stadium legislation neared passage, Pittsburgh's hockey team, the Penguins, increased their lobbying for a new facility. On the eve of the vote, a legislative aid argued that the measure would "provide the strongest taxpayer protections in the country."[180] On February 3, 1999, legislation was passed funding four new stadiums in Pittsburgh and Philadelphia. It was celebrated in news coverage. Once funding was assured, opposition voices were more prominently represented than in the coverage leading up to the vote.[181]

The construction process in Pittsburgh was not without controversy, but it was tame compared to Cincinnati. Some vendors were upset at the bidding process, prompting unsuccessful court challenges. In an ironic twist, some of the structural steel for the Steelers's project came from Texas, home of their former Super Bowl rival Dallas Cowboys. Yet construction generally continued without controversy about overruns. Minority groups correctly complained about lower than agreed levels of minority representation, but these complaints failed to draw the emotional response that was evident three decades earlier.[182] Attempts to bring minority contractors and vendors into the process were circumvented by behind-the-scene deals that resulted in "passing business through to other white-owned companies." The allegation of such action was reported early, but the Sports and Exhibition Authority did not take tangible action to address the issue until March 2002, months after both ballparks were unveiled.[183]

When PNC Park opened, public response was positive. Citizens attending the early games spoke in awe about the new ballpark's beauty. Many of the ballpark features were designed to replicate the Forbes Field experience, bringing back many older fans' memories of the ancient home that served Pittsburgh baseball fans until it was phased out in 1970. The ballpark received occasional accolades, including a "best ballpark" story in the May 2004 *Reader's Digest*.[184]

Heinz Field was not as impressive for the average fan, but luxury sections featured amenities that kept the wealthiest patrons happy. Pittsburgh's deep love of the Steelers limited complaints regarding seat license fees and somewhat spartan restrooms.[185] Several vocal fans did complain, however, feeling the old stadium was better for them personally. A lawsuit against the Steelers disputed the fairness of seat license distribution. When the Rooney family announced an intention to increase their commitment from $76.5 million to $123 million it gave some residents a comfortable belief that cost overruns would not be shifted to taxpayers as had occurred in Cincinnati. Dan Rooney bragged that "our deal, basically, is the best deal for the public in the league."[186]

The opening regular season game, scheduled for September 16, 2001, was cancelled after the league postponed all games after the September 11, 2001, terrorist attacks. The Steelers played their first regular season home game on October 7, 2001, beating Cincinnati by a 16-7 margin. Politicians who supported construction felt vindicated, but there were signals that the overt boosterism that accompanied construction had a political price. The political dynamic of stadium building had changed since Forbes Field and Three Rivers Stadium were built. No longer could politicians happily ride the coattails of popular sports teams.

Allegheny County Commissioner Bob Cranmer chose not to run again, citing negative public reaction to his aggressive support of Plan B as a reason for backing away from public service.[187] He later accepted a position as vice president of business development with L. Robert Kimball and Associates, an engineering and architectural firm that was founded by the in-laws of Art Rooney II, the Steelers president.[188] Tom Murphy barely edged out Councilman Bob O'Connor in the mayoral primary. He explained vocal support of stadium building was a reason for the close vote. Murphy's 2001 victory was his last as mayor.

He would not run in 2005, with little chance of convincing a skeptical electorate to give him another term. The frequent suggestions that economic revitalization would follow stadium construction never materialized and Murphy's political stock fell. By 2003 Pittsburgh was on the verge of bankruptcy. In August Murphy laid off 731 workers, including police and crossing guards. He also announced closure of twenty-six city pools, four senior centers, and nineteen recreational centers.[189] State-level oversight was implemented to control economic hemorrhaging. A national economic downturn caused some of the city's problems, but the touted financial benefits of stadium construction were nothing more than rhetorical alchemy. For the second time in less than thirty-five years, Pittsburgh received powerful evidence that taxpayer-funded ballparks would not resolve its economic woes.

The citizens of Allegheny County will see no more than a marginal payoff on their investments. Future regional income from sports facilities is generally limited to rent, taxes on gate receipts, and possible shared income from nongame event revenue. The Pirates had negotiated a rent of $100,000 per year, less than $3 million over the 29 1/2 year lease. The Steelers pay a healthier $250,000, less than $7.5 million over the 29 1/2 years of their contract. In short, rent revenues cover 2 percent of the cost for both facilities, less if financing was included.

The new agreements gave the teams virtually all revenues from naming rights, stadium advertising, skybox rentals, and seat license sales. The Pirates promised to contribute $44 million to ballpark construction, but $30 million of that figure was covered by a naming rights agreement with PNC Bank. Of the $262 million cost, about $14 million would be paid by the team.[190] The Steelers signed a $57 million naming rights agreement with Pittsburgh-based Heinz Corporation. Some of the Steelers's commitment was also paid by approximately $40 in seat license sales, an expense absorbed entirely by season ticket holders. The combined $97 million total was over $20 million more than the team's initial construction commitment. The Steelers also made a deal with Coca-Cola for an undisclosed amount to sponsor the stadium's retail and entertainment plaza. The Pittsburgh Sports and Exhibition Authority listed final costs at about $263 million, with the Steelers kicking in around $105 million, almost $30 million more than they initially pledged. Presumably, any remaining team balance would come from skybox, ticket, and advertising revenues, making it unlikely that they would have to make dramatic financial sacrifices.[191]

On the field of play, the Pirates and the Steelers failed to distinguish themselves in 2001. The Steelers, a well-managed team, were headed in the right direction. In 2002 they made the playoffs. The next year, the team was an uninspiring 6-10, but in 2004, they posted the league's best regular season record and came within one game of reaching the Super Bowl. On February 2, 2006, they were crowned Super Bowl champions after defeating the Seattle Seahawks by a 21-10 margin. The Pirates continue to struggle despite their new park. With another losing season in 2006, they have not fielded a winning team in fourteen years. Baseball's highly competitive free-agent bidding and consistently lackluster on-field performance offer little indication that Pittsburgh will ever reemerge as "a city of champions" in the manner that they did in the late 1970s.[192] The Steelers may bring championships back to their new facility, but the notion of multiple championships returning to Pittsburgh is not expected, even by the most optimistic area fans.

As the city struggled to dig itself out of financial problems, Penguins principal owner Mario Lemieux indicated that without a new arena, the city's professional hockey team could be sold and presumably moved out of the city.[193] Lemieux was led to believe that a new arena would be funded after PNC Park and Heinz Field construction, but those signals came from political officials whose tenure was over or whose power base had diminished. Political turnover has allowed leaders to step away from informal verbal commitments made by others. An NHL labor dispute that canceled play for the entire 2005 season gave officials even more breathing room.

The NHL franchise has pinned its hopes on gambling revenue, an odd funding source for such ventures, gaining league approval to use funds obtained from a slot machine parlor to build a new arena.[194] Governor Ed Rendell signed legislation to bring 61,000 slot machines to venues throughout the state, a move that promised eventual property tax relief, but regional allocation of gaming permits remains uncertain.[195] The Penguins want to obtain one of the few state licenses, but they must compete with several other entrepreneurs to obtain a license.[196] Calls to build have been tempered. Local officials are struggling to provide basic human services, with consolidation of firehouses on the table in 2005. This has further complicated calls to build a new facility. To intensify pressure, on January 18, 2006, the team was put up for sale. Owner Mario Lemiuex said he hoped the team would remain in Pittsburgh, but cautioned that "without a new arena, it is impossible for the franchise to stay here."[197]

If the new ballparks on Pittsburgh's North Shore offered evidence of economic payoff, the odds of new arena funding might increase. In 2002 San Francisco-based Del Monte entered a complex agreement with Heinz. Part of the deal would involve moving some of its operations into a newly constructed regional headquarters between both ballparks by 2005. The deal offered a glimmer of hope for better economic times next to the new ballparks, but the regional economy still sputtered along. Because two cycles of new stadium construction were followed by economic struggles, future leaders may shift away from a sports-based development strategy altogether.

Yet, current leaders regard sports as a highly valued cultural indicator, so millions of gambling dollars could be pushed into a new hockey arena rather than into other areas. A new ice rink would spell the death of the first retractable-domed arena in North America, but its limited amenities and cramped seating have been repeatedly cited as problems. A new indoor venue is unlikely to be a huge economic engine, but it would have the potential to attract a more diverse range of events than football or baseball venues.

The behind-the-scenes campaign to construct new facilities, despite overwhelming voter rejection in a referendum, helps to feed an unhealthy distrust of political solutions to community problems. As fans attend Steelers and Pirates games, they will certainly enjoy some aspects of the new facilities. But they are not likely to forget that the choice of whether to build, renovate, or let teams try to move elsewhere was taken out of their hands by legislators and community leaders bent on fully controlling the political process. The press's role as a conveyor-belt for pro-construction leaders may have diminished the level of anti-stadium discourse after the failed referendum, with some citizens regarding opposition as futile. Public mistrust of media institutions may result after exposure to journalism that favored community elites.

The Pittsburgh case study offers a mixed set of messages. The decision to construct Forbes Field and Three Rivers Stadium were largely unquestioned by journalists of the day, but such a position was tougher to justify in the 1990s. More recent coverage offered evidence of a desire to educate the public early in the process that was admirable. Nevertheless, the tendency to favor the stadium agenda, despite evidence that a reluctant public wanted to move in another direction, suggests that media professionals struggle to satisfy the desires of powerful leaders.

The dramatic shift of coverage in 1998 and 1999 to a more intense pro-stadium position suggests that key elites may have a potent influence in media coverage decisions. As the referendum failed at the polls, local media backed off from attempts to determine why the public responded as it did on election day. It was unclear whether the public wanted two stadiums, one stadium, a major renovation of Three Rivers Stadium, or no new construction at all. Such a clarification could have been achieved with more aggressive media follow-up, but the message of such investigation might not have been a comfortable one for pro-stadium elites.

Pittsburgh is often insecure about how it is perceived. Nevertheless, it is a vibrant city with a multitude of unique assets that extend well beyond sports-based real estate. Its move to build new stadiums should keep it on the sports pages for years to come. Whether it can maintain a national reputation as "major league" in other areas is less certain, however. With the severity of recent fiscal problems, Pittsburgh's future will be dependent on how it faces political and cultural challenges that are entirely unrelated to its shiny new sports infrastructure.

7

BOSTON

History, Mystery, and Political Football

THE BOSTON AREA provides visitors with a unique mingling of historic quaintness and cutting-edge modernity. The old ships in Boston harbor offer a dramatic contrast to the world-class robotic research taking place at the Massachusetts Institute of Technology on the nearby shores of the Charles River. Many of Boston's buildings might buzz with high-tech efficiencies, but individuals in these offices can look upon the waterways below and see the synchronized motions of the Harvard sculls repeating an activity that reflects ancient tradition. Harvard may not be a hotbed of athletic prowess today, but that institution shaped the direction of modern athletics.

The 1869 Cincinnati Red Stockings paved the way for professional athletics to prosper, subsequently prompting new commercial opportunities and construction of more elaborate ballparks throughout America. Boston was part of that process. The construction of Fenway Park in 1912 marked the city's commitment to the first era of brick, concrete, and steel ballparks. Before that, the Boston Americans, the forerunners of the Red Sox, played in the wood-framed Huntington Avenue Grounds about a half mile away. In 1903 the team distinguished itself as the first World Series champion of the twentieth century. Subsequently, the team was given the informal moniker "Pilgrims," but this was never a formally recognized name. The official name was the Boston American League Baseball club.[1] John I. Taylor, the team owner, renamed them the "Red Sox" in 1907 after giving some thought to the name "Speed Boys."

On the surface, New England's culture and history appeared to limit the potential for regional advancement of professionalism in athletics. The Puritan ethos that produced Jonathan Edwards's and Cotton Mather's homilies emphasized stoic self-sacrifice and piety. Leisure for leisure's sake was frowned upon, but properly calculated recreation was tolerated and eventually accepted by New Englanders. A philosophic requirement was that it allowed for greater subsequent productivity or that it contributed to one's moral development.

A competing cultural dynamic that involved profitable colonial-era trade with old world merchants offered one avenue for acceptance of mercenary compensation in athletics. The historian David Cressy compellingly argues that active recruitment of old world labor by John Winthrop and his colleagues contributed to successful commercial trade with England. Colonial New England may have been imbued with the trappings of Puritanism, but Cressy argues that "from the employers' view, [actively recruited] servants were a valuable investment."[2] This commercialism created an environment where paid athletic endeavor could be philosophically reconciled.

The Yale versus Harvard rivalry further encouraged bending the rules of amateurism toward the direction of professionalism. This heated Ivy League rivalry included high-level political maneuvering and low-level pranks. In 1933, Harvard's young athletes were so determined to demonstrate their superiority that they kidnapped Yale's bulldog, bringing him to their Cambridge campus. The unfortunate creature was subsequently photographed licking the boots of the famed John Harvard statue after it was smeared with hamburger grease to achieve the desired effect.[3] Harvard alumni, coaches, and administrators bent accepted rules of amateurism to achieve on-field success. One early action included awarding academic scholarships to questionable students who possessed substantial athletic abilities.[4]

The emergence of social Darwinism, Progressive Era concerns over the "feminization" of boys, and the influx of immigrants further eroded New England's ability to remain an enclave of amateur athletics.[5] Some Irish immigrants created bachelor subcultures that resulted in athletic sponsorship from local pubs. After spending time in Boston and contributing to professional baseball's popularity there, both Albert Spalding and George Wright moved away to establish sporting good companies. Spalding established his firm in Chicago. Wright's company, Wright and Ditson, moved to nearby Providence, Rhode Island.[6]

New England and Early Twentieth-Century Stadium Construction

The first fully steel-reinforced concrete stadium in America was constructed in the Boston area. It had little to do with professional baseball, however. Instead, Harvard's alumni, in an orgy of pride for their gridiron legacy, provided resources for a football field that was to become the model for collegiate and professional football.[7] Constructed in 1903, almost six years before professional baseball moved into its first fully fireproof ballpark, Harvard Stadium was lauded in the *Boston Herald* as a "monster amphitheater for football games." A project that might take more than a year to finish today was completed in six months. Among the creative tactics that made this possible was an on-site foundry and extension of rail lines into the construction site.

With no comparable architectural parallel in North America, reporters struggled to explain the structure to a curious public, describing it as similar in design to "the old Greek or Roman amphitheaters." One reporter referred to scientific tests that demonstrated the superiority of steel-reinforced concrete as both "stronger and more economical than stone." The Boston media cited spectator safety and crowd management as principal concerns, while joking that Harvard Professor I. N. Hollis's meticulous design and supervision of the work provoked some to suggest abandoning the "stadium" moniker for the more personable "Holliseum."[8]

The university's student newspaper, the *Harvard Crimson,* was enthusiastic about this project, featuring front-page photos and stories. Boston's commercial media demonstrated less excitement. They tended to give the stadium placement in less-visible locations.[9] The new stadium received a brief front-page mention in the *Boston Herald* after a stadium-opening loss against Dartmouth. A paragraph describing the partially completed stadium was relegated to page 5, and no major ceremonies or festivities related to the facility's opening were mentioned.[10]

Fenway Park's construction in 1911 and 1912 received more intense media coverage. Like many ballparks of this era, it was constructed with unique dimensions and quirks that set it apart from other ballparks. Many analyses suggest that Fenway Park was uniquely tailored to fit in its urban location. Although generally true, Fenway's design could have been less unique if not for architectural choices made early in the design process. Shaughnessy and Grossfeld indicate that "Fenway could have been more symmetrical, but concessions to the street layout had to be made once the Taylor family called for team offices on the Jersey Street side."[11]

One of Fenway's most unique features, "The Wall" (now the "Green Monster"), was vastly different than it is today. The wall's height was visually minimized by an outfield hill that sloped ten feet upward. It also contained various advertisements rather than a plain green background. The purpose of this huge barrier was not to prevent an inordinate amount of home runs, as is its primary function today, but rather to keep fans from peering into the ballpark without paying admission.[12] The high hill created some odd fielding situations. Left fielder George "Duffy" Lewis had mastered the art of fielding on this hill in Fenway's early years. He was portrayed in newspaper cartoons as a "mountain climber making catches amidst sheep and snowcaps."[13] The left field area became affectionately known as "Duffy's Cliff."

The Taylors broke ground on the Fenway Park project on September 25, 1911, to positive media coverage. Prior construction of ballparks in other cities cultivated a public desire to read about such issues. The front-page coverage in Pittsburgh and Philadelphia offered evidence that a stadium could bring community pride. After Pennsylvania's projects were completed in 1909, the future of haphazardly constructed major league ballparks were numbered.

Some of the publicity for this project could have been fueled by self-interest rather than broader national trends, however. The Red Sox were controlled by John I. Taylor, the son of General Charles Taylor. Charles Taylor was editor and publisher of the *Boston Daily Globe*.[14] General Taylor hoped to sell his control of the Red Sox to someone else and profit as a landlord. John I. Taylor had developed a reputation as a carefree playboy. This may have had some bearing on his father's decision to sell the Red Sox. The transfer to new owners was regarded as favorable to American League Commissioner Ban Johnson who hoped to cultivate a positive reputation for his fledgling organization. Red Sox historian Frederick George Lieb asserted that "this deal was engineered by Ban Johnson, and . . . he was behind the scenes all the time during the brief [James] McAleer, [Robert] McRoy, [Jake] Stahl ownership."[15] The Taylors remained influential in Red Sox operations despite their sale of the team. John I. Taylor was appointed the club's vice president, and General Taylor served as a member of the team's board of directors.

Continued involvement of the Taylors made this deal feasible because it allowed family control over Fenway area development. Charles Taylor was a major stockholder in the Fenway Realty Corporation. Prudent development of property in Boston's western wetlands area had the potential to increase land values in this sparsely populated neighborhood.[16] John I. Taylor's role as team vice president was primarily focused on supervision of ballpark construction. Such oversight gave General Taylor more direct control over Fenway area real estate. Rail transit was scheduled to be installed, in part because of Taylor's ballpark. This made the surrounding property ripe for commercial and residential development. Years prior, Frederick Law Olmstead hoped to develop much of the area as a public park, but profit took priority. Some evidence suggests that Fenway development faced opposition because of Olmstead's desires, but such opposition was not reported in news coverage of the ballpark project.[17]

General Taylor's chosen name for Fenway Park was likely the first attempt to use "naming rights" for commercial gain.[18] "Fenway" was more than a section of Boston; it was also the name of Taylor's real estate firm. The name helped to build recognition of Fenway Realty Corporation and exposed citizens to Boston's Fenway section. Both of these outcomes benefitted Taylor. Fourteen years later, Chicago chewing gum magnate William Wrigley renamed his team's ballpark Wrigley Field, a step that raised the visibility of his commercial product.[19]

Shaughnessy and Grossfeld described *Boston Daily Globe*'s ballpark construction coverage as "exhaustive."[20] The overall coverage was more detailed than rival Boston newspapers, but the publicity that this project received had limits. At times, ballpark construction news was simply inserted into the closing paragraphs of stories unrelated to construction. A September 16, 1911, story focusing on transfer of the team to new management offers an example of this strategy. The article closed with a paragraph about the ballpark. According to the article, the ballpark would be "the very best in the country" and it could be "reached as quickly" as the Huntington Avenue ballpark.[21] Overall reporting marked an unprecedented level of media coverage for a Boston ballpark up to this point, but the amount of total column space was not nearly as dramatic as today's stadium coverage.

After Taylor's initial construction announcement, an October 15, 1911, story in the *Boston Daily Globe* offered a large architect's drawing of the ballpark. According to the *Globe,* it would cost $1 million to build and would accommodate 28,000 fans.[22] The final construction tally was actually closer to $650,000. The ballpark would be built by the Charles Logue Building Company with design assistance from Osborn Engineering Company, the same company responsible for design of the Polo Grounds and, later, Yankee Stadium. The facility was constructed with brick, concrete, and steel, but outfield bleacher sections were built with cheaper wooden materials.

Inaugural coverage of Fenway Park was limited by several factors. First, rain forced cancellation of the original opening date twice. Second, news about the sinking of the Titanic broke as the original ballpark opening was scheduled. The Titanic's coverage squeezed all other news to less-prominent locations for at least a week. Advance coverage of the ballpark's opening game was pushed to the internal pages of the sports section. On Sunday, April 21, 1912, the Titanic sinking was still the city's lead story, but the opening game at Fenway Park earned above-the-fold placement on the *Boston Daily Globe*'s front page.[23] Boston's first game, an April 9, 1912, exhibition with Harvard's baseball team drew only 3,000 fans, but the April 20 regular season game was reported to include 24,000 fans. Photos of the latter game showed enthusiastic fans packing the ballpark with overflow crowds standing in the outfield during the game.[24]

Fenway was not an immediate landmark, but in its first few years it was a venue that Boston citizens seemed to enjoy. The team's World Series victory during Fenway's inaugural season helped to emotionally link the city to their team, but the ballpark was not a revered part of Boston yet. Fenway achieved Taylor's developmental goal. Property values increased dramatically, prompting speculation in 1917 that new Red Sox owner Harry Frazee would tear down the park, "move to Braves Field, sell the property and reap a gigantic profit."[25]

Braves Field was built in 1915 and was home to the rival Braves until their departure in 1953. After this move, it was transferred to Boston University where it remains a useful facility today. The Braves struggled with attendance, not topping the million mark until 1947. Braves Field contributed to the problem. It was built with cavernous dimensions at the end of the "dead-ball" era. When the home run became a defining fan attraction, Braves Field was poorly suited to entice attendance. Ron Smith, author of the *Ballpark Book,* described the field as "an outdated, oft-renovated dinosaur" that was "the victim of bad timing and ownership without vision."[26]

Boston Globe sportswriter Harold Kaese indicated that the same issues that prompted Fenway Park construction, also led to Braves Field. James Gaffney, the team's majority owner, sought real estate profits, too. Gaffney took over the Braves after experience in New York City as a building contractor. He had strong Tammany Hall connections, so he was savvy in both real estate and politics. To maximize profit, Gaffney placed the ballpark in the property's back, selling smaller commercial parcels that fronted the site. According to Kaese, "He was able to sell the frontage at a handsome profit."[27] Gaffney's real estate profits did not result in team turnstile success. Instead, the Red Sox typically outperformed the Braves in attendance. Fenway Park's more cozy dimensions may have contributed to the attendance disparity.

Fenway Park's first massive revision took place in 1934, shortly after Tom Yawkey purchased the team. A May 8, 1926, fire damaged some of the bleachers before Yawkey took control, but Bob Quinn, the struggling team owner, collected insurance money and never replaced the stands. One *Boston Globe* reporter speculated that the fire may have been instigated by the "cash-strapped" owner. The Red Sox were not a good ball club, so they did not draw many fans. Ironically, New York Yankees owner Jacob Ruppert held the Fenway Park mortgage through the 1930s. As part of the deal that sent Babe Ruth to New York in 1920, Ruppert extended a loan to former Red Sox owner Harry Frazee at better terms than he could obtain from a bank.[28] The loan obligation remained with the team when Frazee sold the team.

Yawkey purchased the team from Bob Quinn shortly after his thirtieth birthday.[29] Several analyses heaped effusive praise upon him for his extensive 1934 renovations, but the decision was inspired by necessity. If changes were not made, the Red Sox might fold because of diminished public interest, leave town, or simply linger as a community embarrassment. Beyond that, Yawkey inherited millions from his grandfather's timber and mining empire, so Fenway renovation did not substantially diminish his personal fortune. Historians Stout and Johnson argue that "what Vanderbilt was to the railroad and Carnegie to steel, Yawkey was to lumber."[30]

Previous owners left Fenway in poor shape. The 1926 fire rendered the wooden outfield bleachers useless. At a bare minimum, Yawkey would have to replace this section and repair smoke damage in other areas. Renovations were further complicated by another fire in 1934. Some individuals speculated that the fire was intentionally set. This Depression Era renovation was the largest privately funded construction project in metropolitan Boston. With jobs hard to come by, many workers wanted to keep the project going for as long as possible. Completion might mean daily soup kitchen visits rather than a paycheck. Under such conditions, it is not difficult to understand how a fire may have been set.

The new Fenway opened up on April 17, 1934, to rave reviews. "Duffy's Cliff" was replaced by the massive thirty-seven-foot high wall that later became known as the "Green Monster." It was referred to as "The Wall" for fifteen years because billboards for various products interrupted the green background until advertising was phased out in 1947. With vast personal wealth, Yawkey may not have needed the revenue, but it helped to bring in extra cash at a time when he was spending lavishly on the ballpark and player acquisition. He spent $1.25 million on the makeover, almost double Fenway's original $650,000 cost in 1912. Yawkey was also pushing hard to acquire high-caliber players with the hope he could win a championship.

The renovation thoroughly modernized Fenway Park, but it also locked Yawkey into a long-term tenancy. Later he would regret that constraint. In 1958 he lobbied the city to extend the park into Landsdowne Street when construction of the Massachusetts Turnpike threatened to change the neighborhood. His expansion request was rejected. As the 1960s unfolded, Yawkey saw more and more teams obtaining new ballparks. Some teams received publicly owned land, others were offered taxpayer-funded facilities. Yawkey seemed convinced that some taxpayer funding was in order even if Boston politicians were unwilling to accommodate him.

Despite his inability to gain such subsidies, when Yawkey died in 1976, Fenway Park was a cherished part of Boston history. The nation's bicentennial brought national attention to Boston. The unveiling of the Faneuil Hall Marketplace further contributed to Boston's image as a historic city. A city that previously lacked confidence began to more proudly revel in its past. Boston had rebounded from the urban mistakes of its West End modernization program. It had rebuilt its downtown center, but at its core, it was a city with an abiding respect for its history.

Boston's pride in its role as a historical locale would present problems for those wishing to replace Fenway Park in the 1990s. After Yawkey's death, team control was transferred to his wife, Jean, until she passed away in 1992. From 1992 until 2002, when ownership was transferred to a group headed by John Henry, the team was held by the Yawkey Foundation, a charitable trust. The Yawkeys' hand-chosen administrator, John Harrington, headed the foundation. Attempts to sell the team were complicated by Harrington's calls to replace Fenway.

Professional Football in Boston: From Stadium Itinerants to Suburban Tenants

For more than seventy years the Red Sox were paragons of geographic stability. However, Boston's football teams had a long history of stadium problems. These difficulties prevented New England from cultivating and maintaining a strong professional football franchise until the Patriots were established in the 1960s. Even after the Patriots won the hearts of many New Englanders, the stadium situation still festered, remaining unresolved until 1970.

Unlike many team owners, Billy Sullivan did not have deep pockets. He began his career as Boston College's first sports information director and worked as publicity director for the Braves until the team moved to Milwaukee in 1953. The move was prompted by the promise of a subsidized ballpark and poor attendance.[31] After the Braves's departure, Sullivan became president of an area petroleum company, but he never lost his enthusiasm for sports.

With the Yawkey family firmly controlling the Red Sox, Sullivan saw little opportunity for advancement in local baseball.[32] This belief was reinforced in April 1958 when Sullivan made an attempt to construct a suburban multisport facility that would house the Red Sox and a yet to be established professional football team. His proposal was released less than seven months after Sullivan's alma mater, Boston College, opened a 26,000 seat stadium to much fanfare.[33] The proposal was prematurely released before formal meetings were set with Red Sox owner Tom Yawkey. Using his public relations skills, Sullivan did his best to put a positive spin on this early release, but did not succeed in placating Yawkey.

Ballpark models were displayed and front-page coverage was achieved. According to a cautiously supportive editorial, "The architectural plans have just enough bizarre touches needed to heighten the fashionable appeal of the palace." The plans included a retractable roof, $5,000-a-year deluxe boxes, a nearby golf range, an adjacent bowling alley, and a glassed-in nursery to provide on-site child care.[34] Despite the visionary nature of the plan, it died a quick death when the Red Sox curtly indicated that they preferred to stay in Fenway Park. Despite the setback, Sullivan determined that Boston was ready to support professional football. Several football teams failed to catch on in years past, but Sullivan believed that the emergence of television cleared the path for more enthusiastic regional support.[35] After failing to acquire an NFL team in the late 1950s, he paid $25,000 and settled for a less prestigious AFL franchise in 1959.[36]

Unlike the Red Sox, the Patriots struggled to find a permanent home. The first Boston area game, an August 13, 1960, exhibition contest, was played at Harvard Stadium. The game would mark the beginning of a ten-year odyssey that would have the team haphazardly moving from one venue to another. The Patriots's regular season home opener took place before 21,597 fans in Boston University Stadium, the same place where Sullivan worked for the Braves before the university purchased the facility. In an effort to permanently resolve the stadium issue, in 1962 Massachusetts Governor John Volpe appointed Sullivan to chair the Greater Boston Stadium Authority. The appointment did little to move construction plans forward. In 1963 the Patriots moved to Fenway Park where they remained until 1968. The team then moved to Boston College's Alumni Stadium for a single season and then struggled to find a home in 1970.[37]

The Patriots's attendance was constrained by the stadium situation. Their venues were smaller than other professional football facilities. Because of football's revenue-sharing arrangement, low attendance limited visiting teams' game-day profits. When the AFL was in its infancy, the struggle for survival pushed the stadium issue to the back burner. But as the AFL established credibility and eventually planned to enter into an NFL merger, team owners and league officials grew increasingly impatient with the Patriots's situation. Some team owners bristled at the small payouts that followed Boston games. If AFL teams were going to share attendance revenues with more prestigious NFL markets, then Boston, one of the AFL's large market cities, would have to correct its stadium capacity problem. Boston was the nation's sixth largest television market. Because market size generated higher national ratings, league officials did not want to move the team unless no stadium solution could be found.

Billy Sullivan, worn down after years of lobbying and bickering with city and state leaders, regarded this as an opportunity to secure a permanent stadium deal that would improve his bottom line. He had been pushing since 1960, but unlike Tom Yawkey, he did not have sufficient personal wealth to bankroll construction. On May 15, 1968, AFL and NFL owners unanimously approved a measure requiring stadium capacity "in the vicinity of 50,000 by 1970." Sullivan was described as "pleased by the warning." He announced that this requirement was "far overdue and fully justified." He predicted he "could get a stadium underway quickly."[38] For the next two years unpredictable and often heated discourse unfolded with neighborhoods, politicians, and civic leaders.

Media coverage focused on political elites and Billy Sullivan. The public was generally frozen out. On the heels of the football owners' policy announcement, Massachusetts Governor Volpe asserted that a new stadium was needed "if we are to retain our major league sports teams." Other political leaders argued that "we can't afford to lose the Patriots" while reminding citizens that "we have lost several football teams in the past."[39] Despite the political support, a state proposal to purchase a stadium site and lease it to the team failed to gain momentum. A year earlier, a governor's proposal passed in the House, but was defeated in the Senate.

Sullivan may have believed that he could use league regulations for subsidy leverage, but the twists and turns of Massachusetts politics rendered the assumption suspect. Any effort that involved subsidies raised complicated political questions. Boston area politics was uniquely parochial. City councilors represented neighborhoods, forcing them to consider the quirky political fallout of their specific communities. Such a political system encouraged cautious horse-trading and stonewalling. Statewide decisions were often driven by similar prejudices and local self-interest. In such an environment, legislators in western Massachusetts could reflexively vote against Boston-area spending unless incentives for cooperation were somehow built into the legislation. *Boston Globe* sportswriter Bob Ryan passionately argued that "everything in Massachusetts must come down to back-scratching and quid-pro-quoing in some way, and you can never get a straight answer from a major politician."[40]

Elite-driven attempts at urban renewal further clouded progress. The bulldozing of Boston's West End in the early 1960s, remained firm in the memories of citizens faced with the prospect of stadium construction in their neighborhood.[41] The West End project had early media support, but urban scholar Thomas O'Connor argued that once it was underway, the ruthless displacement of citizens created "such a wave of horrified revulsion that the future of any 'urban renewal' projects in Boston was much in doubt."[42] After the West End was bulldozed, reporters were more inclined to examine construction proposals with greater skepticism.

In such a setting, stadium building was an uphill battle. Boston's neighborhoods typically responded with disdain to proposals that involved increased traffic and the potential for future inconveniences. The aggressive construction policy of the past intensified the likelihood of opposition. In 1968 legislators suggested sites in Dedham, Fenway, and South Station. Dedham was favored because it did not tie up already valuable commercial land and it was near rails and highways.[43] By January 1970 the Massachusetts State Legislature had killed twenty-three different stadium proposals.[44] Sullivan was running out of options. To enhance his negotiating leverage, he publicized outside offers to lure the Patriots. Invitations from distant regions trickled in throughout 1969 and in early 1970. A January 17, 1970, report listed "Tampa, Memphis, Birmingham, Seattle, Toronto, Montreal, and North Carolina" as viable relocation options. If a stadium solution was not forthcoming, the team would "weigh offers" from these locales.[45]

As 1969 concluded, the Patriots lacked a stadium lease and were unable to work out a deal with an area university. Baseball's move to a longer playoff system diminished the possibility of cooperation from the Red Sox. The team was fearful that a torn-up field could jeopardize their success if they qualified for postseason play. Substantial political concern and the subsequent publicity generated for the Patriots irritated the Red Sox. When confronted about the Patriots, General Manager Dick O'Connell irately barked, "we own Fenway Park and we pay taxes on it. . . . I'll listen to hear what they have to say, but I'm sick of hearing about the Patriots. I've been hearing their crying and begging and threatening to leave for 10 years."[46]

The Patriots faced the 1970 season without a home field. The team attempted to strong-arm Harvard University into using its historic football field. Harvard refused to cooperate because, according to Harvard's president, it would "cause serious disruption of our athletic activities and a very serious problem of congestion." The Harvard Business School, located adjacent to the stadium, opposed the proposal because it increased "traffic and parking problems on autumn weekends."[47] Despite some evidence that the Red Sox might allow the Patriots to use Fenway Park for another year, Sullivan stated that all options were exhausted.[48] He set a March

15, 1970, deadline for resolution. If a solution was not found, he said the Patriots would relocate.

Some politicians proposed using eminent domain to take over Harvard Stadium. On January 27, 1970, the Massachusetts Joint Legislative Committee on Federal Financial Assistance voted 20-1 to use eminent domain to force Harvard to accommodate the Patriots. Massachusetts Governor Francis Sargent criticized the university's "provincial point of view," but said he would veto such legislation since it could not be justified legally.[49] Presumably, a court challenge would favor Harvard and waste time that could be better spent addressing other stadium options.

Harvard's tax-free status was frequently cited as a reason that the university was obligated to help the Patriots. Sullivan argued that unlike many urban areas, the area was unable to afford stadium subsidies, in part, because tax exempt institutions such as Harvard prevented leaders from collecting taxes on vast areas of land. Mayor Kevin White argued that "the least that the school can do in exchange for this tax exemption is to render a helping hand so that Boston can retain one of its most prestigious and entertaining attractions."[50]

As the issue was being debated, a front-page *Boston Evening Globe* article touted the economic benefits of sports to the region.[51] This three-part series was intended to educate citizens on the value of professional sports to the community. The final piece in this series focused on the ability of sports teams to bring Boston revenue from noncity residents.[52] This boosterism was offset by criticism of the Patriots for limited financial commitment to construction. In a column advocating voluntary public contributions to fund a new facility, Harold Kaese openly criticized local politicians and questioned the Patriots' commitment to the region. Kaese rhetorically asked "if in 10 years they have contributed so much as a bag of cement towards the construction of a new stadium, where is it?" Kaese offered to donate $10,000 if Patriots's management and more than 4,500 citizens and businesses stepped up to the plate.[53]

News coverage surrounding the Harvard decision was mixed but suggested that Harvard acted arrogantly in shutting out the Patriots. Stories more frequently quoted voices that were critical of Harvard, and many opinion columns attacked the decision.[54] Mayor White argued that Harvard's action reflected "the university's hardened indifference to community problems."[55] An editorial-page cartoon featured a caricature of Billy Sullivan in front of the famed John Harvard statue with an arrow labeled "Harvard" piercing his chest. The *Boston Globe*'s editorial board and opinion columns supported Harvard's right to lock out the Patriots.[56] The editors argued that "Harvard baiting is a . . . form of amusement more time-honored than . . . professional football and probably on a level of antiquity with public execution of witches." They sternly advised "public officials . . . to get cracking at last on a responsible plan to build a stadium."[57] Letters to the editor also favored Harvard.[58] In one of the few news articles to inject public voices into the stadium issue, Harvard students supported the decision to keep the Patriots off campus.[59] Another article focused on lobbying Massachusetts Governor Francis Sargent. It included quotes from a few citizens. One stated "this town will be bush league if the Patriots go." Another threatened the governor with the chant, "We'll have a stadium in September or Sarge will go in November."[60]

After Harvard formalized their lockout in a February Harvard Corporation vote, other ideas began to emerge. Compelling legal evidence was unearthed supporting Harvard, so the issue quickly dropped from public view. New proposals were then offered. So many options were suggested that the public was certain to be confused. One called for Fenway Park expansion to make it more football friendly.[61] Another suggested a $5 million renovation of White Stadium, a high school facility.[62] Southern New Hampshire, the Dover Street Railroad Yards, and East Boston were also mentioned as stadium locations.[63]

After these ideas were pulled off the table, Boston Redevelopment Authority Chairman John Warner prepared a $16 million proposal for a 55,000 seat stadium at a site near Neponset Circle in Dorchester. The plan was pitched as "the last hope for keeping the Boston Patriots in Boston."[64] The plan called for "a spartan-like bowl with no architectural frills."[65] It was opposed by Boston politicians and Dorchester residents. State Senator George Kenneally said he received "a lot of calls from constituents . . . worried that their streets will be turned into parking lots."[66]

The Neponset plan ran into financing problems. Governor Sargent's desire to avoid all taxpayer subsidies complicated matters. Some individuals proposed a shared arrangement between the University of Massachusetts and the Patriots.[67] Financing turned out to be tricky, however. After numerous ideas failed, Bill Veeck, owner of Suffolk Downs Race Track, offered a proposal that he said would eliminate subsidy. Veeck's formula required state approval for twelve additional days of racing, with the net proceeds allocated to retiring stadium bonds. Veeck contended he would not profit from the arrangement, but concession revenues and added publicity might enhance Veeck's bottom line. The idea was attacked for several reasons, but the most publicized was that it would not fully fund a new stadium, forcing a need for future subsidy.

Veeck was a legendary thick-skinned promoter, but the brutal nature of Massachusetts politics had him confessing that "I should have known better than to get involved . . . especially in an election year."[68] New York sportswriter Red Smith, in a nationally distributed column, attacked Massachusetts legislators. Smith peppered his column with sarcasm. He concluded that since "the state government contributes nothing and takes about $7 million a year from Suffolk, Veeck had the naive notion that nobody would mind seeing the stadium project helped."[69]

The Boston City Council Committee on Home Rule voted to abandon the Neponset site for another city location. As this occurred, Billy Sullivan looked more aggressively outside the city for alternate sites.[70] A day after the city council abandoned the Neponset site, *Boston Globe* sports columnist Bud Collins reported that the tiny community of Foxborough wanted to host a new stadium. According to Collins, one of the most important benefits of the site was its distance from Boston because "Massachusetts pols [are] . . . the masters of obstruction."[71]

Other sites were discussed and many small communities expressed active interest in hosting a stadium. Billy Sullivan continued to remind the public of the many offers he received from distant cities, but he also stated that local interest was strong. On April 3, 1970, Sullivan stated that in ten days he "had 60 offers of land in New England." Sullivan gloated that "what they say in effect is, 'the Lord put this land here for a stadium.' "[72] By April 4 site selection had become so uncertain that a *Boston Globe* editorial quipped that "every cow pasture in eastern Massachusetts and southern New Hampshire is under surveillance as a possible site."[73]

A day later the Patriots ended the debate, selecting Foxborough. Sullivan made the decision contingent on citizen approval, knowing in advance this would not be a problem. The deciding factors were land donation by a wealthy businessman and an excited citizenry that wanted to host an NFL franchise. Unlike Boston proposals, the Foxborough site drew few local objections. A preliminary head count conducted by Foxborough selectmen showed that residents favored hosting the stadium by a 2900 to 400 margin.[74] This site had reasonable highway proximity and an ability to draw from both Boston and Providence markets. After the residents approved the stadium site in a "special town meeting," debate about site selection ended.[75] As a stopgap measure, Harvard later negotiated a deal with the Patriots allowing them to play the 1970 season in Harvard Stadium. This took pressure off the team as Foxborough plans moved forward.

Funding was finalized on September 19, 1970, and ground was broken the following Wednesday.[76] Construction controversies that occurred on other stadium sites were not generally reported in Foxborough. The stadium's projected cost, a paltry $5.5 million, was less than one-quarter the total of other recently constructed facilities.[77] Architectural strategies and limited amenities helped to significantly limit expenses. Because public funds were not used, journalistic scrutiny may have been tougher to justify.

The stadium's first game, an exhibition contest against the New York Giants, took place on August 21, 1971, approximately eleven months after groundbreaking. The *Boston Globe* did not hype the opening, keeping it off the front page on game day, but they offered a special section ten days before the stadium was unveiled. The publication was extremely positive, praising those responsible for construction, financing, and design. Advertisements were abundant. Governor Sargent was credited for bringing investors together.[78] Foxborough received positive press coverage. Stadium amenities were also highlighted. One article speculated that the stadium would lead to a building boom in Foxborough. Gerald Rodman, a Foxborough selectman, emphasized media coverage as a rationale for support. He rhetorically asked, "How can you put a price tag on the number of times Foxborough will be mentioned on national TV?"[79]

Foxborough is often touted as one of the best examples of private-sector stadium financing. Days after groundbreaking, Will McDonough argued that it "seems sure to be a forerunner for many other stadia around the nation."[80] Instead, future construction was typically driven by subsidy rather than private sector ingenuity. Clearly, the Patriots's commitment to cost containment was outstanding, not because they wanted to cut corners, but because of their inability to attract subsidies. James Quirk and Rodney Fort argue that this construction "should be studied by anyone who thinks that the free enterprise system can't work to keep costs down."[81]

Such analysis does not examine the perspective of NFL owners. Taxpayers benefitted when private funding eliminated subsidies, but for team owners, Foxborough was not a long-term success story. Cost containment resulted in a facility with far fewer amenities than a typical NFL stadium.

Press areas were limited and fan seating was austere. Cold aluminum benches were substituted for more comfortable chairback seats. Amenities such as posh skyboxes were lacking. The stadium allowed the Patriots to remain in metropolitan Boston, but years later it is probable that no NFL owner would have swapped stadium arrangements with the Patriots.

Construction placed a heavy burden on Billy Sullivan. To complete a facility with private funds, Sullivan made deals that diminished his percentage of team control. By the early 1970s his ownership status was sufficiently diluted that he lost decision-making control of the team. He had parceled out stock to enough individuals that they eventually could outvote him. Although other issues may have contributed to Sullivan's awkward situation, the stadium project was his most prominent single expense and obligation.

Years after stadium completion, Sullivan lamented that in his deal making, "I saved the stadium, but I lost the ball club."[82] To regain team control, he had to ante up $10 million in 1975, buying out shares of several people, including two New York investors. Sullivan explained the absurdity of his personal situation, stating "I owned this thing originally, lock stock and barrel, for $25,000. . . . I ended up spending $10 million to buy back what I once totally owned. That's how smart I am."[83] Sullivan was eventually forced out of the NFL after his Stadium Management Corporation declared bankruptcy.[84] The league stepped in, released $4 million in contingency funds to meet team payroll, and sought new leadership.

Future NFL owners would take Billy Sullivan's lesson to heart. By the 1990s they would also consider the many political difficulties faced by Sullivan as his privately funded stadium became a reality. The changing economic landscape in professional sports made it more likely than ever that a replacement for Billy Sullivan's stadium would include some form of taxpayer subsidy.

The Patriots and Red Sox Push for Modern Facilities

The Patriots went through several ownership changes in the 1980s and 1990s. Victor Kiam, owner of Remington Products Corporation, purchased the team in 1988. He was the first NFL owner to be given an offer to play in a rent-free facility. Kiam rejected the proposal since it would have required extending his commitment to the Foxborough stadium for nineteen years. As this offer was extended, Kiam indicated that he wanted a new stadium and hinted at moving the team if taxpayer support was not forthcoming.[85]

Boston media regarded Kiam's quest for a new stadium as quixotic in light of the difficulties faced by Billy Sullivan two decades earlier. In a 1988 opinion column, Leigh Montville mockingly suggested a cooperative arrangement to build a massive complex that would serve the Patriots, the Bruins, and the Celtics. He sarcastically parodied Kiam's rhetorical appeals to local leaders. According to Montville, "All of this is possible, Victor. Yes it is. The vision is shared. The vision is within reach. . . . .Hell will freeze over any day now. Then we can get started."[86] Michael Madden also mocked Kiam's effort, calling him a "fuzz-cheeked novice . . . speaking like a Rotary Club president in Phoenix." According to Madden, "All the buzzwords that fool the rubes in Memphis and Birmingham and Orlando and Jacksonville" would not succeed in Boston.[87]

The barbs aimed at Kiam may have furthered his resolve. His early lobbying included soft-peddling the stadium idea on local talk shows and orchestrated attempts to compare his situation to other areas.[88] In March 1989 Kiam spoke to reporters at a Baltimore hospitality suite while munching on crab cakes and examining that city's new ballpark plans.[89] The strategy brought limited progress. In August Mayor Raymond Flynn announced that the Boston Redevelopment Authority would hire HOK Sport "to lay the groundwork for a possible new stadium." Flynn indicated, however, that if a stadium was built "it'd have to be privately financed."[90]

After Kiam's soft-sell failed to produce a subsidy, he became more aggressive. In December 1989, he indicated that he would only stay in the current stadium for "three or four years." If progress was not made, he'd sell the team to "someone from another city seeking a franchise."[91] However, he struggled with public relations issues. Kiam was criticized for failing to act quickly after an embarrassing locker room incident involving player harassment of a female reporter.[92] He also faced criticism for renaming the facility "Foxboro Stadium," a perceived slap at former owner, Billy Sullivan.[93] Before the change, the stadium was renamed Sullivan Stadium after Schaefer, a beer company, did not renew a naming rights deal. The "Sullivan Stadium" renaming took place during Billy Sullivan's final years with the team. Kiam denied that the change was intended to diminish Sullivan's stature, but he struggled to convince a skeptical public. His company did not need negative publicity. Since Kiam positioned himself as a corporate spokesman in advertising, adverse publicity could cut into Remington's market share.[94] Kiam was also burdened by limited personal funds. After three years of failed lobbying, he stepped away from NFL ownership.

Kiam transferred the team to James Orthwein on May 11, 1992. Orthwein continued the stadium push and said he was an interim owner. Will McDonough reported that Orthwein "moved into the picture to bail out his friend/partner [and minority owner] Fran Murray for two years."[95] Presumably, Orthwein would hold the team while local leaders developed a strategy to purchase the team. Nevertheless, he was from St. Louis, a city stung in 1988 by the loss of their NFL team. His goal was to establish a franchise in Missouri. The arrangement might allow him to cultivate ties with NFL owners, giving him an inside track on an expansion team. If he intended to sell the team to locals, Orthwein's probable motivation, to maximize resale price, complicated attracting taxpayer support for a new stadium.

Orthwein paid $106.5 million to buy the team, but an expansion franchise would cost at least $140 million.[96] If Orthwein could boost the team's value to more than $140 million, it would make sense to sell the franchise. Without a new stadium, however, it might be more cost-effective to simply move the team to St. Louis. Transferring the Patriots to Orthwein seemed to be a clever way to steer legislators into taking action on the stadium issue. Individuals with more insight about area politics knew that the situation could only get more complicated.

As the Patriots's sale was consummated, the Red Sox began to make overtures for ballpark subsidies. Construction of a new hockey and basketball facility was also under way. The potential for the Patriots to move out of New England kept the stadium issue alive, but getting political action was clouded by the complexity of a multiteam sports landscape. Politicians began talk of constructing a massive complex that would simultaneously serve as a convention center and sporting venue.[97] Red Sox management indicated that the multiplex concept would be acceptable only if one section was designed for sole use by the Red Sox. Politicians countered that convention center space was a greater priority than athletic facilities. One option discussed was temporary use of the multiplex by the Red Sox while Fenway Park received a thorough two-year refurbishing. Red Sox President John Harrington cautioned in 1993 that renovation would fail to permanently address the Red Sox problems because Fenway Park "has only 10 to 20 years of life remaining because of structural deterioration."[98]

The community's affinity for Fenway Park and its ability to generate respectable revenues despite its small size kept most discourse focused on the Patriots's situation in the early 1990s. Cleveland Browns owner Art

Modell made a somewhat surprising NFL Expansion Committee announcement. The league awarded new teams to Jacksonville, Florida, and Charlotte, North Carolina, in 1993.[99] Rumors began to intensify that James Orthwein's St. Louis connections would prompt westward relocation. Orthwein was already involved in a St. Louis stadium construction project that was intended to house an NFL expansion franchise. With knowledge of this public, some speculated that this could be the last season of football in Foxborough. Baltimore officials made an effort to lure the Patriots, too.

When Robert Kraft, a paper and packaging magnate, took over the team on January 14, 1994, he was perceived as a local savior. The team's official Web site credited Kraft, a Brookline native, with "saving the team from a possible move outside of New England."[100] As Orthwein was making plans to take over the team in 1992, well-connected reporters argued that a move out of the Boston area was probable. Will McDonough asserted that "either a new stadium has to be built or the Patriots will be sold out of town." McDonough was so confident of the claim that he advised readers they could "bank on it."[101]

Public sentiment regarding Kraft would briefly change during his drive to build a new stadium. Before Kraft took over, he was critical of new stadium plans for the football franchise. Part of the reason may have been self-serving. One of his firms, Foxboro Stadium Associates, was responsible for stadium management when Kiam and Orthwein owned the team. By December 1994, after taking the reins as team owner, Kraft argued that building a new sports "megaplex" in Boston "may be essential to keeping the team in Massachusetts."[102]

Kraft decided early in his tenure that the team's financial viability was predicated on a new stadium. His stadium management experience put him in an ideal position to understand the revenue potential of a well-designed new facility. As a result, Kraft lobbied hard. In one NFL pre-game show, he described the Foxborough facility as a "high school" stadium that was totally inadequate for modern professional football. He had little desire to follow the private sector path carved out by John I. Taylor, Tom Yawkey, and Billy Sullivan. Instead, Kraft believed that the next facility needed a subsidy. He was willing to pay construction costs but believed that much of the land acquisition and surrounding infrastructure could be borne by taxpayers.

Billy Sullivan made multiple attempts to publicize his ability to profit if he moved the Patriots, but he was emotionally wedded to metropolitan

Boston. With several NFL teams receiving record-breaking subsidies during the 1990s, Kraft and other team owners had even greater incentive to consider outside offers. Al Davis's courtroom success further cleared the way for more flexible franchise movement. Subsidized stadium deals elsewhere prompted Robert Kraft to pursue new facilities. His initial goal was to remain in the Boston area, but after failed negotiations with local politicians, Kraft began to consider other opportunities.

Foxborough Stadium hampered the team's ability to maximize profits. Concession options and skybox amenities were limited. The aluminum bench seating hurt the owner's abilities to generate game-day income, as separate seats in other NFL stadiums fostered more food and beverage consumption. Skyboxes were part of the stadium design, but this "premium" arrangement was considerably less luxurious than NFL skyboxes elsewhere. The facility was so spartan that fans and reporters routinely laughed about inadequacies. The *Boston Herald*'s Gerry Callahan recalled his first visit in 1971. He joked that a trip to the stadium bathroom could be harrowing and traumatic, recollecting that "after my first experience in the [stadium] men's room, I just kind of sat there like Marlon Brando in *Apocalypse Now*."[103] Plumbing problems also reportedly prevented players from access to hot showers on occasion.[104]

Kraft was determined to gain taxpayer support. At a bare minimum, he expected help with land acquisition and surrounding infrastructure. His demands were not as aggressive as other NFL owners, but in the crucible of Massachusetts politics, satisfying Kraft would not be easy. Kraft threatened movement to either Connecticut or Rhode Island to try to gain leverage advancing the sports megaplex. Citizens reacted with a jaded yawn. Boston's Mayor Menino joked that "next week it's Maine," publicly making light of Kraft's relocation attempt.[105]

During Kraft's early years as Patriots's owner, much of the sports infrastructure headlines focused on replacement of the Boston Garden, an aging facility that had served the Bruins and later the Celtics since 1928. When this arena's replacement was completed in 1995, the push to address baseball and football facilities intensified. Recognition of Sullivan's inability to get Boston officials to move on stadium construction should have preempted attempts to propose a Boston site for the Patriots. Sullivan's equally tough time with the state legislature in the 1960s suggested that the new owner would face a profound challenge with state subsidies. By the mid-1990s, however, franchise free agency had given team owners greater leverage, prompting Kraft to believe that he could turn Sullivan's earlier inner-city failure into a success.

He pushed hard in 1995 and 1996 to establish a stadium site in South Boston. The NFL offered to build an indoor NFL theme park if the Patriots obtained funding for a city-based project.[106] Kraft made several mistakes that hurt his ability to gain momentum. He underestimated opposition intensity in South Boston. He further underestimated the ability of provincial Boston politicians, whose ability to get reelected was dependent on neighborhood support, to block his plans. Equally important, he made tactical mistakes with allies. He harshly criticized Governor William Weld, a supporter of his construction agenda, for releasing South Boston stadium plans instead of consulting him in private.[107]

The South Boston stadium push was sharply criticized by local citizens and politicians.[108] It drew mixed reviews from the press. In the *Boston Globe,* Bob Ryan supported Kraft's plans, but Dan Shaughnessy criticized Kraft's "thinly veiled threats" to leave the Boston metropolitan area.[109] According to Ryan, the poor facilities in Foxborough meant that "the paying customer is, sadly, not as important as a guy sitting in front of a television set 3,000 miles away."

Boston Mayor Thomas Menino was willing to listen to Kraft's plans but preferred a convention center on the South Boston site. Menino cautioned that South Boston's citizens were an important part of the process, allowing himself an exit strategy if political fallout became intolerable.[110] After political resistance appeared to stall Kraft's plans, Governor Weld attempted to broker an acceptable substitute, offering the Patriots state-owned land at a former incinerator site in Boston's South Bay. Weld proposed a land giveaway instead of a monetary subsidy to make the deal palatable to reluctant state legislators who would have to sign off on the deal. Newly elected House Speaker Thomas Finneran opposed this, suggesting instead that a sale at "fair market" prices would better serve taxpayers.[111]

Kraft attempted to make the South Boston site work despite evidence that support was waning.[112] Kraft believed that legislators, not the public, would decide the issue. He pinned hopes on an alliance between Governor Weld and Mayor Thomas Menino. Weld supported Kraft, but Menino opposed South Boston construction.[113] Kraft was unable to sway Menino. In early 1997 Menino argued that the Red Sox situation deserved greater attention.[114]

Sensing a repeat of the 1970 site selection debacle, cities on the outskirts of Boston expressed a desire to accommodate the Patriots. Quincy, Worcester, Springfield, Randolph, and Uxbridge offered interest, and political leaders in Providence began to more actively court Kraft.[115] NFL Commissioner Paul Tagliabue made a pre–Super Bowl assertion that an unresolved stadium situation would hurt the team's long-term viability. He also explained that the NFL hoped to situate teams in Los Angeles and Cleveland. He suggested that other sites might be considered, including Pequot tribal land near the Connecticut–Rhode Island border.[116] With the Patriots set to play in the 1997 Super Bowl, few seemed concerned that the tribal land scenario had little chance of occurring or that Tagliabue's mentions of Cleveland or Los Angeles constituted a team relocation threat. Regardless, some players and fans indicated that they would not mind seeing a new stadium in or near Providence. Meetings between team officials and Rhode Island leaders did not appear to worry Boston area citizens or politicians.

Coverage of the Patriots in the Super Bowl did little to increase project support. After the Patriots were defeated, the *Boston Herald* suggested that momentum for stadium construction was lost. Robert Kelly, Boston City Council president, indicated that he and others were relieved they did not have "to deal with Bob Kraft the hero."[117] Opinion columns argued that the South Boston project would not work while calling for owner financing of any construction in the city.

After hopes were raised that the Massachusetts Port Authority would provide a long-term lease for stadium land in South Boston, the U.S. Army announced that a five-acre parcel would not be available for stadium parking. Vocal public opposition further complicated Kraft's plans.[118] Boston Mayor Tom Menino sidetracked the issue even further, again suggesting that the Red Sox ballpark issue required attention. At least one reporter suggested that the mayor dragged the Red Sox into the equation to forestall moving forward on the football project.[119] This argument gained credibility when John Harrington stated "we've got no deadline and no timetable. We are not doing a lot of effort on this."[120] The Red Sox received headlines for eventual plans to address their ballpark inadequacies, but the team was in no position to offer tangible plans early in 1997.

After Menino's involvement, Red Sox management expressed some willingness to move away from their neighborhood rather than to renovate or build new in the same area, despite the Fenway site preference by Menino and other political leaders. South Boston was suggested by John

Harrington. Movement was predicated on a belief that "rebuilding Fenway would be too complicated, too costly, and, ultimately, inadequate, for the team's needs."[121] But the team's move to this position took months to unfold. In the meantime, the football situation held greater prominence. By late February it became apparent that political support for the South Boston plan was not forthcoming. Wisely, construction within Boston was abandoned. Kraft said "the people have spoken and I have heard them. . . . Now we are literally back to the drawing board."[122] Kraft invested approximately $4 million of his team's funds to pursue the city site and had nothing to show for the effort and little chance of winning over a mercurial Boston political system.

Before the South Boston failure, Foxborough repeated its desire to remain the team's host. Renovation was suggested by several individuals. The Foxborough site also seemed to be the favorite of many Massachusetts legislators. Thomas Finneran, the newly installed House Speaker, supported a Foxborough plan, but cautioned that subsidies would be very difficult to justify. According to Finneran, "We have more serious challenges that affect six million citizens, not just the Kraft family."[123] In response to subsidy uncertainties, Kraft announced ticket price increases that would bring in an additional $3 million in revenue for his team.[124]

Finneran continued to insist that subsidies be entirely avoided. As the House Speaker dug in his heels, the Patriots announced they would consider a move to Providence. Kraft indicated that his preference was to stay in Massachusetts, but Rhode Island would be seriously examined. Rhode Island officials used media as a self-promotional platform. A *Boston Herald* article spoke of Providence Mayor Vincent Cianci "mugging for Katie Couric on *The Today Show*."[125] By late September, a Providence move appeared likely. Will McDonough argued that "there really is no comparison between the [Rhode Island] offer on the table . . . and the Massachusetts counterproposal."[126] Rhode Island would reportedly provide a $135 million subsidy for land and infrastructure, whereas Massachusetts would offer a less-generous renovation package. Opposition to Providence subsidies hurt the feasibility of a move. A Brown University public opinion poll revealed 57 percent were "against the state paying so much for a football facility."[127]

Kraft pulled out of the Providence deal before it could backfire on him, but in doing so, faced a tough Massachusetts legislature. Despite nearly losing the team to another state, Finneran showed little willingness to accommodate the Patriots. Kraft responded with an indication that he might revisit future proposals from Rhode Island. He cautioned that "I'm not going to . . . let anyone put me in a position to do something that isn't good for this franchise long-term." Boston's mayor cautioned that he was not interested in providing a stadium site for the Patriots, arguing that a professional football facility "isn't the economic engine that people think it is."[128] Kraft announced plans to broaden the appeal of the Foxborough site, suggesting that the area could be expanded to include a NASCAR track, a waterslide park, and shopping outlets.[129]

A Foxborough renovation was just one of several possibilities for the team. Kraft left the door open for outside offers. As 1997 concluded no single idea seemed to gain momentum. As an uncertain stadium situation was unfolding, a lavish NFL television contract was announced. The NFL would receive about $2.2 billion per year for the next eight years. Reporters quickly noted that even if players gobbled up 70 percent of these revenues, each owner would still receive at least $12 million a year from the deal.[130] The effect of this announcement was to raise expectations for owner contributions to any future construction projects. Citizens and politicians may have also been lulled into a secure feeling that the team would be shielded from the type of financial crisis that plagued Billy Sullivan. In early 1998, political solutions to the Patriots's stadium subsidy requests were moving further away from Kraft's desired outcome.

On February 10, 1998, Senate President Thomas Birmingham suggested that instead of renovation, the Patriots should consider a long-term stadium solution. He told reporters that the team might be better served with a new $200 million stadium on land next to the existing stadium. Birmingham's announcement marked the first time in almost a year that new construction was put back on the table. Patriots management did not greet the idea with enthusiasm because Birmingham presumed that the team would pay the entire $200 million construction expense. *Boston Globe* reporter Tina Cassidy wrote that "Kraft . . . has said he cannot afford that." A Patriots spokesman asserted the idea "seems like a long shot at best."[131] An op-ed piece argued against subsidies not just for the stadium, but for roads surrounding the stadium. The author argued that "it is absurd enough that the state, the same state that . . . just avoided a slashing of special education, is even considering paying $52 million . . . to repair roads for Foxborough Stadium when Kraft now shares in a new $17.6 billion National Football League television contract."[132]

With the cautious political climate, state legislators hammered out a formula that called for $52 million in subsidies for what was likely to be a renovation. Funds would cover road work and surrounding infrastructure but could not be used for stadium renovation or construction. The funding was predicated on the logic that such improvements could benefit citizens, but stadium subsidies would only benefit the team owner and ticket holders. State legislators presumed that a $50 million figure suggested for stadium renovations would be covered entirely by Kraft. He tried to negotiate an earlier $70 million deal which passed through the Senate, but it fell through in the House. The key sticking point was the state's purchase of land and subsequent rental to Kraft for below market rates. House Speaker Thomas Finneran countered with a $57 million infrastructure package. Kraft deemed the proposal inadequate. He expressed dismay at the prospect of renovation, but public opinion was positioned against him. A poll showed that "55 percent opposed using tax money to keep the Patriots, while just 34 percent favored the idea." The poll also revealed that 58 percent opposed construction subsidies for a new Red Sox ballpark.[133]

Kraft's position was hampered by the Red Sox. They were now more aggressively exploring subsidies. The Red Sox could not claim the same level of television revenues as the Patriots. Beyond that, their century-long regional tenure made them a more revered part of the community in the eyes of many. In March 1998, the Red Sox hired numerous consultants, including HOK Sport Facilities Group and three local companies. Among them were two urban design firms and a historic preservation consultant. Their mission was to determine the best strategy for approaching the team's long-range infrastructure needs.

A Beacon Hill Institute poll revealed that "only 20 percent of respondents said they favored a new ballpark," and 58 percent were willing to subsidize Fenway renovation. Although a team spokesman indicated they didn't "have a specific plan right now," reporters announced that the Red Sox were "determined to move slowly and are concerned about frightening the neighbors with large-scale expansion and rebuilding plans." Citizens announced formation of a grassroots group named "Save Fenway Park!" They promised a report that would explain "why rebuilding Fenway is the most viable option in terms of economics and urban planning."[134]

Many citizens, including Mayor Menino, offered vigorous support for Fenway Park renovation. Despite his skepticism about a new ballpark, Menino promised to keep "an open mind" as consultants moved forward with feasibility studies.[135] The Red Sox were more cautious than the Patriots in their approach to community relations. They periodically suggested that a new ballpark in the same neighborhood might be a better long-term strategy. According to the Red Sox, new construction would include recreating the best features of Fenway Park and citizen input would be considered if this occurred. Although coverage before 1998 favored renovation, media support for new construction gained momentum. An April 16 *Boston Globe* editorial suggested that "it is better to start anew than to renovate the life out of the old ballpark."[136]

The Red Sox tended to repeat the idea that renovation of Fenway Park was less likely while cultivating expectations that taxpayer subsidies would be required in any construction scenario. The team deflected attention from the Patriots's stadium issue, but did not seem to be in a hurry to push a specific plan forward. The Red Sox hoped to maintain positive community relations, and, as such, held back on a specific construction strategy. A July 6, 1998, *Boston Globe* article revealed a poll by pro-renovation activists in which a mere 9 percent supported new ballpark construction. The article offered quotes from area businesses suggesting that they would be hurt if Fenway Park was replaced by a new facility.

The Red Sox suffered another setback in December when members of the Fenway Action Coalition, staunch critics of new construction, accused the team of treating "Fenway neighbors like campesinos in a Banana Republic" after cancellation of a meeting. A Red Sox spokesman indicated that a children's Christmas party at the ballpark prompted the cancellation and indicated that the team held meetings with other groups, including Save Fenway Park!, and the Red Sox made other public relations errors. One included an announcement a week before Christmas in 1998 to prohibit street vendors from the front of Fenway Park, eliminating a commercial institution that had been part of Fenway lore for generations. Although unrelated to construction, the decision hurt the team's attempt to position itself as a good neighbor. They struggled with a prior reputation as unresponsive and callous to those in the Fenway area. Such a reputation was difficult to shed. While difficult to address all constituencies, the team also appeared to lack a tangible strategy for minority inclusion. This population was frequently noted as marginal patrons at games. The team finished 1998 with no specific plans for Fenway Park.

As baseball season concluded, the Red Sox situation was overshadowed by an announcement that the Patriots would be moving to Hartford,

Connecticut. Robert Kraft was stung by failure to gain House approval for a Senate-negotiated $70 million infrastructure subsidy in Foxborough. As Finneran and state-level officials bickered about the philosophic problems of stadium subsidies, Connecticut Governor John Rowland quietly forged a personal relationship with Kraft. Rowland appeared poised to demonstrate that his state was an emerging economic force. Nevertheless, the city of Hartford was unable to retain a less-prestigious National Hockey League franchise, losing it to another city earlier in the decade.

Although the Massachusetts House was willing to offer Kraft a $57 million subsidy, the deal paled in comparison to the Connecticut offer to provide $350 million in subsidies for a brand-new stadium in downtown Hartford. The deal was reported to include various guarantees, including 90 percent of stadium-related revenues, subsidies for unsold skyboxes, and land development opportunities for Kraft.[137] A study by KPMG Peat Marwick asserted that the project "would create 4,600 jobs during construction . . . [and] 2,700 permanent jobs." Connecticut officials argued that the stadium could be paid for "by fans attending Patriot games—not by taxpayers who never go to the stadium."[138] Armed with figures that might convince taxpayers this was a prudent move, Connecticut legislators approved Rowland's plan.[139]

Boston media appeared stung by the team's tactical shift. News coverage retained a fact-based tone, but opinion columns were peppered with insults that were more often directed at Patriots's management and Hartford's citizens than at House Speaker Thomas Finneran, the hard-line opponent of stadium subsidies.[140] Some individuals were skeptical that the deal with Connecticut would ever come to fruition. Sportswriter Dan Shaughnessy concluded one piece with the prophetic assertion that "I still say the Pats never will play a game in Hartford."[141]

The stadium arrangement in Hartford faced several difficulties, despite overwhelming passage of stadium subsidies. Cost estimates had to be adjusted upward to confront inflation. Public opposition became more evident as citizens had time to contemplate the decision.[142] In addition, the NFL, on the heels of losing teams in large-market Los Angeles and Houston, became increasingly uncomfortable with the long-term ramifications of franchise shifts away from top-ten media markets because such shifts could damage future television revenues. Finally, site-related difficulties emerged. Environmental cleanup costs at a CTG Resources, Inc., steam plant threatened to raise basic infrastructure costs substantially beyond the

$55 million already allocated for that purpose. The company expected a $48.8 million payout to simply move from the site, a figure that was almost double what the state was willing to pay.[143]

The agreement between Connecticut and the Patriots allowed the team to back out if the state could not clearly demonstrate the ability to complete construction by 2002. The contract obligated the team to "establish an office with marketing, public relations, and community affairs staff in Hartford. . . . no later than April 2" if the team did not exercise its "sole and absolute discretion" to terminate the agreement.[144] The April 2, 1999, deadline was also set as the timetable for a report by Connecticut's governor. After presentation of the progress report, Patriots officials were granted thirty days to consider whether to continue with the agreement.[145]

Uncertainties regarding the Hartford site gave Massachusetts legislators a narrow window to move forward with plans to lure the Patriots back to the Bay State. In a surprise reversal of long-standing opposition to a Boston football stadium, Mayor Menino indicated that he could be convinced to support a stadium within the city limits. After a mid-April indication that a Boston incinerator site might be feasible, talk shifted to a more practical location in Foxborough. The NFL actively supported a move that would keep the Patriots in Massachusetts, offering highly attractive loan terms. Under the terms of Kraft's agreement with Connecticut, team management could not legally negotiate with Massachusetts, yet the media became an ad hoc negotiating tool that was used frequently by political and civic leaders to convey messages to Kraft.

Analyzing such media coverage might be complicated by a lack of referendum, but examining the *Boston Globe* from April through July 1999, a period when the Massachusetts legislature worked to establish a subsidy agreement with Patriots and the Red Sox released new ballpark plans, reveals unique nuances in Boston-area coverage. Opinion content was balanced between opposition and support, with slightly more backing for ballpark subsidies, and a bit less than a third taking a neutral stand. News reporting also featured the highest level of neutrality of any examined city, with almost one quarter of the quotes expressing ambivalence. A high level of quoted experts and the uneasiness over possible team relocation probably led to this outcome. When opinions were offered in news stories, pro-stadium voices were quoted four times more frequently than opponents, the highest level of any region, suggesting that the potential Hartford move caused an uneasy situation for civic leaders and possibly reporters.

When it became clear that Hartford would have difficulty meeting the 2002 deadline, Kraft exercised his option to terminate the contract in April. Although no stadium plans were set, it was presumed that a deal would be worked out, with Kraft receiving a $70 million infrastructure subsidy for his Foxborough project. If such an agreement could not be reached, team officials suggested that a sale or relocation would take place. The $70 million subsidy was approved by state legislators on May 18, 1999, and signed by Governor Cellucci six days later.

Boston-area coverage celebrated the decision, whereas Connecticut media reacted with disappointment. Kraft turned his back on a $374 million subsidy in order to stay in his home state. Opinion columns tended to speculate that Kraft's decision was more rooted in concern for his long-term legacy than bottom-line profits. If Kraft's primary concern was immediate profits, the Hartford deal was more attractive. The political controversy surrounding the issue was finally put to rest on December 6, 1999, when 93 percent of Foxborough residents voted to approve construction of a $275 million facility on land adjacent to the present stadium. Sewer, roads, and infrastructure costs would be subsidized by state taxpayers, but stadium construction would be paid for entirely by Kraft with financial assistance from the NFL.

As the Patriots moved forward, the Red Sox struggled to convince an unenthusiastic public to approve ballpark subsidies for their team. The Red Sox cautiously moved forward on plans in a manner that reflected team president John Harrington's personality. By 1999 it became evident that the team had to make specific plans or face long-term arrangements in a facility that Red Sox management considered hopelessly obsolete. The issue was complicated by arrangements made by Tom and Jean Yawkey to transfer the team to a family trust after their death. In essence, after Jean Yawkey passed away, the team was not owned by anyone. Instead it was managed by the Yawkey Trust, which was supervised by John Harrington. Because 53 percent of the team was controlled by the Yawkey Trust, much of the team's sale price would benefit local charities. Nevertheless, attempts to sell the team were clouded by an inability to lock in a more profitable ballpark deal, the political whims of minority owners, and other complications.[146]

The Red Sox's long record of community philanthropy limited public calls to speed up the sale. Since the 1950s, the Red Sox raised millions of dollars for the Jimmy Fund, an anti-cancer philanthropy that provides direct benefits to the Dana Farber Institute. In Yawkey's early years as team owner, philanthropy was limited and the team's public relations were suspect on several fronts.[147] But when the Braves left in the 1950s, the Red Sox took over fund-raising for the Jimmy Fund, a move that helped solidify the team's emotional bond with the community. Ted Williams was among the first ballplayers to sell his autograph, but the proceeds from these autographs were directed to the Jimmy Fund charity. For many years Fenway Park restricted ballpark advertising for commercial purposes. One exception was the many signs and boxes throughout the ballpark that encouraged fans to contribute their spare cash to the Jimmy Fund.

Harrington announced an intention to sell the franchise in December 2000. Many believed that until Fenway's future was resolved, the team sale would be put on hold. But Harrington worked to complete a deal. Sale progress was slow and was not resolved until February 27, 2002, when ownership was transferred to a group headed by the former Florida Marlins owner, John Henry, for a record-breaking $700 million. The transfer was preceded by a congressional inquiry launched by U.S. Representative Bill Delahunt of nearby Quincy after concerns that the charities expected to benefit from the sale might have been "shortchanged." The Henry bid was not the highest, yet Major League Baseball approved it.[148] To make the deal work, Henry sold the Marlins to the Expos owner, Jeffrey Loria, for $158 million, who, in turn, sold his franchise to Major League Baseball.[149] The exchange troubled some sports analysts, who perceived the sale as a sign of collusion, but John Harrington denied any impropriety.[150]

Before this deal was finalized, Harrington attempted to lock in a stadium deal to maximize the team's value. Although hints and suggestions of a new ballpark slowly unfolded from the mid-1990s onward, tangible replacement plans were held back until May 1999. Part of the rationale for this cautious approach was the volatility of Boston's political landscape. But this caution was also ingrained in Harrington's personality. The team's subsidy expectations were considerably more ambitious than his NFL colleagues. Robert Kraft turned down a $374 million stadium subsidy in Hartford after plans were put in place for a $70 million subsidy. Red Sox management appeared to set minimal expectations at $200 million. They also hoped to obtain taxpayer protection from cost overruns that could have doubled this figure. If not for public opinion and political leadership that appeared stacked against moving the team from Fenway, it is likely that the team would have pushed harder to move out of the neighborhood.

In 1998, the Red Sox seemed poised to state their position on Fenway Park, frequently suggesting that new construction would be needed to remain financially competitive. During this year, professional consultants were hired to present a case to the citizens and leaders of Massachusetts.

By 1999, Red Sox management was ready to put its case on the table. Unlike the Patriots, who seemed to treat the public with monolithic uniformity, the Red Sox chose public relations strategies that were designed to appeal to diverse constituencies. Approximately two months before releasing design plans to replace Fenway Park, the team hired BSMG Worldwide, a public relations firm with expertise in campaigns targeted at women.[151] The team also obtained endorsements from former athletes shortly after the ballpark plans were released. The team made the expected rounds within the business community and worked to be sensitive to supportive political leaders. In addition, the Red Sox made multiple attempts to cultivate local citizens.

The overall public relations strategy was not without flaw, however. In its attempt to carefully avoid errors, management often excluded outside input. Steve Wolf, president of Fenway Community Development Corporation, expressed frustration with team attempts to micromanage the issue. Wolf, a civic leader and Red Sox fan, offered skepticism that the team would truly involve the community in the planning process. He offered an alternative to the careful orchestrations that were intended to minimize controversy: "Instead of presenting us with their idea of a perfectly baked cake, why not let us help them figure out the ingredients?"[152]

Red Sox management unveiled plans on May 15, 1999, that called for a "new Fenway Park" that would attempt to replicate the features most cherished by Red Sox fans. On the day that plans were unveiled, the *Boston Globe* provided John Harrington space for an op-ed column that articulated the Red Sox position on phasing out Boston's ancient landmark. In the column, Harrington argued that numerous consultants advised the team to seek new construction because the structural integrity of the old facility was insufficient to support the type of additional seating that would be needed to make the team more financially competitive. He concluded suggesting that the team would work with community members to find "the best way to preserve the Red Sox experience for both our current fans and for generations to come."[153]

Despite arguments by some that the ballpark, not the "curse of the Bambino," was a reason that the team was unable to achieve a World Series victory after fielding winning teams for most of the twentieth century, team executives took steps to pacify those moved by the tradition and charm of Fenway.[154] The team planned to install a replica of the original "Green Monster" in the outfield, transfer "Pesky's Pole" to the new facility, and even move the sod from the old ballpark so that it would be replanted in the new structure. The new venue would need a larger footprint than the old facility, requiring more land and presenting unique architectural challenges. To ensure that the new ballpark did not overpower the existing architecture of the neighborhood, the team agreed to situate the playing field twenty feet below street level. The facility was estimated to cost $545 million. Team officials stated that with the proper support, the ballpark could be completed by 2003.[155] New owners would be on board in a few months, but before that the future of Fenway Park took several interesting political twists and turns.

The Legislation Aftermath: The Red Sox Dilemma and the Patriots's Progress

As with many Boston political issues, when John Harrington attempted to get a new ballpark on track, local constituencies conspired to undermine his plans. A local hotel owner presented evidence of expansion plans made as early as 1990, complicating the team's legal ability to use eminent domain. Other businesses complained about possible displacement. A health care facility targeted for ballpark use was regarded as a possible environmental hazard because medical waste from decades earlier might have been beneath the property. Save Fenway Park!, a grassroots group, provided repeated vocal opposition to a new ballpark. This highly energized group was particularly difficult to suppress, in light of their enthusiasm, the region's rich preservation heritage, and the community's passion for sports tradition.

A final complication was the vocal opposition of Stephen Mindich, a weekly newspaper publisher, whose property was a target for eminent domain takeover.[156] Mindich became a difficult adversary, using his distribution network and press leverage to repeatedly attack team plans. The *Boston Phoenix*, his publication, framed the issue as a David versus Goliath battle that could be won at the grassroots level, prompting many residents to more vigorously challenge new construction in their neighborhood. On the eve of a legislative vote on a ballpark subsidy the *Boston Phoenix* offered a special section entitled "Fenway Pork" that offered readers mobilizing information and arguments intended to sway citizens to oppose the subsidy plan.[157]

The Red Sox quest for subsidies was also hurt by dramatic cost overruns on a massive multibillion-dollar Boston road project informally known to the public as the "Big Dig" and a financial crisis involving Harvard-Pilgrim Healthcare, the state's largest healthcare provider. Both crises left state and city legislators uncertain about available revenue and put the public in a skeptical mood about public funding. Hesitation by Red Sox management further hampered chances of new ballpark construction. *Boston Globe* columnist Eileen McNamara offered a February 16, 2000, political analysis that argued "if the team delays delivery much longer, its plans for public financing of a new ballpark could be stillborn."[158]

Despite the pessimism, the *Boston Globe* sportswriter Will McDonough described the Red Sox as "upbeat" and on target to push legislation through the state legislature before the summer session concluded on July 31, 2000. According to McDonough, the team established a conservative timetable that set groundbreaking for 2002 and project completion for 2004 or 2005.[159] A month later, McDonough suggested that a new ballpark was a most important element if the Red Sox were to compete with the rival Yankees. After comparing known financial records of both teams, McDonough concluded that "until the Red Sox get into a new ballpark that can produce more revenue, they'll be chasing the Yankees in vain."[160]

As this unfolded, Boston coverage tended to favor pro-stadium voices by a wide margin, while limiting public participation. The coverage was unique in its balanced involvement of politicians, civic leaders, sports officials, and experts. Boston reporters appear to maintain a more diverse Rolodex than some media markets, a clear benefit to its readership. But typical citizens were less likely to be included in stadium-related articles than in Cincinnati or Pittsburgh.

The Red Sox were able to meet their deadline, receiving state-level approval on July 29, 2000, for a plan that offered them $312 million in taxpayer subsidies. According to the agreement, which was methodically hammered out in multiple closed door meetings, the state would offer the Red Sox $100 million in infrastructure subsidies unrelated to ballpark construction. The city would provide $212 million, with $140 million allocated to site preparation and land acquisition and $72 million for construction of a parking garage adjacent to the ballpark. The 3,000-car garage would be controlled by the Red Sox but would provide a mechanism for recouping the city's initial investment. According to the plan, the city would eventually be refunded by parking fees, ticket surcharges, and ballpark concession taxes. The garage could possibly create a revenue stream that could help the Red Sox offset some of the estimated $353 million that the team would pay for ballpark construction. The total project cost was estimated at $665 million.

Because the agreement held the Red Sox responsible for all cost overruns, the project never moved forward. Two major problems, the potential for astronomical environmental costs in cleaning up the Harvard-Pilgrim medical facility and the uncertainty of land acquisition costs, put the brakes on progress. Harrington tried to seek liability limits for overruns, but failed as skeptical taxpayers and cautious politicians were reluctant to face an uncertain outcome.

The stadium subsidy legislation, although agreed to by Harrington and the Red Sox, created a Trojan horse for the team. It offered them a generous handout, but unlike stadium funding arrangements in some cities, it made the franchise responsible for factors that could not be predicted. With no assurance of an adequate return on investment, the financial community, even those supporting the Red Sox, steered clear of heavy financial involvement. The team's conservative management style and Boston's high real estate development costs brought new construction plans to a halt. Some citizens and political experts doubt that a new ballpark will ever be built in the Fenway area. The expense and uncertainty of building in Boston's Fenway section prompted talk of construction in other parts of the city, but little occurred that would suggest that the Red Sox would be playing outside of their old home any time soon.

Before locking in a new ownership group, Red Sox management reacted with frustration. In October 2000, John Harrington unveiled plans to sell the team. Weeks later he sought assistance from corporate friends to obtain political concessions on the initial ballpark agreement. He sought legislative amendments that would cap the team's portion of construction-related liabilities and property tax relief that would freeze the team's tax expenses at current levels into the foreseeable future. As the national economy languished and local government struggled with revenue issues, the probability of such concessions diminished. Sale of the Red Sox was regarded as political leverage because "a new owner could take the team out of town."[161]

Once a new ownership group was established and it was clear that the

Red Sox were not leaving, a more sober examination of the Fenway Park issue emerged. The Red Sox maintain the highest ticket prices in baseball, something that might perplex teams with newer facilities. The new owners seemed to intuitively know that the public's willingness to pay such premiums was in part because of the historical reverence attributed to the Fenway surroundings. Tinkering with that issue had the ability to kill a golden goose at a time when attendance declines might be evident in other cities. The failure to win a World Series for longer than any other team suggested that intangibles such as history and tradition were important to fans. Even if it was a bit run-down, Fenway Park was regarded as an important part of what made the franchise unique.

Because the new team owners paid $700 million for the storied franchise without the assurance of new ballpark construction, as had occurred in other cities, the automatic linkage between high franchise value and a new stadium deal has been broken. After all, in the long history of American baseball, no other professional franchise had been sold for a greater sum. Furthermore, Boston did not command the same broadcast revenues as New York or Los Angeles. This did not mean that the new owners would quietly back off of subsidy requests. In 2003 team accountants reported a franchise that was losing money, and owners blamed a high payroll and stadium limitations, among other things.

Yet many other owners would trade their problems for the income-generating advantages enjoyed by the Red Sox, and the new owners appeared to understand this fact. Despite that, the price paid for the team required an effective plan to bring in new revenues. The team's chief executive officer, Larry Lucchino, helped to increase the value of the Baltimore Orioles with a program that emphasized respect for the historic past. His management tenure in Baltimore was punctuated by meticulous creation of Camden Yards, a new park that recreated the feeling of a bygone era. Lucchino knew that the right atmosphere could generate profits. Shortly after his introduction to Red Sox fans, he spoke of making the local ballpark a "better, warmer, more hospitable place."[162] After making a first round of improvements, he coined the team's stewardship of the ballpark "the Camdenization of Fenway Park."[163]

Lucchino also understood public perception. Even though his boss, billionaire John Henry, periodically entertained clients and partners on his lavish yacht, Lucchino made sure that luxury was not publicly flaunted in day-to-day team management. In celebrating the official takeover of the team, he quickly told reporters that the champagne that was being toasted was "just Korbel." Carefully clarifying that "we don't want to waste valuable reserves on vintage. We've got a lot of better places to spend that money now." Among the first moves taken by the new owners was to gain a city approval to add "about 150 new 'dugout' seats on the field and along the first and third baselines." The seats were in place for the 2002 season and added about $200 per seat to the team's revenue picture for each game. The new group talked about further expansion of the ballpark, with the possibility of an additional 10,000 seats.[164] They later backed off those ambitious plans, but were reluctant to commit to a long-term plan to preserve Fenway.

The new owners were regarded with skepticism, but their careful approach on the Fenway issue helped to limit problems with both casual fans and ballpark activists. Instead of pushing for a brand-new facility, they shifted gears and avoided discussion of the Harrington plan, focusing instead on a public posture that emphasized a desire to preserve Fenway Park if such a move best served the fans. They steered away from open talk of a new ballpark and instead hired the architectural consultant Janet Marie Smith to examine the long-term viability of Fenway Park.

Although Smith was instrumental in overseeing Camden Yards construction, management was careful to avoid rhetoric about replacing Fenway. In a June 12, 2002, interview, principal owner John Henry stated they were "moving closer and closer to a time in which we can definitely say we can attempt to renovate Fenway. There's been nothing brought to our attention that's acute or dangerous or couldn't withstand another 30 or 40 years of use." Reporter Scott Greenberger described the interview as "the clearest signal yet that the Red Sox will stay, instead of moving a new park next door, as the previous owners wanted."[165] In January 2003, Smith stated that her architectural analysis would "probably take six to twelve months," indicating that "neighborhood residents and preservation groups will be consulted about any plans."

The new owners worked diligently to uncover other revenue sources from the existing ballpark. One of the plans for the 2003 season placed seating atop the Green Monster. The 280 "Monster Seats" were described by Lucchino as "some of the coolest seats in baseball." The $50 per game seats would generate $1.1 million of revenue annually, in addition to the more than $7 million worth of revenue created by the addition of "dugout" seats that were installed in 2002. New signs and scoreboard expansion provided other potential revenue streams. Another gives the team greater latitude for game-day merchandising on Yawkey Way, the street adjacent to the ballpark. The owners made plans to set up new barbeque and picnic areas by entrance gates facing this road and also designed new concourses under the stands.[166]

More in-stadium advertising and a closer examination of how new media revenues could be generated also took place. The *New York Times,* the *Boston Globe*'s parent company, invested $75 million into the new ownership agreement, and team co-owner and chairman Tom Werner presided over Red Sox programing at the New England Sports Network, the cable broadcast outlet for the team, closely linking the interests between area media and the team.[167] Such affiliations may lead to real or perceived conflicts, yet from an owner's perspective such arrangements minimize the potential for negative coverage, regardless of how this issue unfolds.

Not all citizens in the region were convinced that the new owners' renovations were on the right track. *Boston Globe* columnist Dan Shaughnessy argued that the renovations were a "way to court favor with suspicious and provincial New Englanders," but determined that "it was difficult to believe that a savvy park builder like Lucchino can come to Boston and arrive at the conclusion that Fenway can be saved."[168] Some members of Save Fenway Park! expressed regret at conversion of Yawkey Way into the team's commercial zone, but others with a preservationist impulse saw it as a necessary tradeoff to save the ballpark from the wrecking ball. Vendors who had been chased out of that area during Harrington's closing years were probably less than happy with this arrangement. Some residents regarded fan seating on Fenway's Green Monster as absurd. In a letter to the *Boston Globe,* Belmont resident Joan Graham wrote that the new seats "are making a mockery of an aging and beautiful ballfield." Graham admitted that "I love Fenway, but it's time to retire her after 90 years. . . . Don't subject her to any more humiliation."[169]

New management may have retained Fenway Park, but area fans know that the $700 million team cost will force decisions based primarily on bottom-line self-interest. Shortly after the 2002 season, a price increase was announced, with field-level seats priced at $70 per ticket.[170] Cheaper seats would be available, but Red Sox fans would continue to pay the highest ticket prices anywhere. Owners hoped to determine whether the infrastructure subsidies promised to the Red Sox in the new stadium package could be used for renovations of the existing ballpark.[171]

It appears that Fenway Park will remain the home of the Red Sox for some time. That future may have been aided by recent on-field events. In 2003, the Red Sox lost a heartbreaking championship series to the much hated Yankees, prompting some Boston-area fans to declare the Red Sox and their home "cursed." A year later, they entered the playoffs as an underdog wild-card team, but defeated the Yankees. Just days later they swept the St. Louis Cardinals in the 2004 World Series to bring a championship crown to Boston.

The 2004 victory prompted the local businesses to pitch in and assist the Red Sox in making Fenway Park more fan friendly. In November, the team unveiled plans to add approximately 1000 new roof-level seats, widen concourses, and add concession stands. Over a million dollars in improvements were planned for the area around the stadium, with the Red Sox and other local businesses picking up most of the expenses. In November, city Public Works Commissioner Joseph Casazza indicated that the city would allocate $100,000 to improve lighting and landscaping. Although the team made no long-term guarantee regarding Fenway Park after the World Series victory, Larry Lucchino proudly mentioned the team's 145 consecutive sellouts when announcing future renovation plans, despite maintaining the league's highest ticket prices. The team raised prices for loge box seats from $70 to $80 for the 2005 season.[172] On April 11, 2005, the Red Sox unveiled their championship banner at Fenway Park, and after an emotional pregame ceremony, pounded their hated rivals, the Yankees, by an 8-1 margin. To rub salt in the wound, the celebration was captured in full color on the front page of the *New York Times*.[173]

Three weeks earlier Mayor Thomas Menino bluntly indicated that city finances would not be available to renovate the Fenway Park neighborhood.[174] Menino was prepared to spend $212 million in city funds for a new ballpark a few years earlier. Despite the mayor's pullback, the Red Sox announced, a day later, that Fenway Park would be their permanent home. John Henry called it "a historic day for baseball and a historic day for Boston."[175] Larry Luchino asserted "you will not find a government dollar in Fenway Park or for the exclusive benefit of the Red Sox."[176] The remark appeared to offer an opening to lobby for neighborhood improvements that might benefit the Red Sox and their neighbors.

The activism of Save Fenway Park!, *The Boston Phoenix*, and other citizen groups made it difficult for team management to bulldoze a regional landmark. Now that the team has won a championship, demolishing the ballpark might be a tougher challenge. The financial uncertainties of construction in metropolitan Boston further contribute to a reluctance to move ahead on new ballpark construction. The formulaic conformity of new ballparks may further contribute to a desire to save this unique venue, particularly if the team can retain its top-tier ticket pricing.

Yet the vagaries of team ownership could imperil Fenway Park's future years from now. John Henry may be fully committed to self-financed Fenway Park renovations, but new ownership will eventually enter the picture. Ten or twenty years from now, that could change the ballpark situation. The city's reluctance to dedicate resources to the Fenway area could foster an environment in which new construction becomes more likely, potentially costing the city substantially more. However, this scenario would likely take many years to unfold.

Although lacking the historic charm of Fenway Park, the Patriots's suburban stadium became available for occupancy in 2002. Relocation threats prompted Massachusetts legislators to provide infrastructure subsidies that may not have been as lavish as the Hartford alternative, but they were acceptable to Robert Kraft. Holding the line on subsidies almost cost the region an NFL team, but in taking a firm stand, legislators were able to get the Patriots to pay the full cost of stadium construction, minus $70 million in state-generated infrastructure costs. The new stadium was not a Taj Mahal, as is the case with some heavily subsidized facilities, but it was a vast improvement over what it replaced.

Kraft was portrayed as a villain during his Connecticut courtship, but his eventual commitment of personal resources to the area and a championship winning team assuaged most fans' feelings about his brief flirtation with Hartford. As the new stadium opened, the Patriots's owner appeared to have built a secure legacy. In their last season at run-down Foxborough Stadium, the team made the playoffs, advanced to the 2002 Super Bowl, and beat a heavily favored St. Louis Rams team. The symbolism of a Patriots victory seemed to lift the spirits of a nation rocked by terrorism a few months earlier. The red, white, and blue of the World Champions appeared to mesh with the patriotic fervor that emerged after terrorists attacked New York and Washington on September 11, 2001.

The new facility was christened two days before the one-year anniversary of this horrific event, and the nation's president watched on, flipping a ceremonial coin to determine how the game would begin. NFL Commissioner Paul Tagliabue also attended. The prime minister of Japan was on hand, giving the event an international flavor. Bob Kraft was in his glory as the Patriots dismantled the Steelers by a score of 30-14 on a brisk New England evening. ABC Sports veterans Al Michaels and John Madden praised Kraft for his ability to get this new stadium built. After inking a naming rights agreement with CMGI, a high-tech company that later fell upon hard times, a revised agreement was made with Gillette, a pioneer in sports-related advertising. Gillette Stadium was a dramatic improvement over the bare-bones stadium it replaced.

In the first full season at the new facility, Kraft's team failed to make the playoffs, but after a one season slump, the team won back-to-back Super Bowl crowns in 2004 and 2005. In 2005, the Patriots defeated a Philadelphia Eagles team whose facilities were much more lavishly subsidized by Pennsylvania taxpayers. For a single year, the Boston metropolitan area featured championship teams in both baseball and football. These on-field successes suggest that management decision making, coaching excellence, athletic ability, a little luck, and other intangibles ultimately determine on-field success or failure, not taxpayer subsidy levels.

Nevertheless, the battle for stadium subsidies was not over, as profit margins, not on-field victory, are often the primary motivator for new stadium construction. As the Boston metropolitan area's two teams hoisted championship trophies in late 2004 and early 2005, powerful political forces in the nation's largest city were carefully setting a strategy for what might become the most expensive stadium construction project in North American history.

8

NEW YORK, PART ONE

Stadium Origins to the Modern Era

NEW YORK HAS A BRASH ARROGANCE that is detested by many, but such an attitude often inspires its inhabitants to act as national leaders on many fronts. Carl Abbott's historic analysis of boosterism described Chicago as "notorious throughout the [old] Northwest as a loudmouthed city."[1] If Chicago was filled with "loudmouthed" civic boosters, as Abbott suggested, New York might be a city of loudmouths with more ability to amplify their message. New York's position as a commercial center gives its citizens a unique platform. Its role as a media center makes it impossible for those uninterested in this city to avoid hearing about its unique features. Major broadcast networks cover New York–based stories in greater detail than distant cities, in part because it is more convenient and cheaper. Because it is home to a powerful corporate community, the primary media revenue stream, it also receives more reporting resources.

Anyone looking for evidence of New York boosterism can find it by talking to a cab driver, watching local news, or reading a newspaper. Boosterism is woven into the fabric of New York. In an article on reduced city tourism, *New York Post* columnist Cindy Adams demonstrates ebullience that is typical of New York boosterism. Adams argues, "We are the capital of the world. . . . We are Attitude City . . . We've got it all. If we ain't got it, you don't need it. . . . The boonies have Motel 6. We have The Plaza, Pierre, Waldorf, St. Regis, [and] Four Seasons. . . . They have Main Street. We have Wall Street."[2] The column is peppered with celebrity names and nationally known landmarks to let others know of New York's superiority to other locales.

Ironically, many New Yorkers come from distant locations, and some of the city's most jingoistic civic boosters are transplants. Power in New York can be tricky and unpredictable. At times, it is transparent. At other times, power is elusive. The trappings of power can be highly visible, easy access to a coveted restaurant table or routine contact with heavy hitters. At other times, power takes on a less visible dimension. Power is often shared in uneasy alliances with competitors, and big plans can take years, if not decades, to unfold. It is rare when a single individual can exert dramatic change. New York's vast size and complexity conspire to wear down even the most persistent individual. Yet its vibrance and energy can be intoxicating. Visitors and citizens alike typically realize New York is a special place with a unique allure.

Big Apple landmarks often become globally recognizable. Skyscrapers became a defining feature of New York in the twentieth century. The Empire State Building, the Chrysler Building, and the now destroyed World Trade Center are architectural achievements that reflect the era of their construction. Surrounding landmarks have become powerful symbols for various constituencies. Ellis Island and the Statue of Liberty have emotional appeal for immigrants. Wall Street is a defining symbol of the financial community. Broadway has become a symbol for performing arts. St. Patrick's Cathedral reflects the power and stature of America's Catholic Church. Yankee Stadium has become a symbol of grandeur and tradition for sports fans.

Early New York Stadium Construction History: An Overview

Steven Riess argues that New York "has historically been the center of organized sport in America, the locus of national media, and the urban area most intensely studied by sports historians."[3] New York has often served as a leader in shaping the sports landscape. In the earliest days of organized professional sports, New York led the way in construction of venues that linked sports entertainment to admission fees. The first baseball admission fee began in a game between New York and Brooklyn on the Fashion Race Course in nearby Long Island in 1858.[4] New York also opened the first commercial ballpark, the Union Grounds, in 1862. The facility was located in Brooklyn's Williamsburg section. The spectator model established in these early years became further entrenched in the American psyche when twentieth-century New York–based corporations created and perpetuated a paid rights–based model for sports broadcasting. The emergence of modern media systems heightened the importance of the ballpark as a symbol of a community's commitment to "major-league" status.

Nineteenth-century New York's coverage of sports venues paralleled the low-key coverage found in other cities. Early New York stadium coverage was limited. The *New York Times* and *New York Herald* did not provide any coverage of the opening of the Union Grounds on May 15, 1862. Both papers understandably focused more prominently on the Civil War. These newspapers offered little sports coverage. The emergence of sports pages did not occur until urban citizens became more comfortable with the penny press and team sports gained popularity.

The Union Grounds was formerly a skating rink that was converted into a ballpark by William Cammeyer, the property owner. His initial strategy was to offer free rent in exchange for the ability to pocket admission proceeds. This arrangement ceased when Brooklyn's Union Nine refused to play unless given a share of the gate revenues. The result contributed to the emergence of American sport as a profit-making institution. When Cammeyer renovated the ballpark in 1869, the work received some press coverage. It marked one of the first instances where an athletic facility seemed to be regarded as a potential symbol for civic pride. On April 19, 1869, the *Standard* asserted that "these grounds, if properly managed . . . could be made not only to prove very profitable, but a credit to the section in which they are located."[5] Ballpark capacity was a mere 1,500 people. The New York Mutuals moved into the venue in 1871. This team, underwritten by the infamous "Boss Tweed," included professional ballplayers who were given no-show jobs in City Hall. Henry Chadwick, the inventor of the "box score," frequently served as official scorer at games in this ballpark. For years the Mutuals were one of the nation's best baseball teams. They were typically regarded as the best East Coast team.

Washington Park became a popular baseball site after the Union Grounds closed. First opened in 1881, its capacity was 2,500. Located on a Revolutionary War battle site, it was the initial home to the Brooklyn Superbas, a team later renamed the Trolley Dodgers, or the Dodgers. The team name was derived after fans casually applied a nickname that reflected neighborhood characteristics. A trolley line complicated street crossing in the ballpark's neighborhood, so anyone heading to a game, including players, had to "dodge" trolley cars. Washington Park offered a more casual and less-organized environment than today's ballparks. When fan turnout exceeded seating capacity, local spectators used their own portable seating. Two fires forced facility repair. Charles Ebbets was a ticket seller and maintenance worker at this ballpark. He eventually bought the team and in 1912 he moved them to Ebbets Field.

Brooklyn was a hotbed for baseball, with a number of ballparks briefly established during the nineteenth century. The Capitoline Grounds, Eastern Park, Ridgewood Park, Ambrose Park, and the Satellite Grounds were some of the many ballparks that sprouted up for brief periods. Eastern Park was a rowdy environment that hosted the Wonders and the Bridegrooms in the 1890s. The Satellite Grounds was a haven for black ballplayers, and Ridgewood Park was used briefly by the Trolley Dodgers for some games.[6]

The team moved into a new Washington Park across from the original location in 1898, remaining there until Ebbets Field was built. The second Washington Park marked a significant improvement over the first ballpark. It was built at an initial cost of $60,000, a large sum for ballparks of this time. A $22,000 renovation in 1908 expanded its capacity to 20,000. On April 11, 1908, the *Brooklyn Eagle* described the various ticket options, which included 25-cent outfield seats and more appealing seats for 75 and 50 cents. Charles Ebbets, the team owner, was such a mercenary that seats were made available a mere 15 feet from home plate.[7]

During the Progressive Era no facility could match the aura of the legendary Polo Grounds. The Giants were the city's most popular team, the Yankees were relative newcomers to baseball, and the Dodgers were from outlying Brooklyn. The Polo Grounds's Manhattan location gave them an advantage in both media coverage and in fan loyalty. Despite that factor, coverage of Polo Grounds construction was limited. It is likely that the simple origins of the Polo Grounds contributed to this rather sparse coverage.

The original Polo Grounds were first used for baseball on September 29, 1880, when the New York Metropolitans hosted the Washington Nationals. The park was located on 110th Street between Fifth and Sixth Avenues. The grounds were used by newspaper magnate James Gordon Bennett Jr. and his buddies for polo, not baseball; by 1883, baseball supplanted polo but the name remained. In 1884, the Polo Grounds were split into two ballparks and separated by a canvas barricade. The new field was built over a garbage dump, so it was not a popular site and attracted fewer fans than the original field. The first Polo Grounds were quickly dismantled in February 1889 after New York politicians, upset at the limited number of tickets received for an 1888 Championship game, decided to take action. Giants owner John B. Day made a last-minute offer to donate $10,000 to "city charities" to prevent the field's demise, but the offended politicians were intent on teaching the team owner a severe lesson for his transgression.[8]

After the team was evicted, the Giants played ball in Jersey City and Staten Island. They later moved to Manhattan Field in September 1889. Manhattan Field was so close to the new Polo Grounds, a facility that was completed in 1890, that one Giants player hit a home run into the Polo Grounds, drawing simultaneous applause from fans in two ballparks. The new Polo Grounds was initially called Brotherhood Park and used by the Players League. This league dissolved at the end of the 1890 season, paving the way for the Giants to move into Brotherhood Park in 1891.[9] Shortly after they moved into this facility, it became known as the Polo Grounds.

Constructed on 155th Street and on the shores of the Harlem River, by 1908 the facility evolved into a massive 30,000 person capacity wooden structure. At the time it was eclipsed in capacity only by Harvard Stadium. The vast wooden ballpark suffered serious fire damage in 1911, and a new facility was rebuilt on the same land, where it remained a landmark for more than fifty years. An effort to change the facility's name to Brush Stadium, in honor of team owner John Brush, failed miserably in 1911. Fans and press continued to refer to the site as the Polo Grounds, so the name change was dropped.[10] Until the wrecking ball hit in 1964, the Polo Grounds name stuck. The name has not been reused since, but in a brief moment that mixed nostalgia and commerce, thought was given to using the name for a San Francisco ballpark. This facility is now inhabited by the Giants, a franchise originally established in New York. The idea died a quick death when Ralph Lauren could not be coaxed into paying a substantial sum for the naming rights.[11]

Stadium Construction in New York: From the Progressive Era to Shea Stadium

If New York City was a national leader in many aspects of professional sports, it was a laggard in media coverage of stadium-related issues in the early twentieth century. Coverage of such construction was typically less prominent than the reports offered in other cities. New York's preeminence as a commercial capital for the sporting industry may have lulled reporters, and possibly citizens, into a belief that sports infrastructure was not important.

When a new ballpark was built in the New York market, its opening was covered, but typically with less enthusiasm than in another city. The gulf between limited stadium-related reporting in New York City and coverage of other venues outside New York further widened when concrete and steel stadiums began to emerge in 1909. *New York Times* reporting tended to focus much more on game coverage itself, integrating comments about a ballpark into a game-related story. The *New York Tribune* and *New York Herald* seemed to follow a similar pattern.

The 1886 opening of a Staten Island ballpark provided an exception to this overall trend. The ballpark served the New York Metropolitans. It was one of the first examples of a major Manhattan newspaper's coverage that offered a ballpark opening as evidence of civic pride. A brief *New York Times* article provided game coverage, but led the story with a focus on the ballpark itself. The headline called the new ballpark, located in the upscale St. George area of Staten Island, "one of the finest baseball fields in the country." The article explained how the grandstand overlooked the bay. It also emphasized fan comfort and good spectator sight lines.[12] The positioning of the story on page three demonstrated that the New York publications of the era still considered new stadium construction less significant than many other issues. Ballpark coverage by major New York newspapers after this unusual burst of enthusiasm tended to downplay infrastructure and focus more intensely on game reporting and team strategy.

New ballparks were regarded as an index of progress in other cities, but in New York, they appeared to be considered an expected part of commercial sport, not a tangible symbol of progress. Even in the early years, it is probable that a fancy "world class" stadium was not needed to demonstrate the civic pride that came with attainment of major league status. New York's citizens might have imperiously assumed that they were "major league" and did not need tangible evidence such as a new stadium to demonstrate this.

It is also possible that the city's diverse cultural landscape limited focus on sports infrastructure. New York newspapers had a multitude of cultural products competing for space. Central Park, a massive park designed by Frederick Law Olmstead, siphoned off some leisure-oriented column space. Broadway shows, the Philharmonic, the public library, and museums were some of the entertainment options that received routine coverage. Celebrities and business elites provided another form of competition. If sports editors had to make a choice between coverage of a notable sports figure or sports construction, the victor was personality rather than place. The rapid influx of immigrants further complicated reporting, as editors struggled to satisfy a diverse readership. Other construction projects, crime reports, house fires, and human interest stories may have collectively conspired to further minimize coverage of sports-related construction.

In addition, New York City fielded more professional teams for each sport than any other American city. This divided fan loyalties, making it more difficult for an entire city to rally around a specific franchise. In cities such as Pittsburgh and Cincinnati, a single team may have simplified the linkage between sports coverage and civic pride. In the early years Boston, Philadelphia, and Chicago may have fielded two professional baseball teams, but until the 1950s New York always had at least three. Furthermore, in most years one of these two-team cities fielded one very weak team that was not popular with local fans. New York's ability to frequently field several competitive teams complicated the coverage choices of reporters.

As the Progressive Era unfolded New York was slower to move forward on construction of modern concrete and steel facilities than other major cities. Pittsburgh and Philadelphia's use of steel and concrete construction in 1909 did not inspire New York owners to follow their lead. This suggests that Gotham's teams may not have felt the need for the enhanced status that a new facility might provide. Owners may have created an enjoyable environment that would keep patrons away from the nearby nickelodeon or amusement park, so die-hard sports fans did not seem agitated by the existing ballparks. Because it was more cost efficient to simply add wooden sections as needed, owners were satisfied to take a path of least resistance. New Yorkers were rabid sports fans despite lagging behind some cities in stadium technology. Giants and Dodgers fans were legendary for their enthusiasm during the Progressive Era.

As a result, New York did not enter the concrete and steel era of stadium construction until a severe fire forced a team owner to rebuild. The Polo Grounds, New York's most popular baseball venue, was primarily a wooden facility when it was decimated by fire in 1911. The Polo Grounds fire was prominently covered in New York newspapers. It was an exception to the tendency that downplayed ballpark infrastructure issues. Coverage of the April 14 fire was on the front page of almost every daily newspaper in the city. The *New York Tribune* speculated that the fire was caused by a cigarette that ignited peanut shells after a game on Thursday, April 13.[13] They indicated that the blaze was discovered by a night watchman a few minutes after midnight and that Giants manager John McGraw was among the first to be contacted because he was in a nearby pool hall that he owned at the time. McGraw was hopeful that the debris could be cleared quickly and that the Giants could play later that day in the heavily charred facility.[14]

McGraw's reaction offers an indication of the little regard that some in the New York sporting community had for sports infrastructure. The Polo Grounds were so severely burned that playing ball any time soon was unwise and unlikely. Further evidence of this attitude could be found in follow-up stories. Two days after the fire gained front-page headlines, a *New York Times* reporter joked about the fire in game coverage. The reporter wrote, "Maybe it is a good thing that the fire at the Polo Grounds burned up the Giants' bats. With a new collection of smooth ash sticks, the hometown team won its first victory of the season at the American League Park yesterday."[15] Another *New York Times* feature, offered three days after the fire, focused on fan disappointment regarding the blaze. The story argued that "New York without its Polo Grounds would not seem the same to the vast army of baseball fans." Though generally serious, the story contrasted this tone with accounts of "youngsters who furnished . . . comedy . . . while the stands were burning down with their shouts 'get a score card; you can't tell the players without a score card,' and 'fresh roasted peanuts; get 'em while they're hot.' "[16]

In the months ahead, the team played its games in the same facility used by the New York Highlanders, a financially insecure team that was later renamed the Yankees. The fire prompted Brush to build a new concrete and steel facility. Even though the ballpark was only partially completed, Brush opened the new Polo Grounds to the public on June 28, 1911. Construction continued as the Giants finished the season. The team moved in a mere two and one-half months after the old ballpark caught fire.

Stew Thornley, author of the most comprehensive historical overview of the Polo Grounds, indicates that "Brush had ambitions for a stadium . . . that would surpass all others in terms of size, structure, and design." To achieve this goal, he designed the box seats to replicate the royal boxes in Rome's Colosseum. The ballpark attracted attention in the building community, receiving a write-up in *Architecture and Building* magazine in 1912. It was also called "the mightiest temple ever erected to the goddess of sport" in the April 1912 issue of *Baseball Magazine*. The new stadium capacity was 38,281. Subsequent additions expanded ballpark capacity to over

55,000 by 1923. In keeping with New York's reputation as a communication mecca, the Polo Grounds became the first ballpark to use a public address system. The microphone was not managed by an announcer, but instead attached to the umpire's mask.[17]

The construction of a more modern Polo Grounds pushed other owners to consider their sports infrastructure needs. The Highlanders were not financially stable enough to build a facility of similar stature. The Superbas, owned by Charles Ebbets were better positioned. After struggling through land acquisition issues, the Superbas opened Ebbets Field on April 6, 1913. The *New York Times* kept Ebbets Field opening stories off the front page, instead putting it on the sports section's first page.[18] The *New York Tribune* offered a front-page crowd photo and an adjoining story.[19] Both papers gave brief preview stories on the ballpark's inaugural day, but once christened, coverage fully shifted to the field of play.[20] Construction coverage before the opening was limited. Four days before opening, brief stories about ballpark inspection appeared.[21]

A major ballpark construction project did not occur again in New York City until team owners Jacob Ruppert and Tillinghast Huston made the commitment to build Yankee Stadium in 1921. Prior to Yankee Stadium construction, the Yankees played in Hilltop Park, a run-down facility that was built on uneven land previously owned by the New York Institute for the Blind. It had a masonry foundation, but the park's construction above this foundation was spartan and entirely wood. Ironically, Yankee Stadium, a replacement for this wooden facility, was built on an old saw mill site on the Harlem River shores of the Bronx.

The Yankees were the last major league team to construct a fully concrete and steel stadium. Yet they were the first team to officially call their facility a "stadium." It was a term that reflected a transition from the more rural term "ballpark" to a more openly urban terminology. Yankee Stadium was opened to the public on April 18, 1923, with much fanfare. New York Governor Al Smith threw out the first pitch and sat in the owner's box. Music was provided by the Seventh Regiment Band under the direction of John Phillip Sousa.

The *New York Times* provided front-page coverage of the opening-day festivities and offered several sports section feature stories. Other papers, including the *New York Post*, provided front-page reporting, too. With a reported 10,000 fans turned away due to excess capacity, it is likely that this news coverage was popular. The opening-day crowd was listed as 74,200, which some subsequent analysis speculates was inflated. The attendance figure remains an opening-day record for a New York City ballpark. With fire codes and the existing stadium situation, it is unlikely that this attendance figure will be broken at any present venue.

The *Times* described the festivities and the overall enthusiasm of the crowd. In keeping with the majesty of the day, Babe Ruth guided the Yankees to victory with an opening-day home run. The newspaper account described the park as one that "towers high in the air. . . , a skyscraper among baseball parks." The analogy might seem unimpressive today, but in 1923, the skyscraper was the pinnacle of urban construction technology.[22] It was also an apt analogy because Yankee Stadium was one of the first ballparks to truly revel in its bigness. It was a massive facility that made the celebrated ballparks constructed a decade before look small.

Yankee Stadium made a profound architectural statement that, when combined with the assembly of a championship caliber team that included Babe Ruth and local hero Lou Gehrig, put the Yankees in serious competition to draw fans from the traditionally more popular Giants. A week after the Yankees christened the stadium, U.S. President Warren Harding attended a game, offering evidence that the stadium had elevated the stature of the ballclub significantly.

It is probable that Yankees co-owner Jacob Ruppert intuitively knew the statement that this grand edifice would make.[23] Ruppert was a brewery owner and a former four-term U.S. congressman with a wealth of political and commercial connections. Such connections were important because the strength of Tammany Hall politics could make life exceedingly difficult for those without the right contacts. Ruppert and his partner Tillinghast Huston's ability to fund stadium construction during Prohibition serves as a testimony to the extent of Ruppert's wealth and abundant connections. After all, during the 1920s a brewery was not a legal enterprise.

Ruppert had power but was not a towering figure in New York City politics. He had a pragmatic understanding that when he took over the Yankees, he had a second-tier team that needed something special to draw fans. Years after the success of Yankee Stadium, Ruppert stated that when he bought the team in 1915, "We got an orphan ball club, without a home of its own, without players of outstanding ability, without prestige."[24] The new stadium and Babe Ruth's signing as the 1920 season approached were probably the two most important steps taken to acquire prestige.

It is likely that Ruppert, aware of the Giants's stature within the community, reveled in Yankee Stadium's location right across the river from the Polo Grounds. After all, the intensely competitive John McGraw, the legendary Giants manager, believed that the Yankees would be unable to attract fans if they were chased out of the Polo Grounds that they shared with the Giants from 1913 until 1922. McGraw believed that if the Yankees were unable to find a Manhattan location, they would be out of business in a few short years.

Although McGraw got his wish, the Yankees left Manhattan, the team did not wither and die. The new stadium, just a stone's throw from the Polo Grounds, became a daily reminder of the rival Yankees. Giants fans would have to see it when attending their team's games. Such visibility was fine with Ruppert, whose competitive intensity rivaled McGraw. From an architectural standpoint, Yankee Stadium was vastly superior to the bathtub-shaped ballpark on the other side of the river. Initially, mass transit to the stadium was available, but not convenient. By 1926, new subway lines simplified the stadium commute from any point in Manhattan.

The Yankees expanded their popularity after Yankee Stadium's construction. Because the project was fully funded by the team owners, newspaper coverage of the project was predictably positive. On the field, championships contributed to this popularity, but the improved respect that followed construction may have aided press coverage received by the team. The signing of local sports hero Lou Gehrig, a Columbia University product, in June 1923 helped to solidify the bond between team and community. The stadium itself made it possible for new fans to feel as though they were part of an emerging tradition. Years later, the monuments in the outfield, the classic overhead facade, and the total stadium environment helped to reinforce loyalty and sway some former National League fans across the Harlem River to the Bronx.

The Giants and rival Brooklyn Dodgers were still popular decades after Yankee Stadium construction, but the majestic ballpark on the banks of the Hudson helped to make both teams less prominent in the total sports landscape. New York City had the capacity to support three high-quality baseball teams, but the eventual departure of the Giants and Dodgers to the West Coast would mark a distinctive moment in sports history. It would be the first time in the post–World War II era that baseball teams left a community despite both popularity and profitability. The Braves left

Boston for Milwaukee before the Dodgers and Giants moved to the West Coast, but the trek to Milwaukee was the result of years coping with empty seats in Boston.

Although impossible to determine the role of Yankee Stadium's construction in the departure of the Giants and Dodgers, it was clear that Giants management did not want to share the spotlight with another nearby team. At the same time, Dodger owner Walter O'Malley had grown tired of trying to cut through the red tape presented by New York's powerful construction czar, Robert Moses. O'Malley wanted a new stadium, even considering a domed facility. He was willing to pay for it, but various attempts to work within the system were a struggle for O'Malley. He was repeatedly denied city help in his attempt to acquire land via eminent domain.

Moses argued that land could not be obtained for a new stadium unless it was part of a considerably larger public works project.[25] Although Moses acted as though he was taking a moral high ground, his decision was more motivated by a personal desire for housing and highway projects in Brooklyn. Moses was willing to bulldoze neighborhoods and displace citizens, but only when such actions fit his needs. A long-range goal of Moses was to create a municipally controlled stadium in a more wide open section of Queens. Such a maneuver would put him, not team owners, in control. In addition, the ballpark location would be better suited to motorists, which would help Moses to further push his highway construction agenda forward. Beyond that, Brooklyn had become increasingly cramped and residential, making it tougher to justify stadium construction as part of the total mosaic of land use policy. Even so, if Moses wanted to accommodate O'Malley, the outcome could have been very different.

Inner-city ballparks, Moses believed, reflected a bygone era that relied on mass transit instead of the modern automobile. After an initial rebuff by Moses, O'Malley's attempt to connect the project to a new railroad terminal made the use of eminent domain increasingly unlikely as long as Moses controlled land-use decisions. A railroad terminal may have linked ballpark construction to a larger public project, but Moses had no desire to move the New York metropolitan area into greater reliance on mass transit. For Moses, the future of America was linked to expanded automobile use and new urban highways. This policy had underlying class and ethnic implications. Affluent, entrenched white citizens were much better prepared to take advantage of this emphasis. Minorities and low-income, ethnic whites, in contrast, were likely to be locked into a specific neighborhood as highways supplanted the streetcar and the railroad.

Robert Caro provides ample evidence that Moses could help O'Malley but lacked the political desire to do so.[26] In an August 20, 1955 *New York Times* article, Moses taunted O'Malley's desire for an Atlantic and Flatbush Avenues site, asking "Then, if you don't get this particular site, you'll pick up your marbles and leave town?"[27] Although O'Malley denied that desire, in approximately two years, the pieces were in place to move the Dodgers to Los Angeles. Two days after winning the 1955 World Series, O'Malley said, "We don't want to go anywhere else. I am now more confident than ever that something will turn up that will enable us to build a new home befitting a world champion."[28] He made numerous attempts to push New York legislators to help him purchase stadium land at fair market value, with eminent domain as a weapon. O'Malley hoped that he could capitalize on the team's on-field success and suggested that a moderate level of political cooperation would keep the Dodgers in Brooklyn.

After several futile efforts, O'Malley changed his tactics. In August 1955, O'Malley announced that the Dodgers would play seven home games at Roosevelt Stadium in Jersey City during the 1956 season. The move was likely taken to push New York politicians into recognizing O'-Malley's seriousness. It is likely that he wanted to also demonstrate that the Dodgers were not wedded to Brooklyn, but the tactic had negative consequences. *New York Times* sports columnist Arthur Daley subsequently argued that "O'Malley's frantic reach for the extra dollar had gone beyond the bounds of decorum and common sense."[29] A Brooklyn fan was quoted stating that O'Malley's attempt to shift games to New Jersey was "a dirty trick."[30]

O'Malley may have been disappointed by adverse publicity, but his tactic did prod the city's Board of Estimates to publicly recognize O'Malley's demands on August 19, 1955. Nevertheless, instead of moving to quickly appease the Dodgers's owner, the board chose to further study the issue as part of a larger development program in the area.[31] Continued failure with ballpark construction prompted the Dodgers's owner to become more serious about options outside of New York. Throughout the process he continued to stress his desire to control and fund construction of his own ballpark. His difficult and circuitous negotiations with city officials prompted him to avoid pursuit of construction proposals that he could not fully control.

In February 1957, O'Malley traded his Fort Worth, Texas, minor league farm club to William Wrigley, obtaining the Chicago Cubs's minor league team, located in Los Angeles. The move prevented territorial conflict with other owners, but would also motivate Los Angeles politicians to respond politically now that O'Malley controlled the rights to this burgeoning West Coast market. Los Angeles officials, enthusiastic to establish themselves as a major league city, pushed hard to convince O'Malley to move. New York's politicians acted with lethargy. Some Los Angeles officials also considered a plan to lure the Washington Senators to Los Angeles.

O'Malley's negotiations with Los Angeles officials initially centered on building a publicly financed ballpark, something he resisted in New York. During this process, O'Malley had the firm support of powerful Los Angeles politicians and media professionals. Among the more rabid supporters was *Los Angeles Times* sports reporter Paul Zimmerman, later a writer for *Sports Illustrated,* as well as the newspaper's editorial staff. On September 29, 1957, hours before the league's relocation deadline, the newspaper offered an enthusiastic editorial pushing for approval of an O'Malley land swap that would give him the rights to a substantial portion of land at Chavez Ravine, the eventual site of Dodger Stadium. Once negotiations in New York became intractable, O'Malley moved his team to Los Angeles, albeit with no stadium deal firmly established. Instead, the Los Angeles city council approved the land swap. O'Malley exchanged less desirable land that he obtained from Wrigley. The deal was approved by the city council just hours before the National League's October 1 franchise relocation deadline.

O'Malley had to settle for less than he might have received if given more time to manipulate California's political leaders. Cognizant of powerful press support, several political leaders indicated that they would do everything possible to help advance O'Malley's ballpark plans, but direct ballpark subsidies were not part of the council approved plan. The city offered funding for site preparation and connecting roads, and stadium construction was left to O'Malley and Dodgers's management. He was more comfortable with Los Angeles civic leaders and might have been coaxed to accept a municipally funded stadium. However, his eventual resolution, land acquisition, was precisely what he could not obtain in Brooklyn. His first years in California were spent in the cavernous and, ironically, publicly owned Los Angeles Coliseum.

New York officials may not have considered public stadium funding in the 1950s, but a philosophic shift was taking place. More cities were considering publicly funded ballparks. This trend reflected an emerging demand of baseball ownership. The Dodgers's arrangement may have been a largely privately funded affair, but San Francisco's Candlestick Park, completed in 1960, relied entirely on municipal funding. By 1961, the idea of subsidy for a New York ballpark began to gain political leverage. Robert Moses, although weakened by political squabbles, still had the power and capacity to bring such a project to fruition. His answer to the baseball void created by the departure of the Dodgers and the Giants was to attract a new team with the construction of a publicly funded stadium in the Flushing Meadows section of Queens.

Moses hoped that such a project would solidify his legacy. If linked with the enthusiasm of the 1964–65 World's Fair, set to unfold in Queens, he believed that the stadium could be part of a massive park that might replace Manhattan's famed Central Park as the city's most coveted public asset. Total acreage available for the Flushing Meadows park exceeded Central Park by 50 percent. In addition, the location was near the center of New York's five boroughs, unlike Central Park. With much of the city's affluent population moving eastward into Long Island, Moses believed that the park that would be heavily used for generations to come.

Shea Stadium construction coverage was often overshadowed by the New York World's Fair, another pet project of Moses. At times stadium construction was intertwined with World's Fair coverage, but a few stories focused exclusively on this new facility. In 1962 the *New York Times* offered a general description of the stadium and political attempts to have the stadium named after prominent attorney William Shea.[32] Tangible construction issues gained prominence in 1963. One article emphasized assembly of the world's largest escalator system within the facility.[33] Others focused on funding, construction timetables, and concerns about on-site hiring bias.[34] No stadium-related articles received front-page coverage in the *New York Times* during these two years. In addition, articles did not challenge whether stadium construction should take place and the general public was typically squeezed out of the reporting process.

Shea Stadium's limited coverage might be attributed to the New York press, its relationship with Robert Moses, and the political landscape during that period. The press was reluctant to intensely investigate high-level city officials unless the smell of scandal was impossible to avoid. The press might report small instances of corruption, offering the public a sense that the press served a watchdog role. But big stories involving important individuals often required overwhelming evidence or the investigation might cease. Shea Stadium did not appear to fit the profile of something that should gain reporter attention under this criteria. No blatant corruption or improprieties could be found on the surface, so further digging was unlikely.

The 1964–65 World's Fair was a separate but related story, prompting reporters to investigate that event further. Reporters worked harder to cover the event, to the detriment of Moses legacy. Robert Moses was often a beneficiary of New York City reporting tendencies that favored elites with sound reputations, but Moses had gradually tarnished his reputation later in his career. The problems he faced earlier, when linked with problems related to the World's Fair revenue shortfalls and attendance problems, left him open for press criticism.

Over the years, Moses displaced thousands of individuals with little controversy because he kept projects tightly insulated from the press and moved rapidly with demolition and subsequent construction. By the time the press may have reacted to a Moses project, it was often too late. The bulldozers had moved in, the displaced families were moved, and a potentially contested area was reduced to construction rubble. Unless a reporter wanted to do extensive research, something that many newspapers were unwilling to support, Moses moved ahead without challenge. Even in cases when a reporter conducted an investigation, Moses was given greater opportunity to defend his position than a less-prominent politician might be afforded.[35]

In most municipal projects, the people Moses displaced were low-income or lower-middle-class individuals who had no prior media access. In the 1950s and early 1960s, the New York press often reacted as a lapdog, not a watchdog, when it came to high-level city administration. Although exceptions could be found, the media did not tend to challenge officials unless a pattern of impropriety emerged. This lasted until the roof caved in on city finances in the mid-1970s. Even then, the press reaction was often reflexively supportive. The comfortable relationship that Robert Moses had with the press began to break down in the early 1960s.

Moses's reputation was first tarnished by negative coverage of his handling of parking lot construction in Central Park's Tavern on the Green facility.[36] His mistake was trying to jam a project down the throats of affluent citizens. A *New York Times* editorial published less than a year after the controversy speaks volumes about how the press covered Moses and other high-level political leaders with sound reputations. A Moses project was under a federal investigation by led by Home Finance Administrator Albert Cole. The 1957 editorial argued: "Mr. Cole had better face the fact that New York City is not going to drop Bob Moses as a public servant as long as he is willing to keep working for the city. . . . It's possible to find a mistake and failure here and there. But look at the long, long record of successes. You don't bench Babe Ruth because he strikes out once in a while. . . . The Federal Government is not going to change Mr. Moses. It had better try to get along with him, for that is the way we will travel farther [and] fastest for the public good."[37]

It might have made more sense for Moses to milk the Shea Stadium construction issue for more extensive coverage early in the process, but that was not his style. Moses did not like to struggle through the ugly battleground of consensus-building once a project was in the works. Beyond that, Moses's large ego prompted him to develop grander visions about coverage of his World's Fair. He believed that this event would define his legacy. Moses's staff, anxious to please their boss, worked to massage his ego when lining up coverage for that event. They pushed beyond local media reporting to secure national magazine articles and network television coverage. The local press was part of the process, but Moses and his staff had less patience with them, treating them shabbily at various intervals. In one case, Moses walked out on the *New York Times* editors early in a luncheon at a site that he determined. The meeting was arranged to "clear the air" with several new editors who had replaced his former friends at the newspaper.[38]

Local newspapers tended to fall in line with Moses's desires up until then, so Moses responded to a skeptical press corps by attacking them at every turn. He seemed much more focused on the overall success of the 1964–65 World's Fair than the stadium project. This might seem odd with the scope of the stadium project, but throughout Moses's career he juggled various big projects with little fear of political fallout. When the press attacks began, the World's Fair received more media scrutiny than stadium construction.

The New York City press corps may have believed that the stadium was a larger part of Moses's desire to build a long-standing legacy that would continue beyond the fair's closing date. After repeated daily attacks by Moses, it is possible that many of these reporters had little desire to help perpetuate his legacy. Despite a lukewarm press reception, the building did contribute to the future design of several stadiums throughout the country. Ron Smith describes Shea Stadium as "the trigger for the so-called cookie-cutter ballpark explosion in the late 1960s and '70s."[39]

Yankee Stadium Renovation and the Departure of the Giants

The decision to renovate Yankee Stadium in the 1970s was not the brainchild of team management but of Mayor John Lindsay. It is doubtful that the huge renovation project would have ever taken place without Lindsay. At the time, the Yankees were owned by CBS, a profitable broadcasting company that did not need a subsidy. Issues surrounding this dramatic renovation drew more coverage than the initial construction of Yankee Stadium in the 1920s.

The mayor approached team President Mike Burke in 1970 with a clear mission to acquire Yankee Stadium and devote resources to major renovation. Although the city was struggling financially, Lindsay improved the project's possibility of success by framing it as one that would place the Yankees on equitable terms with the Mets. Lindsay did not suggest the Yankees would be receiving a subsidy from the city. Instead, he told Burke that he wanted to provide the Yankees with the same level of financial help that was accorded to the Mets when their ballpark was constructed less than a decade earlier. He suggested spending $24 million on the project, a sum that matched the city's earlier commitment to the Mets.[40]

The mind-set of Yankee management shifted from tenants in a privately held facility to a belief that they were entitled to a share of city resources. The stadium was owned by Rice University, with the land owned by the Knights of Columbus.[41] Lindsay's renovations were so extensive that they would require the Yankees to play outside of their stadium for at least two seasons. Yankee management had reservations about renovation because of concerns that the surrounding neighborhood offered a less than desirable atmosphere for their fans. Lindsay incorporated 6,000 new parking spaces into the plan to limit such apprehensions. The Yankees also proposed a more detailed examination of the stadium issue, but Lindsay instead preferred to take an incremental approach that would simply move ahead without expert analysis.

In his initial public pronouncement on renovation plans, Lindsay argued that a key concern was to keep both the Yankees and the Giants, the region's NFL franchise, in New York City. The Giants shared Yankee Stadium with the baseball team, but were discussing the possibility of moving out of the forty-seven-year-old facility. To finance ballpark renovation, the city would fund 25 percent through the capital budget, and 75 percent would emanate from "anticipation notes" that would be paid off with parking, concession, and lease-related revenues.[42]

The decision to renovate Yankee Stadium was greeted with opposition by several columnists and political leaders, but Bronx legislators and residents almost universally praised the project.[43] Dick Young, one of New York's most influential sportswriters, argued that the stadium's attendance problems were caused by "a lousy neighborhood," something that renovation could not resolve. He suggested moving both teams to New Jersey and bulldozing the stadium so that "some decent dwellings" could upgrade the area.[44] One city councilman received headlines for suggesting that the city abandon Yankee Stadium to devote city resources to a much newer Shea Stadium. He further argued that the city should work out an agreement to share the facility with the Yankees, Mets, Jets, and Giants.[45] Months later, Mets chairman M. Donald Grant stated that he would try to move to New Jersey if forced to share with the Yankees.[46] This threat seemed to solidify the commitment to stadium renovation in the Bronx.

After New York Governor Nelson Rockefeller approved the city's plan to purchase the stadium, news coverage intensified.[47] The Yankees decided to stay put and take advantage of the city subsidy, but the Giants were lured into moving to a New Jersey Meadowlands location after being actively courted by New Jersey officials. The Yankee renovation and the Giants Stadium project both received front-page headlines, a level of reporting that had not been rivaled in New York newspapers since the Polo Grounds fire in 1911. Yankee Stadium coverage mixed pro-subsidy sources with political opposition who argued that the stadium was obsolete.

After the Giants Stadium decision, coverage took a different trajectory. The Giants signed a thirty-year lease in August 1971 and were enthusiastic about their "first real home."[48] Up to this point, the Giants were always tenants in ballparks constructed for baseball teams. Football stadium reporting focused more intensely on civic pride and the loss of a cultural institution to New Jersey. Many New Yorkers regarded New Jersey as a cultural wasteland. These residents contrasted the suburban focus on shopping malls to world-class events found only in New York. Some cosmopolitan residents sneered at New Jersey culture as an oxymoron.

Early articles resonated with confidence about the possibility of retaining the Giants. Once the team's departure to New Jersey appeared inevitable, a shift in tone occurred. Some articles focused on threats to take specific action if the Giants did move. Others discussed legal options to prevent the move or to cause a more difficult move for the team. Mayor Lindsay pushed to evict the team from Yankee Stadium when the city obtained the title to the facility.[49] Officials also threatened litigation if the Giants retained their "New York" name.

Another strategy was attracting a new football team. One article suggested that the city seek an expansion NFL franchise. A less plausible proposal, broached by the city's deputy mayor, involved luring a Canadian Football League team. The deputy mayor sought out individuals willing to invest in this idea.[50] The Canadian commissioner looked at the proposal with pessimism, arguing that the league would lose its unique Canadian identity if such a relocation were to transpire. A 1974 proposal to bring in a World Football League franchise was also discussed, but the league's economic demise preempted the proposal.[51]

As stadium renovations moved forward in the Bronx, the Giants became sporting vagabonds. The Yankees played exclusively in Shea Stadium during renovations. The Giants were forced out of Shea Stadium to another site after the city vindictively punished the team by locking them out of a temporary rental situation in Queens. The Giants considered several alternate sites, including Princeton's Palmer Stadium and the Yale Bowl, two relics built before the United States entered World War I. Although far from ideal, the Giants shifted to New Haven, playing in the ancient Yale Bowl until Giants Stadium was completed.

The Giants's move across the river intensified the importance of keeping the Yankees in New York. The decision was based on psychic factors, not rational economics. The city's urban core was on the decline and finances were bleak. If one of New York's most impoverished neighborhoods could be revived and perhaps thrive, it might lift the spirits of a population that was questioning its future. The psychological dimension of retaining Major League stature made it easier to justify the vast sums of money that were being thrown into the project.

As construction moved forward, evidence suggested that Lindsay knew from the outset that his initial estimates were inadequate. He pegged the project at $24 million in March 1971, but cautioned that expenses could balloon to $27 million. By November 1973 Lindsay said that renovation and acquisition costs had risen to $39.8 million, almost sixteen times the original $2.5 million cost to construct the stadium five decades earlier.[52] Days later, funding approval was granted by the city's Board of Estimates. As the approval was made, costs were feared to be closer to $50 million. Charges swirled that Lindsay had concealed the project's real cost.[53]

Less than two months later, Lindsay was replaced by Abe Beame. On August 10, 1974, the new mayor pushed to contain costs so that they would not exceed $55 million.[54] By 1975 the figure increased to $66.4 million. Inflation and engineering difficulties were cited.[55] Shortly after this estimate was offered, the city dropped plans to demolish decaying properties surrounding the stadium, abandoning the urban renewal component of the renovation, an idea that helped make the total project more acceptable to the public. The move was supported by many New Yorkers but vigorously opposed by area residents whose hopes for broad-based community improvements were pinned on riding the coattails of stadium renovation. The *New York Times* reported that some of the funds saved in this cost-cutting measure would be used to buy equipment for the team.[56] Five days later, Yankees General Manager Gabe Paul claimed that various inaccuracies surrounding the stadium renovation issue put the team in a negative light. Anger that financial constraints squeezed out neighborhood renovations but took care of the Yankees was palpable. South Bronx residents criticized project priorities after renovations were completed.[57]

Renovations proceeded even though resources were so limited that all other large city-funded construction projects were aborted. The fiscal crisis was so intense that by 1975 the city was deferring routine maintenance on buildings throughout the city.[58] Yet by this time, New York was so far into the project that backing out would have provided the entire nation with a clear indication of the city's weakened financial status. On the eve of the April 15, 1976, reopening of the stadium, Mayor Beame estimated that costs had spiraled to more than $70 million. An incomplete tally from the city's Public Works Authority estimated final costs at between $91.4 million and $97.4 million, approximately 400 percent more than the initial low-end estimate.[59] Neil Sullivan pegged the final renovation cost at $100 million (about $450 million in 2005 dollars), but some have argued that the cost may have been as high as $150 million.[60] It is unlikely that a definitive renovation expense total will ever be known.

The *New York Times* did not avoid putting unpopular cost overrun news on the front page. It was an era of uncertainty, and the landscape changed from a decade earlier when the press deferred to Robert Moses, allowing him to tightly control the city's construction agenda. The city was in an economic crisis, and an uneasy press tried to make sense of this uncertainty. Frustration was evident in opinion columns as the project progressed. Although construction was intended to revitalize the morale of a city facing financial hardship, the renovation became an often discussed example of the city's inability to manage its affairs. Suburban residents looked at the project as a validation that their decision to leave the city was prudent.

The Yankee Stadium project demonstrated how important sports had become as an index of a community's major league status. This massive renovation was prompted by a desire to demonstrate to the nation that New York was a vibrant leader, not a weakened dinosaur. City leaders wanted to show that they could keep up with less populous cities that had successfully completed stadiums. According to Sullivan, "Cities kept building stadiums as a sign of confidence in the future. . . . [Recessionary] downturns were particularly hard on New York, but it too kept building. To do otherwise would be to admit that the city was in an especially grim position. Lindsay would have to admit that the city could not compete with . . . the Sunbelt, and he could not concede that."[61] New York's fiscal meltdown rattled the psyche of a city that was normally a confident national leader.

Widespread sports coverage made it easier for politicians to favor sports-related projects, even though New York's diverse cultural landscape could prompt reallocation of such resources to renovation of museums, theaters, local landmarks, or a multitude of other venues. Broadway shows and museums might attract tourists, but they do not garner the kind of extensive routine daily coverage outside of New York as sports do. If New York did not have a crisis of confidence in the 1970s, it might have been more cautious in its approach.

Even though the nation was struggling through a recession, high inflation and a fiscal meltdown, stadium construction continued at a brisk pace during the 1970s. New York's impending loss of its football team, the Giants, to New Jersey intensified the resolve of city leaders to complete the Yankee Stadium project at almost any cost. Even though New York still had the Mets and Jets, loss of the tradition-rich Yankees to suburban New Jersey might have been psychologically devastating to some citizens and political leaders.

The Yankee Stadium renovation created a gem in the Bronx, but cost overruns and the failure to address the surrounding neighborhood problems had long-term political consequences. News coverage moved into a more skeptical mode. The combination of a skeptical media and a public that was largely excluded from the decision-making process may have put a damper on new stadium-related construction in the New York metropolitan area for years to come.

Major stadium construction proposals were avoided by city officials for at least a decade. In 1984 the Jets moved from Shea Stadium to the New Jersey Meadowlands, agreeing to serve as co-tenants in Giants Stadium. Before the move, the Jets owner, Leon Hess, periodically expressed his displeasure with Shea Stadium's amenities. Hess was a petroleum executive with a chain of local gas stations that were noted for their clean, bright appearance.[62] His decision to move out of Shea Stadium came after frequent attacks of Shea Stadium's cleanliness, particularly the restrooms. Hess bristled at the thought that potential gas station customers might associate the city-controlled stadium's uneven atmosphere with his business's sparkling clean environment.

New Jersey's ability to attract a second NFL team gave some individuals at the New Jersey Sports and Exhibition Authority the confidence to believe that they could also host a Major League Baseball team. By 1987, they received authorization from the New Jersey Senate to offer a referendum on whether taxpayers wanted to pay for a new 45,000-seat ballpark. The facility would be funded through $185 million in general obligation bonds. Construction would not occur unless a team was committed to play at the site.[63] Robert Mulcahy, III, the state's Sports and Exhibition Authority chief, announced selection of a 246-acre site near the Meadowlands Sports Complex before receiving state approval for the ballot initiative. New Jersey leaders believed that isolation of a specific site enhanced their chances of attracting a major league team.[64] Talk of luring the Yankees occurred, but the state gave more serious consideration to attracting an expansion franchise after baseball commissioner Peter Ueberroth indicated expansion teams would be considered in the near future.[65]

The baseball stadium referendum never gained momentum. Coverage was considerably less profound than in other urban areas several years later. The public did not regard the idea with any level of enthusiasm and area journalists did not seem to manufacture public interest. New Jersey's electorate was divided by small communities and the state did not have a single urban center that could serve as a core for civic pride. Its division as suburban terrain for New York and Philadelphia complicated chances of passage. The Northern New Jersey site location stifled enthusiasm in South Jersey communities, whose primary urban allegiance was to Philadelphia.

On the eve of the vote, the *New York Times* offered op-ed coverage to Anton Campanella, president of New Jersey Bell and a supporter of the plan, and U.S. Representative Robert Torricelli, a referendum opponent.[66] A front-page story in the same publication announced an agreement to extend the Yankee Stadium lease through 2032 in exchange for $90 million worth of infrastructure improvements to transportation and the neighborhood surrounding the stadium.[67] The agreement effectively diminished New Jersey's chances of attracting an existing team and may have eroded already weak public support to an even greater degree. The initiative was defeated by a two-to-one margin, a level so overwhelming that talk of Major League Baseball in New Jersey generally ceased. Approximately a decade later, minor league baseball came to New Jersey, and minor league teams were also installed in Brooklyn and Staten Island.

Perhaps to keep the crosstown Mets satisfied with their ballpark situation on the heels of the Yankee agreement, Shea Stadium received a facelift and minor renovations during the off-season in 1988. Calls for new construction or major stadium renovations in New York City failed to gain even modest traction until the 1990s. Even then, team owners and city leaders were unable to gain public support or form meaningful political coalitions for any new proposals.

The 1990s and the Push to Build New Ballparks

CBS sold the Yankees to a little-known Cleveland shipbuilding executive named George Steinbrenner as Yankee Stadium renovations were nearing completion. The network paid $14.9 million for the team, but sold it for a mere $10 million. Tax laws allowed the network to do slightly better than breaking even after player deprecation and other deductions were included, but it was one of the few times in the modern era that a major sports franchise diminished in value. The Yankees were a wounded team with no star players and an uncertain future.

George Steinbrenner made a name for himself by bidding on free-agent players. Marvin Miller, baseball's labor leader, was changing the future of baseball economics, and Steinbrenner was among the first to respond. If Marvin Miller changed the dynamic for ballplayers, George

Steinbrenner changed the dynamic for fellow owners. In attracting such baseball superstars as Jim "Catfish" Hunter and Reggie Jackson, Steinbrenner was able to build a championship-caliber team that brought World Series crowns back to the Bronx.

Rival owners were now pushed to bid against Steinbrenner for talent. When Steinbrenner took ownership of the Yankees in 1973, he had the benefit of a meticulously renovated stadium, a generous lease agreement, and a team in the nation's largest media market.[68] Unlike football, which shared broadcast revenues equally, baseball's media bidding structure was localized, giving the Yankees a dramatic edge in accumulating revenues. To compete with the Yankees, other owners had to come up with some strategy to attract the best players. Because the economics of each media market could not be changed, small market owners eventually looked to new stadiums to keep pace.

As other teams earned more stadium revenues, Steinbrenner began to look at Yankee Stadium as a liability. Its limited number of skyboxes and older construction offered fewer amenities and creature comforts than newer ballparks. Even though Yankee Stadium had the potential to generate revenues comparable to newer parks because of its New York setting, Steinbrenner was confident that he could earn more money in a new stadium.

Steinbrenner thanked the city for the generosity of taxpayer subsidized renovations early in his tenure as Yankees's principal owner, but he never really liked his inherited arrangement in the stadium's run-down Bronx neighborhood. During the 1980s he intensified his talk about problems with the neighborhood and suggested that the perception of South Bronx crime chased suburban fans away. Talk of moving the team to New Jersey began to surface.

In the early 1990s, the Yankees were a difficult tenant for the city, often arguing that the city owed them money for their Yankee Stadium tenancy because of an agreement that gave them substantial latitude over facility maintenance costs and the ability to deduct such costs from their rent total. By 1993 the city claimed that the team owed $6.1 million, but the Yankees argued that the city owed them $8.7 million.[69] The team took a hard line with the city. Yankee officials often reiterated claims that the Bronx location caused attendance problems because suburban baseball fans were reluctant to travel to the stadium neighborhood. At the same time, U.S. Representative Guy Molinari, whose district included Staten Island, extended an offer to consider moving the team to this outer borough.[70]

Despite questions about the Yankee's rent status, New York Governor Mario Cuomo met with George Steinbrenner to discuss the possibility of a new ballpark at a thirty-acre railyard situated on the western edge of midtown Manhattan. Rupert Murdoch, president of News Corporation, the parent company of the Fox media empire and the *New York Post,* was rumored to be included in these talks as a way to "give the vastly expensive project a financial anchor." Murdoch's interest was reported to be either in building an "entertainment center, television studios, or an arena" on the site.[71] Reporters seemed unconcerned about the meetings. Harvey Araton, a sports columnist for the *New York Times,* called Steinbrenner's "tormenting [of] New York politicians . . . the nicest thing he has done for his baseball team in more than a decade."[72]

The railyard talks did not gain momentum, even though some believed that it was the only long-term solution that would keep the Yankees in the city.[73] Steinbrenner had periodically discussed moving to New Jersey as he would take aim at his displeasure with the South Bronx. In spite of this, Cuomo opened talks with the Yankees about stadium renovation.[74] Approximately $150 million was considered to make the stadium more appealing to the team.

The 1993 elections changed the stadium dynamic. New Jersey's governor-elect, Christie Todd Whitman, was perceived to be much less likely to offer the Yankees generous subsidies if they moved across the river than was lame-duck Governor James Florio. The incoming governor's press secretary indicated very early that New Jersey was willing to talk with Yankees management, but that "the line in the sand is that we won't use public money."[75] Another new player, New York City's mayor-elect Rudolph Giuliani, was described as a "Yankee nut" who occasionally shared the owner's skybox with Steinbrenner before being elected mayor.[76] As Giuliani took over, Cuomo backed off of his negotiations, suggesting that the Yankees's future hinged on the new mayor's public policy agenda. Giuliani attempted to push stadium renovation plans forward, but as estimates increased, Major League Baseball's labor problems conspired to sabotage both public opinion and political support. A baseball labor dispute cancelled the 1994 season and put stadium renovation plans on hold. After the strike was settled, the public was in no mood to support baseball subsidies.

Giuliani made several attempts to subsidize construction for the Yankees and Mets, but was unsuccessful in each effort. In April 1998 a 500-

pound steel beam crushed a seat below, prompting fears that Yankee Stadium's physical condition could present a major safety hazard and force eventual replacement of the facility. Media coverage initially suggested the stadium's days were numbered, but the nature of coverage changed after a couple weeks. The follow-up on the steel beam accident was one of the most intense periods of media coverage for the stadium issue before emergence of the 2012 Olympic bid, but within several weeks the stadium issue shifted to the background of New York's highly varied media agenda.

The incident caused national media to follow the New York stadium issue more closely. ESPN and Fox Sports Network offered coverage, and CNN and major networks reported the event. Comedy Central's news parody, *The Daily Show,* offered satirical commentary from anchor Craig Kilborne. Following a humorous news story, Kilborne remarked that the Yankees's owner could not be reached for comment because he was "at Sears returning a blow torch and a hacksaw." *New Yorker* magazine presented a comic of individuals at an upscale bar, with one person asking the other "Am I a bad person if I don't care what happens to Yankee Stadium?"[77] *Time* magazine offered an essay on New York Mayor Rudolph Giuliani that focused other issues but concluded with satirical comments about his relationship with George Steinbrenner.[78]

Even though local coverage was not as intense as what transpired in smaller media markets, unlike most other cities, New York's several-week spotlight brought national attention to the issue. After a thorough city inspection, reopening of the ballpark, and philosophic reflection about the physical decay of other New York structures, the pendulum appeared to swing back to support for continued maintenance of Yankee Stadium. Some individuals reflected on the physical decay of some New York facilities that continue to serve the city. The condition of public schools, including one in which a brick fell and fatally injured a youngster, was cited. One individual compared the call to replace Yankee Stadium as illogical as replacing the entire Brooklyn Bridge after a snapped cable caused a fatality several years earlier. Support for a new stadium never gained momentum, so the issue was pushed to the background.

Attempts to place the stadium issue on the ballot resulted in political maneuvering between New York's city council and the mayor. Giuliani opposed a ballot initiative because such a move would have meant certain defeat for his ballpark construction plan on Manhattan's West Side. The city budget was held up briefly, and the mayor considered plans to change the city charter as a technical procedure to eliminate the issue from the ballot, but the issue died when a judge ruled against permitting the issue to go before the voters in November 1998.

News Coverage: The New York Media and Yankee Stadium

Stadium-related coverage in New York has been limited historically, but the combination of two events in April 1998 caused sustained coverage for a brief period. The first event was the falling 500-pound steel expansion joint, which was followed by the closing of Yankee Stadium for safety inspections. This event prompted intense debate about the future of Yankee Stadium. The other event was Mets co-owner Fred Wilpon's announcement that he wanted to work with the city to replace Shea Stadium. The combination of events prompted front-page coverage in all the New York newspapers. The events also received sufficient coverage levels to motivate the *New York Times* to create a Web site location that listed various stadium-related stories. The New York press appeared comfortable with a cycle of somewhat aggressive coverage, followed quickly by limited coverage after a lack of subsequent dramatic action. This cycle unfolded in this three-month period, making it a good illustration of how the New York press has handled the stadium issue before a more public emergence of the 2012 Olympic bid in 2003.

New York Times coverage in the three months following the 1998 stadium beam incident generally excluded public input from reporting. Four percent of the news article quotes were from citizens rather than from officials. Not one individual from these categories actively supported new construction. Such public exclusion from the dialogue suggests that news routines and contacts are pre-determined and difficult to change. Some evidence suggests that greater public involvement is possible within the context of the *New York Times* newsroom. A humorous article speculated on the possible role of the Yankees's owner in the falling beam, and many indicated that they believed he may have orchestrated this construction-related problem. Of the quotes evaluated from news articles, more than two-thirds were from politicians. Some quotes came from political spokespersons. Political voices were heavily privileged, and they offered three-quarters of the pro-stadium quotes.

New York Times news articles favored institutional voices who advocated construction, but opinion content was dramatically skewed against construction. News articles were almost twice as likely to offer a pro-subsidy voice. Even though the *New York Times* staff and the public were opposed to stadium subsidies, news content failed to reflect that tendency. Opinion content countered this disparity. Only two opinion articles favored construction, whereas sixteen were opposed. Two pieces offered mixed opinions.

The eight-to-one ratio of anti-stadium opinion to pro-stadium pieces offers a sharp contrast to the Cincinnati case study, which offered a nineteen-to-one pro-stadium ratio in the final weeks before the referendum. Overall, however, the tone of New York stadium opposition appears to offer a more assertive anti-stadium posture than the couched support of Cincinnati columnists. In Cincinnati, opinion columns contained admissions that a subsidy was not fair, but offered a reluctant claim that they were needed to maintain major league stature. In New York, the attitude tended to be that such subsidies were foolish and entirely unnecessary.

One piece argued that the Yankees did not need a new stadium because "Mr. Steinbrenner is making money hand over fist." It documented specific figures that put the Yankees at the top in revenue generation for *all* teams. The article offered ways that the Yankees were manipulating maintenance bookkeeping to ensure a "city rent in the last decade that is a paltry average of $210,000 per year."[79] Based on an absurdly conservative average of two million fans per year, readers could calculate rent payments at about ten cents per ticket. Another piece explained stadium subsidy horror stories in other cities and pointedly argued that "Mr. Steinbrenner should be told to pay for his own ball park."[80] The editorial desk was more cautious when examining the Mets and Yankees projects. The editors offered a reluctant willingness to listen to owners, but skeptically argued that "when club owners in lesser markets raise huge amounts of private capital to finance stadiums, owners and politicians have to explain why that will not work in the city."

An article favoring stadium construction was cautionary. It specified that New York City should support limited subsidies to the Mets because their management offered a willingness to accept responsibility for some costs associated with their proposal. Harvey Araton argued that such a policy would send a clear message to the Yankees that the city "would be rewarding professionalism, a willingness to compromise."[81] The other pro-construction article suggested that the stadium may be too old to renovate, arguing metaphorically that "even the vain and wealthy eventually face the reality of too many face lifts."[82] Both pro-stadium articles were produced within a week of the steel beam accident. After this time, the publication's opinion columns and editorials moved more aggressively in the direction of subsidy opposition.

It is difficult to determine precisely why the *New York Times* would strongly favor voices that are in direct contrast to the opinions of the publication's editors and staff. Communication scholarship tends to demonstrate that institutional actors with greater power are given more extensive media access. These individuals are frequently integrated into the fabric of daily news gathering routines. Former Mayor Giuliani and his staff were among the most vociferous construction advocates and by virtue of their role in city management, they were typically available to reporters on a daily basis. It is likely that coverage simply reflected typical media routines. Just as the Washington press corps offers more extensive presidential coverage, the New York press is more inclined to quote the mayor's office than individual city council members. The heavy use of political voices provides evidence that New York coverage is more reliant on institutional voices than any market examined.

Explaining why the stadium issue did not gain the kind of momentum of other cities is problematic. New York's diverse cultural landscape is probably one reason for limited stadium coverage. The tendency to pull in experts who are almost always critical of stadium economics may have reduced citizen concern for the issue. Another possibility may come from community-based research, which concludes that coverage of conflict tends to "contribute to the legitimation of the conflict and/or certain points of view that are part of the conflict."[83] Although reporters might seek out conflict to attract an audience, in this case, decision makers at the *New York Times* may have determined that the issue did not merit further legitimation. Conversations with area residents suggest that the surge in stadium publicity surrounding the 2012 Olympic bid in early 2005 was perceived by some as annoying, particularly because many residents felt they were frozen out of the process. In a market-driven media environment, it would be economically rational to tone down or minimize coverage that has the capacity to irritate potential customers.

New York media is difficult to compare to other markets. The newspaper environment is extremely competitive, yet the contrast between the more prestigious *New York Times* and the two tabloid-style newspapers, the *New York Post* and the *New York Daily News*, is dramatic. Suburban newspapers such as *Newsday* or the *Star Ledger* have more in common with newspapers elsewhere, but neither has caught on as a popular option within New York's five boroughs. The *New York Times* has a reputation for providing in-depth coverage of national, global, and local issues. The *Times* favors high culture, even though more recently, as with most of today's media, it has expanded its popular culture emphasis. But there are limits to how far the *Times* will go to achieve a populist readership. Sports opinion is less edgy and more highbrow. The columnists tend to dabble in sociology, psychology, and economics. The tabloids, with an edgier, more assertive tone, focus to a greater degree on personalities and controversy.

One might expect more stadium-related coverage in the *New York Times* because of the political and economic nature of the issue. Nevertheless, a case could be made that the *New York Post* or the *New York Daily News* would provide more extensive coverage due to the personalities involved. After all, George Steinbrenner and Rudolph Giuliani have been a frequent source of tabloid headlines. Yet, in all publications, none seemed as aggressive with the issue as smaller market publications. Boston, Pittsburgh, and Cincinnati routinely offered periods where the issue was a lead story for several days each week. In contrast, from 1995 to 2002, it is difficult to find long-term sustained stadium coverage in any New York publication. However, the emergence of the issue as part of the 2012 Olympic bid in 2003, 2004, and 2005 changed that dynamic. Brief periods of enthusiastic coverage were visible in 2005.

In general, the tabloids may occasionally offer splashy lead stadium coverage, but the content is more driven by enticing graphics than a desire to offer in-depth information. The tabloid's typical lead article when focusing on the stadium issue is almost always less than seven hundred words. The *New York Times,* in contrast, may relegate the issue to less visible internal pages and use less striking headlines, but this publication has a better chance of offering more depth, periodically exceeding a thousand words in a story. The *New York Post* differs from the other publications because its editorial staff was an early supporter of a new stadium on Manhattan's West Side as a replacement for Yankee Stadium. This editorial position did not prevent *New York Post* columnists and invited opinion commentators from offering occasional opposition to new construction. As an example, Phil Mushnick, a popular sports and media columnist, was consistent in his opposition to Manhattan stadium subsidies.

The *New York Post* also seemed to do a more effective job of involving the public in the process than the *New York Times,* but they were less objective. No newspaper appeared to work hard to facilitate public dialogue about this issue. All newspapers fell short on public input, but the *New York Post* seemed more willing to seek out average citizens to solicit a superficial set of public views. In some instances, this use of the public may actually be a circulation building strategy rather than an attempt to involve the public in the democratic process.

Conclusion: The Yankees Push to Replace Yankee Stadium

The Yankees were never able to mobilize substantial public support for replacing Yankee Stadium. Many Yankee fans regarded the ancient landmark as a larger-than-life shrine that contains the trappings of Yankee legends. Even though the dramatic renovation of the 1970s changed the ballpark physically, with the facade moving from the top of the stadium structure itself to beyond the outfield, it was still the same hallowed ground where Babe Ruth, Lou Gehrig, Joe DiMaggio, Mickey Mantle, and Reggie Jackson electrified several generations of fans. It was hard for most fans to get excited about the shiny new skyboxes a new stadium would bring, particularly when few affluent fans would be the beneficiaries of such amenities. Nevertheless, the Yankees never lost hope that a new stadium could be built, one that they believed could bring in more revenues than the old relic.

In 2001 the Yankees announced ambitious plans to build an $800 million retractable-dome stadium in the Bronx, but the plan required splitting costs with taxpayers. The proposal went nowhere. In the closing days of July 2004, the Yankees scaled back plans, offering to pay all $700 million of costs for an open-air facility. If all moved as hoped, construction would begin in 2006. Ed Skyler, Mayor Bloomberg's press secretary, proclaimed "a new facility will have to be built completely with private money. If there is any accompanying investment in public infrastructure, it would have to pay for itself and wouldn't cost the taxpayers a dime."[84]

By January 2005, estimates had risen to $800 million for the 50,000 seat ballpark, but the Yankees still agreed to ante up the full cost of stadium construction, a more substantial commitment to stadium building than any baseball team in history. If the plan moved forward, the public would be on the hook for about $300 million. Despite that, the mayor's office felt a payback on investment would occur. State and city resources were expected for infrastructure and nonstadium improvements, including new parking garages, a ferry terminal, a train station, and new parkland to replace park acreage that would be eliminated by construction.[85] Early in the process, Michael Bloomberg was upbeat about the plans. He praised Steinbrenner and the Yankees for being "smart, aggressive, and rather than just go out and . . . try to stop other projects, their whole focus is trying to get something that is viable and that works."[86]

The remark was as much a compliment to the Yankees as it was a backhanded swipe at Cablevision, owners of Madison Square Garden. The local cable company was locked in a heated battle with the mayor and the Jets over the fate of stadium construction on Manhattan's far West Side. It was a battle of economic titans over what could be the largest stadium deal ever. Billions of dollars were at stake, and the mayor, a billionaire himself, was not used to losing. The battle made the Yankees's proposal look comparatively minor. At stake was the future of the last major undeveloped parcel in one of the world's most coveted real estate markets. Hosting rights for the Olympics and the Super Bowl were also on the line. The project was so big and so complex that it would pull in some of the nation's most powerful figures.

9

NEW YORK, PART TWO

The Olympics, the Jets, and Manhattan

ON MAY 2, 2001, the *New York Post* used public reaction to questionable journalism to solicit street-level opinions about a new stadium for the Jets. The news article indicated that the Jets might contemplate a move to Los Angeles but failed to cite a specific individual directly involved in considering such a move. The story was based on speculative remarks by someone described as one of the owner's "social chums." The huge graphics and headlines in this "exclusive" story took up three times more space than the rather superficial article.[1]

The story was not even carried by the *New York Times* and was subsequently refuted by Jets's management. Yet in the uncertain times of today's fast-paced news environment, these unsubstantiated rumors were reported on several national news outlets, including MSNBC and Fox News.[2] As part of the coverage, the *Post* included highly visible opinions from seven citizens who offered specific input about the team's stadium situation. The front-page headline about the possible move to urban rival Los Angeles may have generated newspaper sales from a community that often purchases a newspaper to read while riding mass transit. The journalistic reputation of the News Corporation chief, Rupert Murdoch, has been challenged by some analysts, and, on occasion, he has been accused of placing profits ahead of news values. Nevertheless, this reporting provided evidence of a shift away from baseball infrastructure to a focus on football and, later, to more intense coverage of 2012 Olympic hosting opportunities.

The genesis of this tactical change was made public in January 2001. After several failed attempts to help the Yankees and Mets move into new ballparks, Rudolph Giuliani, then mayor, shifted gears, offering a proposal to build an indoor football stadium that would attract the Jets to Manhattan. The *New York Times* reported that the structure would be part of a major "sports corridor" that Giuliani suggested "would pay for itself many, many times over." The retractable domed stadium would be built adjacent to the Jacob Javits Convention Center and would expand convention and exhibition capacity on nonfootball dates. In addition, the mayor proposed that the neighborhood would become home to a new Madison Square Garden. He excitedly talked of attracting the 2012 Summer Olympics, NCAA Championship games, and Super Bowls. Giuliani appealed to New Yorkers's sense of grandeur, arguing that moving forward on this project would "create the most famous sports facility in the world."[3]

Most New Yorkers did not regard the plan with the enthusiasm he desired. While touting the plan, Giuliani worked to bring minor league teams to Brooklyn and Staten Island. Two heavily subsidized ballparks were constructed for affiliates of the Yankees and Mets, but these projects were small, with funding levels that paled in comparison to major league construction. The quest for a large new stadium did not move forward despite Rudolph Giuliani's aggressive efforts, yet as his administration came to a close, he worked to authorize legislation that would help the Mets and Yankees achieve their long-term goals.

Just days before leaving office, on December 27, 2001, he introduced legislation that authorized using $1.6 billion in city bonds to build new retractable dome ballparks for both New York baseball teams. The city was expected to recoup this record-breaking commitment though $50 million debt-service payments made by each team over the course of a thirty-five-year lease that included "no escape clauses." Despite concerns of multibillion-dollar deficits as a result of a sluggish economy and recent terrorist attacks, Giuliani confidently insisted that the stadium deal "would pay for itself." Giuliani believed that the retractable domes would help bring other events to the city. He predicated this legislation on approval of the incoming mayor, arguing that "I can't imagine why he won't support it." To give the teams leverage they did not previously have, Giuliani built in an amendment that allowed each team the "right to leave the city on 60 days notice if either team finds that the 'city does not intend to proceed with the stadium project.' "[4]

The stadium controversy fell into the hands of a billionaire media mogul who, early on, indicated a desire to build new sports facilities. Giuliani's successor, Michael Bloomberg, faced an uphill battle as an advocate of new stadium construction, particularly after terrorist attacks destroyed the city's World Trade Center complex on September 11, 2001. The enormity of this event prompted many citizens to focus on rebuilding the city's financial center before willingly entertaining any thoughts of new stadium construction. Beyond that, a stagnant economy after September 11 placed burdens on the city's overall ability to provide basic services.

In the 2001 New York mayoral election Michael Bloomberg was the only candidate among a long list of contenders to admit supporting new stadium construction, but he took this position before the tragic events of September 11.[5] Bloomberg, a political outsider, received an important endorsement from Giuliani in October 2001. Giuliani's courage and decisiveness as the September 11 tragedy unfolded earned him dramatic political capital, even though many New Yorkers may have opposed some policy positions. With Giuliani's support and a sizeable campaign war chest, Bloomberg defeated Democratic opponent Mark Green on November 6, 2001.

To win in the aftermath of the September 11 tragedy, Bloomberg downplayed the stadium issue substantially. He invested approximately $50 million of his own money and millions from like-minded supporters. He ran an aggressive campaign that focused on rebuilding New York's financial district and the need to stabilize an ailing metropolitan economy. Early in his administration, Guiliani's stadium ideas were put on the back burner. In 2002, Bloomberg told reporters "at the moment, everybody understands that given the lack of housing, given the lack of school space, and given the deficit in operating budget, it is just not practical to build stadiums."[6]

But as Bloomberg spoke of confronting more immediate problems, he made decisions that would keep the stadium issue active for years to come. He maintained close ties with NYC2012, the umbrella organization hoping to attract the 2012 Olympic Games to the city. His next step was appointment of Daniel Doctoroff, the founder and president of NYC2012, to the role of deputy mayor of economic development. Doctoroff quickly resigned at NYC2012 to begin his focus on New York's urban infrastructure. This appointment had potential implications for sports-related construction. *Crain's New York Business* reporter Steven Viuker described his job as one where he would "continue to push for the Olympics project, along with reconstruction of the World Trade Center site and, possibly, new stadiums for the Yankees and Mets."[7]

A key piece of the Olympic push was a $3 billion project that would add to the construction plate of a city already planing major rebuilding after the September 11 attacks. Doctoroff would put a new stadium on Manhattan's West Side, expand the adjoining convention center, and divert a subway line to the massive facility. Early on, the stadium alone was projected to cost $1.2 billion, more than any stadium project in the nation's history. Transportation-related infrastructure accounted for much of the balance. To offset sticker shock, proponents suggested that some costs would be absorbed by the Jets who were looking to leave their New Jersey home which they shared with the Giants. In March 2003 analysts projected that the team and the league might add $600 million, a figure that increased as political pressure intensified.[8]

Involvement with the Olympic issue was not initiated by the Bloomberg administration. Yet once the administrative pieces were in place and political fallout from September 11 subsided a bit, Bloomberg attacked the idea with vigor. Rudolph Giuliani initially looked at the Olympics as yet another way to push stadium construction forward, particularly as his final term as mayor began to wind down. In his 2000 "State of the City" address, he boasted that "we have a terrific plan to get the Olympics for New York City in 2012. . . . The core proposal is to build a stadium on the West Side of Manhattan that could be used as an Olympic Stadium."[9]

The 2012 hosting plan was unveiled in a more overt manner via a splashy newspaper insert on July 1, 2002. The insert, included in the Sunday *New York Times,* came in the form of a two-sided, fold-out poster. The text was light on financial details, emphasizing the feel-good environment that the Olympics would bring. It advised citizens that the Olympics would take place "in a safe, yet relaxed and comfortable atmosphere," while telling New Yorkers "if you log onto NYC2012.com and show your support, you can make it happen." The insert indicated that 84 percent of New Yorkers "want the 2012 Olympic Games to come here." The basis for these claims were a commissioned survey that any reputable pollster would challenge as methodologically flawed. A more objective poll, conducted by Quinnipiac University, revealed much less certainty. That poll revealed 69 percent of New Yorkers supported hosting the 2012 Olympics, but support declined to a mere 37 percent if taxpayer subsidies were required.[10]

After several cities jumped into the bidding process, the choice for a U.S. representative came down to New York and San Francisco. Slick promotional videos featuring local celebrities were produced in an effort to sway the United States Olympic Committee (USOC) voters and the broader public. Billy Crystal was featured in the New York effort, and Robin Williams was the celebrity of choice for California. Doctoroff made several media appearances on the eve of the USOC decision, but many of these appearances were limited to New York outlets. Even though the competition between the two cities was considered close by most Olympic experts, it appears that Doctoroff was looking ahead to the potential fallout that might occur if the city won and he did not adequately court local citizens. WCBS, WABC, and WNBC all featured brief appearances with the deputy mayor.

On the Thursday before the decision, Doctoroff made a national appearance on CNN's Financial Network at the Nasdaq financial center where "he helped kick off the trading day." His emphasis was not sports infrastructure. Instead he explained a plan to transport athletes and spoke about how the games would be funded. He stated that television rights, ticket sales, and sponsorship revenues could be used to fund "the largest single investment in parks and recreation in the city's history." However, no figures were offered.[11]

The San Francisco proposal featured a greater use of existing sports facilities, but New York boasted stronger financial potential and a more geographic concentration of athletic events. Ultimately, New York's stature as financial and media centers eclipsed the California effort. San Francisco appeared to involve their community more directly in the planning process, but ultimately the Big Apple's money and influence held sway.

Hopes for new stadium construction rose considerably on November 2, 2002, when the USOC chose New York as the nation's sole candidate to compete for the 2012 Olympics's hosting rights. The potential of attracting the Olympics and relocating the Jets to Manhattan briefly revived stadium discussion. After the USOC bid was secure, and New York's competition moved to the international stage, Doctoroff stepped into the limelight for a brief period, appearing on national programs more frequently.

He was seen, for example, on the *Today Show,* the nation's highest rated morning program. The shift in emphasis may have been a recognition that national support for the Olympic movement was an important dimension in landing federal subsidies if New York managed to win the international competition. The 2000 Winter Games in Salt Lake City captured federal subsidies of $1.3 billion, but political fallout resulted after a bribery scandal tarnished the hosting decision. Senator John McCain (R-AZ) reacted to these Olympic expenditures by stating "it's outrageous and it's got to stop."[12]

Doctoroff's appearances were heavy on emotion and symbolism and light on detail. In a November 2, 2002, *CBS Evening News* piece, he emphasized the concentration of immigrant families in the city. Doctoroff optimistically asserted that "there is no place on earth that brings more people from more places together, and it all works." He did not explain the stadium issue; instead, the CBS reporter Lee Cowan quickly described the Olympic costs at $1 billion dollars, approximately one-sixth of what experts regarded as the total estimated cost of hosting the event.[13] Doctoroff's *Today Show* appearance was brief and failed to focus any detail on key infrastructure issues. Instead, he offered generalities, quickly asserting that "we've got a great spirit in this city right now, and . . . that spirit will enable us to do magnificent things." NBC's Ann Curry followed the interview quickly, stating that "Doctoroff also said that as much as $6 billion would have to be raised to pay for the Olympics in New York, most of it private money."[14]

An orchestrated parade of athletes took place on November 6, 2002, and a same-day press conference featured Bloomberg and Doctoroff touting the games. These events gained some local attention, but the Olympic issue moved into the media shadows rather quickly. Because a final hosting decision would not occur until July 6, 2005, Doctoroff stepped off the national stage shortly after winning USOC approval. The 2012 host city would be determined by the International Olympic Committee (IOC), based in Lausanne, Switzerland. Although the USOC endorsement did not assure a successful Olympic bid, it gave city officials new leverage to push stadium construction forward. Realizing this opportunity, Doctoroff asserted that subway construction on Manhattan's West Side would "begin by mid-2005, regardless of the city's Olympic quest."[15] Doctoroff further stated that the project could move ahead even if the city was not chosen as a host city.[16] In every public pronouncement on the issue, he appeared to believe that such construction would lead to economic growth.

The NFL helped to add credibility to the stadium proposal. League Commissioner Paul Tagliabue suggested that New York could serve as a Super Bowl host if the proper infrastructure decisions were made. In response to this overture, the New Jersey Sports and Exhibition Authority, the organization responsible for nearby Giants Stadium, began to push for a major renovation of their facility, with the hope that they could attract the event. Giants co-owner Robert Tisch used Super Bowl leverage to push renovation plans ahead. According to Tisch, "Without the renovation of Giants Stadium, they won't come. It's a fact, and rightfully so." He further argued that even if the event did not come to New Jersey, renovations were expected. After all, Tisch said, unlike other NFL teams, "We're not asking for a new stadium."[17] Co-owner Wellington Mara suggested that hosting such an event might "provide perhaps the best opportunity to get the renovations at Giants stadium."[18]

Renovations were initially projected to be in the neighborhood of $200 million, but as 2003 began new estimates raised the total to about $225 million.[19] By September, the Giants told Sports and Exhibition Authority officials that renovations would cost $290. Sports Authority President George Zoffinger argued that adequate renovations could be achieved at a lower cost. The team and the authority struggled through negotiations that covered everything from naming rights, to ancillary nearby construction, to how to finance the renovations. The Giants expressed a willingness to finance the $290 million improvements in exchange for a $6 million flat fee rental per year and the ability to keep revenues from profits earned for other events that they would stage in the off-season.[20] In December 2004, the Giants further altered their strategy, offering to pay the entire cost to build a new stadium, initially projected to cost $700 million, with the caveats that they would pay no rent and maintain full control over all events in the facility.[21]

Even with a new stadium, the Jets hoped to leave New Jersey. As secondary tenants in Giants Stadium, they regarded the Super Bowl hosting opportunity as a chance to bring that event to a venue they would control in Manhattan. To improve the chances of obtaining a new home, the Jets hired Jay Cross, currently the team president, on July 25, 2000. Cross was not known as a football guru. Instead, he had a record of getting sports facilities completed under difficult circumstances. His experience in getting a Miami basketball franchise a new arena before moving to New York was every bit as important to owner Woody Johnson as gridiron expertise.

The Jets later hired Bill Lynch, a former New York City deputy mayor, to "help win over elected officials, community leaders, and members of the city's labor elite." Lynch planned to involve players, coaches, and team officials in the effort, and polling began to determine how to counter the message of community opposition groups. Lynch was optimistic about his chances in 2003, stating that "I want everyone to be wearing a Jets cap in this city. I want New York to become a Jets town."[22] Whether Lynch's goal would be achieved hinged on the combined effort of the Jets, the Olympic hosting issue, and the outcome of the battle between community activists, self-interested business executives, and political leaders. Lynch stepped away from the Jets situation in 2004 to assist Democratic presidential nominee John Kerry, but to maintain lobbying momentum, the Jets continued to hire individuals who could help them. The Jets allocated $150,000 to retain Kieran Mahoney, a political advisor to New York Governor Pataki, and Michael McKeon, former chief spokesperson to the governor. They also put Jeff Burley, counsel to the state's Republican party, and Ken Sunshine, former staff worker for Sheldon Silver, state assembly speaker, on their payroll.[23]

When possible, city officials downplayed stadium funding realities. Ironically, the same economic growth arguments used in other cities and ridiculed by New Yorkers were applied to stadium construction in this instance. Doctoroff argued that "there has not been a time in the city's history when relatively virgin areas did not grow and develop after the extension of mass transit and public investments."[24] In 2003 and 2004 the word stadium was virtually eliminated from Doctoroff's vocabulary, yet the construction of a stadium remained the foundation upon which his West Side plans were focused. Press conferences on the issue were sparse until 2004, and the result was limited media coverage in comparison to other cities.

Nevertheless, city officials made various presentations on the project, often controlling the information flow. In one instance, a Crain's Breakfast Forum, sponsored by *Crain's New York Business,* offered networking contact with Daniel Doctoroff on February 26, 2002, but at a cost of $50 per person. Approximately one year later, on February 10, 2003, a presentation at the Javits Center offered about 300 citizens a chance to see the plans, but democratic input was not built into the process. Part of the presentation included a Bloomberg administration statement that the plans would move ahead even if New York did not receive the 2012 Olympic bid.[25] A September 23, 2004, public hearing allowed more substantial public input, with 140 people registering to step up to the microphone. The crowd of about 700 people included vocal supporters, such as Cristyne Nichols, president of the city's tourist bureau. She argued that the convention center expansion and stadium construction would bring $1 million per day to the city. Assemblyman Adriano Espaillnat countered the job-creation rhetoric by stating, "We don't want our kids selling peanuts and Cracker Jacks at a stadium."[26]

To deflect public criticism, proponents made dramatic claims about how the project would be financed. The NYC 2012 Web site argued that the Olympics would cost the taxpayers "nothing." The site offered citizens little more than superficial press releases. In a *New York Times* op-ed piece, Manhattan attorney Wendy Fried stated that the materials available on the NYC 2012 Web site "gives one the feeling that being a candidate for Olympic host city is a lot like running for class president." She lampooned the available information as "breathless optimism" and "public relations fluff of the highest order."[27] The limited content was likely by design, but stadium opponents did their best to make any available information public.

Early media coverage vastly underestimated Olympic hosting costs. A 2001 *Newsday* article on Doctoroff listed total costs at $1.3 billion, and a 2002 package on the *CBS Evening News* offered a $1 billion figure. In the *Newsday* article, Doctoroff touted the benefits of Olympic deadlines, arguing that such timetables "create a magical sense of purpose, something that allows a city to get things done that it otherwise would not accomplish."[28]

In response to vague official claims, HellsKitchen.net, an activist Web site, offered a much wider range of resources that typically attacked the pro-stadium position. The Hell's Kitchen activists took an aggressive posture to any media coverage related to West Side stadium construction because such construction was likely to profoundly change the complexion of their neighborhood. Because many of these neighborhood activists regarded stadium construction as a major threat, they held little back. Their webmaster and site owner, John Fisher, was occasionally quoted in area media, through his personal involvement with the Clinton Special District Coalition, which provided him with materials for the site. Fisher admitted in 2003 he was fighting an uphill battle. He indicated that New York media often "give the impression it is a done deal," and they often fail to include opposition voices. When they do, Fisher asserted, "it's usually at the end of articles or broadcast clips [that are] . . . about one tenth as long."[29]

Nevertheless, his Web site offered articles about specific details and expert opinions related to stadium construction. He also highlighted opportunities for activism within the city. When officials planned meetings that allowed for a public forum and subsequently cancelled them, these cancellations were highlighted to ensure public knowledge of official behavior.

Anger at limited visibility for activists in mainstream press coverage was also offered. Some articles uncovered unseemly activity or questionable ethical lapses of leaders involved in the stadium construction issue, in an overall strategy to go for the jugular with city leaders.

Fisher was diligent about posting articles that would cast a negative light on Olympic hosting, while simultaneously e-mailing individuals on an electronic listserve as new information became available. Fisher and his Hell's Kitchen activists added e-mail addresses to their listserve in an effort to inform journalists or mobilize the public. With the aggressiveness of a tenacious New Yorker, he directly critiqued writers who investigated the issue.[30] He was periodically quoted as a stadium opponent. Among the various items posted on his Web page was the 600-page NYC2012 proposal to the USOC, a document that might not normally make its way into a public forum. The Web site's edgy demeanor ridiculed the NYC2012 authors' "warm and cuddly" document as something that fails to show "its destructive teeth."[31]

Other Web sites sprouted up, including nowestsidestadium.org, a site that included recruiting and lobbying links. The lobbying link encouraged opposition to fax local political leaders through quick links to standardized opposition letters. In addition, the site offered a list of organizations opposed to the West Side stadium and actively solicited organizations to list themselves on the site. Another Web site, newyorkgames.org, pushed an agenda that opposed the West Side stadium, but favored hosting the Olympics, adding a unique wrinkle to the opposition.

Numerous New York City activists threatened pro-stadium power brokers, but none were more damaging than the Dolan family. The Dolans had deep pockets and a vested interest in keeping a retractable-domed stadium out of Manhattan. A key part of the family's Cablevision empire is Madison Square Garden, host to many of Manhattan's concerts, sporting, and cultural events. They would lose millions if a competing facility was placed a few blocks away. The unfolding feud between the Dolans and the Bloomberg administration exposed stadium construction as, first and foremost, a high-stakes real estate venture. The passion of sports fans had much less to do with this battle than the ability to reshape Manhattan's real estate landscape.

The Dolans were an ironic opponent. In 1982, Gulf and Western, the previous owners of Madison Square Garden, worked out an agreement that exempted them from paying city taxes, a deal worth $11 million a year by 2005. When the Dolans took over, they continued to reap these benefits, in addition to a state-sanctioned break on their electric bill was worth an additional million dollars a year.[32] The Dolans have fought among themselves and had a rocky relationship with Cablevision shareholders and subscribers. They were not particularly popular with New Yorkers, but in a pitched battle with a billionaire mayor, they were intermittently portrayed as underdogs. One *New York Post* letter to the editor, asserted that "as a Cablevision subscriber. . . , I can't stomach the Dolans. However, Bravo for their bid to derail the stadium."[33]

Cablevision poured some of their tax exemption savings into a campaign against the mayor's plans. In 2004 alone, Cablevision spent $7.6 million in advertising and lobbying to kill the project. Their adversaries, the Jets, spent $6.2 million.[34] Most of the almost $14 million was spent on television, radio, and print advertising. Influential political voices were also put on the payroll of each organization. Paradoxically, the Dolans tried to pitch the stadium as something that would drain revenues from other city services.

The Jets did what they could to ensure that the project would not be attacked as a stand-alone stadium. Mixed use development has emerged as a buzzword in Manhattan real estate circles. Plans for the stadium were consistent with this trend. Full-page print ads offered the slogan "More than just a stadium."[35] It was part stadium, part convention center, but planners added other creative wrinkles. It would be home to "four or five high-end restaurants, a community theater, a museum, an open-air market, a ground-level café, and retail space." Jets management regarded the mixed-use dimension of the plan as "the project's strongest selling point."[36] It provided a rationale for why the project could bring economic growth when combined stadium and convention center projects elsewhere had not. Such an eclectic mix was essential to sell the project because the economic track record of stadiums and convention centers were shaky at best and economic performance could be easily challenged by opponents.

The word "subsidy" was taken off the table in public remarks, and even the term "stadium" was minimized to avoid correlations with stadium-related research. Bloomberg asserted that hosting the 2012 games would be "done literally without any public monies whatsoever." Doctoroff told several sources, including WNBC reporter Gabe Pressman, that the 2012 hosting plan would not use "any money from the existing budget." If new taxes were needed, Doctoroff claimed, they would be paid for from "tax revenues that get generated as a result of investment in infrastructure on the West Side." He emphasized "private funding" in his public presentations, making his best attempt to sidestep the subsidy issue. Doctoroff repeatedly told citizens that "no existing tax revenues will be used to finance the Olympic Games."

The deputy mayor's choice of the word "existing" was a carefully measured attempt to sidestep the subsidy issue. The funding mechanism employed for the new stadium, the necessary transportation infrastructure, and surrounding development was a relatively new idea called "tax incremental financing," more commonly referred to as a "TIF" by real estate professionals. The idea anticipates a growing tax base presumed to occur through increased property values after new development. In theory, the plan uses those newly acquired revenue streams to provide ongoing financing required to service debt obligations created by the initial construction. In short, the projected tax obligation of a given development site is determined before construction begins, and if higher tax revenues are achieved by the newly created "TIF zone," this becomes "found money" that can be applied to project funding. The concept is an optimistic leap of faith that, if unsuccessful, forces taxpayers to make future sacrifices to finance the initial project.

In an ideal scenario, such a plan might work, but the history of TIFs is less than stellar. Neil deMause uncovered information regarding the checkered history of TIF projects. In California deMause revealed "a study of 38 TIF districts [which] found that only four had generated enough property value growth to justify their tax subsidies, [while in] . . . Chicago, a similar survey determined that the city's 121 separate TIF districts had cost $1.3 billion in taxpayer subsidies to developers, while generating just $362 million in new revenues." Because New York's proposal was about ten times the size of the largest TIF ever, the potential downside prompted concerns in various corners, including developers of the World Trade Center site.[37]

In response to such concerns, city planners and their consultants referred to the financial plan for the stadium project as a "PILOT." The term is an acronym for "payment in lieu of taxes." The PILOT, as part of the city's bureaucratic structure, became a formalized funding mechanism over a decade earlier, but its use was generally to negotiate lower tax costs to attract businesses or to prevent their movement out of the city. In past PILOT arrangements revenues went straight to the city's general budget rather than to fund specialized projects. Doctoroff tried to deflect TIF and PILOT comparisons, arguing that "the precise structure may be different than a classic TIF, but the concept of using incremental revenues . . . is still exactly what we're planning to do."[38] The relatively arcane terms may have confused some citizens, taking some edge off of public scrutiny, but ultimately, how a PILOT differed from a TIF was never fully explained.

The mayor's office indicated they would use PILOT revenues to fund stadium construction. Because past PILOT revenues were previously plowed into the city's general fund rather than dedicated to specific projects, a battle between the city council and the mayor's office would unfold if construction moved forward. The administration was savvy in determining how to find revenue streams that might be in technical compliance with his promise to avoid tapping existing revenue streams. In the early years of the Bloomberg administration, amounts squirreled away in the PILOT program increased dramatically, giving the mayor a chance to make a case that the revenues created by new PILOTS were not existing revenues. However, the mechanisms for control of those revenues were not fully clear, and might be determined by litigation. The mayor's office contended they could allocate these funds as they saw fit, whereas some city council members argued that they had to be involved in the process.

In describing the Olympic bid, Doctoroff carefully focused on projects that appeared to be privately funded first, recognizing that such a strategy might allow him to sidestep the larger subsidy issue entirely, or at least minimize its prominence. It was a pattern he fine-tuned. When outlining the Olympic projects in one interview, Doctoroff highlighted the "roughly $2.7 billion. . . . all of that paid from television rights, sponsorship revenues, and ticket sales" that would be part of "the largest single investment in parks and recreational facilities in this city's history. . . , [including creation of] almost a dozen new facilities." He then shifted to the $1.5 billion Olympic Village project in Queens, indicating that it would be "all privately financed by developers, just like any other building or set of buildings in New York would be financed."[39]

The final piece of the Olympic hosting picture, the stadium project, was generally the last part to be explained, often allowing Doctoroff to rush through this explanation. The strategy often let him to use the clock to his advantage. In a November 10, 2002, interview, for example, after going through less controversial financing issues, host Gabe Pressman asked him "*Quickly,* [emphasis added] how much would the last piece be?" Even though this was the largest piece of his three-part plan, he was able to downplay its significance. When Pressman tersely asked about "the stadium" as the program was closing, Doctoroff was very quick to deflect the focus, arguing that "we're not really talking about a stadium. What we are really talking about is expanding the convention complex." As time ran out on this interview, Doctoroff adroitly asserted that this project would be funded through "private financing from the Jets, as well as bonds that would be bought by private investors, and that would be repaid out of new tax revenues that get generated." The interview concluded as Doctoroff finished this sentence.[40]

The administration minimized the term "stadium," and the Jets followed a similar approach. In an article touting the benefits of the facility, Jay Cross described the structure as "a convention center that also holds football games."[41] Simone Sindlin, chairwoman of the West Side's Community Board 4, stated that city officials were "instructed to drop the word stadium from their lips. I call it the 900 pound gorilla in the room."[42] Yet if they deflected stadium-related criticism by selling a convention center addition, they faced scrutiny from convention center experts who indicate that such additions rarely bring an economic windfall because convention center expansion has been undertaken by numerous cities at a brisk pace.

New York's comparatively higher hotel costs might be willingly absorbed by some conference hosts, but the majority of conferences and conventions involve less than glamorous, cost-conscious organizations. In those instances, even New York's lure as a cultural center is unlikely to make a huge difference. Trade shows for plumbing fixtures might make cost considerations a higher priority than cultural amenities, so with many cities already overbuilt in conference space, New York's ability to routinely fill up the Javits Center is limited. Heywood Sanders, a convention center expert, saw little benefit to expansion. Even with the additional space of an indoor stadium, in 2001 Sanders argued that "there would be essentially no change in its [the Javits Center's] business, and maybe even a decline as the competition gets tougher."[43]

By 2005 his diagnosis had not changed. Amid a sea of data, he confidently asserted that "the overall conference marketplace is declining in a manner that suggests . . . a recovery or turnaround is unlikely to yield much increased business for any given community." Sanders concluded that "in city after city . . . the new private investment and development that these new facilities were supposed to spur—and the associated thousands of new visitors—has simply not occurred." He suggested more rigorous scrutiny of growth projections and greater citizen input because the opportunity costs of such investments often come at the expense of "any number of other priorities [that] may be likely to yield far greater bang for the buck."[44]

Despite evidence that stadium construction was not an economic panacea and convention center expansion was, at best, a breakeven proposition, top New York officials decided to follow the philosophic path of other cities, claiming economic benefits as a rationale for construction. Daniel Doctoroff argued that hosting the 2012 Olympics "would create 135,000 jobs and pump $12 billion into the local economy."[45] Perhaps the most problematic issue challenging the project was the lack of support for such rosy projections. To create the economic growth required to fully fund the project without tapping into existing taxes, the administration made construction of nearby high-rise commercial complexes part of the plan. According to Bloomberg's officials, the project was expected to create 28 million feet of commercial space over the next thirty years.

These projections exceeded the current commercial stock available in most American cities. One reporter indicated that "during what was arguably the biggest real estate boom in the city's history, between 1996 and 2002, only seven towers were built in Manhattan, for a total of 6.5 million square feet."[46] To suggest that more than four times that amount would be consolidated to this somewhat small slice of Manhattan appeared overly optimistic, particularly in light of aggressive construction plans for the World Trade Center site.

The city was unlikely to find sufficient corporate dollars to fully underwrite development of this magnitude. At a minimum, New York would have to issue some bonds to move the project forward, even if this was done under the umbrella of some bureaucratic entity. This would have made area citizens responsible for financing if it did not create sufficient economic growth. In his 2003 state of the city address, Michael Bloomberg suggested that such public funding was a probable requirement to make the project function. While talking about the convention center expansion (i.e., the stadium), Bloomberg argued that "the public sector can pay for improvements—with revenues generated by future economic activity."

To generate the level of economic growth needed to sustain such a project without tapping "existing" tax revenues, as was promised, quick construction of new office buildings and housing might be needed to finance the project's debt servicing commitment. The Jets were, in a sense, an economic albatross. Their share of the stadium funding would be drawn from PILOT revenues, forcing the city to cover any ancillary expenses somehow. In short, the Jets would not be enhancing the city's property tax coffers in a direct manner.[47] Possible increases in sales and income taxes might bring some new revenues eventually, but usable city property tax income would not improve unless ancillary construction could produce new ongoing revenue streams. Because of a tight economic timetable, a Robert Moses-type of bulldozing of housing stock and less upscale commercial properties to erect skyscrapers might have occurred, possibly causing a backlash against the injustices of such actions. Bloomberg's plan was further complicated by estimates that the subway extension infrastructure could not be done until 2009.

Lower Manhattan's World Trade Center reconstruction further clouded West Side development. If both sites simultaneously enhanced real estate stock by a vast level, this increased space could raise vacancy rates or suppress rental levels elsewhere. Incoming real estate revenues could go up on Manhattan's West Side, giving Doctoroff and his colleagues raw statistics to argue that they had succeeded, but future rental income could drop in other sections of the city. Some speculated that constraint prompted Bloomberg to limit his focus on lower Manhattan until the stadium issue was resolved. *New York Post* real estate reporter Steve Cuozzo suggested that attracting the 2012 Olympics may "explain why the mayor, who found every reason to try freezing office development in Manhattan after September 11, wants to see giant office buildings sprout on Manhattan's far West Side."[48] Construction plans for the former World Trade Center site in downtown Manhattan inched forward despite the mayor's West Side vision.

Bloomberg, an astute businessman, appeared to understand the tenuous nature of his proposals. He prepared citizens for future sacrifices as he aggressively pushed forward on the stadium front. In his 2003 state of the city address, he optimistically stated that "we've laid the foundation for New York's recovery." Yet he followed with the caution that "the task hasn't been painless. Nor will the course ahead be easy." He concluded that "our willingness to do whatever it takes . . . pulled us through the darkest days in the nation's history. Animated by that spirit . . . let's continue to build the next New York."

During 2004 the stadium issue ping-ponged in a number of different directions. The Giants pushed for major stadium renovations in the New Jersey Meadowlands and then shifted gears, adopting plans for a brand new stadium. The West Side stadium plan moved in and out of focus, with the Bloomberg administration mobilizing resources as opponents did their best to undermine construction. Plans for basketball and hockey arenas moved forward in Brooklyn and New Jersey, and the New Jersey Sports and Exposition Authority uneasily worked on plans to ensure that their sports complex would not become irrelevant.

In January, Lewis Katz, then owner of the New Jersey Nets, a National Basketball Association team, reached an agreement to sell the franchise to New York real estate developer Bruce Ratner for $300 million. Normally, such a transaction would have little to do with stadium construction, but Ratner had plans to move his team from New Jersey to a new arena that he would build in Brooklyn. Successful construction would add another sports facility and would include tax incentives that could begin a chain reaction of requests for similar deals.

The *New York Daily News* headlined their front page "Bum Deal" with a subhead "Nets-to-Brooklyn All About Money, Nothing About Basketball." Sportswriter Mike Lupica was highly critical of the deal, pointedly stating that claims that a new arena would not cost taxpayers "a dime" should be weighed against the reality that "only one taxpayer ultimately benefits from new ballparks and arenas, and that is the taxpayer who owns the team." He further argued that the Yankees and the Mets "will be in there wanting to know how much the city plans to give them when they get around to building their ballparks."[49]

Ratner planned an aggressive construction agenda that would include housing and other development surrounding the proposed arena. Newark was simultaneously working with the New Jersey Devils, a professional hockey team, that would move them out of the Meadowlands. The potential departure of both teams from the Continental Arena and prolonged talks that might pull the Jets from Giants Stadium added pressure to the New Jersey Sports and Exhibition Authority. During 2004, their control over professional sports entertainment appeared to be rapidly eroding, making them an increasingly unpredictable player in the high stakes sports construction game.

On March 24, 2004, the Jets entered into a "memorandum of understanding" with the Metropolitan Transportation Authority (MTA) and the Empire State Development Corporation to begin laying the procedural groundwork for stadium construction. The agreement included a timetable that would begin construction in June 2005, a month before the IOC made its 2012 hosting decision.[50] The next day, New York Governor George Pataki and Mayor Bloomberg held a meeting that included much fanfare and press coverage. Both signed a memorandum of understanding "to agree to support all necessary legislation to enable the Javits Center expansion . . . and to seek a comprehensive agreement, on terms mutually acceptable, for the financing and redevelopment of the entire Hudson Yards redevelopment area."[51]

The plan called for the city and state to split the estimated $600 million cost for stadium infrastructure, with the most important component a huge platform that would serve as a foundation. The Jets agreed to pay $800 million for stadium construction, the most ever spent by a single team to build a sports facility. A final complication, securing the development rights for the land, would be later worked out with the MTA, who had jurisdiction over the property. The whopping $1.4 billion estimate for construction alone exceeded expenditures for any single stadium project in the United States by a wide margin.

Bringing a football team back to New York and possibly attracting the Olympic Games gained a mixed response. The Bloomberg administration and their supporters were thrilled. Others reacted with apathetic indifference. Yet a nonbinding signing ceremony caused an uproar in the West Side neighborhood adjacent to the construction site. A front-page editorial in the *Clinton Chronicle,* the West Side's local newspaper, argued that "everybody knows that development will come to the Far West Side," but rhetorically asked "why are the mayor and Governor rushing the process? We remind them that in our democracy, a development process was put in place to assure that development proceeds at a sane pace and takes public needs into consideration. Their joint announcement of a 'deal' was premature and thus misleading."[52]

The newspaper also offered anti-stadium comments from assemblymen Richard Gottfried and Scott Stringer. Gottfried called the announcement of "a done deal . . . a shameful disrespect for those who would be the stadium's neighbors." He further argued that "stadium traffic would tie up transportation throughout Manhattan and damage important industries like the Broadway theater community."[53] Stringer criticized the "secretive drafting of the plans, avoidance of official public input, and the assertion that the stadium plan is indelibly linked to the Javits Center expansion," while arguing that "the shaky finances and widespread unpopularity of the stadium proposal have the potential to doom other parts of the proposal."[54]

The Bloomberg administration continued its fight, as stadium opponents fought vigorously against it. Bloomberg cited jobs as a key reason to support construction, whereas opponents pushed a variety of agendas. Meanwhile, George Steinbrenner unveiled plans to replace Yankee Stadium. July headlines touted a new $750 million ballpark that, according to a team source, would be "more like the place that Babe Ruth and Joe DiMaggio played than it is today." The Yankees were willing to pay the entire $750 million construction bill, but expected "$450 million in public money to improve transportation and put up a hotel and conference center nearby."[55] By 2005, the Yankees upped their share to $800 million. What was not clear was whether a creative funding mechanism would somehow limit the team's financial commitment.

The chaos of stadium and arena politics continued to swirl. By October, Ratner told Brooklyn neighborhood newspapers that he might keep the Nets in New Jersey, a move that could derail the larger Brooklyn development plan.[56] However, Ratner was able to maneuver a deal with political officials that was to his liking. On February 18, 2005, Ratner entered into a twenty-three-page memorandum of understanding with city and state officials that would set future ground rules for Brooklyn basketball arena construction and ancillary development.

The press release on this complex nonbinding pact was issued by the mayor's office two weeks later. State and city agreed to ante up $100 million each in "capital contributions to fund site preparation and public infrastructure improvements on and around the arena site, including streets, sidewalks, utility relocations, environmental remediation, open space and public parking." Bloomberg framed his support of the plan as a major victory for area residents, asserting that "the jobs and housing will have the greatest lasting impact. . . . Development is not just about construction buildings. It's about building a stronger future for this great city and state." The arena would be designed by trendy architect Frank Gehry, and the total project would include housing, offices, and retail space. Ratner's firm, Forest City Ratner Companies, would "relocate and reconfigure the Long Island Rail Road Yard. . . , [an MTA property, while] building and maintaining the overbuild platform."[57]

The memorandum of understanding spelled out that a publicly controlled not-for-profit local development corporation would be established as the property's leasing agent, using PILOT payments to service the tax-exempt bonds needed for construction. Ratner's company was expected to "pay rent . . . equal to the debt service" on the bonds.[58] In an ironic twist, the site was in the same area coveted by Walter O'Malley for Ebbets Field relocation; the memorandum specified that eminent domain laws would be used to facilitate construction. The memorandum itself was light on details of how developers and political officials would resolve land issues with the MTA. Six days after the memorandum was signed, the MTA drafted a five-page document that asserted that nothing "shall obligate the MTA to sell or lease MTA Properties" to any of the involved parties. The authority asserted that it could open the process to competitive bidding and that any agreement with their agency to lease or buy MTA controlled property "must be based on fair market value."[59]

Just sixteen days before the Nets agreement was inked, nearby Newark entered into an agreement with the New Jersey Devils hockey team to build an arena. The city promised $210 million for the project, and the team would pay $100 million. The move to Newark and the Nets departure, if successful, would diminish the relevance of the Meadowlands Sports Complex. The Continental Arena would no longer have a major sports team, and without sporting events, the property could be rendered completely irrelevant or possibly given a second life as a venue for concerts, trade shows, tractor pulls, and an assortment of less high-profile purposes.

As long as that arena was a part of the metropolitan area commercial property stock, venues might have to compete with a low-ball competitor, potentially depressing the income possibilities of nearby facilities. Once all of the arenas were functional, the impact would be difficult to determine. New York's Madison Square Garden might feel the pinch more than other venues, but it is also possible that revenue opportunities for the Javits Center would be strained. Local residents might be convinced to attend more activities, keeping revenue levels healthy across the board. But such increases in arena and stadium usage could come at the expense of other cultural venues such as Broadway theaters or local cinemas. How New York's tourist base might react to a new entertainment landscape was equally uncertain.

Feasibility studies related to the West Side stadium did not generally devote tremendous attention to this multiarena environment, save one that focused on the broader region. Yet in 2004 and 2005, economic projections were a major factor in the stadium construction debate. As expected, the conclusions drawn from local analyses tended to reflect the agendas of those responsible for commissioning them. A 2003 Ernst and Young report commissioned by the Jets projected the creation of 18,000 temporary construction jobs and 6,700 permanent jobs.[60] The Jets-sponsored report estimated that the new stadium would generate $72.5 million in annual tax revenue, generating $27.5 million more tax revenue than the estimated debt-servicing obligation for the city and state's $600 million commitment to the project. It was adopted as a benchmark by the Bloomberg administration and roundly criticized as inaccurate by stadium opponents.[61]

Another economic forecast, this one offered as the city's sixty-five-page report was presented to the IOC, suggested that hosting the Olympics would create 135,000 jobs and have a total economic impact of $12 billion. These claims, made by Daniel Doctoroff, reflected the deputy mayor's agenda. It included an assertion that the city would immediately benefit to the tune of $1.8 billion if awarded the 2012 games. Because the figures were speculative and contingent on a scenario that could not be controlled by city officials, these figures did not gain further momentum. The likelihood that the vast majority of any created jobs would be part-time positions over a relatively short period rendered continued use of these claims potentially dangerous for stadium proponents. These rosy estimates offered pro-stadium advocates short-term headlines but were quickly dropped after their release.[62] An off-the-cuff economic analysis offered by Bloomberg ten weeks later claimed "the project would create 42,000 construction jobs and 17,500 permanent jobs."

The City's Independent Budget Office (IBO), with overall city management as a goal, issued a July 1, 2004, report that was used by individuals on both sides. It more conservatively estimated a new stadium would create 3,586 permanent jobs and $28.4 million in annual taxes, a substantial downgrade from Jets's projections and subsequent pie-in-the-sky estimates given by Doctoroff and Bloomberg. The IBO concluded that a stand-alone stadium "would yield just 1,179 jobs and $9.2 million in new tax revenues," offering credibility to the argument that a combined convention center and stadium would bring greater benefits than a stadium alone.

The IBO report noted that as part of a $5.9 billion capital budget, a $300 million expenditure is "a relatively modest sum," but cautioned that "alternative uses of these resources could easily yield higher returns." The report concluded that an Olympic hosting opportunity could improve the revenue picture, but failed to speculate on the amount, cautioning policy makers on the potential for lost MTA revenues.[63] The assertion that tax revenues would more than cover the city's $300 million infrastructure expenditures was cited by supporters, whereas the job estimates and cautionary rhetoric was pointed to by opponents.

The Regional Planning Association (RPA), with a goal of encouraging economic vitality for the entire metropolitan area, including suburban New Jersey and Connecticut, offered a less optimistic assessment in its July 2004 report. Their analysis concluded that the IBO report was generally accurate, but argued that some benefits gained by the city would draw resources from other facilities, and as a result would provide "no net gain to the region as a whole." Because the unit of analysis for this report was shifted from the city itself to the broader metropolitan area, the conclusions were more negative. The RPA suggested a continued shared arrangement between the Jets and Giants, indicating that this could serve the New York Sports and Convention Center's "proposed functions . . . including playing host for the Olympics, Final Four, Super Bowl, and other major events." However, the RPA cautioned that "there would be no benefit to the region of having the Jets relocate from New Jersey to New York City. Even the benefits to New York City alone are suspect." The RPA argued that New Jersey or Queens would be a better stadium site, and recommended that "17 days in 2012 [the Olympics] should not drive the planning for a crucial part of the City for the next 50 years."[64]

The outcome of the RPA's position paper gave New Jersey Sports and Exhibition Authority executives an opening. On November 16, 2004, New Jersey Governor James McGreevey stepped down amid scandal, and Acting Governor Richard Codey, a sports enthusiast, took over. In his first day on the job he mentioned a variety of agenda items, ranging from overhaul of the state's mental health system to funding for stem cell research. Among a long list of possibilities was new stadium construction for the Giants.[65] New Jersey was tempted with the possibility of hosting a Super Bowl earlier by NFL officials, and, despite losing the 2008 bid, appeared to believe they might succeed if the right steps were taken.

Codey had big plans for New Jersey sports. A week before taking over, he talked about a new Giants Stadium, a new professional soccer field, and a vast $1.3 billion retail and entertainment facility in the Meadowlands area that was already in the planning stages.[66] Less than two weeks after taking over as governor, he boasted "I'm going to invite Penn State into the Big East."[67] As December began, formal talks between the Giants and the New Jersey Sports and Exhibition Authority heated up, with the goal shifting from stadium renovation to successful completion of a new stadium.[68] Three weeks later, the Giants offered to pay all construction costs for a $700 million stadium in exchange for full control over operations and no rent.[69]

Although the new governor may have been an avid sports fan, New Jersey Sports and Exhibition Authority President, George Zoffinger, was appointed by the previous governor with an eye on limiting sports-related subsidies while guiding the authority to profitability. One of the ways to do this was an ambitious proposal to develop a huge retail and entertainment complex on the land. The Xanadu project, as it was called, promised to add almost 5 million square feet of retail, entertainment, and office space to the Meadowlands area. The Giants were uneasy about the impact that the new complex would have on game-day parking and revenues. They lobbied to obtain more land for practice space, a hall of fame facility, a corporate office building, and other potential commercial projects, including, possibly, a hotel. Over time, they agreed to pay a rental fee as part of their agreement with the state, but they pushed hard to limit rent and to structure the rental terms in a manner that was most advantageous to them.[70]

The retail and entertainment complex appeared to be the biggest negotiating obstacle. The Giants wanted assurances that the complex would be closed on game days, something that the Sports and Exhibition Authority was unwilling to do. Jeff Tittel, director of the Sierra Club's New Jersey chapter, further complicated negotiations with a vow to drag the authority into court for the potential environmental damage that might be caused by entertainment-based construction. His primary concern was the Xanadu project, but the proposed stadium could be painted with the same broad brush of environmental scrutiny.

Governor Codey tried to remain upbeat but expressed dismay that the previous administration did not resolve disputes between the Giants and the authority over the Xanadu project. He asserted that the Giants had a right to block elements of the Xanadu project. Nevertheless, authority officials attempted to get team officials to sign a document that would allow the complex to remain open on game days. Pat Hanlon, a spokesman for the Giants, angrily told a reporter that "there's no way in hell we're going to sign off on Xanadu before we come to an agreement with them about how we coexist, especially on the day of the game."[71]

Speculation periodically emerged that the Giants might be coaxed into a shared arrangement with the Jets. As this unfolded, New Jersey officials made it clear that legal action would follow any attempt to move. The Giants argued that even though their lease ran through 2026, a key element of their agreement was to maintain the facility in "state of the art" condition. John Mara, the Giants's chief operating officer, stated this would require a $300 million authority investment, which the team had legal grounds to insist upon.[72] By March, the Giants stated that a deal to share a West Side stadium with the Jets was possible. Mara argued that the team's goal was to remain in New Jersey, but that if the Jets approached them "we'd have to listen."[73]

As discussions in New Jersey alternated between resolution and meltdown, the Jets and the mayor's office worked to coax Manhattan plans forward. If negotiations between the Giants and New Jersey officials seemed ugly, it was tame compared to the unfolding drama in Manhattan. The West Side controversy rose to prominence in 2005. A fact-finding visit by the Olympic site selection team contributed to this burst of attention. Bloomberg administration construction targets, simultaneous stadium construction proposals in New Jersey, a plan to build a Brooklyn basketball arena, election year politics, and public outcry over budgeting resource allocations were some of the many factors that made sports construction one of the top local issues in 2005. Dozens of unrelated issues, timetables, and personal agendas appeared to coalesce in a bizarre political stew that could only unfold in a metropolitan area as large and as complex as New York.

The battle was tough and personal in 2004 and 2005. The Dolans used a variety of resources to paint the Bloomberg administration and the Jets in the most negative light possible, and Bloomberg and Jets executives did their best to sling political mud at the Dolans, bringing anything negative about the Cablevision empire to the surface. The Dolans's strategy was to portray stadium expenditures as funds that could diminish city services, such as schools and firehouses. Paradoxically, tax breaks enjoyed by the Dolans could be regarded as a drain on city services, but philosophic consistency was less important in this battle than bottom-line profitability. During 2000, as stadium plans were being formulated, Cablevision's Madison Square Garden hosted almost 700 different events, reaping $140 million in profits.[74]

The Dolans did not pull any punches in their feud with Bloomberg and Jets management. As the Jets attempted to close in on a sweetheart deal for stadium land in 2005, Cablevision offered to develop the same land for a substantially higher amount. The MTA's dire need for cash forced what was up to then a closed bidding process wide open. This move had the potential to kill the entire project. In March, to ratchet up the acrimony, Cablevision banned pro-stadium advertisements from its cable system, a move that made it increasingly difficult to drum up public support for West Side construction.

Bloomberg, the Jets, and stadium supporters attempted to portray the Dolans as greedy businessmen who were acting to preserve a monopoly for Madison Square Garden. Bloomberg assailed the Cablevision team for undermining the 2012 Olympic hosting effort. According to Bloomberg, blocking the West Side stadium could cost New York and the nation the 2012 Olympic hosting rights. As a result, the mayor argued that "this company says to hell with America. We don't care."[75] Bloomberg boycotted all events at Madison Square Garden to further show his displeasure. Ironically, he traveled to New Jersey to attend Jets games instead.[76]

The Jets launched their own attack against Cablevision. Their Web site prominently displayed a link to the New York Sports and Convention Center site, which, in turn, made news coverage available. Featured stories often placed Cablevision in a negative light. In early March articles included a shareholder lawsuit against Charles Dolan, critical coverage of Cablevision's pro-stadium ad ban, and a Standard and Poor's downgrading of Cablevision's stock. The final article suggested that the stock was downgraded because of their foray into West Side development.[77] The Web site also offered a convenient lobbying tool, allowing individuals from anywhere to send multiple pre-written e-mails directly to influential New York political leaders by simply entering personal information and clicking the send button.

If an assault on the company's stock value and pseudo-grassroots political lobbying was not bruising enough, the Jets hired attorney David Boies to take legal action against Cablevision for causing project delays and for preventing the team from advertising on local cable channels. Boies was previously retained by the U.S. Department of Justice in a high-profile antitrust case against Microsoft and was lead attorney for presidential candidate Al Gore during the 2000 election controversy. Boies alleged that Cablevision's ownership of Madison Square Garden allowed them "to charge New Yorkers more for every event" because of their monopoly position.[78]

As the groundwork for legal action was being set, the Jets used league influence to solidify its cause. In February, league officials pulled the 2005 NFL draft from Madison Square Garden, its traditional home since 1995. The 2005 event would take place in the Javits Center. A league source asserted the move was taken because "they're fighting one of our owners."[79] The team also pushed the league to accelerate their decision on hosting rights for the 2010 Super Bowl, adding an element of economic leverage that could not be matched by the Dolans.[80] The NFL gladly complied, tentatively approving the Jets stadium as the host venue if construction was completed by 2009. The Super Bowl hosting news received national attention.

The stadium construction issue was amplified by visiting Olympic officials in February 2005. The visit was punctuated by a lavish campaign estimated to cost $15 million, approximately $1.15 million per visiting Olympic dignitary. Advertising was placed on phone booths and billboards, on top of 13,000 taxis, on 4,000 city buses, and in 7,000 subways where public service spots were normally posted. Splashy television ads were run on local television, with stations donating time for NYC2012 commercials.[81]

The wining and dining of Olympic dignitaries was considered a success, but ultimately Bloomberg needed the Jets's support on the West Side project to make New York more appealing to the IOC. Olympic officials had never granted hosting privileges to a Third World country, so selecting an affluent city based on huge stadium expenditures was bound to backfire unless the construction could be justified for another purpose. France had a relatively new stadium, the 80,000 capacity Stade de France, built to host the 1998 World Cup. England expected to christen a new Wembley Stadium in 2006 and gained approval to break ground on yet another stadium. New York's stadium situation lagged behind, but to construct a new stadium for the express purpose of attracting the Olympics might be perceived as damaging to the broader philosophic goals of the Olympic movement. Olympic officials might have been as mercenary as other sports organizations, however, they were reluctant to make that visible to the global community. This created a marriage of convenience between the Jets and the mayor.

Bloomberg did everything he could to solidify the Jets's position in the stadium sweepstakes, but was undermined by Cablevision's surprise $600 million offer to develop the same land that he wanted for a stadium, amid much fanfare. The mayor hoped that the Jets could get development rights for a minimal cost, but in doing so, the MTA, owners of the property, would be shortchanged. The MTA was in an awkward position. The authority's chief, Peter Kalikow, was appointed by the governor, yet was responsible for management of a the nation's largest transportation network. It impacted virtually every city resident in some manner, so Kalikow could be castigated if he curried favor.

However, the MTA needed state and regional funding, so Kalikow's job required walking a delicate political tightrope. The governor, who had veto power over the MTA budget, recommended a $19.2 billion allocation that was $8.4 billion short of their desired needs.[82] The mayor, eager to ease the MTA's financial strain, lobbied the governor to support "the kind of investments we should be making in infrastructure."[83] Pataki's lackluster MTA support made Kalikow's ability to secure powerful political allies more important than ever. For Kalikow, leaving a few hundred thousand dollars on the table to win a much bigger budget battle might be a risk worth taking, but the political tea leaves were exceedingly difficult to read. The MTA was in a difficult bind. It was in debt and struggling to implement an ambitious maintenance and construction agenda. As the nation's largest transit system, routine operational costs were staggering. The potential for fare hikes agitated New Yorkers, yet not addressing maintenance issues might lead to service disruptions and further infuriate citizens. If the MTA could not extract maximum value for the land, the entire transit system might suffer.

Initially, the MTA tried to hedge its position by keeping the real estate appraisals from public scrutiny. State assemblyman Richard Brodsky, chairman of the assembly's Committee on Corporations, Authorities, and Commissions, subpoenaed the MTA's Executive Director Katherine Lapp and Chairman Peter Kalikow, ordering them to appear at a Manhattan public hearing.[84] A day after this threat unfolded, an uneasy Bloomberg used his weekly radio show to assert that failure of the West Side project would sink future ballpark projects from moving forward for the Yankees and Mets.[85] Some stadium-weary New Yorkers wondered why that would be a problem.

The threat of a hearing coaxed the MTA to make their appraisals public. The Jets conducted their own appraisal that set the land's development rights value at $36.9 million, but offered to pay $100 million to build the stadium on approximately one-third of the land's surface area. The MTA was not pleased. They had appraised the property's value at $923.4 million and hoped to obtain at least $330 million to develop the stadium footprint;

the authority assumed it could sell or lease the remaining land for residential or commercial development.[86] Rezoning would be needed for such ancillary construction.

The Jets and the Bloomberg administration managed to keep outside developers from expressing interest in alternative West Side development plans. Some developers confessed, off the record, a fear that their involvement in anything that might jeopardize the stadium could hurt their own ability to move forward on other city projects. Some cited the Bloomberg administration's input on zoning issues as a particular deterrent.[87] One privately admitted "everyone, including me, is scared to cross him on this. I've got too many things cooking in this town."[88] In such an environment, Bloomberg, Doctoroff, and the Jets mistakenly thought they would be able to cajole the MTA into giving them a massive discount on the land's value.

Initially, the Jets proposal would be scrutinized by an independent arbitrator, but the cash-strapped MTA opened the parcel to competitive bidding once Cablevision's $600 million offer was on the table. Failure to do so could have exposed the MTA to lawsuits. The Jets had a decided advantage, however. Kalikow indicated that the MTA's priority was to raise the most money possible, not to help Bloomberg host the Olympics or to give a sweetheart deal to a football team. Nevertheless, Kalikow also stated bids would be predicated on existing zoning laws that were already crafted to support a stadium. He cautioned that bids should be made "on a where-is, as-is basis," because zoning issues could invalidate the viability of some types of construction.

The Bloomberg administration suggested use of zoning regulation as a defense mechanism, with Deputy Mayor Daniel Doctoroff ominously stating that rezoning "isn't likely to happen."[89] In the dog-eat-dog world of New York real estate, zoning laws can be used as a carrot, a stick, or a negotiating tool. Councilwoman Christine Quinn suggested the bidding process was skewed, asserting "I don't know how the administration can argue that it wants the MTA to get fair market value. . . . They want what is best for the Jets' pocketbook."[90]

The bid deadline was March 21, with a March 31 decision date established. The ability to line up architects, urban planners, and consultants on short notice conspired to make the process exceedingly difficult for anyone but the Jets. Local developers understood that undermining the mayor's pet project could complicate other development projects; not surprisingly, local developers chose to follow rather than lead as the bid deadline approached.

The March 21 deadline brought five bids, but only three were viable. One came from the Jets for $720 million, another was produced by Cablevision for $760 million, and another was submitted by TransGas Energy Systems for $1.05 billion. Two other bids were tossed because they did not contain a required $25,000 deposit. The energy company's bid included a complex array of contractual obligations, so even though it offered the highest total payout, insiders critiqued it as the weakest proposal. Despite the MTA's cautious warnings about rezoning, both the Jets and Cablevision bids required zoning adjustments to work.

The *New York Post* argued that the Jet's bid was superior, whereas the *New York Times* more cautiously suggested that some analysts gave the edge to Cablevision. The complexity of each bid made an apples to apples comparison impossible. The Jets's bid had a $280 million dollar payout from the team, with $440 million in payments from six city developers who would be partners in high-rise commercial construction on the remaining nonstadium parcels. Binding agreements were not obtained from the developers, an issue that could have worked against the Jets. From the MTA's vantage point, the total payout from the Jets's proposal was potentially more lucrative than the Cablevision bid. The Dolans's plan allocated approximately $350 million of their bid to platform construction. Because the city and the state would be subsidizing the platform, the entire $720 million of the Jets proposal, if contractual details fell into place, would bring the MTA about $310 million more than the Cablevision bid. Cablevision's willingness to make payment in an "all-cash, non-contingent" form closed the gap, particularly because $440 million of the Jets bid was not guaranteed and was contingent on the actions of the Jets's development partners.

City and state commitments to stadium construction, in effect, served as a tie-breaker. If half of the $600 million stadium platform subsidy promised by the city and state was shifted to MTA coffers, the Cablevision project was likely to be more lucrative than the Jets plan. If the full value of the city and state subsidy was factored into the total picture, rather than in its impact on the MTA alone, the Jets bid would bring a net gain of $120 million to the table, a mere $20 million more than the Jets's initial bid. However, the uneasy political position of the MTA and the enthusiasm of the Bloomberg administration to build a stadium made a reallocation of platform subsidies unlikely. Peter Kalikow, the MTA chief, needed allies to lobby for future funding, and his MTA agenda could be jeopardized by undermining Bloomberg. The NFL's promise of a 2010 Super Bowl opportunity, when linked with the unknown possibility of Olympic hosting, politically skewed matters further to favor the Jets's proposal.

But Cablevision's focus on commercial property might have brought greater long-term tax revenue streams. Jeremy Soffin, a spokesman for the Regional Planning Association, argued that Cablevision's noncontingent bid "outperforms the Jets both economically and from an urban design standpoint." But Cablevision's lack of real estate development experience added a dimension of risk. Their far from philanthropic motives further clouded the picture, as follow-through might be lethargic. Ultimately, their goal was to retain a venue monopoly, not to develop property. This choice may have added a back-door tax on citizens attending events at Madison Square Garden because rental prices might be inflated because of their monopoly status.

Nevertheless, the Cablevision proposal was crafted in a manner more in line with the Regional Planning Association's suggested mixed-use strategy that could be flexibly tailored to market conditions. Unlike the stadium plan, Cablevision's alternative would allow a street grid through the land and potentially make greater public use of the waterfront property. A sports facility was strikingly absent from the proposal, but the housing and commercial space appeared to better capitalize on the benefits of a waterfront location.

Matt Higgins, Jet's vice president, bluntly asserted, "It doesn't matter what figures Cablevision pulls out of thin air, because their proposal isn't real."[91] Bloomberg emphasized stadium construction as an engine for job creation, claiming that in every parade he attended, "They've screamed at me from the sidelines from beginning to end: 'Get the stadium. Those are my jobs.' "[92] Rumors swirled that integration of commercial development into the Jets's bid was orchestrated by the Bloomberg administration.

A developer confessed, anonymously, that each of the involved developers was "dependent on city government for all the deals we're doing." Another developer admitted that he was sworn to secrecy during the process and that they never met simultaneously as the Jets's bid was being coordinated. One developer suggested that their involvement helped the MTA to better "compare apples to apples" than would be possible in a straight battle between Cablevision and the Jets. Two developers privately confessed that the city might have been better off with stadium construction in Queens instead of taking on a heated political battle in Manhattan.[93]

The Queens option had been suggested for years, but the Bloomberg administration was fixated on Manhattan. On March 1, as MTA proposals for the West Side were being fine-tuned, Bloomberg indicated for the first time that he might consider stadium construction in Queens, but simultaneously argued that Queens construction would hurt the 2012 Olympic proposal. He asserted that when "you put in a bid, you have to follow the rules and deliver what was promised."[94] Jets management reacted cooly to the idea, but did not seem concerned that political pressure would push Bloomberg to abandon his Manhattan plans.[95]

Bloomberg's more flexible posturing may have been driven by election-year politics. The mayor was up for reelection, and his popularity was shaken by a single-minded dedication to the Manhattan stadium. A Quinnipiac University poll reported that if the election was held in early March, Bloomberg would have been edged out by Fernando Ferrer, former Bronx borough president, by an eight-point margin. Veteran political consultant Hank Sheinkopf argued that "the stadium has become the catch-basin for all social-class arguments." Three other candidates trailed Bloomberg by a margin of five point or less.[96]

City Council Speaker Gifford Miller, another mayoral candidate, attacked the stadium plan. He argued that the decision should be made by voters.[97] That would make the stadium debate a more central election issue, a move that would hurt Bloomberg's reelection chances. Virginia Fields, Manhattan borough president, and Congressman Anthony Weiner of Brooklyn suggested consideration of a Queens stadium. Fields spoke of a less ambitious convention center expansion and a Queens stadium as viable alternatives. Like Bloomberg, she spoke of a stadium as a job-creation tool.[98] Democratic front-runner and eventual party nominee Ferrer tried to gain traction with the stadium issue. He prominently cited a Quinnipiac Poll showing Manhattan support for stadium construction at an anemic 27 percent with opposition at a more robust 64 percent.[99] He also accused Bloomberg of rigging the bidding process to favor the Jets.[100]

On March 31, 2005, MTA Chairman Peter Kalikow announced that the Jets were chosen as the winning bid, ending weeks of suspense and drama. In typical New York fashion, the MTA decision did not even come close to settling the issue. Feeling the bidding was fixed, a bitter Ferrer held a news conference on the steps of city hall, proclaiming "I know a farce when I see one." Bloomberg countered, "it will be a very positive thing. . . . I'm not doing it for the election. I was not hired to run for re-election."[101] Nevertheless, the challenges facing Bloomberg were daunting. The platform subsidies had to next pass through the legislative process to receive a $300 million state allocation. The governor, Assembly Speaker Sheldon Silver, and Senate Majority Leader Joseph Bruno had to sign off on the construction as members of the Public Authorities Control Board.

Because the vote required unanimous approval, any of the three political leaders could undermine the project. Once Bloomberg realized this, he pushed hard to lobby Silver, whose constituency included lower Manhattan, an area rocked by the September 11 terrorist attacks. In the months preceding the vote, Bloomberg met with Silver at a golf course and at one of his favorite Kosher restaurants. He also attended several intimate family functions. Speculation emerged that Silver had the ability to gain huge benefits for his district in exchange for his support.[102] Previous political donations to Bruno's party, including a $65,000 personal donation to the state Senate Republican Committee, gave the mayor perceived leverage with the Senate majority leader.[103]

Stadium plans were challenged by a barrage of lawsuits and threats, including one from Cablevision. Attorney Randy Mastro justified their filing by asserting that "the MTA, at the behest of the mayor's office, stacked the deck in favor of the Jets at the expense of all New York taxpayers, subway riders, and commuters."[104] Other lawsuits were possible. New Jersey Attorney General Peter Harvey expressed concern that his state would be harmed by the construction. Harvey contended that "serious questions have been raised as to whether the city's transportation and sewer infrastructure can handle the strain."[105] Within the city, two advocacy groups, the Straphangers Campaign and the Tri-State Transportation Campaign, filed lawsuits for feasibility studies that underestimated the impact on transportation infrastructure during game days. Various West Side activists also entered the fray because construction could radically reshape their neighborhood.[106] Perhaps to limit such complaints, in early February, the Jets scaled back the stadium's original design so it would be less imposing. Bloomberg suggested this new design "shows that the developers are listening to the community and trying to accommodate everybody's desires to the extent that is possible."[107]

The New Jersey Sports and Exhibition Authority added yet another potential complication. They came to terms with the Giants on April 13, 2005, to build an 80,000-seat facility that could be shared with the Jets. According to the initial agreement, the Giants would pay $750 million for construction and annual rent of $6.3 million per year. The state would pick up the tab for $120 million in old stadium debt and offer between $30 to $40 million in infrastructure improvements. New Jersey's sports-crazy governor, Richard Codey, argued that the deal would save taxpayers money because they would be relieved from having to pay for improvements that were needed to bring the stadium up to the "state of art" standards required by the lease.[108] Although the Giants appeared to be on track for a new stadium, Mayor Bloomberg and the Jets worked feverishly to beat the Olympic clock, which, if allowed to tick through July, could fully undermine West Side construction. Legal squabbles had the potential to delay the Public Authorities Control Board's vote. Bloomberg set May 18 as a deadline for state officials to move forward, but any one of the three members could stall if they desired.[109]

To accelerate a decision, Jay Cross asserted if a deal was not finalized in May, a tight construction timetable would force him to call the NFL and cancel plans to host the 2010 Super Bowl.[110] Cross attempted to take the edge off his threat by involving himself in community affairs. In one such instance, he accompanied Freeman McNeil, a former Jets running back, to an elementary school near the proposed stadium site. McNeil told the youngsters, "You children are our future. That's why I'm doing all I can to get that stadium built on the West Side." Cross cheerfully remarked, "We hope that we're going to be your neighbors pretty soon."[111] A few weeks later Cross warned that delays could prompt the team to consider New Jersey options.

Bloomberg tried to rachet up the pressure, cautioning state leaders that they could be blamed if New York was not chosen by the IOC because a stadium deal was not in place.[112] Reverend Al Sharpton, a minority leader, arranged a closed-door meeting with Silver, encouraging him to support stadium construction. According to Sharpton, a positive vote would "provide jobs to those who are too often left behind."[113] The Hell's Kitchen/ Hudson Yards Alliance fought the stadium by distributing flyers, making phone calls, and drumming up grassroots support. Their leader, John Raskin, worked with colleagues to coordinate a May 14 rally in McCaffrey Park. The May 18 deadline passed without a vote, and on May 23, Governor Pataki agreed to a second delay.[114] On the same day New Jersey Governor Codey said he would not sign a lease renewal with the Jets, arguing that "if New York doesn't get the Olympics, that puts us in a much better position." Before the delay, New Jersey authorities and the Jets came close to a ten-year agreement that included an escape clause.[115]

On June 2, the State Supreme Court dismissed challenges to the MTA decision to allow the Jets to develop the railyard property. Cablevision vowed to appeal. Environmental challenges were not yet confronted, but the legal decision put pressure on the Public Authority Control Board to determine the project's fate. The board met four days later in a contentious Albany convention room packed with vocal supporters and opponents. Angry union members shouted down stadium opponents as both sides waved signs and made noise. State troopers were dispatched to prevent mayhem. Earlier that morning, the mayor's office issued a press release praising the IOC for putting New York "in the top tier of bidding cities" and asserting that "New Yorkers and Americans are counting on us." Even though the IOC gave much higher marks to London and Paris, the drama of the pending decision was palpable.

When it became clear that Bruno and Silver would not support the Manhattan stadium, a mix of moans and cheers reverberated through the room. Without unanimous support, the West Side stadium's fate was doomed. Silver argued that West Side development plans might shift the nation's financial capital away from downtown, a move that would diminish the significance of the September 11 rebuilding effort. In a news conference he pointedly asked, "Am I supposed to turn my back on lower Manhattan as it struggles to recover? For what? A stadium?"[116] Silver indicated possible willingness to support a Queens stadium, but was deeply concerned about the long-range impact of extensive ancillary commercial office space that was part of the West Side proposal.

Bloomberg was stung by the decision. Both Doctoroff and Bloomberg's private sector pedigrees hampered their ability to navigate politically sensitive waters, particularly at the state level, and they finally reached a bureaucratic impasse they could not bypass or avoid. Their use of the Olympic bid to push deadlines on political leaders caused irritation, and a last-ditch attempt to offer subsidies to businesses relocating in lower Manhattan failed to sway Silver.[117]

Bloomberg reacted with extreme disappointment, but within a week released an alternate plan that would put a new Olympic stadium in Queens, next to the Mets's current home. The Mets would abandon Shea Stadium for a new ballpark initially projected to cost $880 million. They would pay the lion's share of construction costs; the state and city would invest about $180 million. If New York won the 2012 hosting rights, taxpayers would pay an additional $108 million to convert the stadium to

Olympic standards, but NYC2012 would commit approximately $142 million of the anticipated $250 million total conversion costs.[118] The Mets and the Yankees quickly agreed to share the Yankees's new facility in 2012 if the Olympic bid was successful. Such a scenario, if successful, would put the Yankees on a more secure path to complete their project and give them added leverage in the stadium sweepstakes.

This shared arrangement was enticing because the Yankees continued to push for a new stadium even before the West Side plans fell through. In April the *New York Daily News* offered an "exclusive preview" of the new park's design. It gushed about the amenities that would be part of the new ballpark. According to Randy Levine, president of the Yankees, groundbreaking was anticipated in 2006, and the 50,800-seat ballpark would be ready in time for the 2009 season. The team said the facility would have "all the amenities of a state of the art shopping mall" and would have "six times the space for concession sales." If the retailing opportunities did not excite fans, the stadium would be "constructed to replicate the original Yankee Stadium." The Yankees would pay for all ballpark construction costs. The city and state would provide $300 million for infrastructure needs and parkland conversion.[119]

Even though the construction would be paid by the Yankees, how some of it would be paid had an ironic twist. Major League Baseball instituted a "luxury tax" for teams that wanted to spend lavish amounts to attract free-agent players, with the hope that it would make small-market teams more competitive against wealthy teams. The Yankees, as the biggest spending team in baseball, traditionally pay the most in luxury taxes. Nevertheless, the league allowed teams to deduct stadium-related costs, in effect, permitting the Yankees to spend money on a stadium that would have been otherwise directed to small-market teams in the form of a luxury tax.[120] New York taxpayers might get some break from a sports subsidy, but teams in small-market cities would lose economic ground to baseball's most valuable franchise.

As the Olympic hosting issue was gaining momentum, the Yankees organized a June 15 press conference to showcase their building plans. To maximize positive spin, the team leaked details to the *New York Post*. They reported that the plan had "plenty of political support" and was "designed to boost the economic fortunes of the South Bronx" with "little public funding." This rosy report estimated city and state commitments at $100 million.[121] The next day, the *New York Times* offered a more cautionary assessment, which suggested a $135 million city contribution, $70 million from the state, and uncertainty about financing for a rail station that would presumably be part of the MTA budget. According to the report, the state would fund new adjoining parking garages rather than direct stadium construction.[122] A few days later, Bloomberg estimated city and state contributions at $235 million for the Yankees's project. Sales tax breaks on construction materials for both the Yankees and Mets were projected to provide a possible $22 million exemption for the Yankees alone.[123] Energy-related tax breaks promised further benefit. In addition, placing the stadium on heavily used parkland had the potential to irritate local residents.

Regardless, the Yankee situation took a back seat to the 2012 Olympic bid, so for a very brief period, the Mets's situation jumped ahead of plans from the typically more popular Yankees. HOK Sport worked with New York officials to solidify design and conversion strategies, and Doctoroff and Bloomberg readied themselves for a flight to Ghana, where they would pitch a revised bid to IOC officials. IOC President Jacques Rogge praised the "quality and dedication of the New York team," and Bloomberg expressed optimism that New York could still prevail.[124] A report that a $12.5 million toxic cleanup would be needed near the Queens stadium site slowed momentum a little, but, despite an underdog position in the Olympic sweepstakes, Bloomberg and NYC2012 officials moved forward with enthusiasm.[125]

The mayor was rewarded for his resilience. In late June, with the Manhattan stadium issue off the table, public opinion began shifting in his favor. A Quinnipiac University poll revealed that he moved ahead of Democratic rival Fernando Ferrer by a 13 percent margin and 61 percent of New Yorkers supported his revised plans to build in Queens.[126] The state legislature even cooperated with him, permitting the issue of $75 million in bonds for the Yankee and Met projects respectively, and unanimously authorizing use of parkland for the Yankees's project.[127]

Olympic plans moved forward with optimism. Even though oddsmakers considered New York a longshot, a Norwegian IOC executive board member called "the new solution . . . as good as the old one," and said the Big Apple had a serious chance to host in 2012. Doctoroff reported visiting all but two of the 115 IOC's voting members.[128] The odds of New York hosting the games improved after the Queens relocation was announced.[129] In a special *New York Post* column, Bloomberg cheerily told citizens that the hosting challenge "helped galvanize support for goals that all New Yorkers share: more parks, housing, open space, and jobs."[130]

However, Bloomberg's good fortune was short lived. The Olympic hosting venue shifted to Singapore, where the New York delegation worked feverishly to influence the IOC's site selection vote. The July 6 vote unfolded with London edging out Paris for the 2012 hosting rights. New York finished a distant fourth, beating only Moscow. Although Paris was the favorite before the vote, the British delegation worked around the clock and sent its heavy hitters to lobby IOC officials, including Prime Minister Tony Blair.

The decision, though not shocking, had dramatic implications for Big Apple stadium policy. Although Bloomberg indicated that ballpark plans for the Mets would move forward regardless of the Olympic outcome, its future is less certain, and the political rationale for new construction is not as compelling. The Yankees seem likely to prevail. Despite Yankee Stadium's storied history, the dramatic renovations decades earlier have been cited as a rationale for abandoning the old park. Because of these changes, many preservationists no longer regarded Yankee Stadium as a historic landmark.[131]

However, some baseball fans disagreed and vowed to fight the plan. More ominous was community opposition, which has been vocally against construction. In a nonbinding vote on November 22, 2005, Bronx Community Board 4 voted 16-8 against the stadium plan. At issue was the loss of community parkland. The proposal would require construction on twenty-two acres of heavily used Macombs Dam and Mulally Parks. To offset the loss, the initial plan called for some recreation areas on parking garage rooftops and creation of new parklands in less central waterfront areas, which would require navigating a pedestrian tunnel to cross the Major Deegan Expressway. Later, plans were revised, and previously promised preservation of Yankee Stadium was abandoned to ensure some useful parkland in proximity to neighborhoods. Residents have been vocal in their opposition at public meetings, with Gregory Bell, chairman of Bronx Voices for Equal Inclusion asserting that the most recent plan has "no benefits for the community."[132]

On August 16, 2006, stadium groundbreaking plans moved forward. Construction of a new megamall somewhat near the proposed ballpark is now under way and has the potential to affect the Yankees's situation. Without Cablevision directly involved, press coverage of community resistance has been minimized. However, the taxpayers' role in such construction may force more careful scrutiny. Stadium expert Neil deMause estimates that the hidden cost to New Yorkers for both the Mets and Yankees's construction is likely to exceed $800 million.[133]

Not surprisingly, the Jets pulled back from Manhattan development plans, failing to meet agreed MTA deadlines.[134] The MTA has suggested mixed use development of the land, with a shift of their headquarters to the far West Side to provide an anchor tenant for the newly created office space. A six-acre park would be installed, too.[135] Meanwhile, the Jets briefly flirted with a Queens relocation, but New Jersey Governor Codey pushed his stadium deadlines forward. He took charge in negotiations, pushing the authority president George Zoffinger aside.

Codey maintained a hard line, refusing to give the Jets additional time to play Queens against New Jersey, and the Giants made concessions that made the deal more attractive. This forced the Jets to make a quick decision. Codey indicated that if the Jets came back after New Jersey stadium plans were fleshed out, they would be regarded as secondary tenants. Unwilling to risk unforseen complications in Queens, the Jets safely decided to work with the Giants. By committing early, they were assured being treated as equal partners and were in line to receive a sweetheart deal for offices and practice facilities.[136] On November 10, 2005, both teams unveiled an enclosed oval preliminary design with a capacity of nearly 90,000 seats.[137] Revised construction estimates that exceed $1 billion and a possible debate about whether a retractable roof should be integrated into the final design may complicate matters, but overall, the joint agreement appears to be moving forward.

However, the dramatic profits that have been estimated could have New Jersey legislators rethinking Codey's proposed contractual terms with both NFL teams. In January 2006, *New York Times* reporter Charles Bagli disclosed a confidential document that estimated annual revenues for advertising and premium seats alone at $183.9 million per year. Both teams received development rights for 75 acres of prime real estate in exchange for $6.3 million in rent and fees. Although the state would not subsidize a penny of stadium construction or maintenance, they would forfeit parking, suite, and advertising revenues previously collected by the sports authority. New Jersey taxpayers would also provide both teams with twenty acres for training facilities, $30 million for infrastructure, and $100 million in debt relief on the old stadium.[138]

Brooklyn's basketball arena could be jeopardized by community opposition to large skyscrapers that have been woven into the project, but Bruce Ratner's development team continues to push ahead.[139] Construction has begun on the New Jersey Devils's Newark arena, but in June 2006 the city's mayor-elect threatened to cut off funding for the project. A variety of problems have prompted officials to switch construction managers and contractors. The city has spent about $85 million on a project that is expected to cost as much as $350 million. The Devils are expected to pay $100 million for their share of construction.[140]

Across the river, Bloomberg won reelection by a twenty-point margin, clearly benefitting with the removal of the West Side stadium issue from the election agenda. He outspent his rival, Fernando Ferrer, by a ten-to-one margin, investing more than $30 million in advertising alone. His administration remains committed to stadium construction, and to bet against the billionaire mayor would be unwise. *Time* magazine named Bloomberg one of America's five best mayors in 2005, citing a falling crime rate and "an unprecedented level of transparency" as reasons for his selection. Bloomberg told *Time* that stadium building was "investing in the future."[141] While lobbying for stadiums, Bloomberg told *New Yorker* author John Cassidy that "the city and state can't pour money in unless there is an economic benefit." Bloomberg has argued "it would be a tragedy if we let the naysayers stop us from doing things."[142]

New Yorkers perceive their region as different from all others. This "exceptionalism" may allow supporters to marginalize economic comparisons to other cities. Bloomberg and Doctoroff, with grand visions for New York, have shifted gears to emphasize sports construction in the Bronx, Queens, and Brooklyn. Rudolph Giuliani's sixty-day escape clause for the Mets and Yankees, brokered during his closing days as mayor, could have long-term implications, although a move by either team is highly unlikely. If either team meets unexpected resistance in their stadium ambitions, the escape clause could force competition between New York City and a nearby suburb in the distant future, but that is not likely any time soon.

Even without a single stadium project in progress, New York has enjoyed economic success. As 2005 closed, the city was on track to issue five times more permits for residential real estate development than a decade earlier.[143] Like other cities, it struggles to meet education, infrastructure, and basic citizen needs, but tourists are visiting in record numbers, despite high hotel costs.[144] In the complex, fast-paced world of metropolitan New York, the future could involve construction of three, four, or even five major sports facilities, but only one facility might move forward as planned. Conventional wisdom suggests that, at a minimum, two sports facilities will be constructed, with at least one of them an arena, though metropolitan New York does not need such construction to validate its stature.

The lure of Olympic glory has dazzled New York's leaders. The chance of hosting future Super Bowls raised the stakes further. Local media were also deeply drawn into the issue. In June 2005, as the Olympic struggle and the Yankee ballpark issue came to a head, New York's three major newspapers offered at least eighty-eight related news articles and thirty opinion pieces, a volume somewhat more intense than other major league cities. City officials did not succeed in obtaining the 2012 Olympic games, but some leaders may look with optimism to hosting in 2016 or 2020. If the Olympic showcasing of China in 2008 is dramatically successful, New York insiders could fight harder to show off the Big Apple globally, despite being snubbed in 2005. Should they chose that path, they would have to battle several American cities and the skepticism of USOC officials who may believe that stadium uncertainties cost the nation a hosting opportunity.

Regardless of how this unfolds, stadium construction is on track in New Jersey and appears likely to succeed in the Bronx. The intoxicating allure of stadium construction has moved from smaller cities and has taken root in the nation's largest metropolitan area. As these vast stadium plans move forward in both New York and New Jersey, history will ultimately determine whether the leaders who pushed for such construction were visionaries or lemmings.

10

THE NEW CATHEDRALS AS A REFLECTION OF OUR BROADER CULTURE

THE GRUESOME REALITY of hurricane Katrina entered American homes as news crews covered the aftermath of this tragedy. The Louisiana Superdome served as host to numerous Super Bowls, but its role was now an emergency shelter. While citizens watched in horror as government officials repeatedly botched aid delivery efforts, political leaders in San Antonio jockeyed to gain the upper hand in luring the New Orleans Saints to Texas. Before water was delivered to some of Katrina's victims, San Antonio officials were announcing the possibility of an incentive package, including guaranteed sellouts, that might lure the NFL team to San Antonio. City Councilman Chip Haas boasted, "We believe that can easily be done."[1]

Although Louisiana residents had deeper concerns, team owner Tom Benson's business ties to San Antonio and his personal actions kept discussion of permanent relocation to that city alive. Benson fired Arnold Fielkow, his executive vice president of administration. Fielkow was instrumental in obtaining a ten-year $186.5 million state inducement package in 2002 to keep the Saints from contemplating a move, but his vocal support of remaining in Louisiana just three years later was cited as a likely reason for Benson's sudden dismissal of his former friend.[2]

Rumors also swirled that the team might be headed to Los Angeles. Stories suggesting that the Rose Bowl and the Los Angeles Coliseum might be willing to house the Saints added fuel to such speculation.[3] League officials discounted such talk and indicated, for the moment, they would try to keep the team in Louisiana.[4] But much of the public was skeptical; a letter in *USA Today* argued that "if Tom Benson were openly leaning toward L.A. instead of San Antonio, then [NFL Commissioner Paul] Tagliabue would probably be offering to drive the Mayflower moving van."[5] After league officials and the NFL Players' Association lobbied for continued play in Louisiana, speculation was put to rest for 2006. On December 30, 2005, Benson said he would keep the Saints in Louisiana for another year. New Orleans columnist Peter Finney wrote that this was Benson's "first positive public statements on New Orleans. . . . Until Friday, he had been acting like some weapon of mass destruction intent on abandoning his home town."[6] As a result, the long-term prognosis for the team remains uncertain.

Some argued that converting the Superdome into a hurricane shelter was a mistake, and others suggested it might need to be fully replaced. As this occurred, Florida officials proposed building a new stadium that would serve as a hurricane evacuation center. State Representative Susan Goldstein suggested that it could serve as a "safe environment," rhetorically asking "what taxpayer would vote against it?" A driving force behind the proposal was Goldstein's admission that "we could still find a way to keep the Marlins here."[7] The Marlins spent much of 2005 trying to get ballpark subsidies, but lack of success had the team contemplating deals elsewhere. Major League Baseball's top executives approved their relocation search in November.[8]

As these events were unfolding, other teams worked on stadium deals that would presumably improve their bottom line. The St. Louis Cardinals were completing a $377 million ballpark that had team officials paying about 77 percent of the tab. However, elimination of a ticket tax before construction allowed owners to put money that previously went to local needs into this project. As their stadium was nearing completion, owners argued that high stadium costs hindered their ability to spend money on players' salaries. Paradoxically, in 2004 team owner Bill DeWitt argued "the new stadium will provide us with increased revenues and the ability to have a higher payroll," prompting one area sportswriter to ask "is it too late to put the old Busch [Stadium] back together again?"[9]

Washington, D.C., entered into an agreement with Major League Baseball, but an attempt to hold team owners responsible for cost overruns on a $535 million ballpark had the potential to kill the deal.[10] Local officials planned to fund the project, but total cost estimates ballooned to $667 million by 2006. The team agreed to kick in $20 million and later pushed for arbitration to minimize further cost to them.[11] The Oakland Athletics began a push for a new ballpark, too, exploring options that might move their stadium dreams forward. For 2006, they planned to limit seating capacity in their current ballpark to a mere 34,179, closing their entire upper deck.[12]

The Minnesota Twins kept lobbying after repeated failures to get subsidies for a new $478 million ballpark.[13] The Minnesota Vikings also fought an uphill battle for stadium subsidies, proposing a $675 million facility in Anoka County.[14] This was initially sidetracked by calls for a referendum, but was later pushed to the sidelines after several team members were accused of engaging in a bizarre sex cruise on Lake Minnetonka. The national attention these allegations received caused palpable anger. One irate resident wrote, "Do the Vikings deserve a new stadium? Does Hitler deserve to be canonized? If we give these overgrown, lecherous, promiscuous, overpaid, spouse-abusing, substance-abusing embarrassments to this state a new stadium, then we all deserve to have our heads examined."[15] Team owner Zygi Wilf apologized profusely and subsequently fired his head coach, but the public now had powerful ammunition to oppose the team's subsidy request, so supportive legislators pulled back.

Other NFL teams fared better. The Cowboys worked out a deal with Arlington, and contractors were clearing away more than 100 homes and 1000 apartments to construct a $650 million stadium. The NFL team would pay a total of $60 million in the next thirty years for their new home.[16] The Phoenix Cardinals were ready to unveil a $370.6 million stadium, also contributing less than 10 percent of the total project costs.[17] The Giants and Jets appeared on track for their new home in the New Jersey Meadowlands but were on the hook to pay for construction.

The Indianapolis Colts may have arranged for the best deal of all. They agreed to pay $100 million of the total costs for a $625 million retractable roof stadium that was set to open in 2008. They were given $48 million from the city to break their existing lease. They also received $34 million as a forgivable loan from the NFL and were promised all naming rights income.[18] If these rights bring $50 million, they could pocket $32 million and be on the hook for a $250,000 annual rental fee, less than $5 per season ticket sold per year. Despite that, owner Robert Irsay stressed the team's "risk" on groundbreaking day, explaining, "We have a very difficult road ahead of us—one that we think we'll be successful in."[19] While lobbying for this stadium in 2002, NFL Commissioner Paul Tagliabue told the *Indianapolis Star*'s editorial board that stadium-related scholarship is insufficient and often poorly prepared. Tagliabue argued, in particular, that economic claims made by scholars were off base. He confidently stated that "when I retire and get some time to write in academic journals, I'm going to do a little writing about what's been done by some economists that, if it was me, I would be embarrassed to publish."[20]

A few months later, in ABC's Super Bowl pregame show, Tagliabue hinted that San Diego, the host for the 2003 game, could forfeit future hosting opportunities unless steps were taken to build a new stadium. The Phoenix area quickly jumped in, making a case that its willingness to build a new stadium put it in a position to displace San Diego as a future Super Bowl host.[21] Arizona was awarded hosting rights in 2008, and future bidding has been made more enticing to cold weather cities with the selection of Detroit's Ford Field as host in 2006. Metropolitan New York and Indianapolis now look with optimism at hosting possibilities. Kansas City officials proposed a $312 million renovation of Arrowhead Stadium, speculating they might be able to host this event if they could add a roof to their plans.[22]

Although San Diego's finances have been severely strained and the city has faced political upheaval, the Chargers continue their push for a new stadium. The team hired the former Super Bowl director Jim Steeg as executive vice president. In a press release for a luncheon introducing Steeg, participants were encouraged to "ask Steeg about the plans for a Super Bowl quality stadium."[23] Because taxpayer money is not available, the Chargers proposed picking up the full cost of a $450 million stadium and up to $175 million of traffic-related expenses in exchange for sixty acres of free land at the current Qualcomm Stadium site. The team hoped to use that land to build condominiums, a hotel, offices, parking, parkland, and retail shops. They hoped to line up a partner to finance the development and then put the issue up to a public vote.[24] The team has since retreated, backing out of the plan, so talk of a departure from San Diego after the 2008 season, presumably to nearby Los Angeles, has intensified.

It is within this context that the stadium issue continues to affect cities throughout America. League officials have more lavish resources than a typical academic scholar will ever see, but the logic of stadium-related scholarship will not be undermined by league-generated commentary. The realities of new stadium construction do not support growth claims of partisan local documents, but league officials in both baseball and football have a decided advantage over academic analysts in access to the public. Although researchers may struggle to bring their work to a wider audience, in an information-rich society, the public has the ability to cut through the rhetoric and determine whether the arguments made by team owners and league officials are credible. The "quality of life" arguments may have validity, but claims that substantial economic growth follow taxpayer investment have less merit no matter what form of analysis is employed. At the core of the subsidy issue is public perception and regional boosterism. Declining cities cling to a hope that a "major league" image will help them to retain the luster of yesteryear, and growing metropolitan areas hope that a new team will somehow validate their emerging national stature. But without a threat of some sort, most stadium subsidies would not occur.

For some cities, failure to build could result in the loss of a Super Bowl, an All-Star Game, or an Olympic hosting opportunity. For many other cities, a major hosting event is less likely, but the loss of a team to another city is a deep concern. In each case, threats force urban leaders to make difficult choices. More secure and culturally diverse cities fare better in attempts to hold off taxpayer subsidies, but metropolitan New York, with its enormous cultural capital, has been pulled into the subsidy game. The recent carrot of Olympic and Super Bowl hosting opportunities seemed too tempting to pass up for some city officials, as was the potential for a legacy that included presiding over decisions that would reshape the city for generations. These deals are often moved forward by real estate and labor interests who benefit from such construction. Despite lukewarm public response, big egos, boosterism, and power politics make stadium construction highly tempting, even in New York.

History as a Barometer for Stadium-Related Policy Formulation

How historians will regard our recent obsession with stadium construction is uncertain, but several generations from now, sociologists, anthropologists, and urban scholars are likely to put a negative spin on this preoccupation. Examination of how this issue has unfolded since the emergence of the professional sports stadium might provide some clues about how we will be regarded long after today's new ballparks have been replaced.

Some historians suggest that events and activities occur in cycles with accompanying policy moving in a fluid, pendulum-like manner. Unfortunately, such an analysis often oversimplifies reality and fails to consider broad philosophic shifts that may occur within a culture. In the case of the stadium issue, building booms may have occurred in cycles, but the funding and subsidy patterns are not so simple. In the Progressive Era and before World War II, stadium subsidies were rare and team owners had considerably less clout. This dynamic changed in the second half of the twentieth century. When one looks at the public's role in new ballpark construction, broad-based public input has typically been pushed to the margins in every era of stadium construction. News coverage bias favoring selected community leaders has existed throughout the history of this issue. This is not a recent development.

The linkage between civic pride and ballpark construction emerged during the Progressive Era. Before then, isolated evidence could be found linking community pride to ballpark construction, but it was not a common theme. Until the steel and concrete era supplanted the rickety wooden structures that served the early pioneers of team sports, there was little reason for a community to have deep pride in its ballparks. Progressive Era coverage tended to support a hierarchical society in a manner that was consistent with the managerial imperatives of the time. The rise of Taylorism, a scientific approach to factory production, shifted labor from craftsmanship to specialization. In the same manner, ballpark construction emphasized the specialized skill of the architect and various building trades. Specialized equipment used by players was another reflection of the time, as was the introduction of turnstiles and other features that gradually allowed ballparks to become more lavish.

Construction coverage in 1909 focused on the specialized box seating and new building supplies that were necessary for project completion. These materials were obtained from a diverse range of vendors and shipped to the community via railroad. Citizens may have developed a sense of awe for these projects. More importantly for leaders of the day, the public may have been prompted to accept scientific management in the workplace even if workers were exposed to traditional apprenticeships and old labor methods in prior generations. Coverage of stadium construction helped reinforce broad sociological changes as they unfolded.

Media coverage also helped to cultivate baseball as an important cultural institution. Recognition of the local ballpark as a symbol of civic pride helped to cement the relationship between a community and its team. The owner became a local figurehead and received positive coverage throughout the process. Because taxpayer subsidies were not sought, press coverage steered clear of critical remarks about team owners. Nevertheless, owners were established as mercenaries, much as others in the business community. Publicity about renting the stadium for other entertainment performances gave Progressive Era citizens a firm understanding that the profit motive was the driving force behind new ballpark construction.

Team owners made a number of savvy moves to solidify their position within the community as Progressive Era ballpark construction unfolded. Many of these moves involved inclusion of key leaders in the process. The ceremonial involvement of important politicians in opening day events and carefully orchestrated stadium inspections from league officials helped enhance team owner credibility at a time when some citizens may have looked with suspicion on the cultural stature of professional athletics. Such coverage also served as a latent lesson in community power. Owners may not have been at the top of the pecking order, but they gained credibility through publicity that chronicled their limited access to more powerful dignitaries.

Visits from national political leaders, such as the nation's president, worked to further heighten this credibility. Such visits also served to build a sense of civic pride that allowed citizens to believe they were involved in a community activity that was truly special. The opening of Yankee Stadium in 1923 involved New York's popular governor as well as world renowned maestro John Philip Sousa. As the 1920s began, the Yankees were not as popular as the rival New York Giants, but a winning team and a luxurious new stadium changed that dynamic. A blend of political and cultural institutions helped the Yankees to eventually solidify their role within the community. The serendipitous timing of Babe Ruth's on-field exploits and the construction of Yankee Stadium helped a team with less prestige to win the hearts of many sports fans in the nation's most powerful city. After ballpark construction was completed, successful teams and compelling personalities such as Ruth, Gehrig, and DiMaggio created an environment that served to shift Big Apple allegiances. The Yankees were able to position themselves as the city's number one baseball team when Horace Stoneham moved his Giants to San Francisco. Without construction of a new and impressive stadium in 1923, the sports landscape may have been different and a change in fan loyalties may not have occurred.

The second era of stadium construction differed in many ways from the Progressive Era. After World War II civic leaders were more profoundly integrated into the process. Planning became more important. Unorganized, impromptu ballpark construction was now a distant memory. Taxpayer subsidies gradually emerged as a core ingredient in arranging construction. Even though the public was not a major part of stadium-related decisions, the subsidy component opened the issue to greater levels of public scrutiny. Pittsburgh offered one indication that the public could be woven into media coverage of stadium building. The civil rights marches that used the stadium as a backdrop demonstrated the symbolic power of sports within a community.

Coverage during Riverfront Stadium's construction showcased the power of media institutions to shape public policy on stadium issues. *Cincinnati Enquirer* management was at the forefront of pushing for construction. When it looked as though taxpayer funds for stadium planning would stop, executives at the *Enquirer* actively rallied the business community for support. Without their involvement, policy may have moved in a different direction. Such involvement raises questions about whether opposition voices were pushed to the margins in news coverage. After all, the executives at the *Cincinnati Enquirer* were publicly committed to this project, and examples of stadium opposition in the newspaper during this era were rare.

New York and Boston coverage of stadium construction during this era demonstrated the political difficulties of publicly sponsored stadium projects. The site selection debacle in the Boston area's football stadium planning and New York Mayor John Lindsay's miscalculated Yankee Stadium construction estimates revealed the limitations of political officials in major urban areas. Both projects took place at a time when large American cities faced financial and social crises. In both cities, key political leaders were unable to inspire public confidence in urban management. In Boston, the result was team movement to suburban Foxborough. In New York, the result was an expensive renovation of an area landmark at a time when essential city services were under siege. In light of what transpired as the Yankee Stadium project unfolded, it was not surprising that the city lost an NFL franchise to neighboring New Jersey in the 1970s.

The Current Landscape: Boosterism and the Desire to Hold On to Major League Status

The third era of stadium construction reveals a shift in power from political and civic leaders to sports franchise owners. By the late 1980s, team owners were making demands for both new stadiums and a larger portion of the stadium revenue streams. Metropolitan areas that were insecure about their "major league" status typically caved in to such demands. Up-and-coming cities with sports-friendly local leadership and a desire to demonstrate their ascent to the "major leagues" might ante up as well. Cities with greater confidence resisted multimillion-dollar subsidies, at least initially. In some cases, cities that did not acquiesce to such demands lost their teams. Houston lost its NFL franchise to smaller Nashville, but later paid a very high price to get an expansion franchise. Los Angeles lost two NFL teams to Oakland and St. Louis.

During this period, more focus was placed on team voices than ever before. Public resistance to subsidies intensified, but nervous political leaders often gave team owners what they wanted to avoid political fallout associated with the loss of a major league team. A few metropolitan areas, such as Boston and Los Angeles, refused to cave in to subsidy demands. In metropolitan Boston, subsidy was minimized, and the outcome was positive. In Los Angeles, professional football has not returned, but is likely to do so at the expense of another city. In other areas, such as Pittsburgh and Cincinnati, generous subsidies were given, so teams remained in place. New York's situation exposed stadium construction as real estate development deals with power politics at their core. The opportunity costs of building more conventional structures on Manhattan's West Side diminished the potential of stadium construction, but the project was ultimately killed because two powerful state legislators opposed it. Sheldon Silver's concern that such construction would challenge redevelopment of Manhattan's financial district after the 2001 terrorist attacks ultimately led to its demise. Bronx construction is likely to move forward despite local opposition to use of public parkland, but the outcome is not certain.

During stadium campaigns, team owners and their allies were often key political donors, offering support for those willing to back their cause. This alliance of money and power serves to make resolution of the stadium issue exceedingly difficult. Even with strong public opposition, building continues at a brisk pace as the third major era of stadium construction begins to wind down. New York's immersion into the high-stakes stadium building game marks a watershed for this era, and Los Angeles may eventually follow.

In some complicated and esoteric issues, the public may have an insufficient level of expertise to comment on public policy in a coherent and responsible manner. However, the stadium issue is one in which the public can be easily educated and should be regarded as participants in the decision making process. Such public involvement might complicate the lives of team owners and selected political leaders, but the result of not incorporating the public into the process could be lower levels of political efficacy in cities where individuals are locked out of the process. Furthermore, the ramifications of behind-the-scenes maneuvering might be more corrosive over time than civic leaders and team owners might realize.

In contrast to less populous cities, a stadium is unlikely to have a dramatic impact on how New York perceives itself. This region's intense belief that it serves as a national cultural center appears to be partially responsible for less initial media coverage of the stadium issue than other cities. Downplayed coverage may be desired by those planning new construction. However, the West Side stadium project eventually gained coverage similar to smaller cities. New York's media practitioners and their customer base seem to regard blind imitation of trends in other cities as unacceptable, but when a large global event such as the Olympics was injected into the dynamic, New York became intensely drawn into the stadium issue.

It is not surprising that until this development, New York tended to provide less media focus on stadium construction issues than was apparent in Boston, Pittsburgh, and Cincinnati. Boosterism in New York is predicated on its perceived role in setting trends, not a demonstrated capacity to parrot building trends that have become commonplace elsewhere. Because new stadium construction would place New York in an imitative mode, it would conspire to make such construction less appealing for many of its citizens. Some New Yorkers might enjoy visiting other cities on occasion but would react with horrified revulsion if asked to use these locales as a routine source for establishing trends in their own community.

The reason for this is rather simple. In many ways, New York regards itself as more than just a national city. It is a world city, a metropole that projects culture on a global scale. Arts and other forms of cultural entertainment dwarf those of smaller cities. Nonprofit cultural institutions, art galleries, auction houses, commercial theaters, and motion picture and televison production institutions sustain New York elites with forms of cultural capital that render them if not impervious then less bound up with the stadium as the ultimate source of civic pride.

When the economists of culture and arts James Heilbrun and Charles

M. Gray compared direct per capita expenditure on the arts in New York with Minneapolis–St. Paul and five other small to medium-sized U.S. cities, they found "the differences in magnitude to be striking." According to their data from two decades ago, "The arts in New York annually generate $182 of direct expenditure per capita, compared with only $15.24 in Minneapolis–St. Paul and $9.96 in the six cities as a whole." The five other cities included Columbus, St. Louis, Salt Lake City, San Antonio, and Springfield, Illinois. With a budget of $103 million in 1998, New York City's Department of Cultural Affairs actually outspent the National Endowment for the Arts, and the city's capital budget claimed to have funds in the range of $164 million available, if necessary, for construction projects by cultural institutions.[25]

The lack of a New York stadium referendum may have contributed to less extensive early coverage, but minimal enthusiasm for the 1987 New Jersey ballpark referendum, a vote that would have directly affected the New York sports power structure, suggests that even if an initiative was part of the media landscape, it would not have altered a tendency to downplay this issue. Limited discussion with individuals in metropolitan New York tends to support the hypothesis that stadium construction is not perceived as an important regional concern.

Evidence of an exceedingly strong commitment to cultural assets unrelated to sports suggests that stadium coverage limitations in New York may accurately reflect public priorities on this issue. Media practitioners in New York might not be unfairly suppressing coverage of the issue. However, with the enormous scope of the New York 2012 Olympic project, there was a danger that civic leaders were working behind the scenes to minimize coverage so that relative silence on the stadium subsidy issue would be interpreted as consent. A brief spike in coverage of the Olympic stadium issue suggests that New York media try to counter elite attempts to work below the radar screen. However, the limited follow-through on public resistance to the new Yankee ballpark suggests a below-the-radar leadership strategy may be unfolding.

Boston, another large market city, generally reacted with self-assurance when confronted with owner threats regarding stadium subsidies. Boston's boosterism appears to be localized, but a more broad-based regional boosterism could be uncovered that ties into the area's focus on history and heritage. The local/regional dichotomy further complicated New England's unique brand of boosterism. The citizens of Foxborough used their suburban football stadium as a platform for small town boosterism. Other areas regarded their neighborhoods as sufficiently developed and not in need of a new stadium to define their cultural identity.

Even though the Boston area was faced with possible NFL franchise relocation, opinion content leaned against stadium subsidy. Despite that, negative voices in Boston's news coverage were pushed to the sidelines more than in any other city. Boston coverage favored pro-stadium voices by more than a four-to-one margin during the period analyzed, and more than one in five voices were neutral. Inflammatory statements had the potential to push the Patriots to the highly subsidized Hartford stadium plan. Opinion expression in the Boston area may have been constrained by this reality. Under such circumstances, civic and political leaders may have minimized public pronouncements about subsidy opposition.

But *Boston Globe* news coverage of social issues unrelated to stadium coverage provided not-so-subtle arguments that were anti-stadium subsidy in nature. These indirect attacks of stadium subsidies would not have been uncovered in a simple quantitative comparison of stadium stories. As an example, one news story focused on lack of affordable housing for the poor and the efforts of Julie McKinney, a local Habitat for Humanity director. Her attempt to raise $300,000 to pay for unexpected construction-related expenses was contrasted with pending approval of $70 million in infrastructure support at the site of a new stadium for the Patriots. The article closed by stating that "while John Harrington was selling Bostonians on a new ballpark and Bob Kraft was accepting taxpayer contributions to his new stadium, Julie McKinney was wondering where in the world she would find enough money to build . . . a roof."[26]

Boston-area public opinion was complicated by possible team relocation and emotional nostalgia for an old ballpark. Despite both issues, one public opinion poll taken as these issues were unfolding revealed that residents opposed stadium subsidies but were willing to assist with nonstadium infrastructure subsidies. According to the poll, conducted by RKM Research for the *Boston Herald,* 60 percent of those questioned "opposed . . . public spending on the bricks and mortar of a stadium, while just 32 percent support[ed] it." Infrastructure support for public transit, parking, and roadways surrounding a stadium site received more enthusiastic support, with "62 percent supporting the idea and 30 percent opposing it."[27]

Once ballpark legislation was crafted that made Red Sox management responsible for cost overruns, new construction became unlikely. For many baseball fans, this was regarded as a victory. Some citizens regarded the thought of a shiny new facility as something that would be incongruent with the city's reverence for history. This attitude made it possible for Save Fenway Park! to mobilize grassroots interest in preservation. This activism was justified because Fenway Park as an historical landmark served as a tangible way of presenting Boston's uniqueness to the rest of the nation. Many citizens were subsequently convinced that a new ballpark should be constructed, but only after a carefully orchestrated campaign presented the new ballpark as an attempt to preserve the historic charm and tradition created by the old ballpark. For now, Fenway's future appears to be secure, as local leaders have authorized limited ballpark expansion and unique merchandising opportunities for the Red Sox that includes game-day closure of Yawkey Way for team-related commerce.

Some Boston-area decisions have been predicated on parochialism. Regardless, such insular decision making may have paid unexpected long-term dividends. Parochialism is one element that allowed the Boston area to cling to tradition in a way that tends to elude other regions. If the wrecking ball was put to more heavy use in all areas of construction, as frequently occurred in other cities after World War II, Boston may have sacrificed much of its uniqueness.

Boosterism of a very traditional nature was exposed in Cincinnati and Pittsburgh. These small market cities gave readers access to a greater number of pro-stadium voices in opinion columns, suggesting that new stadiums construction may be equated with civic boosterism in markets with fewer cultural resources. Cincinnati's citizens may feel that they were duped in the construction of Paul Brown Stadium, but they know that they were, at a minimum, invited into the process, however flawed that process might have been. Citizens in Pittsburgh may not have a similar feeling. Instead, they know that the decision to build was initially triggered by the Allegheny County RAD Board, a collection of appointed bureaucrats. The board members were not elected and were somewhat shielded from political fallout. RAD Board members are rarely examined by journalists in routine reporting assignments, and their names are largely unfamiliar to anyone except those who are well connected or exceedingly attentive.

Just as the steel titans of an earlier era guided policy without much input, local political and civic leaders in Pittsburgh have succeeded in getting their way without pushing hard to understand what alternatives might have been more palatable to the public. The result has been the construction of two state-of-the-art facilities, but another by-product may be a public that is more skeptical about the governing system that triggered the construction. In both Cincinnati and Pittsburgh, the long-term effect of stadium subsidy and subsequent construction could be diminished citizen trust in area leadership.

Skepticism of this nature can manifest itself in unanticipated ways. The heavy administrative hand of Pittsburgh steel magnates during the Progressive Era was countered by public resistance to their philanthropic efforts. Such philanthropic actions may have been part of a series of good-faith efforts intended to improve the quality of life for the less affluent in the city, but many of these citizens reflexively chased less-cultured commercial recreation in part because of a deep-seated uneasiness about the intentions of more powerful affluent citizens.

The popularity of baseball in the early twentieth century was one result of these citizen choices. Baseball became an acceptable activity for both elites and the broader public for vastly different reasons. For elites, it inculcated a set of ideologies that served their capitalist mind-set. For others, it provided an opportunity to bind with fellow citizens in a ritual that may have been influenced by elites but was not fully controlled by them. Pittsburgh's Barney Dreyfuss may have been friendly with Andrew Carnegie, but the steel titan did not measure his community stature by his ability to obtain skybox seating at major sporting events. That dynamic has changed in recent decades.

Team owners have been the short-term beneficiaries of this trend, with NFL attendance steadily increasing from more than 14 million fans in 1994 to more than 17 million in 2005 and baseball attendance exceeded 73 million in 2006. Both were all-time records. However, fan support is no longer as deep as it once was. Now that the trappings of sports spectatorship have become a more tangible measure of one's status in the community, those unable to play or attend the game may turn away entirely or watch only when convenient. Evidence of this is unfolding.

Television ratings for professional team-oriented sports have slipped in recent years. *New York Post* media critic Phil Mushnick argued that as the 2002 World Series drew to a close, "I have heard from at least a dozen life-long baseball fans who claimed that [they] didn't come close to making it through any of this year's first six . . . games." The opening game drew a 9.4 rating, an all-time low for a first game telecast. In the Nielsen ratings for that week, the game had fewer viewers than NBC's *Good Morning Miami*, a program that was kept off the air during the February 2003 sweeps because of concerns about its ability to attract viewers. Ratings have not improved since. *USA Today* described the 2005 World Series as "the least watched in history."[28]

The case for football may be stronger, but the NFL should be uneasy about fan loyalty, too. In the same week as the 2002 World Series, Monday Night Football managed to break into the Nielsen's top twenty, but just barely. The 49ers versus Seahawks game, held at a shiny new Seattle stadium, ranked 20th overall and was eclipsed on the same night by four different shows.[29] The NFL and the networks have taken substantial steps to limit ratings slippage. For the first time, in 2003 NFL playoff games were shifted from afternoon to prime time. The NFL also has worked harder to broaden their audience base, running promotional spots at the end of network soap operas. The result seems to have achieved success, with the 2005 Super Bowl attracting the fifth-largest audience ever.[30] Nevertheless, nine months later, CBS had the lowest ratings ever for their regular season Sunday NFL broadcasts, drawing just 6.4 percent of all households.[31]

Multiple cable channels have siphoned off sports audiences in many areas, complicating comparisons across decades. But in many instances today, other network programs have jumped ahead of traditional professional team sports. As this has occurred, alternatives such as golf and auto racing have increased their market share at the expense of team sports. A substantial increase in cable programming for extreme sports, such as ESPN's X-Games, suggest that the coveted youth demographic is not loyally locked into passive acceptance of an established sports paradigm. Even pseudo-sports such as professional wrestling have made inroads on the youth market in a manner that draws spectators from stadium-oriented team sports. In 2001 *New York Times* reporter Jere Longman reported that "average television sports audiences" for pro team sports had declined 22 percent since 1990, but the insight of several industry insiders and academic experts was unable to pinpoint why this had occurred.[32]

In such a complex media environment, alienating fans with subsidy demands may be damaging in the long-term. Visits to Internet chat rooms and blogs offer evidence of a fan backlash against the arrogance of major league sports. The stadium issue is sometimes embedded into the vitriol, but other factors also irritate long-time sports fans. Trends in sporting good sales may provide even more ominous evidence that stadium-oriented sports may face a difficult future. Sales of skateboarding equipment now outpace sales of baseball equipment in sporting goods stores. Soccer has also emerged as more popular with youth than in generations past. Participation in youth soccer tripled from 1980 to 1995.[33] Baseball participation among youth has declined with approximately 300,000 fewer participants in 2004 than in 1996. In Maryland, the number of Little League teams dropped from 2,003 to 1,721 in the past three years.[34]

Football may be the most secure sport in revenue production, but it is not safe from future declines as a new generation of sports fan emerges. *Street and Smith's Sports Business Journal* reported that football participation among youth declined 9.6 percent from 1995 to 2000, but skateboarding rose a dramatic 102.2 percent and snowboarding rose by 53.6 percent.[35] The NFL and Major League Baseball now must compete against Tony Hawk and other extreme sports icons as well as the emergence of NASCAR as a commercial force.

Traditional sports insiders are not likely to back down without a fight. Major League Baseball and the NFL have both involved themselves in public service and initiatives that involve youth in their sport in some manner. The NFL has launched its own cable network and has succeeded in placing it in 50 million TV households. They also signed an agreement with Sirius, a satellite radio provider, to broadcast games and have entered into licensing agreements with video game manufacturers, credit card companies, and a fantasy sports league.[36] Baseball has made a number of similar moves.

The dedication of $3 million in resources to construct a New York City Little League field offers further evidence that some individuals are willing to push hard to ensure that traditional sporting institutions retain their popular appeal.[37] Nearby Bergen County, New Jersey, recently poured $5 million into refurbishing Overpeck Park for their Little League.[38] In 2002, Acting Massachussetts Governor Jane Swift signed legislation leasing state owned property to Mini-Fenway, Inc., for construction of a $7.5 million mini-replica of Fenway Park for Little League play. In this instance, plans have been funded through private donations.[39]

Many other communities have overseen multimillion-dollar construction projects for local ballpark renovation or new minor league ballparks. In fact, minor league subsidies have contributed to a 29 percent increase in minor league fan attendance over the past nine years and a resurgence in baseball interest at small and mid-sized cities throughout the nation.[40] On the football field, construction has followed a similar trajectory. Valdosta

High School in Georgia allocated $7.5 million to a renovation of its football facility, and Lafayette Jefferson High School devoted $8 million in private funds to a football stadium with a high-tech video scoreboard and an athletic complex. But that pales in comparison to two Texas high schools. Each has built separate football facilities at a cost of over $20 million apiece.

These efforts might help preserve the status quo in sports, but there is no assurance that the public will continue to support baseball and football with the same enthusiasm and passion as prior generations, particularly if such support requires sacrifice of other community resources. Shortly after moving the Browns to Baltimore, team owner Art Modell told a Cleveland reporter that "the pride and presence of a professional football team is far more important than thirty libraries."[41] Presumably, his remark was intended to suggest that Cleveland-area residents needed to make greater collective sacrifices if they intended to retain an NFL franchise. Yet if cities cut back on libraries and other quality-of-life services, it is hard to imagine no animosity toward team owners who ultimately benefit from stadium-related subsidies.

In the short term, major league owners may win, but the long-term outcome is much less predictable. If the value of major league team sports is diminished as a publicly marketable commodity, it is possible that media emphasis of these sports will also change. For stadium subsidy, brief campaigns may be an effective way to gain temporary public support, particularly when the threat of team relocation is made. Owners and select community elites may gain slightly more than 50 percent support at the ballot box, getting precisely what they want from less connected citizens, but such orchestrated victories may be Pyrrhic. The elite voices may have successfully controlled the news agenda, receiving the bulk of quotations, but they cannot alter the fundamental street-level outcome of their policy victories.

The result of stadium subsidies, tax revenues funneled to team owners, and the ironic increase of ticket prices after these subsidies are arranged are embedded in media messages that are interpreted by less-privileged opinion leaders throughout each community. Because of this, it is unlikely that broad-based, long-term public satisfaction for a policy that transfers millions of dollars in taxpayer resources from all citizens, including the lower and middle class, to a select group of wealthy citizens can be sustained indefinitely. Owners who have obtained their desired subsidy may feel tangible short-term benefits, but an erosion of community support may occur as the novelty of a shiny new ballpark wears off and the bills for such facilities continue to be paid.

If the American economy weakens substantially, falling into an extended recession, long-term disenchantment with such subsidies may be intensified. The softening of the American economy between 2001 and 2003 prompted cities contemplating stadium construction to move with caution, but new stadium construction has been gaining steam in some areas since. Failure to consider an uncertain economic landscape could be a recipe for political suicide. In Missouri, earlier overtures by the legislature to fund a baseball complex for the St. Louis Cardinals faced intense pressure. Sensing public distaste for such subsidies, the Missouri legislature intentionally kept it off the agenda in their final 2001 session. Eric Stern, a reporter for the *St. Louis Post-Dispatch,* described the stadium subsidy as "one of the most politically unpopular ideas they will be facing [in 2002]."[42] Missouri politicians steered clear of outright subsidies but quietly crafted legislation that brought tax relief and desired infrastructure support to the Cardinals. Team owners threatened to move to suburban Illinois, but public pressure forced the team to pay for a greater share of construction than they might like.

Fan loyalty allowed the Cardinals to maintain the seventh highest ticket prices of all major league franchises in their old ballpark, and they were competitive enough to advance to the World Series in 2004. The team attracted more than three million fans as the old ballpark closed and did so since 1998.[43] The old Busch Stadium was enjoyed by fans, too. A *USA Today Sports Weekly* survey released in February 2003 of more than 7,000 baseball fans voted the old facility fourth favorite of all major league ballparks, a result that may not occur for the new ballpark.[44]

The principal owner of the team, Bill DeWitt, is no stranger to the stadium construction issue. His father owned a majority stake in the Cincinnati Reds, selling the team in 1968 as the Riverfront Stadium project moved forward. DeWitt subsequently held a minority role in the Texas Rangers, an ownership arrangement that made him a financial partner and personal friend of the current president of the United States. In both Cincinnati and Texas, the taxpayers picked up millions in expenses for ballpark construction.

Cincinnati is a case where the teams stayed put, but poor management has caused a boomerang effect for new stadium construction. Instead of positive national publicity for the region, the heavy subsidies brought derisive coverage. On February 18, 2003, NBC produced a television package for its evening news segment called "The Fleecing of America" that highlighted Cincinnati because "taxpayers are stuck paying for thousands of empty seats" after sports fans reacted appropriately to many seasons of futility on the field. Cincinnati's woes moved to a more global scale when the *Financial Times,* a publication more likely to focus on the economics of European sports, offered a lengthy article on the subject on February 22, 2003. In the article, Harvard law professor Paul Weiler suggested that the lawsuit filed against the city's football team might have some chance of victory despite league attempts to frame the lawsuit as absurd and frivolous.[45] A legal victory of any type would mean even more negative publicity for Cincinnati and could cause a franchise exodus.

The relocation of the Montreal Expos to Washington, D.C., has the capacity to bring some of the sobering realities of stadium subsidies to the more direct attention of national leaders. The Redskins move to Maryland in the 1990s was done in a manner that limited subsidies to $70.5 million in infrastructure support, but the baseball relocation scenario will not follow such a path and has the potential to be somewhat messy. Washington, D.C., was pitted against Portland, Oregon. As plans took shape, the Washington ballpark was projected to cost as much as $436 million. As the mayor, Anthony Williams, put his ideas on the table, the city was "bracing for deep budget cuts in basic services."[46] Portland was struggling with one of the nation's highest unemployment rates. One Portland reporter indicated they were contemplating "drastic cuts in everything from medical benefits to the school calendar." To keep high school sports from the budget axe, private donations were solicited.[47]

After Washington became Major League Baseball's choice, the team was renamed the Nationals amid great fanfare. By the end of March 2005, the city's Chief Financial Officer, Natwar Gandhi, indicated that the new ballpark cost could be as high as $581 million.[48] The debate over land acquisition costs has intensified and will move the cost even higher.[49] The ballpark is expected to be completed in 2008 or 2009 and costs will likely exceed $650 million. During the interim, the Nationals play in Robert F. Kennedy Stadium. The proximity of the Nationals to the corridors of power make this a potential watershed in prompting federal confrontation of the stadium issue.

Political action is unlikely without public outcry, however, as national leaders have generally treated sports issues with kid gloves. Stephen

Lowe, an expert on congressional involvement with professional sports, argues that "Congress has failed to move authoritatively regarding professional sports when clear public support was lacking. Yet, the issue directly affects large segments of the American public and Congress has tended to move on issues of public interest. . . . The franchise relocation issue [which is predicated on stadium subsidies,] will present Congress with a huge and unavoidable challenge in the future."[50]

The impact of the September 11, 2001, terrorist attacks and the subsequent war on terrorism had a brief dampening impact on stadium construction, but by early 2003, stadium planning regained momentum. Projects in metropolitan Dallas, New York, and Indianapolis appear to be moving forward, and others may begin, too. Sport, once used by politicians to earn easy political points with the public, has now become difficult terrain for political leaders. Increasing federal deficits might intensify pressure to fund programs that may have been underwritten in prior years by national revenues. Such pressure could eventually bring greater public scrutiny for large capital outlays for recreational activity. Back-door funding approaches might be tried in some metropolitan areas, but the spending levels for these sports projects are too large to fully sneak past taxpayers.

Financing ideas that put a greater part of the construction burden on team owners might emerge unless a strong economy shifts public sensibilities away from bottom-line taxpayer concerns. If these ideas truly put team owners in a position of paying more, progress will have been made. However, if the result is transfer of funding to sports fans in the form of exorbitant seat license fees or a process that allows tax-generated revenue streams to be quietly diverted, then the long-term result could be potential alienation of sports fans and the broader public.

The Ballpark, Public Policy, and the Implications for Future Media Practices

The stadium subsidy issue resonates with many Americans. Media coverage of the issue reflects a variety of institutional and personal biases. Gaye Tuchman's examination of media routines attempts to politely couch such biases as the media's tendency to "frame" an issue, much in the same way that a window offers a framed view of a landscape but limits the parameters of what is viewed. Despite the limitation of a media "frame," media coverage allows us latitude for interpretation within the context of that particular frame. Tuchman asserts that this interpretive ability is limited, however. According to Tuchman, the news reporter's focus on "facticity" distances the public from involvement in the political process while giving special status to facts produced by institutional leaders.[51]

As institutional actors retain their foothold on the media agenda, the public is typically left on the sidelines and kept out of the policy-making process. The stadium issue appears to offer a potential exception to this tendency. The public's familiarity with the sports landscape and the basic knowledge of what is at stake offers the possibility of a more active public role in the democratic process. The outcry regarding subsidies in various media markets suggests that this is a topic with which the public is willing to invest personal capital in order to contribute to a policy outcome. Despite potential public enthusiasm, traditional news routines, as outlined by Tuchman, appear to have curtailed citizen involvement on the stadium issue.

Dramatic public outcry was effective in defeating Pittsburgh's Regional Renaissance initiative in November 1997, but once the debate shifted to implementation of "Plan B," the public was frozen out of the process by reporting that offered advantages to individuals who had routine institutional contact with the press. New York features some of the nation's most talented journalists, but residents with a desire to get involved were also locked out by a media system that confers authority onto a limited number of recognizable community leaders. That a limited number of elite voices receive more profound access to media coverage should be of little surprise to anyone immersed in careful study of media reporting trends. The scholarship of Warren Breed, C. Wright Mills, Gaye Tuchman, Michael Schudson, Ben Bagdikian, Robert McChesney, and many others offer compelling evidence that media patterns have been established for decades that offer a more visible platform to a limited number of powerful individuals.

A greater public role in the stadium issue is needed. If, after inclusive debate and dialogue, a community wishes to allocate vast resources to sports infrastructure, such a decision should be implemented as public policy. But many communities that have built ballparks in recent years may have preferred to allocate such resources elsewhere. The tendency to allow closed-door meetings and carefully orchestrated news conferences to dictate the direction of public policy is simply wrong. The real losers in this issue are the public and the democratic process.

It is possible that the public may make poor choices if given greater input, but it is unlikely that the decisions made by the public could be more flawed than decisions made by many team owners and public policy professionals. Civic leaders who decided to dismantle many historic ballparks during the 1960s and early 1970s subsequently pushed for replacement of all-purpose circular stadiums because they were deemed both impersonal and inadequate as revenue generators. Leaders would be wise to remember that Baltimore's Camden Yards, one of the most unique newer ballparks, was the initial brainchild of Eric Moss, a Syracuse University student, not ballpark professionals or community elites.[52] Although some facilities being built today have the potential to become long-term landmarks, many of them are built with a formulaic routine that make this unlikely. In a few short decades, a public bored with these new cathedrals may be asked to replace them with subsidized versions of the latest trend in new construction.

The cycle for replacement has shrunken from fifty years during the 1960s to a more recent standard of between twenty to thirty-five years. This cycle could further tighten unless substantial public outcry forces change. The creation of sports facilities that are deemed disposable after a single generation creates an ironic paradox that has become the central logic of new construction. Two key arguments are made when building these facilities: attracting tourist dollars and creating a national profile that distinguishes a community from others. It is likely that the opposite has occurred. Because so many cities have bought into new construction, those with newer facilities are less distinguishable from communities who have chosen to preserve the past.

It may seem outlandish, but if an older "cookie-cutter" ballpark was painstakingly preserved, it might have become a future tourist attraction while today's newer ballparks would be regarded as boring. With the exception of Fenway and Wrigley, a commitment to preservation has diminished, but the abandonment of the old in favor of the new may not be in the best interest of a community. Boston's pride in its historic past was created, in part, by its inability to attract substantial federal subsidies at various intervals in its history. As a result, many older buildings remained intact at a time when other cities demolished blocks of old architecture to pursue "progress." It would be wise to consider that athletic facilities that have stood for thousands of years in Rome and Greece remain tourist attractions today, whereas the Milwaukee Brewers and Pittsburgh Pirates struggle to attract fans to new facilities that offer all the latest amenities.

Ironically, the promise of a winning team, an assurance routinely offered by new stadium advocates, may be less likely than typically thought when a new stadium is constructed. Sports, unlike many activities, is a zero-sum game. When the vast majority of teams have new facilities, on-field play will sort itself out with as many winners as losers at every seasons' end. Some evidence has surfaced that provides a counterintuitive spin on the stadium issue; a new facility might actually hinder a team's ability to win. A 2002 study revealed that in the season that a new facility is unveiled, a typical team loses 24 percent of its home field advantage.[53] A look at recent performance should offer limited evidence that these findings may be accurate. It might also suggest that taxpayer subsidy is not a successful strategy for helping a home team.

In 2002, the Patriots won a Super Bowl after playing in a facility that was deemed "unacceptable." In the same year, the Anaheim Angels, a team with an older, refurbished facility, won the World Series. To get there, they had to beat the New York Yankees and the San Francisco Giants. The former plays in a ballpark that was built in 1923, and the latter plays in a newer ballpark that was constructed with minimal taxpayer support.

More recently, the landscape has not appeared to change dramatically. Baseball tends to favor higher payroll teams in larger cities. In 2003 the Florida Marlins, a lower payroll team playing in a football stadium deemed inadequate by team ownership, beat the Yankees to hoist the World Series trophy. In 2004, the Red Sox, playing in the oldest Major League facility in America, won the World Series. They beat a St. Louis Cardinals team that beat all National League rivals, despite playing in a stadium that management described as inadequate.

In football, with the benefits of revenue sharing and a labor agreement that have more effectively held players' salaries in check, the Patriots emerged as an example of how to maintain a winning team, winning Super Bowls in 2002, 2004, and 2005. Team owner Bob Kraft was able to build his new stadium with very clear limits on public funding, unlike competing owners who insisted public subsidies were needed to remain competitive. Kraft received infrastructure support, forcing him to underwrite stadium construction himself. Nevertheless, the dynamic may be changing. In football three of the four finalists vying for Super Bowl supremacy in early 2006 played in heavily subsidized facilities, and in baseball, the White Sox, a team with a relatively new ballpark, won the World Series in 2005.

On-field victories may be important to fans, but to owners, success is also determined by the bottom line. In baseball evidence is mounting that the benefit of a new stadium is fleeting. During the 2002 season, the Detroit Tigers attendance dropped 22 percent from the previous season, despite christening the facility in 2000. New ballparks in Milwaukee and Pittsburgh drew similar results. The Brewers faced a 30 percent decline, and the Pirates's attendance dropped 25 percent. Overall, attendance for all teams dipped by 6 percent despite record-level construction over the last decade.[54] The slide continued in 2005 for new ballparks in Philadelphia and San Diego, with per-game drop offs of about 7,500 and 1,900, respectively.[55] Ironically, the 2005 champion, the White Sox, play in a relatively new facility, but during the regular season many more fans came to see the nearby rival Cubs, a much weaker team, in ancient Wrigley Field. The Red Sox, with a ballpark that also might be described as a rickety anachronism, has managed to consistently sell out, despite maintaining the highest prices in Major League Baseball.

The Yankees, with plans to move to a new ballpark with about 7,000 fewer seats, hope they can increase profits. It is likely that substantial price hikes will be part of that marketing model, but what is less certain is whether fans will pay more to sit in a ballpark that is not constructed on the same hallowed ground where generations of legendary Yankee heroes once played. Even though the newly proposed ballpark has been sold as a very close replica of the old Yankee Stadium, it will be different in the eyes of many fans. If the move is made, as now seems likely, some of the historic magic may be gone. The skyboxes may be more luxurious, the concession stands might be more convenient, but the new ballpark will not have the same sacred aura. George Steinbrenner's move is a dramatic experiment. It is one that may not have the positive long-term outcome he anticipates.

No one can predict the longevity of the current group of professional stadiums, but a twenty-year replacement cycle could be possible if public officials are unwilling to place limits on team owner demands and if media routines continue to place limitations on public input. Involving the public in the process is one way for those involved in stadium construction decisions to avoid the pitfalls of the past. For media practitioners, such involvement has the capacity to increase public demand for their product. Falling newspaper circulation may be the by-product of a multichannel media environment, but some of the declines may also be the result of a grassroots belief that some media practitioners are out of step with the average citizen. A recent Ford Foundation/American Journalism Review examination of public attitudes to newspaper content indicated that 64 percent believed news stories were either "very biased" or "somewhat biased."[56]

The bias issue is problematic. Even the most dedicated and competent reporters can be accused of news coverage bias despite good faith efforts to present material in an honest and thorough manner. But existing media routines conspire to prevent reporters from integrating a broader array of community voices into media coverage of this issue. With today's dominant coverage model, reporters often serve as conveyor belts, delivering the message of elite interests instead of actively engaging the public to participate in the democratic process. The system may be cost-effective, but it does not meaningfully integrate the public into the political process.

Ideally, new media models would balance the desire of elites to control the policy agenda with good faith efforts to better integrate the public into the process. The considerable influence of elites, particularly in stadium issues, makes adoption of such models less likely, but courageous journalists and editors have the capacity to make such models a reality. News routines are one factor, among many, that determine how public policy unfolds. In spite of some public skepticism about the influence of news reporting, over time journalists can powerfully shape how a community perceives an issue.

In New York, few citizens initially regarded stadium construction as an engine of economic growth. Even though such claims have been repeatedly made by selected leaders, these assertions were often neutralized by the voices of experts and opinion columns that challenged the credibility of such claims. But as public officials repeatedly make claims about jobs and economic growth, the possibility that citizens may begin to believe such claims could increase. In smaller cities a greater number of residents seem to perceive stadium building as an engine for economic growth as stadium construction is completed, but a new skepticism may emerge if local economies subsequently struggle with population declines and economic vitality. Pittsburgh's close brush with fiscal insolvency is one such example.

A fundamental difference between Pittsburgh and New York is that one is fighting for respect at the national level and the other is not. The Big Apple can swagger with confidence, but its recent embrace of the stadium may be more rooted in concern about its role globally. As China gears up to host the 2008 Olympics, a symbolic battle of economic powers may be intensified on a world stage. With dramatic trade deficits, a declining manufacturing base, and an inability to balance federal deficits, the United States is in an uncertain long-term global position. New York, the nation's financial capital, now lacks the modern symbolic sports-related trappings of Paris, London, or Beijing. Paris has its Stade de France, the host site for the 1998 World Cup; London will unveil a new Wembley Stadium in 2007; and Beijing broke ground in 2005 on Wukesong Indoor Stadium. New York's stadium plans may suggest its leaders could have some insecurities about the Big Apple's position of long-term global dominance. It may also mark a moment when the stadium-building rivalry has moved from intercity competition to a much broader stage. If New York officials fight hard for a 2020 bid, this might offer powerful evidence that this construction has taken a more global direction.

Conclusion

Media coverage of stadium construction in major metropolitan areas has had yet another impact on public policy that may not be easily perceived. As Major League teams have used media resources to create a culture of stadium construction that is beneficial to the revenue imperatives of team owners, smaller, less publicized sporting institutions have tried to follow suit. Minor league baseball has received millions of dollars in stadium subsidies from small and mid-sized communities in suburban, urban, and rural areas across the nation. Local little leagues and organized football teams have funneled thousands and even millions of dollars in community resources to construct or renovate sports facilities so that the youngsters have a ballpark that better replicates the professional model. A number of high schools have started to sell personal seat licenses just like professional teams, with prices ranging from $150 to $1,500.[57]

Such imitation is hardly new. One model for sports administration came from other institutions' desire to replicate the Ivy League model that was prominent during the Progressive Era. This model gained credibility through sustained media coverage in the late 1800s and early 1900s. Public support for this form of sports administration was fortified by the direct public involvement of President Theodore Roosevelt in 1905. A move to a more blatantly commercial sports paradigm gradually replaced the pseudo-amateurism of this collegiate model. The professional model gained momentum as new ballparks were constructed several years later.

Harvard and Yale may have been instrumental in establishing an athletic model that led to a professional paradigm, but they pulled back from such a system when it became clear that the resources needed to remain on-field leaders would be enormous, and dedication of such resources would offer no assurance of consistent victory. In response, these prestigious institutions have shifted their priorities away from athletics and have focused on areas that have a more profound impact on global policy.[58] Before doing so, these institutions built massive football stadiums in 1903 and 1914. Both facilities may be considered ancient relics, but they are still used today and were sought for use by professional football teams before the NFL gained sufficient power to dictate stadium policy in many communities. Some alumni of these Ivy League institutions have remained wedded to professional sport with an enthusiasm that parallels Theodore Roosevelt's involvement with college football reform one hundred years ago.

More recently, current U.S. President George W. Bush, an alumnus of both Yale and Harvard, has served as an ambassador for baseball, visiting ballparks around the country and inviting children to play T-ball on White House grounds. He threw out the ceremonial opening pitch on April 14, 2005, when the Washington Nationals played their first game in the nation's capitol. He has also made his presence known in NFL venues, visiting new stadiums and offering presidential messages during sports broadcasts. If not for personal experience gained by Bush in a campaign to heavily subsidize a Major League Baseball stadium in Arlington, Texas, it is possible that today's political landscape would be very different in Washington, D.C.[59] Ironically, the free-market fiscal conservatism often espoused by the current administration can be sharply contrasted to the multimillion-dollar taxpayer subsidies that have become the norm in modern-day sports.

It may seem that the managerial structures of media, politics, and sports have become so entrenched and are so interconnected to power that dramatic future change is unlikely. Yet sports, journalism, and politics are in precarious positions. The sporting world is struggling to prevent diminished public interest in the same way that traditional media institutions are battling declining audiences and politicians are fighting to counter citizens' knee-jerk distaste for political institutions. The historic record offers tangible evidence that alterations to the policy landscape will take place. Where the recent foray of big cities into the stadium game will lead our nation is unclear. It is difficult to predict where we are headed, but the paradigms of journalism, sports management, and public policy will certainly change in the years ahead. Failure to understand that the public should have a role in each of these settings may contribute to the eventual decline of the individuals and institutions currently dictating policy in these vastly diverse arenas.

NOTES
BIBLIOGRAPHY
INDEX

NOTES

Preface

1. Wimmer and Dominick, *Mass Media Research,* 152.

2. Ragin, *The Comparative Method,* 49.

3. John C. Craig, "Meeting the Challenge: Why an Editor Chooses to Help Lead a Civic Committee," *Pittsburgh Post-Gazette,* July 4, 1999, B3.

1. Introduction

1. The 1998 NFL broadcast multiyear agreement brought the league $17.6 billion, more than the total spent on *every* major professional football facility ever built. The NFL has inked new deals, effective in 2006, worth $3.735 billion per year. Game coverage frequently includes panoramic city views. Michael Hiestand, "Really Big Bucks Inflate NFL TV Deal," *USA Today,* Apr. 19, 2005, 3C.

2. Michener, *Sports in America,* 419.

3. Fitch IBCA, "Public Finance—Changing Game of Sports Finance," 1.

4. Noll and Zimbalist, "Build the Stadium—Create the Jobs!" in Noll and Zimbalist, *Sports, Jobs, and Taxes,* 5.

5. Angelo Bruscas, "Modern Marvel," *Seattle Post-Intelligencer,* July 14, 1999, C4.

6. Despite active lobbying for a new stadium, the Mariners's legal counsel Bart Waldman made it clear that the team regarded overruns as a public burden. In a letter to the Washington State Major League Baseball Facilities District, Waldman argued that "the magnitude of this burden [$100 million overrun] . . . now exceeds the entire purchase price of the club [and], threatens to undermine the very purpose for which the ballpark was conceived—ensuring the success and competitiveness of baseball in Seattle." Ibid.

7. "Mariners Accept Their Fair Share on Safeco Field" (editorial), *Seattle Post-Intelligencer,* February 19, 2001, B3.

8. Peter Callaghan, "Allen Hides Football Finances Behind Lawyers," *News Tribune,* Sept. 15, 2005, B1.

9. Frank Deford, "Seasons of Discontent," *Newsweek,* January 5, 1998, 74–75.

10. Rosensweig, *Retro Ball Parks,* 2005.

11. Voigt, *American Baseball*, 42.

12. Riess, *Touching Base.*

13. Ibid., 223.

14. Smith, *Sports and Freedom*, 214.

15. Ibid., 218.

2. Stadium History: Religious Roots and the Transition to Secularism

1. Romano, *Athletics and Mathematics in Archaic Corinth*, 1–16.

2. Murray, *Early Greece*, 222.

3. Bowra, in *The Oxford Classical Dictionary*, 524–26.

4. Romano, *Athletics and Mathematics in Archaic Corinth*, 103.

5. Romano states that this facility was constructed in the second century, but some historians trace construction to an earlier date.

6. Romano, *Athletics and Mathematics in Archaic Corinth*, 2.

7. Mumford, *The City in History*, 223.

8. Veyne, *A History of Private Life*, 107. Because work was frowned upon in aristocratic circles, funding for these projects came from a variety of sources, including the expectation of a tribute from middle- and lower-class subjects in exchange for services or protections. A Roman citizen might, for example, pay a healthy tribute to avoid military conscription.

9. Kathryn Lomas, "The Idea of a City: Elite Ideology and the Evolution of Urban Forms in Italy, 200 BC–AD 100," in Parkins, *Roman Urbanism*, 22–41.

10. Laciani, *The Ruins and Excavations of Ancient Rome*, 369–70.

11. Veyne, *A History of Private Life*, 131.

12. Mumford, *The City in History*, 242.

13. Accidental football deaths are chronicled each year and should not be minimized. However, at times Roman sport reveled in death. Laciani describes multiple slaughters for perverse entertainment (*The Ruins and Excavations of Ancient Rome*, 371).

14. Guttmann, *From Ritual To Record*, 29. Guttmann argues that by AD 90, "Gladiators were almost always slaves rather than citizens, a complete reversal of the Greek view of participation." With multimillion dollar salaries abundant in sports, such a correlation may seem absurd. However, modern sports participation is largely passive, and consumption is more the norm than vigorous exercise.

15. Laciani, *The Ruins and Excavations of Ancient Rome*, 379.

16. Mrozek, *Sport and the American Mentality.*

17. Walvin, *Leisure and Society*, 114.

18. Seymour, *Baseball*, 18.

19. Voigt, *American Baseball*, 18.

20. Guschov, *The Red Stockings of Cincinnati*, 6. Guschov provides an insightful examination of the public response to the early transition from amateur to professional baseball.

21. Ibid., 39.

22. Benson, *Ballparks of North America*, xxvi.

23. Riess, *Touching Base*, 51.

24. For a significantly more detailed overview of Progressive Era politics as it related to establishment of ballfields and sports franchises, see ibid., 49–84.

25. George Plunkitt, "New York City's Boss Plunkitt Defends "Honest" Graft, 1905," in Fink, *Major Problems in the Gilded Age and the Progressive Era,* 305–7.

26. This strategy was common during the Progressive Era, but diminished as an effective tactic after World War I. As plans for Yankee Stadium were introduced in the 1920s, opponents unsuccessfully pushed political leaders to cut a road through the property. For a more detailed examination of political ruthlessness in establishing and maintaining a ballpark location, see Riess, *Touching Base,* 66–75.

27. Guttmann, *From Ritual To Record,* 15–55.

28. Taylorism is a science-based management strategy. It involved rationally breaking down production practices to achieve maximum levels of efficiency. Before Taylorism, craftsmanship was more evident in the American workplace.

29. Westcott, *Philadelphia's Old Ballparks,* 74–75.

30. The Baker Bowl's reputation was earned by poor maintenance. Stands from the Baker Bowl collapsed in 1903 and 1927. In 1903, eleven died and more than two hundred were injured. In 1927, no deaths occurred, but a number of serious injuries were reported. Ritter, *Lost Ballparks,* 16.

31. Craig Lambert, "First and 100: Harvard Stadium, With Its Storied Past, Is Football's Edifice Rex," *Harvard Magazine,* Sept.–Oct. 2003, 42–53.

32. For a look at the origins of professional football and how it was perceived its earliest years, see Maltby, *The Origins and Early Development of Professional Football,* and McClellan, *The Sunday Game.*

33. Smith, *Sports and Freedom,* 216.

34. James Pollard, "Ohio State Athletics 1879–1959: The Birth of Ohio Stadium," WOSU Web site. Although this source is no longer available, a revised version can be found at http://www.wosu.org/television/local-programs/program-birth-of-ohio-stadium/.

35. Carroll, *Red Grange and the Rise of Modern Football,* 60–67.

36. Smith, *Sports and Freedom,* 218.

37. Kuklick, *To Everything a Season,* 15.

38. For an example of this frequently run promotion, see the *Philadelphia Inquirer,* Oct. 4, 1905, 15. The Giants beat the Athletics, so the $1,000 was never paid.

39. "Harvard Shut Out by Dartmouth," *Boston Sunday Herald,* Nov. 15, 1903, 1.

40. E. A. Bushnell, "The Dedication Game with Some Impressions by the Post's Cartoonist," *Cincinnati Post,* May 17, 1902, 1.

41. "Record Breaking Crowd at Opening of Ball Park," *Pittsburgh Post,* July 1, 1909, 1. The headline above the collage read "Scenes During Opening-Game at $1,000,000 Forbes Field."

42. Peterson, *Pigskin,* 102–4.

43. Sullivan, *The Dodgers Move West,* 97.

44. Buege, *The Milwaukee Braves,* 14–16.

45. Ibid., 61.

46. Lomax and Armond, "The League That Never Was."

47. Weiner, *Stadium Games.*

48. Caro, *Power Broker,* 1113.

49. Jim Yardley, "Last Innings at a Can-Do Cathedral," *New York Times,* Oct. 3, 1999, 20. Both Hofheinz and Klineberg's remarks were extracted from this article.

50. This point is made in graphic displays that are referred to by tour guides during public Superdome tours.

51. The giant scoreboard was dismantled in 1988 to make room for more seating and skybox facilities for the Oilers's owner Bud Adams. According to Paul Darst, director of Astrodome scoreboard operations for twenty-eight years, "Nobody has come close to matching that scoreboard, and I don't think anyone ever will." Allan Truex, "Keeping Score: Dome's Futuristic Original Scoreboard Was Entertainment in Itself," *Houston Chronicle,* Sept. 30, 1999, special Astrodome Farewell section.

52. Joe Jares, "The Big Screen Is Watching," *Sports Illustrated,* May 31, 1965, 30–31.

53. McKenzie, *Arrowhead,* 26.

54. Ibid., 27–33.

55. Weiner, *Stadium Games,* 59–109.

56. "Numbers," *Time,* Feb. 8, 1999, 21.

57. Dan McGraw, "Playing the Stadium Game," *US News and World Report,* June 6, 1996, 46–51.

58. Richard Acello, "$60 Million Stadium Improvement Program Approved by Council," *San Diego Daily Transcript,* May 16, 1995, 1.

59. Michael Armacost, Foreword to Noll and Zimbalist, *Sports, Jobs, and Taxes,* viii.

60. Delaney and Eckstein, *Public Dollars, Private Stadiums.*

61. Ziona Austrian and Mark Rosentraub, "Cleveland's Gateway to the Future," in Noll and Zimbalist, *Sports, Jobs, and Taxes,* 355–84.

62. *Los Angeles Memorial Coliseum Commission vs. NFL.*

63. David Harris, *The League,* 639.

64. Roberts and Olson, *Winning Is the Only Thing.*

65. Johnson, *Super Spectator and the Electric Lilliputians,* 119.

66. Michael Ozanian, "Suite Deals: Why New Stadiums are Shaking Up the Pecking Order of Sports Franchises," *Financial World,* May 5, 1995, 42–56.

67. Michael Ozanian, "Selective Accounting," *Forbes,* Dec. 14, 1998, 124.

68. Euchner, *Playing the Field.*

3. Stadium Economics: Separating Myth from Reality

1. Bob Kravitz, "Colts-to-L.A. Talk Rekindled: Team, City Deny ESPN Report That Serious Talks with League Are Underway," *Indianapolis Star,* Sept. 9, 2002, D8. Mortensen's remarks were made on Sunday NFL Countdown hours before the Colts's first 2002 game.

2. John Czarnecki, "Colts and Los Angeles," *USA Today Sports Weekly,* Sept. 18–24, 2002, 13.

3. Matthew Tully, "City Slams Report About Colts Leaving," *Indianapolis Star,* Sept. 10, 2002, A1.

4. Matthew Tully, "Most Oppose Using Taxes to Help Colts," *Indianapolis Star,* Sept. 27, 2002, A1.

5. Jennifer Wagner, "Talk Swirls Over Land Near Dome," *Indianapolis Star,* Sept. 23, 2002, A1.

6. Bob Kravitz, "Tagliabue Talks the 'No Move' Talk, but Colts May Still Walk," *Indianapolis Star,* Oct. 9, 2002, D1.

7. Kevin Seifert and Sid Hartman, "Taylor Negotiating for Vikings; 'No Sale,' McCombs Says About Rumors of a Deal, but Talks Are Confirmed," *Star Tribune,* Oct. 5, 2002, 3C.

8. Howard Balzer, "Garage Sale," *USA Today Sports Weekly,* Oct. 16–22, 2002, 12. Sid Hartman, "McCombs Says Relocation a Possibility," *Star Tribune,* Oct. 14, 2002, 2C.

9. Tony Kennedy and Kevin Seifert, "McCombs Wants to Sell Vikings," *Star Tribune,* Oct. 6, 2002, 3C. Kevin Seifert, "Vikings Value Is Variable; Stadium Issue's Resolution Key for Prospective Buyers," *Star Tribune,* Oct. 13, 2002, 2V.

10. Terry Fiedler, "What Price for the Vikings?," *Star Tribune,* Oct. 10, 2002, 1A.

11. Kevin Seifert, "Quick Fixes and Long-Term Plans; New Vikings Owner Brings a Lengthy To-Do List with Him to Town," *Star Tribune,* June 17, 2005, 1C.

12. Jay Weiner, "Commissioner Impressed: Paul Tagliabue Visited with Anoka County Developers and Liked the Stadium Plans," *Star Tribune,* Apr. 7, 2005, 3C.

13. Delaney and Eckstein, *Public Dollars, Private Stadiums.*

14. Robert Baade and Allen Sanderson, "The Employment Effect of Teams and Sports Facilities," in Noll and Zimbalist, *Sports, Jobs, and Taxes,* 92–118.

15. Ibid., 112.

16. Ibid., 101.

17. Dennis Zimmerman, "Subsidizing Stadiums: Who Benefits, Who Pays?" in Noll and Zimbalist, *Sports, Jobs, and Taxes,* 119–45.

18. Rodney Fort, "Direct Democracy and the Stadium Mess," in Noll and Zimbalist, *Sports, Jobs, and Taxes,* 146–77.

19. Ibid., 156.

20. Quirk and Fort, *Pay Dirt.*

21. Ibid., 163.

22. Quirk and Fort, *Hardball.*

23. The agreement with the State of Washington permits the team a $100 million credit to cover past team losses. Although Quirk and Fort argue that the owners of the Mariners have no reason to share profits, some could be shared if it benefitted the team's larger goals.

24. Committee on the Judiciary, *Professional Sports Franchise Relocation.*

25. Ibid., 266.

26. Ibid., 280.

27. Ibid., 281.

28. Ibid., 283.

29. Danielson, *Home Team,* 303–6.

30. Ibid., 306.

31. Euchner, *Playing the Field,* 178.

32. Ibid., 184.

33. Carlino and Coulson, "Compensating Differentials and the Social Benefits of the NFL," 25–50.

34. Sheehan, *Keeping Score,* 15–17.

35. Ibid., 317.

36. Todd Richmond, "New Berlin Wants Packers if Green Bay Doesn't," *Green Bay News-Chronicle,* Sept. 11, 2000.

37. Peterson, *City Limits.*

38. Johnson, *Super Spectator,* 118–19.

39. Associated Press, "University of Michigan to Charge More for Football Tickets," *Daily Collegian,* 16 Mar. 2001, 20.

40. Margaret Hopkins, "Suite Success: Stadium Project is Keystone for Entire Athletics Program," *Centre Daily Times,* Apr. 22, 2001, E1.

41. Ronald Blum, "Average Ticket Prices at $18.99," *Associated Press,* Mar. 30, 2001; Erik Spanberg, "NBA: Why Aren't You Watching?" *Christian Science Monitor,* June 23, 2005, 11.

42. Toma and Cross, "Intercollegiate Athletics and Student College Choice," 633–61.

43. Research from several periods were examined. Cutlip, *Fund Raising in the United States;* Budig, "The Relationship Among Intercollegiate Athletics, Enrollment, and Voluntary Support for Public Higher Education"; Sigelman and Carter, "Win One for the Giver?" 284–93; Robert Mc Cormick and Maurice Tinsley, "Athletics and Academics: A Model of University Contributions," in Goff and Tollison, *Sportometrics,* 193–204; Harrison and Peterson, "Alumni Donations and Colleges' Development Expenditures," 397–413; Rhoads and Gerking, "Educational Contributions, Academic Quality, and Athletic Success," 248–58.

44. Zimbalist, *Unpaid Professionals,* 168.

45. Duderstadt, *Intercollegiate Athletics and the American University,* 128–29. Nevertheless, Duderstadt, former president of Michigan, argues that such a speculative sports-oriented investment might "rapidly lead to bankruptcy in the corporate world."

46. Bast, "Sports Stadium Madness," 3.

47. Lupica, *Mad as Hell,* 55–59.

48. Bob Glauber, "You Gotta Have Heart to Win Our Applause," *Sporting News,* Nov. 14, 1994, 15.

49. Paul Attner, "Running with the Pack," *Sporting News,* Oct. 10, 1994, 9.

50. Richard Hoffer, "The 20th Century: Our Favorite Venues," *Sports Illustrated,* June 7, 1999, 94–97.

51. Richard Jones and Don Walker, "Packers Boss Warns of Move if Stadium Doesn't Get Upgrade," *Milwaukee Journal-Sentinel,* Mar. 1, 2000, 1.

52. Patti Zarling, "Lambeau Tax Vote: It's Yes and No," *Green Bay News-Chronicle,* Sept. 13, 2000.

53. " 'Friends' Spent $420,254 Over Two Months," *Green Bay News-Chronicle,* Sept. 11, 2000.

54. Chicago Bears, "Lakefront Improvement Plan," press release, June 11, 2002.

55. Washington Redskins, "Federal Express Announces Stadium Naming Rights in Deal with Washington Redskins," Nov. 21, 1999.

56. Cagan and deMause, *Field of Schemes,* 176–79.

57. Andrew Cassel, "San Francisco's Stadium Financing Pays Homage to Creativity," *Philadelphia Inquirer,* Feb. 8, 1999, F1.

58. The $27.85 billion figure reflects stadiums and arenas put in use from 1900 to 2000. It was determined by combining figures from Keating, "Sports Pork"; and "Sports Facility Reports." Keating listed all facilities built by 1998 and one from 1999. Facilities opened in 1999 and 2000 were added using Marquette data. Using the Consumer Price index, accumulated totals were adjusted for inflation to reflect 2005 values. Lassiter, "Little Change in Social Security Solvency."

59. Allen Sloan, "The $2.1 Trillion Market Tumble," *Time,* Apr. 24, 2000, 22–26.

60. Mindy Fetterman, "Pampered Pooched Nestled in the Lap of Luxury," *USA Today,* Feb. 13, 2005, A1; "Numbers," *Time,* Mar. 27, 2000, 27.

61. Jonathan Alter, "New Windows on the World," *Newsweek,* Aug. 30, 1999, 50.

62. Jodie Morse, "Cracking Down on the Homeless," *Time,* Dec. 20, 1999, 69–70.

63. The most common levies are hotel taxes, as high as 17 percent in Houston, and car rental taxes. Jim Bradley, a mayoral candidate in Salt Lake City, host of the 2002 Summer Olympics, wryly stated, "We have to raise the car rental tax as high as we can. . . . We have to look at opportunities like that to just screw them [visitors]." "Notebook: Verbatim," *Time,* Aug. 23, 1999, 19; Betsy Wade, "Need an Arena? Tax a Traveler!" *New York Times,* June 18, 2000, TR4.

64. Approximately $3.8 billion was spent on stadiums and arenas that opened up in 1999 and 2000. Using that benchmark, $28.5 billion would be spent in fifteen years, compared to the $27.85 billion cited earlier for total twentieth century expenditure. National Sports Law Institute Reports were used to establish the $3.8 billion figure.

65. Long, "Full Count," 119–43.

66. Ed Hinton, "Not So Fast," *Sports Illustrated,* Mar. 13, 1995, 44.

4. The Media and Stadium Construction

1. Eisinger, "The Politics of Bread and Circuses," 316–33.

2. Roger Noll and Andrew Zimbalist, "Build the Stadium—Create the Jobs!" in Noll and Zimbalist, *Sports, Jobs, and Taxes,* 1–54.

3. Rosentraub, *Major League Losers,* 51–56.

4. Ibid., 55.

5. Sage, "Stealing Home," 110–24.

6. Euchner, *Playing the Field,* 172.

7. Cagan and deMause, *Field of Schemes,* 199.

8. Ian Nuttall, "Live on the Waterfront: Tales of Tourism,
Politics, and Real Estate in Miami," *Stadia,* Feb. 2000, 26–31.

9. Marichal, "Local Politics on the Sports Page."

10. Richmond, *Ballpark,* 128–43. Although Eric Moss formulated the original plans for an old-fashioned ballpark, his name appears on none of the official literature, placards, or merchandise that is part of Camden Yards lore.

11. Boorstin, *The Americans,* 124–34.

12. Cressy, *Coming Over;* Bercovitch, *The American Jeremiad.* The literature and personal letters from the colonial era suggest many reasons for traveling to America. Church elders and entrepreneurs in search of resources for England were most inclined to act as boosters. Cressy offers evidence of religious and secular boosterism, and Bercovitch reveals boosterism with religious overtones.

13. Guschov, *The Red Stockings of Cincinnati,* 47.

14. Kuklick, *To Everything a Season,* 64.

15. Fowler, *Loser Takes All,* 179.

16. Hiebert and Gibbons, *Exploring Mass Media for a Changing World,* 287.

17. Ewen, *PR,* 410.

18. Strauss, "Does Money Tilt the Playing Field?" 16–17.

19. Weiner, *Stadium Games*, 68.

20. The "Green Fan" movement is explained in ibid., 78–83.

21. Ibid., 100.

22. Rosentraub, *Major League Losers*, 54.

23. Strauss, "Does Money Tilt the Playing Field?" 16.

24. After CBS lost NFL broadcast rights to Fox in 1994, some stations abandoned their CBS affiliation. While other variables may have been at play, the proximity of change to the loss suggests NFL program content is highly coveted at the local level. Stacy Perman, "Thrown for a Loss by the NFL," *Time*, Jan. 26, 1998, 52–53.

25. Cathy Booth, "Worst of Times," *Time*, Nov. 15, 1999, 79–80; Joshua Hammer, "Look Out, the Boss Is Back," *Newsweek*, Nov. 15, 1999, 76. Direct quotes are taken from Booth.

26. Entire books have been written on this topic, including Benedict and Yeager, *Pros and Cons*.

27. Schudson, "The Culture of News," 127.

28. Bantz, McCorkle, and Baade, "The News Factory," 65.

29. Pew Research Center for the People and the Press, "Striking the Balance," 1. Pew Center data reveal that media executives were less troubled by commercial pressures than were journalists.

30. Bagdikian, *The Media Monopoly*, 237.

31. Glasser, "Objectivity Precludes Responsibility," 16.

32. Molotch, "The City as Growth Machine," 309–32.

33. Molotch, "The Political Economy of Growth Machines," 29–53.

34. For recent examples, see Morgan, *Glory for Sale;* Fowler, *Loser Takes All*, 1997.

5. Cincinnati: Let's Build Two

1. *Cincinnati Daily Enquirer*, Sept. 2, 1847, 2.

2. Peterson and Barnett, *USA Today*, 27.

3. Flynt is a native of Saylersville, Kentucky. He established his commercial base in Cincinnati and is currently serving as proprietor of a controversial adult bookstore in the area.

4. Guschov, *The Red Stockings of Cincinnati*, 9. "Base ball" as two separate words is correct. Popular usage of the single word "baseball" did not emerge until decades later.

5. Walker, *Cincinnati and the Big Red Machine*, 13.

6. Abbott, *Boosters and Businessmen*, 126–71.

7. Walker, *Cincinnati and the Big Red Machine*, 13.

8. Kansas City, Missouri built the first two-stadium complex after voters approved a 1967 referendum to subsidize the Truman Sports Complex.

9. During the summer of 1999 barbeque products endorsed by Norman "Boomer" Esiason were marketed in the city, including a billboard in one of the residential neighborhoods of Vine Street.

10. Public Library of Cincinnati and Hamilton County, *America's Love Affair.*

11. Bench served as narrator for the Cincinnati Pops Orchestra's 1997 "season opener" where he narrated "Stephen Raineke's musical rendition of Casey at the Bat" on Sept. 6, 7, and 8.

12. "Sign the Apocalypse Is Upon Us," *Sports Illustrated,* Feb. 21, 2000, 26.

13. Kitty Morgan, "Schott in the Afternoon," *Cincinnati,* Feb. 1999, 84.

14. Guschov, *The Red Stockings of Cincinnati,* 9.

15. Ibid., 94.

16. Coombs and West, *Baseball,* 119–20.

17. Much of the information was obtained in a session featuring Cincinnati historians that was part of the Society for American Baseball Research Convention in July 2004.

18. Guschov offers evidence that the 1868 stock issue was not a success, raising only $3,000 (*The Red Stockings of Cincinnati,* 14). Voigt does not provide evidence of this nature, but does indicate that the club incurred some indebtedness in 1868, potentially reflecting lukewarm acceptance of this initial public offering. Voigt does suggest that the 1869 stock issue was a success, indicating that "half" was sold "to members and the rest to new investors." Voigt, *American Baseball,* 24.

19. For 1869 team payroll figures, see Voigt, *American Baseball,* 27.

20. Information provided through SABR Convention's Cincinnati ballpark tour in July 2004.

21. Benson, *Ballparks of North America,* 100. Some historians dispute the death claim, but the collapse did seriously injure fans.

22. Ritter, *Lost Ballparks,* 41.

23. For a detailed examination of the Palace of the Fans, see John Erardi, "Palace of the Fans," *Cincinnati Enquirer,* Apr. 1, 1996, E13, E18–20.

24. "Cincinnati Reds Forever?" *Cincinnati Enquirer,* July 12, 1959, 1.

25. George Amick, "The Stadium Race: As Redlegs Pasture at Crosley Field, Other Cities Build," *Cincinnati Enquirer,* July 12, 1959, 1E.

26. "Milwaukee County Gambles on Stadium," *Cincinnati Enquirer,* July 13, 1959, 2A.

27. "New Frisco Stadium Ready in September," *Cincinnati Enquirer,* July 14, 1959, 2A. The article points out that taxpayers voted to fund $5 million of this $11.5 million project.

28. Cincinnati Planning Commission, "The Cincinnati Metropolitan Area Master Plan and the Official Plan."

29. Tucker, *Cincinnati's Citizen Crusaders,* 201. Tucker provides a detailed description of Robert Acomb's initial riverfront plan.

30. Amick, "The Stadium Race," 1E. Lloyd's remarks are offset by remarks from others that renovation of Crosley Field or a new park at the Carthage site would be best. A front-page sketch of the Carthage Fairgrounds proposal in the *Cincinnati Enquirer* on July 15, 1959, provides further evidence that riverfront development, although popular with select community leaders, was not the clear favorite for stadium development.

31. Tucker, *Cincinnati's Citizen Crusaders,* 212.

32. Gene Russell, "Tickets, Parking Would Buy Stadium Consultant Says," *Cincinnati Enquirer,* Dec. 16, 1965, 8.

33. Bob Firestone, "Officials Eye Pact for Stadium Study," *Cincinnati Enquirer,* Jan. 8, 1966, 1; "Dome Would Cap Deal," *Cincinnati Enquirer,* Jan. 8, 1966, 1; "All on the Ball," AP wirephoto, *Cincinnati Enquirer,* Jan. 8, 1966, 1.

34. Walker, *Cincinnati and the Big Red Machine,* 30. See pages 23–41 for context.

35. Hamilton County Good Government League, *Good Government Bulletin: The Stadium,* 1–4.

36. Pat Harmon, "Reds Objection Fails; Circular Stadium OK'd," *Cincinnati Post and Times Star,* June 15, 1966. The horseshoe shape might seem like an odd request for a baseball enthusiast with no knowledge of Ohio stadium history. The first huge Ohio stadium was a horseshoe-shaped football stadium built in 1922 at Ohio State University. Many Ohio residents consider that stadium a cherished landmark.

37. "Stadium Seats to Be Close to the Field: Proximity Assured as $34 Million Plan Unveiled to Public," *Cincinnati Post and Times Star,* July 9, 1966, 1.

38. Emil Dansker, "Stadium's Press Area Spacious . . . And Oh My!," *Cincinnati Enquirer,* Apr. 2, 1967, 2D.

39. Emil Dansker, "New Stadium Could Handle Varied Events Including Road Race," *Cincinnati Enquirer,* Apr. 4, 1967, 29.

40. Leo Baron, "Vote on Stadium: Petitions to Be Circulated Would Ban Tax Fund Use," *Cincinnati Post and Times Star,* May 8, 1967, 1; "Suit Seeks to Block Stadium; GOP Asks Deadline on Reds," *Cincinnati Post and Times Star,* Aug. 3, 1966, 1. See also "Court to Rule on Funds for Stadium," *Cincinnati Enquirer,* May 18, 1967, 1; "Stadium Bonds OK'd by Judge," *Cincinnati Enquirer,* July 16, 1967, 1; "Court Doesn't Act, Stadium Bonds Legal," *Cincinnati Post and Times Star,* June 6, 1968, 25.

41. "GOP Slows Down Stadium Project," *Cincinnati Post and Times Star,* July 30, 1966, 1. A factor in funding the design plans was the certainty that a $400,000 initial plan allocation would commit the city to a $600,000 payment for a "second installment" of plans by the architect. If an NFL team could have been assured, Republican hesitation would have been tempered, if not eliminated.

42. The NFL and AFL were separate leagues with separate network contracts in 1966. The AFL was generally located in cities that did not have existing NFL franchises. Because the NFL had already established teams in the most populated markets, the AFL was considered less prestigious despite its exciting brand of football.

43. "Fund Drive to Be Made for Stadium Planning," *Cincinnati Post and Times Star,* Aug. 5, 1966, 1.

44. Dennis Breen, "A Stadium for the Ages," *CityBeat,* Feb. 9–15, 1995, 8–13.

45. "Stadium Cost Figure Up, and May Still Go Higher," *Cincinnati Enquirer,* Mar. 2, 1967, 1; "Cost Rise Still Haunts Stadium," *Cincinnati Enquirer,* May 4, 1967, 3.

46. "Council O.K.'s Stadium Pact with County," *Cincinnati Enquirer,* May 11, 1967, 1; Leo Baron, "Vote on Stadium: Petitions to Be Circulated Would Ban Tax Fund Use," *Cincinnati Post and Times Star,* May 8, 1967, 1.

47. "Stadium Cost Figure Up, And May Still Go Higher," *Cincinnati Enquirer,* Mar. 2, 1967, 1.

48. "Need Lease for Reds—Councilmen," *Cincinnati Post and Times Star,* Aug. 6, 1966, 1; "New View," *Cincinnati Enquirer,* Sept. 19, 1966, 22.

49. "Council O.K.'s Stadium Pact with County," *Cincinnati Enquirer,* May 11, 1967, 1; "How Much . . . for the Stadium?" *Cincinnati Enquirer,* June 4, 1967, 9D.

50. Breen, "A Stadium for the Ages," 13.

51. Bob Harrod, "Comment," *Cincinnati Enquirer,* June 30, 1970, 1, special Riverfront Stadium souvenir edition.

52. "Stadium Club Might be Ready by Opening Day, 1975," *Cincinnati Enquirer,* May 23, 1974, 75.

53. "Stadium Boxes," *Cincinnati Post,* Nov. 8, 1973, 19.

54. J. Frazier Smith, "Reds Reject Stadium Club Proposal," *Cincinnati Enquirer,* July 14, 1988, C1.

55. Allen Howard, "City Wants Experts Opinion on Scoreboard," *Cincinnati Enquirer,* May 14, 1977, D2; "Cheap Scoreboard Fix Eyed," *Cincinnati Enquirer,* June 1, 1977, C1.

56. "Private Vendors Must Stay Off Stadium Plaza," *Cincinnati Enquirer,* Apr. 3, 1976, C1.

57. Jeff Harrington, "Home Run for Downtown: Stadium Boosts Area Economy by $2.6 Billion in Two Decades," *Cincinnati Enquirer,* June 25, 1990, D1.

58. Michael Ozanian, "Suite Deals: Why New Stadiums are Shaking up the Pecking Order of Sports Franchises," *Financial World,* May 5, 1995, 42–56.

59. Douglas Bolton, "Stadium Savings Sought," *Cincinnati Post,* Dec. 6, 1993, 5A.

60. Richard Green, "What About Us? City Favoring Reds Brown Complains," *Cincinnati Enquirer,* Feb. 15, 1995, A1.

61. Patrick Crowley and Richard Green, "City Council Softens Stance with Schott," *Cincinnati Enquirer,* Mar. 23, 1994, B1.

62. Patrick Crowley and Mark Braykovich, "City Reassesses Stadium's Worth: New Estimate Doubles Value Filed in March," *Cincinnati Enquirer,* May 21, 1994, B4. City officials claimed that they were readjusting the assessment in response to the school district's concern that they were losing tax revenues on land taxed at below market values.

63. Jack Brennan, "There's No Place Like Home, Brown Says," *Cincinnati Enquirer,* Nov. 11, 1993, A1. An accompanying page one article entitled "Stay or Go? We'll Know January 1" offered political discourse on the potential regional loss of the football team.

64. Barry Hortsman, "We Want Bengals, but Not Tax," *Cincinnati Post,* Apr. 19, 1995, 1A, 4A.

65. Richard Green, Laura Goldberg, and Anne Michaud, "Mayor: It's a Done Deal," *Cincinnati Enquirer,* June 30, 1995, A1.

66. Mark Braykovich and Anne Michaud, "Sales Tax: Residents Won't Pay Alone," *Cincinnati Enquirer,* Aug. 13, 1995, A1.

67. Tim Sullivan, "People Aren't Staid When It Comes to Stadia," *Cincinnati Enquirer,* Aug. 13, 1995, C1.

68. For an overview of the political process that took place as Issue One took shape and a critique of economic claims made by pro-stadium advocates, see John Blair and David Swindell, "Sports, Politics and Economics: The Cincinnati Story," in Noll and Zimbalist, *Sports, Jobs, and Taxes,* 282–23.

69. Linda Vaccariello, "The Selling of the Stadium Tax," *Cincinnati Magazine,* June 1996, 68–74.

70. Geoff Hobson, "Owners Mull Bengals' Fate," *Cincinnati Enquirer,* Mar. 11, 1996, B7.

71. Laura Goldberg, "Schott Says City Owes Her $3.1 Million," *Cincinnati Enquirer,* Mar. 8, 1996, A1.

72. Vaccareiello, "The Selling of the Stadium Tax," 73.

73. For a more detailed analysis of coverage tendencies, see Trumpbour, "The New Cathedrals" (dissertation).

74. "An Enquirer Agenda for 1996," *Cincinnati Enquirer,* Feb. 11, 1996, B6.

75. Peter Bronson, "Owners Deserve a Holding Penalty," *Cincinnati Enquirer,* Feb. 11, 1996, D2.

76. Peter Bronson, "Wrong for All the Right Reasons," *Cincinnati Enquirer,* Mar. 17, 1996, F2.

77. Jon Talton, "It's Time for Major League Attitude Change," *Cincinnati Enquirer,* Feb. 11, 1996, F1. On March 10, 1996, Talton announced his departure from Cincinnati to accept a position in Charlotte, North Carolina.

78. Jim Borgman, "Plan B," *Cincinnati Enquirer,* Mar. 19, 1996, A8.

79. Jim Borgman, "How They Should Have Pitched It," *Cincinnati Enquirer,* Mar. 14, 1996, A18.

80. Jeff Berding, "We Reap Benefits by Investing in Future," Mar. 17, 1996, F1; Timothy G. Mara, "Don't Give Into Big-League Blackmail," *Cincinnati Enquirer,* Mar. 17, 1996, F1.

81. "Vote for a Brighter Future" (editorial), *Cincinnati Enquirer,* Mar. 17, 1996, F1.

82. The concept for the "Nowhereville" sign may have been adapted from a state antitobacco billboard campaign that was popular at the time. The billboard positioned a teen smoker next to a city sign which read "Welcome to Loserville, Population You."

83. Mike Brown, "Recapture Our Sense of Optimism," *Cincinnati Enquirer,* Mar. 17, 1996, F3.

84. Professor Vredeveld indicated nearly 1,000 hours were spent preparing his analysis, which touted the economic benefits of new stadium construction. His findings are consistent with the methodologies utilized by consulting firms often hired to justify stadium construction.

85. Paul Daugherty, "Anyone Want to Spend $500 for This Team?" *Cincinnati Enquirer,* Sept. 13, 1996, D1.

86. Bob Bedinghaus, "We're All Winners," *Cincinnati Enquirer,* Apr. 4, 1996, A17.

87. Tim Sullivan, "They're Your Stadiums, So Speak Up Now," *Cincinnati Enquirer,* Apr. 6, 1996, B1. Gilbert Gottfried is a comedian known for his abrasively shrill voice.

88. Anne Michaud, "Public Input on Stadium Plans Sought," *Cincinnati Enquirer,* Nov. 11, 1996, B9. Of interest is article placement. The public invitation was relegated to a less than prominent location at the bottom of an internal page wedged between a shoe sale ad and a home furnishings store ad. This is in contrast to the front-page placement of many stadium articles.

89. Brown's strategy seemed to be a nonthreat that was framed in media coverage within the context of a potential franchise move. In early December 1997 Brown stated, "I am not threatening anything . . . I hope this gets worked out." By the end of the month, Brown set a firm deadline of January 31, 1997, stating if the deadline were not met, "We would have to look at whatever opportunity was available." NFL Commissioner Paul Tagliabue, cognizant of Cincinnati's strong desire to maintain its "major league" stature, spoke on behalf of Mike Brown's position in a news conference held before the Super Bowl. Geoff Hobson and Lucy May, "Power Play Concerns Bengals," *Cincinnati Enquirer,* Dec. 4, 1997, A1; Rick Van Sant,

"Bengals Give City Deadline," *Cincinnati Post,* Dec. 30, 1997, 1A; Chris Haft, "NFL Enters Stadium Dispute," *Cincinnati Enquirer,* Jan. 25, 1997, D1.

90. The basic issues of contention, parking, land development, and surrounding highway infrastructure are effectively summarized in Lucy May, "Land Deal Unlikely Monday," *Cincinnati Enquirer,* Dec. 14, 1997, B1, B5.

91. Laura Goldberg, Geoff Hobson, and Lucy May, "Bengals Stadium: It's a Go," *Cincinnati Enquirer,* Feb. 1, 1997, A1, A12.

92. Cliff Peale and Barry Horsham, "Development Debate Escalates-City: Bengal Lease Invalid," *Cincinnati Post,* July 1997, 8, 1A. The terms of this lease stipulated that "the county shall make no improvements to the stadium complex without obtaining the prior written consent of the team." County and team officials argued that this did not constitute "veto power," but was rather a "partnership" that was "typical of what a 'major tenant would receive in any major real estate development.' "

93. Lucy May, "City Celebrates Its 'Rebirth,' " *Cincinnati Enquirer,* Apr. 1998, 26, A1, A12.

94. Barry Hortsman, "Reds, County Close to Deal on 'Wedge' Site," *Cincinnati Post,* June 5, 1998, 14A.

95. Geoff Hobson, "Schott Wants Reds to Get Stadium First," *Cincinnati Enquirer,* Apr. 1, 1996, C4.

96. Geoff Hobson, "Finding a Place to Play," *Cincinnati Enquirer,* Apr. 6, 1997, A1, A6.

97. Geoff Hobson, "Welcome to Cinergy: Play Ball," *Cincinnati Enquirer,* Sept. 10, 1996, A1.

98. "Group Pitching Park Adds a Player," *Cincinnati Enquirer,* July 15, 1994, B1, B4.

99. Anne Michaud, "Broadway Stadium Team Builds Facade of Dreams," *Cincinnati Enquirer,* Sept. 29, 1996, B1, B4. Anne Michaud and Geoff Hobson, "New Pitch for Broadway Ballpark," *Cincinnati Enquirer,* Oct. 10, 1996, B1.

100. *Cincinnati Enquirer,* Apr. 6, 1997, A6.

101. " 'Broadway Commons' Name is Tarbell's trademark," *Cincinnati Enquirer,* Oct. 29, 1998, B3. Some Tarbell's detractors sought to imply that he might be making this move as a way to profit in the future. Some also suggested further self-interest in that his business would be improved if the Broadway Commons site was chosen.

102. Jim Borgman, untitled Tarbell cartoon, *Cincinnati Enquirer,* 20 Apr. 1997, A13.

103. The Web site created for this campaign is no longer active.

104. Lucy May and Geoff Hobson, "Deal Done: Wedge Wins," *Cincinnati Enquirer,* July 2, 1998, A1, A13.

105. By mid-October the Broadway Commons proponents raised about $78,000 relying on smaller donations. The pro-riverfront coalition raised $88,500 with approximately four times fewer donors. Lucy May, "Donors Reflect Campaign," *Cincinnati Enquirer,* Oct. 30, 1998, B1.

106. "Build Reds Stadium on the Riverfront," *Cincinnati Enquirer,* Nov. 1, 1998, B2. Paul Daugherty, "No Broadway Means More of the Same," *Cincinnati Enquirer,* Nov. 1, 1998, D1. Cliff Radel, "Broadway Site Most Sensible for Ballpark," *Cincinnati Enquirer,* Oct. 18, 1996, B1.

107. Geoff Hobson and Anne Michaud, "Reds: A River Site, or a Lawsuit," *Cincinnati Enquirer,* Feb. 15, 1997, A1, A13.

108. Richard Green, "Group Pitching Ballpark Adds a Player: Proposed Reds Home Between I-71, Over-the-Rhine," *Cincinnati Enquirer,* July 15, 1994, B1, B4.

109. Indications of citizen displeasure with the stadium issue were obtained via several media sources. This sentiment was further reinforced and confirmed during several personal visits.

110. "Seeing Reds: Latest Threat to Leave Downtown Is Yet Another Insult to Taxpayers," *Cincinnati Enquirer,* Oct. 8, 1997, A14.

111. Tim Sullivan, "Stadium Just More Bad News for Football Fans," *Cincinnati Enquirer,* Feb. 17, 2000, B1.

112. Todd Portune, "Let's Work Together on Plan A," *Cincinnati Enquirer,* Apr. 11, 1996, A13.

113. Richard Green, "Riverfront: Two Pitches," *Cincinnati Enquirer,* Sept. 31, 1994, A1.

114. Richard Green, Laura Goldberg, and Anne Michaud, "Mayor: It's a Deal," *Cincinnati Enquirer,* June 30, 1995, A1, A6.

115. "How the Stadium Fund Went Bust," *Cincinnati Post,* Mar. 6, 1996, 1A. In 1994, a firm with stadium expertise was brought in to offer renovation options and cost estimates. In this case, coverage did not provide expert analysis in arriving at the cited $54 million figure.

116. Dan Klepal, "Stadium Open House II Today," *Cincinnati Enquirer,* Sept. 1, 2000, A1.

117. Mike Rutledge, "Cinergy Demolition Begins—Over Budget," *Cincinnati Post,* Feb. 24, 2000, A1.

118. Skip Tate, "Up, Up, and Away," *Cincinnati Magazine,* Nov. 1997, 48–53. See also Skip Knippenberg, "A Slogan for Those with the Stadium Tax Blues," *Cincinnati Enquirer,* Sept. 12, 1997, E1.

119. Lucy May, "Original Stadium Price: Low-Balled or Best Guess?" *Cincinnati Enquirer,* Sept. 9, 1997, A1.

120. Tate, "Up, Up, and Away," 51–52.

121. "Sanity at Cinergy," *Cincinnati Enquirer,* Dec. 4, 1997, C9.

122. Tim Sullivan, "Vehr Picked a Bad Time to Ask," *Cincinnati Enquirer,* Oct. 7, 2000, D1.

123. A Cincinnati.com poll released on September 30, 2000, of 603 internet respondents revealed only 17 percent willing to support Cincinnati hosting the Olympics with a mere 12 percent willing to spend tax dollars to support hosting the Olympic games. It was a nonrandom sample; hence, it is difficult to draw conclusions regarding how these results meshed with public opinion.

124. Greg Korte, "Bengals Reimburse Buyers: Fans Sued, Charging Stadium Seat Bait and Switch," *Cincinnati Enquirer,* Aug. 21, 2001, B1.

125. Cindi Andrews, "Commissioners Still Waiting for Refund of Extra Stadium Costs," *Cincinnati Enquirer,* June 23, 2003, B2.

126. Cindi Andrews, "Stadium Refund: 14 Million," *Cincinnati Enquirer,* Oct. 13, 2004, 1A.

127. According to a *New York Times* article, the tangible impact of stadium construction is uncertain in the long term, but negative in the short term. John Eckberg, "More Call Cincinnati Downtown Home," *New York Times,* July 30, 2000, section NE, 28.

128. David Ginzburg, vice president of Downtown Cincinnati, Inc., optimistically argued that "80 to 85 percent that I've talked to intend to stay downtown," but one frustrated

executive indicated that he was relocating to Blue Ash. According to the executive, "I've been waiting 15 years for things to get better, and they haven't. They are getting worse." "DCI to Businesses: Stay Put," *Cincinnati Post,* June 14, 2000, 18A.

129. John Johnston, " 'I Built That Stadium,' " *Cincinnati Enquirer,* Sept. 1, 2000, E1.

130. Dan Klepal, "Survey Gives Stadium Passing Grade: Respondents Gripe, Gush Over Amenities," *Cincinnati Enquirer,* Aug. 21, 2000, A1.

131. In the first game ever held in the stadium, an exhibition game, total attendance was 56,180. The stadium has a capacity of 65,600. Tom Groeschen and John Erardi, "Bengals Notebook—Players: Opening Night Electrifying," *Cincinnati Enquirer,* Aug. 20, 2000, C14. Regular season attendance was better, but two of the first three games did not sell out. The only sellout was the regular season opener against cross-state rival Cleveland. Mark Churnutte, "New Stadium No Guarantee of Sellouts," *Cincinnati Enquirer,* Oct. 6, 2000, A1.

132. "Bengals Ticket Sales in 2000," *Cincinnati Enquirer,* Dec. 18, 2000, 8. The precise average below stadium capacity was 6,851.

133. Mark Churnutte, "As Usual, No Sellout, No TV," *Cincinnati Enquirer,* Nov. 28, 2002, B4.

134. Brown was criticized for vetoing Cinergy's transition to a grass surface a year earlier. This was something that was highly desired by the Reds, and baseball fans regarded this move as the last arrogant attempt to get even with the Reds for previous stadium disputes. His concession on this particular issue may have been partially prompted by this criticism.

135. Dan Klepal, "Bengals Dropping Late-Fee Demand," *Cincinnati Enquirer,* June 18, 2000, A1.

136. "Snow, Cold Make Bad Field Worse," *Cincinnati Enquirer,* Dec. 18, 2000. http://bengals.enquirer.com/2000/12/18/ben_snow_cold_makes_bad.html.

137. Dan Klepal, "Bengals Say Pee Wee Play Was Too Hard on Their Turf," *Cincinnati Enquirer,* May 18, 2001, B1.

138. Mark Churnutte, "Fans Will Pay More to Cheer Bengals," *Cincinnati Enquirer,* Feb. 2, 2002, D1.

139. Ken Alltucker, "Census 2000: Counting America," *Cincinnati Enquirer,* Mar. 17, 2001, A1.

140. Cindi Andrews and Dan Horn, "County Joins Stadium Suit" *Cincinnati Enquirer,* Mar. 11, 2004, A1, A10.

141. Kimball Perry and Mike Rutledge, "Bengals Sue County for $30 Million," *Cincinnati Post,* July 27, 2004, 1A.

142. Cliff Peale, "As Team Turns Corner, Hopes and Sales Soar," *Cincinnati Enquirer,* July 18, 2004, A1. Randy Tucker, "Fans Devour New Bengals Gear," *Cincinnati Enquirer,* Aug. 22, 2004, A1.

143. Kimball Perry, "Losing Bengals Winners in Profits," *Cincinnati Post,* Aug. 4, 2004, 1A.

144. Howard Wilkinson, "Bengals Add Marketing QB Issue 1 Strategist to Help Sell Luxury Boxes," *Cincinnati Enquirer,* 26 Apr. 2000, C1.

145. Klepal, "Bengals Dropping Late-Fee Demand," C1.

146. "Bengals Hire Bob Bedinghaus as PBS Director of Development," Cincinnati Bengals Web site, May 18, 2004. http://www.bengals.com.

147. Geoff Hobson, "Dreams of Field Now Realized," Cincinnati Bengals Web site, June 23, 2004. http://www.bengals.com.

148. For an effective example of this, see Geoff Hobson, "No Stadium? Hello Browns; Bengals RIP," *Cincinnati Enquirer,* Feb. 15, 1996, D1.

149. Andy Furman, "Bengals Web Site Curious," *Cincinnati Post,* June 9, 2000, 1B.

150. Chris Jenkins, "League's Web Site Links Teams to Internet to Be Just Like TV: Profit Making," *USA Today,* Aug. 9, 2000, 3C.

151. John Fay, "Lawn at Last: Cinergy Gets Grass," *Cincinnati Enquirer,* Oct. 7, 2000. A1.

152. Ken Rosenthal, "Empty Promises Merit an Empty Park," *Sporting News,* Dec. 9, 2002, 62–63.

153. Cindi Andrews, "Reds Home Done Within Budget," *Cincinnati Enquirer,* Mar. 4, 2003, B1.

154. Stupp, *Opening Day at Great American Ballpark.*

155. Cliff Radel, "Machine Room Strikes Out," *Cincinnati Enquirer,* Aug. 29, 2004, C1.

156. Paul Daugherty, "Bury the Stadium, Praise the Players," *Cincinnati Enquirer,* Sept. 22, 2002, G2.

157. For one example of this argument, see John Eckberg, "A Boom with a View: Stadium Blast Boosts Profits," *Cincinnati Enquirer,* Dec. 25, 2002, A1.

158. James Pilcher, "And This One Is Gone!," *Cincinnati Enquirer,* Dec. 30, 2002, A4.

159. Dan Klepal, "What's Next for Cincinnati's Riverfront?" *Cincinnati Enquirer,* Dec. 30, 2002, A1.

160. John Blair and David Swindell, "Sports, Politics, and Economics: The Cincinnati Story," in Noll and Zimbalist, *Sports, Jobs, and Taxes,* 282–323.

161. Cindi Andrews, "Taxes for Stadium Fall Short," *Cincinnati Enquirer,* June 18, 2004, B1.

162. Kimball Perry, "Stadium Sales Tax Coming Up Short," *Cincinnati Enquirer,* Aug. 24, 2005, 1A.

163. "Clinton's Visit: Text of Speech at Xavier," *Cincinnati Enquirer,* Mar. 24, 1996, B8.

164. Anne Michaud and Richard Green, "Stadium Campaign Lauded," *Cincinnati Enquirer,* Mar. 24, 1996, B1, B12.

6. Pittsburgh: Power Politics and Steely Persistence

1. Tom Barnes, "North Side Restaurant Lures Movers, Shakers," *Pittsburgh Post-Gazette,* Nov. 3, 2002, B1.

2. Bob Dvorchak, "The House That Roared: Steelers and Fans Made the Palace Come Alive," *Pittsburgh Post-Gazette,* Dec. 18, 2000, C1, C10.

3. David H. Lawrence provides a a first-hand overview of the reshaping Pittsburgh after World War II in Lorant, "Rebirth," 372–455. Although the book was written by Stefan Lorant, this particular chapter of Lorant's text was authored by Lawrence.

4. Charles Schwab, as an example, created a lavish retreat in bucolic Loretto, Pennsylvania, approximately 80 miles east of Pittsburgh. His estate featured a golf course designed by Donald Ross with a clubhouse that provided cutting-edge technology, such as a stock ticker.

5. In a clear example of this see Riess, *Touching Base,* 71.

6. Ibid., 49.

7. Riess provides numerous examples of political chicanery that hurt owners. See ibid., 49–84.

8. "Pitt and Tech Elevens to Play Next Season on Oakland Grounds," *Pittsburgh Post,* Oct. 26, 1908, 7.

9. Carnegie Tech's football team played a game against the University of Pennsylvania on the site of the future Forbes Field on October 31, 1908, so reporters thought the site would become a football stadium. It is unlikely that Dreyfuss could have consummated the property deal in October 1908 without the imprimatur of Carnegie, whose influence was vast. News accounts fail to establish a close relationship between Drefyuss and Carnegie, but Benson states Dreyfuss "was guided in his purchase by friend Andrew Carnegie." Benson, *Ballparks of North America,* 312.

10. "Grading of New Baseball Grounds to Be Finished Within Sixty Days," *Pittsburgh Post,* Dec. 23, 1908, 10.

11. "Will Make Plea for Playgrounds: Pittsburgh Athletic Association Maps out Program Along Broad Lines, Wants Stadium Built," *Pittsburgh Post,* Dec. 13, 1908, 6.

12. "World Series Will Not Be Dropped by National and American Leagues," *Pittsburgh Post,* Dec. 15, 1908, 12. The *Pittsburg Press*'s coverage of the early construction of Forbes Field was generally less thorough than that of the *Pittsburgh Post.* The current spelling of Pittsburgh (ending with an "h") was not universally utilized in 1909. The *Press* did not utilize an "h" in its 1909 spelling.

13. "Sports Happenings of the Past Week Brought Up for General Review," *Pittsburgh Post,* 27 Dec. 1908, 3.

14. The flavor of early professional baseball is aptly described in Guschov, *The Red Stockings of Cincinnati,* and the evolution of early ballpark construction is outlined in Benson, *Ballparks of North America,* xxv–xxix.

15. This citation tendency can be found for almost any major city in Benson, *Ballparks of North America.*

16. Voigt, *American Baseball,* 259–60. *Sporting Life,* Jan. 26, 1895. *Sun* (Baltimore), Apr. 6, 1895, Apr. 28, 1895.

17. Ritter, *Lost Ballparks,* 9–18.

18. *Pittsburg Press,* Jan. 3, 1909, sporting section, 1; *Pittsburgh Post,* Jan. 3, 1909, section 3, 1.

19. In one example, a front-page headline announces: "Surgeon Adjusts Brain; Patient's Morals Improve," *Pittsburgh Post,* Oct. 31, 1908, 1. This front page also offers a Democratic presidential endorsement. The same paper gave positive coverage to Republican President William Howard Taft when he visited on May 29, 1909.

20. Still, *Urban America,* 210–11. After World War II, Pittsburgh struggled to retain its declining population base. By 1990 Pittsburgh's population was 369,879.

21. Robert McChesney, "Media Made Sport: A History of Sports Coverage in the United States," in Wenner, *Media, Sports, and Society,* 49–69.

22. Meyer, *The Five Dollar Day,* 149–62.

23. Couvares, *The Remaking of Pittsburgh,* 105.

24. Lubove, *Twentieth Century Pittsburgh,* 51.

25. "Playgrounds," *Pittsburgh Post,* Mar. 13, 1909, 6. For two examples of coverage afforded park-related endeavors, see *Pittsburgh Post,* May 15, 1909, 1; Apr. 25, 1909, 6.

26. Olmstead briefly visited Pittsburgh, preparing a twelve page plan to improve Pittsburgh's parks in 1910. His most sweeping ideas were not considered by area planners until after 1945.

27. Ironically, Kennywood was the product of ultra-rich Andrew Mellon's desire to attract more customers to his Monongahela Street Railway Company. In 1906, the railway company withdrew from day-to-day amusement park management, leasing the park to A. S. McSwigan and Frederick W. Henninger. Kennywood Web Site, http://www.kennywood.com/park_info/history.php.

28. For an overview of the shifting face of labor during this era, see Montgomery, *Worker's Control in America.*

29. Couvares, *The Remaking of Pittsburgh,* 120.

30. Theodore Roosevelt's call for a "strenuous life" represented the essence of this response to a very real fear that young men of privilege could be "feminized" if not challenged by rigorous competition. See Bederman, *Manhood and Civilization.* Kimmel, *Manhood in America.*

31. Perusal of a typical sports section will reveal coverage of some of these affluent activities, which are described in Donald Mrozek, *Sport and the American Mentality,* 103–35.

32. For more detail on boxing and bachelor subcultures see Gorn, *The Manly Art of Bare Knuckle Prize Fighting in America.* By 1909 boxing in Pittsburgh was increasingly controlled by wealthier fans. Working-class boxers frequently became pugilistic cannon-fodder for these moneyed individuals.

33. Some teams were partially owned by newspaper practitioners. See Kuklick, *To Everything a Season,* 14–15.

34. For editorial examples, see the following issues of the *Pittsburgh Post:* Dec. 11, 1908, 4; Mar. 8, 1909, 4; June 1, 1909, 6; June 21, 1909, 4. See also Oct. 9, 1909, 4.

35. *Pittsburgh Post,* Feb. 23, 1909, 12; Feb. 28, 1909, section 3, 1; Mar. 7, 1909, 1; Mar. 28, 1909, section 3, 1; May 1, 1909, 10; May 9, 1909, section 3, 1; June 11, 1909, 8; June 19, 1909, 6; June 27, 1909, 6.

36. G. H. Gillespie, "Forbes Field," *Pittsburg Press,* June 27, 1909. The use of a byline was not as common in Progressive Era news coverage as in today's news reporting, suggesting that this story merited greater attention than many other issues. *Pittsburgh Post* coverage offered a byline for its ballpark story on this same date.

37. James Jerps, "Forbes Field: The World's Finest Baseball Grounds," *Pittsburgh Post,* June 27, 1909, 6.

38. "Baseball: Shower Prevents Baseball Game, Overworked Pirates Enjoy Rest," *Pittsburgh Post,* June 2, 1909, 9.

39. "Pittsburg's Million-dollar Baseball Park," *Harper's Weekly,* May 22, 1909.

40. "Warm Tribute Is Paid to Steel City by Nation's Chief Executive: Taft Asks for Seat Back of First Base at Ball Ground," *Pittsburgh Post,* May 30, 1909, 1. Taft's brother was a part owner of the Cubs.

41. "World's Greatest Baseball Park to Be Dedicated This Afternoon," *Pittsburgh Post,* June 30, 1909, 9.

42. Shibe Park opened on April 12, 1909. It received limited front-page coverage and much less column space and photos on its opening day. *Philadelphia Inquirer,* Apr. 12, 1909, 1;

Apr. 13, 1909, 1, 10. The *Pittsburgh Post* described Shibe Park as "the largest and most ornate monument to sports in this country" on April 12, 1909. Area reporters knew that Forbes Field was a larger project, reporting on February 28, 1909 (*Post,* section 3, 1) that almost three times more steel would be utilized in Forbes Field construction.

43. "Baseball" (editorial) *Pittsburgh Post,* July 1, 1909, 6.

44. The fireworks show took place on Monday, July 5, and was heavily advertised in the newspapers on Sunday, July, 4, 1909.

45. "Audience of 15,000 Sees Hippodrome Open," *Pittsburgh Post,* July 27, 1909, 2. The Hippodrome included animal trainers, human cannonballs, marksmen, and dramatic acts. Many of the props and stage settings were highly elaborate. It was well publicized, with newspaper stories throughout July and August.

46. "Turn First Dirt Today in Hippodrome Open," *Pittsburgh Post,* July 19, 1909, 2.

47. "World's Championship Ball Games Have Boosted the National Sport," *Pittsburgh Post,* Oct. 4, 1909, 10.

48. DeValleria and DeValleria, *Honus Wagner,* 213. The authors paraphrase Mathewson in the first quotation.

49. For examples of this coverage see *Pittsburgh Post-Gazette,* Oct. 1, 1969, 1, 4; Oct. 9, 1969, 33.; Nov. 27, 1969, 1, 9.

50. The stadium authority was initially established in 1964.

51. Lee Linder, "$28 Million Financing of Stadium Challenged," *Pittsburgh Post-Gazette,* Jan. 12, 1966, 1, 7.

52. Thomas Hritz, "Stadium Opening Set for 1970," *Pittsburgh Post-Gazette,* Mar. 30, 1968, 13.

53. "New Stadium Work May Start on April 20," *Pittsburgh Post-Gazette,* Mar. 15, 1968, 21.

54. Thomas Hritz, "Stadium May Cost $30 Million," *Pittsburgh Post-Gazette,* Mar. 19, 1968, 19.

55. P. W. Hutson, "We're Spending Money Not Ours" (letter to the editor), *Pittsburgh Post-Gazette,* Feb. 7, 1968, 12.

56. J. G. Fuller, "Housing Renewal Rated Over Stadium" (letter to the editor), *Pittsburgh Post-Gazette,* Apr. 30, 1968, 8.

57. G. L. Grandy, "Money for Stadium, None for Schools" (letter to the editor), *Pittsburgh Post-Gazette,* May 23, 1968, 16. Letters of stadium opposition seemed to disappear after this letter, which was the first in "The People Speak" section. It is uncertain if the sharply worded editor's note had a chilling effect on subsequent criticism.

58. "A Name for the Stadium" (editorial), *Pittsburgh Post-Gazette,* Apr. 25, 1968, 14.

59. " 'David L. Lawrence' Gains as Name for New Stadium," *Pittsburgh Post-Gazette,* Apr. 26, 1968, 17.

60. Charles Dees Jr., "It's Time to Honor Lawrence Memory"; Erma Echement, "Lets Not Get Into Personalities"; anonymous (author signed as "A Constant Reader"), "Stadium Should be Named for the City" (letters to the editor), *Pittsburgh Post-Gazette,* Apr. 29, 1968, 10.

61. Gerald Lawrence, "Commends Tribute to Renowned Father" (letter to the editor), *Pittsburgh Post-Gazette,* May 21, 1968, 8.

62. "Where Is Lawrence's Legacy?" (editorial), *Pittsburgh Post-Gazette,* June 18, 1968, 12.

The editorial argues that "nothing public has been done to honor the memory of the public official who did most to rebuild this worn-out city after World War II." Years later, the city's convention center would be named in his honor.

63. "Don't Name Stadium for a Politician" (letter to the editor), *Pittsburgh Post Gazette,* May 2, 1968, 12. "Let Us Call It McKechnie Stadium" (letter to the editor), *Pittsburgh Post-Gazette,* May 8, 1968, 14. "Name Stadium for Martin L. King" (letter to the editor), *Pittsburgh Post-Gazette,* May 10, 1968, 10.

64. Among the civic-oriented suggestions were "the Steel City Sports Stadium" and "Pittsburgh Memorial Stadium." Sally Wilson, "Let Fans Decide Stadium Name" (letter to the editor), *Pittsburgh Post-Gazette,* May 10, 1968, 10. Leslie Jones, "Name Stadium for All Personalities" (letter to the editor), *Pittsburgh Post-Gazette,* May 2, 1968, 12. "Name Stadium for War Heroes" (letter to the editor), *Pittsburgh Post-Gazette,* May 16, 1968, 12.

65. George Dorondo, "Name Stadium for the Rivers" (letter to the editor), *Pittsburgh Post-Gazette,* May 6, 1968, 12.

66. Howard Burgwin, "Appropriate Name for Stadium" (letter to the editor), *Pittsburgh Post-Gazette,* May 22, 1968, 12.

67. "Stadium Is Named 3 Rivers," *Pittsburgh Post-Gazette,* Feb. 13, 1969, 27.

68. Thomas Hritz, "Authority Approves Final Stadium Plans," *Pittsburgh Post-Gazette,* Jan. 13, 1968, 1, 4.

69. "Scores to Witness Ground Breaking, Hear Olympic Star," "Stadium Here Today Becomes Reality," *Pittsburgh Post-Gazette,* Apr. 25, 1968, 17. A photograph of Jesse Owens kneeling to greet a four-year-old white child from Pittsburgh's South Side was included in the sports section. The president of the National League, Warren Giles, and the mayor attended this ceremony.

70. " 'David L. Lawrence' Gains as Name for New Stadium," *Pittsburgh Post-Gazette,* Apr. 26, 1968, 17.

71. Alvin Rosensweet, "Lots of Jobs Go Begging These Days: Pittsburgh Area's Shortage of Skilled Workers Critical," *Pittsburgh Post-Gazette,* Mar. 28, 1966, 1, 8.

72. Thomas Hritz, "Stadium Will Cost $27.7 Million; Associated Press, "Violence Marks Negro March in Memphis," *Pittsburgh Post-Gazette,* Mar. 29, 1968, 1, 8.

73. For an example, see Sterling Green, "Racial Probers Fear Split into Two Societies," *Pittsburgh Post-Gazette,* Mar. 1, 1968, 1, 18.

74. "First Negro Ushers Likely at Ball Park," *Pittsburgh Post-Gazette,* Mar. 8, 1966, 20.

75. Joseph Browne, "Contractors Join with Union in Negro Job Plan," *Pittsburgh Post-Gazette,* Apr. 5, 1968, 21. Mayor Joseph Barr was involved in brokering this agreement. One difficult issue for those wanting immediate results was the requirement of 52 weeks of heavy equipment training before union membership could be assured. Individuals were paid while receiving this training, but the pay scale for trainees was not specified in news reports.

76. Although not related to stadium construction, the following article offers the trade union position on this issue. John Moody, "Black Jobs Negotiations Collapse: Plan Rejected, Union-Industry Group Leaves," *Pittsburgh Post-Gazette,* Sept. 24, 1969, 1.

77. "Court Limits Protesters at Stadium Site," *Pittsburgh Post-Gazette,* Aug. 13, 1969, 1.

78. Fred Shilling, "Court Limits, Oks Stadium Pickets; Big March Vowed," *Pittsburgh Post-Gazette,* Aug. 16, 1969, 1.

79. "Stadium Electrical Work Shorted Out," *Pittsburgh Post-Gazette,* Apr. 14, 1969, 1.

80. Bohdan Hodiak, "Still Few Blacks in Unions," *Pittsburgh Post-Gazette,* Aug. 15, 1969, 6. Twenty-six unions were contacted by the mayor's commission in preparing the report.

81. David McConnell, "Work on Stadium Closed to Avoid Possible Furor," *Pittsburgh Post-Gazette,* Aug. 25, 1969, 1.

82. John Moody, "180 Job Protesters Are Arrested," *Pittsburgh Post-Gazette,* Aug. 27, 1969, 1.

83. "Dogs, Sprayers, Clubs: Demonstrators Had Riot Gear Protection," *Pittsburgh Post-Gazette,* Aug. 27, 1969, 5.

84. John Moody, "Black Job Talks Deadlocked: Unions Industry Ask State Study, Negroes Incensed," *Pittsburgh Post-Gazette,* Sept. 16, 1969, 1.

85. Alvin Rosensweet, "Many March in Black Jobs Demonstration," *Pittsburgh Post-Gazette,* Sept. 16, 1969, 1.

86. Robert Simonds, "Supports Efforts of Black Coalition" (letter to the editor), *Pittsburgh Post-Gazette,* Aug. 26, 1969, 10.

87. Miriam Deasy, "Asks Question for Black Veterans" (letter to the editor), *Pittsburgh Post-Gazette,* Sept. 4, 1969, 8.

88. Charles Kindle, "Questions Racism of Building Crafts" (letter to the editor), *Pittsburgh Post-Gazette,* Aug. 26, 1969, 10.

89. For examples see P. Lee, "Why Must Public Give to the Negroes?" *Pittsburgh Post-Gazette,* Apr. 30, 1968, 8. Beafus McAffee, "White Protest Was Beautiful," *Pittsburgh Post-Gazette,* Sept. 4, 1969, 8. Richard Barrow, "Urges Union, Not Closed, Shop," *Pittsburgh Post-Gazette,* Sept. 10, 1969, 8. James Cunningham, "Jobs Conflict: Renaissance Sham?" (letter to the editor), *Pittsburgh Post-Gazette,* Sept. 14, 1969, 12.

90. "Stadium Jobs Agreement Near," *Pittsburgh Post-Gazette,* Dec. 5, 1969, 29. "Black Hiring Pact Expected During the Week," *Pittsburgh Post-Gazette,* Dec. 15, 1969, 31.

91. "New Troubles Brewing on 3 Rivers Stadium," *Pittsburgh Post-Gazette,* July 25, 1969, 19.

92. "20 Workers Balk at 3 Rivers Stadium," *Pittsburgh Post-Gazette,* July 15, 1969, 1.

93. John Moody, "Stadium Scoreboard Dispute is Resolved," *Pittsburgh Post-Gazette,* Apr. 1, 1970, 1.

94. "Work on Stadium Slowed by Pickets," *Pittsburgh Post-Gazette,* Mar. 12, 1970, 6. John Moody, "Site Safety Issue May Bar Stadium Work," *Pittsburgh Post-Gazette,* Mar. 13, 1970, 1. John Moody, "Stadium Fails Union Safety Inspection," *Pittsburgh Post-Gazette,* Mar. 14, 1970, 1. Thomas Hritz, "Concessionaire Demands Stadium Improvements: Finer Eateries to Cost Bucs $1.3 Million," *Pittsburgh Post-Gazette,* Mar. 24, 1970, 12.

95. "Local Beer Asked for New Stadium," *Pittsburgh Post-Gazette,* Mar. 6, 1970, 20.

96. "Ex-Steeler Johnson Named to Stadium Post," *Pittsburgh Post-Gazette,* Feb. 3, 1970, 13.

97. "Stadium Job Talks Nearing Completion," *Pittsburgh Post-Gazette,* Apr. 14, 1970, 21. This article indicated that several black ushers, ticket takers, and ticket sellers had already been hired. According to a city official, "If qualified blacks are recruited for [other] jobs, the unions—Local 508, Service Employees, and Teamsters Local 250—have agreed to accept them."

98. Michener, *Sports in America,* 346.

99. "Authority Approves Final Stadium Plan," *Pittsburgh Post-Gazette,* Jan. 13, 1968, 1.

100. James Daniel, "The Allegheny Club: Its Contribution" (letter to the editor), *Pittsburgh Post-Gazette,* Jan. 13, 1968, 12. (Daniel was president of this club.) Ironically, the forward thinking of the Allegheny Club would be one factor in the call for a new football-only stadium. The club was situated in some of the most valuable stadium real estate (i.e., the skybox area) and attracted some of Pittsburgh's most affluent corporate leaders. As a result, Steelers management could not easily lay claim to revenues generated in this area unless dramatic changes could be made.

101. "Stadium's Special Boxes to Yield $1.4 Million," *Pittsburgh Post-Gazette,* Apr. 30, 1969, 29.

102. Thomas Hritz, "Hike Bucs,' Steelers' Stadium Rent—Kuhn," *Pittsburgh Post-Gazette,* Nov. 27, 1969, 1.

103. Thomas Hritz, "Pittsburgh Fans to Pay Added Stadium Costs," *Pittsburgh Post-Gazette,* Dec. 2, 1969, 1.

104. "Users Should Pay Stadium's Added Cost" (editorial), *Pittsburgh Post-Gazette,* Dec. 2, 1969, 8. Thomas Hritz, "Bucs, Steelers OK Price Hike as Stadium Aid," *Pittsburgh Post-Gazette,* Dec. 3, 1969, 1.

105. Thomas Hritz, "Finer Eateries to Cost Bucs $1.3 Million," *Pittsburgh Post-Gazette,* Mar. 24, 1970, 12.

106. "Stadium Has Silver Lining for the City" (editorial), *Pittsburgh Post-Gazette,* Jan. 7, 1970, 8.

107. "Stadium to Get Super Lights," *Pittsburgh Post-Gazette,* Apr. 21, 1969, 21.

108. "Restaurant Plans River Shuttle Service to New Stadium," *Pittsburgh Post-Gazette,* Apr. 7, 1970, 17.

109. Robert Voelker, "48,846 Fans Open New Stadium," *Pittsburgh Post-Gazette,* July 17, 1970, 1.

110. Smizik, *The Pittsburgh Pirates,* 4.

111. The description of the last game at Three Rivers Stadium was the result of personal conversations with area residents before, during, and after the final game at this venue.

112. An exception to this trend was a *Pittsburgh Tribune-Review* story that quoted several fans who regarded Three Rivers Stadium as a very good venue for football viewing. See Bill Steigerwald, "Saying Goodbye: Emotions Mixed on Stadium's Demise," *Pittsburgh Tribune-Review,* Dec. 17, 2000, G1.

113. "Steelers Say Goodbye: The Old Stadium Shown Respect in Its Final Hour" (editorial), *Pittsburgh Post-Gazette,* Dec. 18, 2000, 12. "Three Rivers Lives" (editorial), *Pittsburgh Tribune-Review,* Dec. 17, 2000, H2.

114. Ron Cook, "Sophie's Choice: Stadium of Dreams," *Pittsburgh Post-Gazette,* Sept. 6, 1991, 11. Even the headline of this article, "Sophie's Choice," cleverly connecting the proposal with a William Styron novel of the same title, may have been chosen to suggest that Masloff was committing political suicide in making this proposal.

115. Tom Hritz, "Put a Good Face on Pie in the Sky," *Pittsburgh Post-Gazette,* Sept. 12, 1991, 7.

116. Tom Waseleski, "If We Build It, They Won't Come—At Least Until the Bottom of the Third—Because They'll be Stuck in Traffic on I-279," *Pittsburgh Post-Gazette,* Sept. 11, 1991, 9.

117. John Craig, "The Pirates' Promise: A New Stadium Might Just Maximize Returns on the Team," *Pittsburgh Post-Gazette,* Sept. 14, 1991, 7.

118. Three letters were published in the *Pittsburgh Post-Gazette* on Sept. 14, 1991, 6. One mocked the stupidity of building an old-fashioned stadium when Pittsburgh abandoned Forbes Field about twenty years earlier. Another offered an ad hominem attack that called Masloff "senile" and called her stadium idea "hare-brained." A final letter simply argued her priorities were wrong.

119. Mark Belko, "Foerster Opposes Tax for New Stadium," *Pittsburgh Post-Gazette,* Sept. 10, 1991, 1.

120. "Dreams of Field—Mayor: Build Bucs a Park and They Will Stay," *Pittsburgh Post-Gazette,* Sept. 6, 1991, 1.

121. "Sophie Faces Reality" (editorial), *Pittsburgh Post-Gazette,* Sept. 19, 1991, 8.

122. Joh Schmitz, "City Tries to Improve 24-Year-Old Stadium: State's $14 Million Would Pay for Half," *Pittsburgh Post-Gazette,* Sept. 4, 1993, A1.

123. Tom Barnes, "Baseball Stadium Idea Strikes Out with Murphy," *Pittsburgh Post-Gazette,* July 24, 1993, B6.

124. Jon Schmitz, "Pirates Go on Block: Murphy, City Have 180 Days to Find Buyer, Keep Team Here," *Pittsburgh Post-Gazette,* Aug. 4, 1994, A1.

125. Ron Cook, "Don't Rule Out Pirates' Move," *Pittsburgh Post-Gazette,* Aug. 5, 1994, C1; Steve Halvonick, "2nd Virginia Syndicate Interested in Bucs," *Pittsburgh Post-Gazette,* Mar. 10, 1995, B1.

126. An example of this fan dissatisfaction can be found in various letters to the editor written throughout 1993 and 1994. For one example, see Mark Brown, "Don't Subsidize the Sorry Enterprise of Baseball" (letter to the editor), *Pittsburgh Post-Gazette,* Sept. 30, 1994, C2.

127. "Bucs Drop to 21st in Salary Average," *Pittsburgh Post-Gazette,* Dec. 8, 1993, D2. The average player salary declined from $1,206,012 to $761,073. Pittsburgh's blue-collar tradition strained the potential for acceptance of such "averages," even with the decline.

128. Tom Barnes, "Pirates in Court for $4.2 Million on City 'Pledge,' " *Pittsburgh Post-Gazette,* Mar. 3, 1993, B6. Tim Reeves, "Court Rejects Pirates Claim to $4.2 Million," *Pittsburgh Post-Gazette,* Aug. 5, 1993, A5.

129. Jon Schmitz, "Prohibited Snacks Hard to Swallow: Firms Protest Stadium Box Ban on Outside Food, Drink," *Pittsburgh Post-Gazette,* Mar. 31, 1994, B1.

130. Jon Schmitz, "Pirates Fans Buy Tickets, But Don't Show Up," *Pittsburgh Post-Gazette,* Oct. 20, 1995, B4. If turnstile activity determined actual attendance, as was Major League Baseball policy before 1993, Pirates attendance would have dropped further to a mere 763,458 in 1995. This is a dramatic attendance drop off from the 2,065,302 mark that was achieved by the Pirates in 1991.

131. Tom Barnes, "City Leaders to Size Up Cleveland's New Ballpark," *Pittsburgh Post-Gazette,* Mar. 23, 1994, B4.

132. According to *Financial World* magazine, the Pirates's value slipped from $95 million in 1993 to $79 million in 1994, to $70 million in 1995. This analysis of all Major League teams

was publicized locally. Steve Halvonick, "Pirates Slip to Last in Baseball Franchise Value," *Pittsburgh Post-Gazette,* Apr. 19, 1995, C7.

133. Mark Belko, "Stadium Concessions Approved," *Pittsburgh Post-Gazette,* Jan. 11, 1996, B4.

134. "McClatchy Contract Puts Shorter Leash on the Pirates," *Pittsburgh Post-Gazette,* Jan. 11, 1996, B1.

135. Steve Halvonik, "Rooney Says a New Ballpark Not a Solution Here," *Pittsburgh Post-Gazette,* Feb. 19, 1995, B1. This article's prominent placement reveals an early attempt to balance points of views on the stadium construction issue.

136. Ed Bouchette, "Steelers Drive for Stadium Upgrade for Financial Health," *Pittsburgh Post-Gazette,* Oct. 10, 1995, A1. Bouchette also introduced Joe Brown, NFL senior vice president of communications and governmental affairs, who said the NFL considered Pittsburgh's stadium among the worst in the league.

137. Ed Bouchette, "Rooney Says Move Will Affect Steelers," *Pittsburgh Post-Gazette,* Nov. 6, 1995, D1.

138. Mark Belko, "Steelers Lobby for Battery Mate," *Pittsburgh Post-Gazette,* Apr. 2, 1996, A16.

139. Robert Zausner, "It Was Tee Time for Ridge and His Biggest Donors," *Philadelphia Inquirer,* June 15, 1997, B1.

140. Mark Belko, "Steelers Remind City of Their Need: NFL Contingent Meets With Murphy to Discuss Wish List," *Pittsburgh Post-Gazette,* July 3, 1996, C1.

141. Mark Belko, "Steelers Stick with Renovation Plan," *Pittsburgh Post-Gazette,* Nov. 22, 1996, C1.

142. Mark Belko, "Architects May Study New Steelers Stadium," *Pittsburgh Post-Gazette,* Dec. 7, 1996, C1.

143. Mark Belko, "New Sports Venues, Part 2," *Pittsburgh Post-Gazette,* Dec. 20, 1996, B9.

144. Tom Barnes, "What's the Game Plan for Football Stadium: Build or Remodel?" *Pittsburgh Post-Gazette,* Apr. 29, 1997, A1.

145. Richard Green, "Riverfront: Two Pitches," *Cincinnati Enquirer,* Sept. 13, 1994, A1.

146. Ed Bouchette, "Steelers Seek New Stadium: Rooney Says Cost of Upgrade Too High," *Pittsburgh Post-Gazette,* Sept. 20, 1997, A1. The initial HOK plans included moving the press box to the upper deck area in order to create more luxury skyboxes.

147. Steve Halvonik, "The Puck Stops Here: Penguins President Tries to Put Fun Back on Ice," *Pittsburgh Post-Gazette,* Dec. 1, 1996, C19.

148. Bill Schackner, "Pitt's New Deal: Asks for $25 Million More to Build Center," *Pittsburgh Post-Gazette,* Oct. 14, 1997, A1.

149. Steve Halvonik, "Poll: 67% Oppose Stadium, But Support Is There to Keep Team in City," *Pittsburgh Post-Gazette,* Nov. 22, 1995, B7.

150. USX was a name change affixed to U.S. Steel.

151. Ridge went on record as an opponent of a sports lottery before he was elected governor and continued his opposition even after the failed ballot initiative. See Tim Reeves, "Ridge, Singel Oppose Lottery for Stadium," *Pittsburgh Post-Gazette,* Sept. 20, 1994, B1; Brad Banisted, "Stadium Lottery Not a Good Bet, Ridge Says," *North Hills News Record,* Dec. 20, 1997, 1.

152. Peter Shelly, "70% Oppose Ridge's Liquor Plan," *Pittsburgh Post-Gazette,* Jan. 27, 1997, A1, 10. For opposition information, see also "House Minority Leader Wants Liquor Privatization Vote," *Pittsburgh Post-Gazette,* Sept. 21, 1997, B10.

153. Peter Shelly, "Ridge Concedes Defeat on Liquor Store Sale: He'll Keep Pushing Plans to Fund Stadiums, Centers," *Pittsburgh Post-Gazette,* Sept. 27, 1997, A1.

154. Bruce Stanley, "Sales Tax for Stadiums a Tough Sell in Pittsburgh," *Altoona Mirror,* June 10, 1997, A3.

155. James O'Toole and Jon Schmitz, "Tax Backers Give More Than $4 Million," *Pittsburgh Post-Gazette,* Oct. 25, 1997, A1.

156. Jon Schmitz, "Campaign '97 / AdWatch," *Pittsburgh Post-Gazette,* Oct. 7, 1997, B2.

157. Since the referendum defeat, the Web site that was used to report and promote this organization's activities (www.goodsports.org) is no longer available for such purposes.

158. The Community Alliance for Economic Development and Jobs Web site was located at www.swpajobs.com. It is no longer an active link.

159. For a detailed overview of media tendencies see Trumpbour, "The New Cathedrals" (dissertation), 2001.

160. Paul Munro, "Call in the Pollsters" (letter to the editor), *Pittsburgh Post-Gazette,* Nov. 12, 1997, A7.

161. Walter Funk, "Double-talk" (letter to the editor), *Pittsburgh Tribune-Review,* Oct. 30, 1997, A7.

162. Frank Vertosick Jr., "Teams Don't Define Us" (letter to the editor), *Pittsburgh Post-Gazette,* Oct. 12, 1997, C3.

163. Mason, "Revenue Sharing and Agency Problems in Professional Team Sport," 213.

164. Bonnie Prutz, "Greed" (letter to the editor), *Pittsburgh Tribune-Review,* Oct. 30, 1997, A7.

165. Christine McKindley, "Make the Players Pay" (letter to the editor), *Pittsburgh Post-Gazette,* Sept. 27, 1997, A7.

166. Tom Schrantz, "Two-For-One Deal" (Sports Mailbag), *Pittsburgh Post-Gazette,* Sept. 27, 1997, C3.

167. Jack Torry, "Tales of Two Stadiums," *Pittsburgh Post-Gazette,* May 19, 1997, A1.

168. Bob Smizik, "PSU Can Blame Itself If It Doesn't Finish at No. 1," *Pittsburgh Post-Gazette,* Oct. 30, 1997, D1.

169. "Stadium Stand: The Governor Spells Out His Position for Pittsburgh" (editorial), *Pittsburgh Post-Gazette,* Nov. 26, 1997, A-22. Creative compromises such as one facility with two separate fields and a shared retail concourse were never introduced into the media coverage. Instead, officials tended to move in the same design direction as other cities. A unique design strategy may have separated Pittsburgh from other areas, likely offering fans outside the region greater reason to visit. David Orlowski, senior vice president for Ellerbe Becket's sports architecture division, indicated that shared facilities were relatively easy to design, but shared revenues limited the appeal to team owners. Jon Schmitz, "Ridge Sees One Ballpark for Bucs, Steelers," *Pittsburgh Post-Gazette,* Nov. 23, 1997, A1.

170. An alternative plan for one new stadium for football and a renovated Three Rivers Stadium for baseball was publicized about a week before final legislature approval on the state stadium subsidy package on February 3, 1999. Earlier options for a Three Rivers Sta-

dium renovation were offered in small weekly papers, but did emerge in the *Pittsburgh Post-Gazette.*

171. Jon Schmitz and Robert Devorchak, "A Diamond in the Rough," *Pittsburgh Post-Gazette,* Mar. 18, 1998, A1.

172. "Plan B: Play Ball! RAD Board Votes 6-1 to Fund New Stadiums, Expansion of Convention Center," *Pittsburgh Post-Gazette,* July 10, 1998, A1.

173. Robert Devorchak, "Plan B Scores a TD: Steelers, Pirates Add Millions for Stadiums, Agree to Long Term Leases," *Pittsburgh Post-Gazette,* June 21, 1998, A1.

174. Robert Jubelirer, president pro tempore of the Pennsylvania Senate, provided information to this researcher indicating that the "stealth legislation" would not have withstood a legal challenge.

175. The assertions here were derived from observation of live coverage of the Pennsylvania Cable Network in late 1998 and through discussions with some political leaders and lobbyists as efforts were being made to secure commitments from legislators. Mayor Tom Murphy did a great deal of lobbying throughout the state during this period. In one example, he presented an overview of stadium construction plans in Cambria County, about 90 miles east of Allegheny County, asking participants to personally contact their legislators to support his plan. Tom Murphy, the Robert and Thelma Gleason Lecture on American Politics and Government, Saint Francis College, Loretto, Penn., Nov. 23, 1998.

176. Sonya Toler, "Third Renaissance Inclusion: Joint Effort to Push for Support of Stadium Funding Plan Announced," *Pittsburgh Courier,* Jan. 27, 1999, B1. During construction limited coverage pointed to potential improprieties in minority-related contract awards. Some firms may have received contracts based on their minority status but then turned the work to nonminority firms, circumventing the spirit of earlier agreements. Although team owners had obtained construction oversight in exchange for responsibility for cost overruns, they did not publicly comment on the specifics of this issue.

177. Such an arrangement was also beneficial for the Steelers because it would prevent upstart professional football leagues from gaining a foothold in Pittsburgh. When the USFL temporarily placed a football team in Pittsburgh, the Rooney family expressed discontent with the stadium authority for permitting usage of Three Rivers Stadium for games.

178. Tom Barnes, "Plan B Cost Estimates Up 10 Percent," *Pittsburgh Post-Gazette,* May 28, 1999, A1.

179. Larry Dunn, "Plan B Is No Good," *Pittsburgh Post-Gazette,* June 28, 1998, C1.

180. Peter Shelly, "Plan B Poised on Threshold: It's a Done Deal—Almost; House Vote Awaited Today," *Pittsburgh Post-Gazette,* Feb. 3, 1999, A1.

181. Frank Reeves and Peter Shelly, "Plan B Wins Big," *Pittsburgh Post-Gazette,* Feb. 4, 1999, A1, 11; Robert Devorchak, " 'We Literally Moved a Mountain in 8 Days,' " *Pittsburgh Post-Gazette,* Feb. 4, 1999, A1. A large photo of stadium supporters celebrating the approval was included in this front-page coverage.

182. Jim McKinnon, "Black Workers Stage Protest at PNC Park," *Pittsburgh Post-Gazette,* June 17, 1999, B1.

183. Timothy McNulty, "Sports Agency Tightens Rules on Contracts: Assuring Minority, Female Participation Is the Aim," *Pittsburgh Post-Gazette,* Mar. 12, 2002, B5.

184. "Best Ballpark," *Reader's Digest,* May 2004, 141.

185. As an example, the men's rooms for the typical fans feature shared stainless steel troughs instead of the privacy of individual urinals that are available in many NFL level facilities.

186. Ed Bouchette, "Steelers Searching for Name to Stadium," *Pittsburgh Post-Gazette,* Mar. 25, 2001, D22.

187. Mark Belko, "Cranmer to Sit Out County Race," *Pittsburgh Post-Gazette,* Jan. 5, 1999, A1. Before the RAD Board vote, Cranmer pressured a RAD Board appointee to resign and replaced this individual with someone who was more supportive of stadium subsidies.

188. Mark Belko, "Cranmer Takes Job with Firm that Serves County," *Pittsburgh Post-Gazette,* Dec. 14, 1999, B1. Cranmer explained that his prior experience in telecommunications and consulting led to this opportunity, not the firm's connections with Allegheny County.

189. Timothy McNulty, "City Budget Ax Falls," *Pittsburgh Post-Gazette,* Aug. 7, 2003, A1.

190. Tom Barnes and Dan Gigler, "Pittsburgh's New Stadium Draws Rave Reviews in Debut," *Pittsburgh Post-Gazette,* Apr. 1, 2001, A1.

191. The *Pittsburgh Post-Gazette* cited $281 million as the cost when work was near completion, with $123 million coming from the team. However, in an e-mail obtained on January 20, 2006, Doug Straley, development director for Pittsburgh's Sports and Exhibition Authority, pegged final costs at about $263 million, with $105 million coming from the Steelers. The September 11 tragedy limited stadium coverage that would have typically clarified such information. Marquette University's National Sports Law Institute lists final costs at $244 million, with the team paying $76.5 million. That $76.5 figure is likely an underestimate, but the earlier offered $123 figure is probably an overestimate. Total construction costs almost certainly exceeded $260 million.

192. Pittsburgh was dubbed the "city of champions" in the late 1970s after local teams won a World Series and a Super Bowl in the same year.

193. Dejan Kovacevic, "Not For Sale; But Lemieux Warns Penguins Could Be Sold, Moved Soon Without New Arena," *Pittsburgh Post-Gazette,* June 11, 2004, B1.

194. Dejan Kovacevic, "Penguins and Slots, OK by Bettman," *Pittsburgh Post-Gazette,* June 26, 2004, B7.

195. Tom Barnes and Bill Toland, "House Approves Slot Machines/Property Tax Relief, Budget Also on Floor," *Pittsburgh Post-Gazette,* July 4, 2004, A1.

196. "The Pittsburgh Casino: Who Is in the Running to Own the Local Casino?" *Pittsburgh Post-Gazette,* July 6, 2004, A1.

197. Dave Molinari, " 'Boots' Won't Try to Buy Penguins," *Pittsburgh Post-Gazette,* Jan. 20, 2006, D1.

7. Boston: History, Mystery, and Political Football

1. Bill Nowlin, "The Boston Pilgrims Never Existed," *National Pastime,* Aug. 2003, 71–76.

2. Cressy, *Coming Over,* 61.

3. Cohane, *The Yale Football Story,* 73.

4. Smith, *Sports and Freedom,* 188–89.

5. During the Progressive Era many New Englanders were concerned that young males

were negatively influenced by female attempts to civilize them. For G. Stanley Hall, a solution was to challenge boys to act aggressively in athletics. Theodore Roosevelt's manly philosophy drew from Hall. See Bederman, *Manliness and Civilization*, 100–12.

6. Voigt, *American Baseball*, 45, 78, 217.

7. For a detailed project overview, see Bertagna, *Crimson in Triumph*, 25–26.

8. "Harvard's Big Stadium, Where Wearers of Crimson and Blue Will Move," *Boston Sunday Herald*, Nov. 8, 1903, 42.

9. Front-page stadium stories were included in the *Harvard Crimson* on Apr. 6, 1903; Sept. 29, 1903; Oct. 5, 1903; Oct. 28, 1903; Nov. 14, 1903 and Nov. 16, 1903. The two November articles included photos. Photos were not common in the 1903 *Crimson*.

10. "Harvard Shut Out by Dartmouth: Beaten 11-0 in the New Stadium," *Boston Herald*, Nov. 15, 1903, 1, 5.

11. Shaughnessy and Grossfeld, *Fenway*, 39.

12. Fenway was constructed during the "dead-ball" era, so home runs were limited. The high wall was created when the ten-foot hill was eliminated during the 1934 renovation and a new thirty-seven-foot wall was installed in place of the previous barrier.

13. Stout and Johnson, *Red Sox Century*, 77.

14. The newspaper was named the *Boston Daily Globe* until 1960.

15. Lieb, *The Boston Red Sox*, 91. James McAleer, previously a manager with the Washington Senators, had been trying to buy a baseball team for several years.

16. For an overview of these early years see Shaugnessy, *At Fenway*, 20–30.

17. For examples of Fenway development opposition, see "Would Keep Parks Sacred," *Boston Daily Globe*, June 27, 1911, 10; "Site in Fens Selected," *Boston Daily Globe*, June 27, 1911, 5. The second article states that "the fight over the site of the [high school] building has gone on about a year."

18. Shaughnessy and Grossfeld, *Fenway*, 36.

19. The Chicago Ballpark, opened in 1915, was originally named Weeghman Park, renamed Cubs Park in 1920, and christened Wrigley Field in 1926. Hartel, *A Day at the Park*, 7–8.

20. Shaughnessy and Grossfeld, *Fenway*, 36.

21. "Next Year Will See Many Changes in Red Sox," *Boston Daily Globe*, Sept. 16, 1911, 2.

22. "New Home of the Red Sox: Plant Ideal in Equipment and Location," *Boston Daily Globe*, Oct. 15, 1911, 7.

23. T. H. Murnane, "Sox Open to Packed Park," *Boston Daily Globe*, Apr. 21, 1912, 1.

24. When capacity crowds prevented seat sales, it was common during this period to place fans deep in the outfield or on the side of the playing field.

25. Stout and Johnson, *Red Sox Century*, 117.

26. Smith, *The Ballpark Book*, 202.

27. Kaese, *The Boston Braves*, 173.

28. Inaccurate historic claims have been made frequently about Ruth's move to New York. Even Major League Baseball continues to report these inaccuracies in officially licensed publications. For an example see Gillette, *Total Red Sox 2000*. For a more thorough historic explanation, see Stout and Johnson, *Red Sox Century*, 137–56.

29. "Schoolboy of 16 Inherits $20,000,000," *New York Times*, Mar. 18, 1919, 6. Yawkey's

thirtieth birthday marked the time when he was legally entitled to take full control of the assets from his father's estate. Yawkey's father was an early owner of the Detroit Tigers. This fueled his enthusiasm for baseball.

30. Stout and Johnson, *Red Sox Century,* 179.

31. The Braves later moved to Atlanta. Greater potential for broadcast revenues prompted the second move.

32. Yawkey tended to surround himself with individuals willing to agree with him. With contrasting personalities, Yawkey and Sullivan might have been a bad fit. Stout and Johnson provide a critical, yet thorough, analysis of Yawkey's management style *(Red Sox Century).*

33. For multipage coverage of the stadium opener see the Boston Daily Globe, Sept. 21, 1957, and Sept. 22, 1957. On April 1, 1958, the *Boston Daily Globe* presented a news story on a career promotion for Sullivan. In the article, Sullivan was credited with assisting Boston College "in bringing Navy's football team here . . . in the dedication of the stadium . . . last fall."

34. "Dream Sports Palace" (editorial), *Boston Daily Globe,* Apr. 2, 1958, 29.

35. The NFL's Redskins got their start in Boston, playing at Braves Field, but shifting to Fenway after facing a rent increase. The team's name was changed from Braves to Redskins when they switched facilities. Keeping a similar theme saved the team the expense of uniform replacement. For a brief history of the various professional football teams that failed to catch on in Boston, see Harold Kaese, "Hub Trio Seeks NFL Team," *Boston Globe,* Feb. 5, 1970, 25.

36. Sullivan worked through Giants's owner Tim Mara and NFL Commissioner Bert Bell to get an NFL team. The deaths of Mara and Bell in 1959 made obtaining an NFL franchise unlikely for several years. Sullivan pushed for an AFL franchise in November 1959. Of the $25,000, Sullivan provided $8,000. Area civic leaders assisted with the balance. See Fox, *The New England Patriots,* 14–24.

37. In some seasons, the Patriots played in two different facilities. As an example, the team used Harvard Stadium for single games in 1960 (exhibition) and 1962 (regular season). For simplicity, the primary stadium used for a season was listed.

38. Associated Press, "New Rule: Stadium Capacity", *Boston Globe,* May 16, 1968, 1. The Patriots were the only team affected by this new league policy.

39. Cornelius Noonan, "Warning Seen as Boost to Stadium," *Boston Globe,* May 16, 1968, 49.

40. Bob Ryan, "At Quiet Time, He's Collecting Their Thoughts," *Boston Globe,* Oct. 28, 1996, D1.

41. For an overview of Boston's West End see Gans, *The Urban Villagers.*

42. O'Connor, *Building a New Boston,* 137. For an example of enthusiastic press support for the West End project see Robert Hanron, "West End Project Could be Spark to Revitalize Boston," *Boston Globe,* Dec. 20, 1959, 40.

43. S. J. Micciche, "Dedham Urged for Stadium Site," *Boston Globe,* May 17, 1968, 29.

44. Leigh Montville, "Buzzards Are Circling as Time Runs Out on Pats," *Boston Evening Globe,* Jan. 27, 1970, 25. The *Globe* published two separate editions on weekdays.

45. Will McDonough, "Pats Admit 'We're Out of Ideas,' " *Boston Globe,* Jan. 27, 1970, 25.

46. Montville, "Buzzards Are Circling as Time Runs Out on Pats," 25.

47. "Excerpts of Pusey Letter to Pats," *Boston Globe,* Jan. 27, 1970, 26.

48. Will McDonough, "Fenway a Must for Pats," *Boston Globe,* Jan. 27, 1970, 25.

49. "Sargent Would Not Sign Bill for Harvard Stadium Takeover," *Boston Evening Globe,* Jan. 28, 1970, 3.

50. *Boston Evening Globe,* Jan. 28, 1970, 3. Before the Harvard debate, the Patriots stadium debate tended to be in the sports section unless the story earned front-page status. As the Harvard Stadium issue unfolded, stories were more frequently in the news section.

51. Charles Claffey, "There's Gold in Pro Sports," *Boston Evening Globe,* Jan. 27, 1970, 1.

52. Charles Claffey, "Boston Benefits as Half Bruins, Celts Fans Not from City," *Boston Evening Globe,* Jan. 29, 1970, 3.

53. Harold Kaese, "$10,000 Offer to Keep the Pats," *Boston Globe,* Jan. 28, 1970, 29.

54. Bud Collins, "Old Snob Job By Harvard," *Boston Globe,* Jan. 27, 1970, 25.

55. Robert Turner, "Patriots Tell State: Stadium by March 15 or We Leave Boston," *Boston Globe,* Jan. 28, 1970, 1.

56. For an article defending Harvard's position, see Victor Jones, "Too Many Actors Present to Label Harvard the Villain," *Boston Sunday Globe,* Feb. 1, 1970, 77.

57. "One Year's Try" (editorial), *Boston Globe,* Jan. 29, 1970, 16.

58. E. A. Siciliano, "Taking the Stadium," (letter to the editor) *Boston Globe,* Jan. 28, 1970, 10; Charles Irwin, "Three Cheers for Harvard" (letter to the editor), *Boston Globe,* Jan. 31, 1970, 6; Bruce A. Durkee, "Pretty Obnoxious" (letter to the editor), *Boston Globe,* Jan. 31, 1970, 6.

59. Crocker Snow, "Sargent Pleads for Pats After Stadium Takeover Voted," *Boston Globe,* Jan. 29, 1970, 1.

60. Gloria Negri, "Sarge, Patriots' Fans Stand Hand-to-Hand on Stadiums," *Boston Evening Globe,* Feb. 17, 1970, 3.

61. George Croft, "Harvard Says Final No to Pats," *Boston Globe,* Feb. 2, 1970, 1.

62. Art Ballou, "White Stadium Bargain Feasible, Backers Say," *Boston Evening Globe,* Feb. 4, 1970, 32.

63. Christopher Wallace, "Last Gasp Stadium Plans Studied," *Boston Globe,* Feb. 6, 1970, 25.

64. "Governor Gets Neponset Stadium Plan," *Boston Globe,* Feb. 9, 1970, 19.

65. "Officials Say Stadium Possible at $16 Million," *Boston Globe,* Feb. 7, 1970, 24.

66. Stephen Kurkjian, "Opposition Builds to Stadium Plan," *Boston Sunday Globe,* Feb. 8, 1970, 1.

67. Will McDonough, "It Could Also Be UMass Stadium," *Boston Globe,* Feb. 10, 1970, 25; Will McDonough, "Bartley Eager to Back Patriots Stadium Plan," *Boston Globe,* Feb. 19, 1970, 55.

68. "Veeck Sorry He Offered Plan to Assist Stadium," *Boston Globe,* Feb. 11, 1970, 43.

69. Red Smith, "Bill Should Have Known Better. . . ," *Boston Globe,* Feb. 13, 1970, 25.

70. Christopher Wallace, "City Counselors Shift Stadium Site," *Boston Globe,* Mar. 19, 1970, 1.

71. Bud Collins, "Foxboro Plus: It's Far from Hub Pols," *Boston Globe,* Mar. 20, 1970, 28. The city that served as the site of the Patriots new stadium has been spelled two different ways. In 1970, the simple "Foxboro" was routinely used by journalists. By the 1990s, references were typically spelled "Foxborough," but the facility was known as "Foxboro Stadium." To ensure uniformity, the current usage "Foxborough" will be employed, with one

exception, throughout this chapter. However, the citations will retain the spelling used at publication time.

72. Ray Fitzgerald, "Foxboro Opens Stadium Drive," *Boston Globe,* Apr. 2, 1970, 33.

73. "The Distant Stadium" (editorial), *Boston Globe,* Apr. 6, 1970, 6.

74. David Taylor, "Foxboro Stadium Site Approved by Patriots," *Boston Sunday Globe,* Apr. 5, 1970, 1.

75. David Taylor, "Foxboro Votes Patriots' Stadium," *Boston Globe,* Apr. 14, 1970, 1.

76. Will McDonough, "Patriots 'Guaranteed' Foxboro Home," *Boston Globe,* Sept. 19, 1970, 1, 21.

77. Leigh Montville, "Pats Stadium to Cost Only $5.5 Million," *Boston Sunday Globe,* Apr. 5, 1970, 81.

78. Bruce Davidson, "The Financing: Making Stadium a 'Good Buy' for Investors," *Boston Globe,* Aug. 11, 1971, 40.

79. Larry Collins, "The Impact: Foxboro Eyes Stadium Bonanza, Hopes to Harness Building Boom," *Boston Globe,* Aug. 11, 1971, 47.

80. Will McDonough, "Stadium Lives Through Onslaught," *Boston Sunday Globe,* Sept. 27, 1970, 88.

81. Quirk and Fort, *Pay Dirt,* 158.

82. Fox, *The New England Patriots,* 167.

83. Ibid., 173.

84. Sullivan's problems were aggravated by concert-related losses that were promoted by his son, Charles, but stadium expenses may have been the reason that he became involved in concert activities.

85. Will McDonough, "Kiam May Prefer Freedom to Free Rent," *Boston Globe,* Mar. 4, 1989, 29.

86. Leigh Montville, "New Stadium? No Problem, Victor," *Boston Globe,* Nov. 11, 1988, 103.

87. Michael Madden, "Nothing to Build On," *Boston Globe,* Sept. 19, 1989, 69.

88. Jack Craig, "Kiam Wasn't Enlightening," *Boston Globe,* Sept. 19, 1989, 70.

89. Will McDonough, "View at Top: Stadium Aside, Kiam Pleased," *Boston Globe,* Mar. 19, 1989, 81.

90. Brian Mooney, "City Won't Pay For Park," *Boston Globe,* Aug. 26, 1989, 30; John King, "City Approves Study on New Stadium Sites," *Boston Globe,* Sept. 15, 1989, 34.

91. Will McDonough, "Kiam Has Bottom Line for Flynn," *Boston Globe,* Dec. 20, 1989, 87. Extracted quotes are from McDonough's column. They are *not* Kiam's words.

92. Derrick Jackson, "Thumbs Down on Kiam Act," *Boston Globe,* Sept. 28, 1990, 17.

93. Paul Harber, "It's Now Officially Foxboro Stadium," *Boston Globe,* June 1, 1990, 71.

94. Kiam was personally featured in Remington commercials that aired on network television. He used a catch line "I liked it [the product] so much, I bought the company."

95. Will McDonough, "It Still May Be a Moving Saga," *Boston Globe,* Mar. 12, 1992, 35.

96. This was complicated by heavy debts and deals that Kiam made to keep the team solvent. Kiam's poor stadium arrangement contributed to the complexity of this sale. Orthwein paid Kiam $23.5 million for his share of the team, assumed $45 million in team-related debts, and paid $39 million to satisfy a previous agreement with Fran Murray, a minority owner.

Ron Borges, "Patriots Complete the Pass; Orthwein Takes it From Kiam," *Boston Globe,* May 12, 1992, 65.

97. Frank Phillips and Michael Rezendes, "Weld to Hire Stadium Panel: New Panel May be Key to Keeping Team," *Boston Globe,* Feb. 26, 1992, 73.

98. Joan Vennochi, "The Gamble on Northern Avenue," *Boston Globe,* May 26, 1993, 47.

99. St. Louis and Baltimore appeared best positioned to win the NFL franchise game but many believed that only one of these cities might be chosen. Whether expansion committee members thought about the consequences of leaving these two cities open is uncertain, but such a move created profitable opportunities for owners willing to move. Modell, a member of the expansion committee, did take advantage of Baltimore's availability in 1995. Morgan, *Glory for Sale.*

100. New England Patriots Official Web site, history page, http://www.patriots.com, accessed June 30, 2001.

101. Will McDonough, "It Still May Be a Moving Saga," *Boston Globe,* Mar. 12, 1992, 35.

102. Richard Kindleberger, "Kraft's Stadium Flip Keeps Pressure On," *Boston Globe,* Dec. 8, 1994, 1.

103. Gerry Callahan, "Pats Stadium Proves to Be Royal Flush from the Start," *Boston Herald,* Jan. 2, 1994, B1.

104. David Nyhan, "Try a Cold Shower Stadium Fans," *Boston Globe,* Jan. 26, 1997, A19.

105. Richard Kindleberger, "Kraft's Stadium Flip Keeps Pressure On," *Boston Globe,* Dec. 8, 1994, 1.

106. David Halbfinger, "NFL Says Theme Park Could Draw 2 Million Visitors a Year," *Boston Globe,* Dec. 10, 1995, 48.

107. Phil Primack, "Kraft Letter Questions Weld's Support," *Boston Globe,* Jan. 5, 1996, 22.

108. Bernard Wolfson and Carolyn Ryan, "South Bay Activists at Odds with Stadium Plan," *Boston Globe,* Dec. 21, 1996, 16.

109. Bob Ryan, "At Quiet Time, He's Collecting Their Thoughts," *Boston Globe,* Oct. 28, 1996, D1; Dan Shaughnessy, "If We Don't Build It, Let Them Go," *Boston Globe,* Dec. 27, 1995, 57.

110. Richard Chacon, "Mayor Open to South Boston Stadium," *Boston Globe,* Dec. 7, 1996, B3.

111. Tina Cassidy and Meg Vaillancourt, "Weld Would Give State Site to Patriots; Pushes for South Bay Proposal as Kraft Is Rebuffed on South Boston," *Boston Globe,* Dec. 20, 1996, A1.

112. Nick Cafardo, "Krafts to Fight for Site," *Boston Globe,* Dec. 22, 1996, C13.

113. Tina Cassidy, "Krafts Court Residents, Count on Politicians," *Boston Globe,* Jan. 15, 1997, 73.

114. Maggie Mulvihill, "Mayor on New Ballpark: Pats Not Only Game in Town," *Boston Globe,* Jan. 3, 1997, 7.

115. Tina Cassidy, "Rhode Island Offers to Help Patriots Find a New Home," *Boston Globe,* Jan. 8, 1997, F2; John Chadwick, "Randolph Offers Site to Patriots," *Patriot Ledger,* Jan. 14, 1997, 1; Jim Bodor and Martin Luttrell, "Uppity Uxbridge Plays Suitor to Pats," *Worcester Telegram and Gazette,* Jan. 17, 1997, A1.

116. Will McDonough, "Tagliabue Addresses Stadium Issue, Super Bowl '97," *Boston Globe,* Jan. 25, 1997, G1.

117. "Super Bowl XXXI: Kraft Sacked by Pats' Loss; Stadium Drive Falters," *Boston Herald,* Jan. 27, 1997, 10.

118. Meg Vaillancourt, "Massport Makes Move on Stadium; OK's Terms for Starting Talks with Patriots on a Lease," *Boston Globe,* Jan. 24, 1997, A1. Angry citizen opposition was reported in this story. Chris Black and Tina Cassidy, "Army Won't Give Parcel for Stadium," *Boston Globe,* Feb. 7, 1997, A1.

119. Joe Sciacca, "Fenway Park Smoke Bomb May Clear the Air of Stadium," *Boston Herald,* Feb. 10, 1997, 6.

120. Joseph Mallia and Joe Guiliotti. "Sox Eye Building Bigger, Better Fenway." *Boston Herald,* Feb. 9, 1997, 1.

121. Tina Cassidy, "Sox Still Want New Site; Harrington Calls Fenway Overhaul Too Costly, Eyes S. Boston," *Boston Globe,* Aug. 11, 1997, A1.

122. Carol Gerwin, "Southie Stadium Scrapped; Kraft Considers Other Sites," *Patriot Ledger,* Feb. 22, 1997, 1.

123. Michael Grunwald, "Beacon Hill Warm to New Stadium at Foxborough; Finneran Cites 'Easiest Deal,' Rules Out Tax Subsidy," *Boston Globe,* Feb. 27, 1997, A1.

124. Nick Cafardo and Ron Borges, "Kraft Is Giving Patrons a Rise," *Boston Globe,* Mar. 12, 1997, C3.

125. Cosmo Macero, "Providence Pushing to Play in the Big Leagues," *Boston Herald,* Sept. 21, 1997, 1.

126. Will McDonough, "Rhode Island on Money for Patriots," *Boston Globe,* Sept. 27, 1997, G1.

127. Tina Cassidy, "Plan May Hold Appeal for Patriots, Team Investment Less Than R.I," *Boston Globe,* Sept. 25, 1997, A1.

128. Anthony Flint, "Menino: Boston Not 'Back in Play,' " *Boston Globe,* Oct. 2, 1997, A13.

129. Tina Cassidy, "Patriots Take Pass on R.I., Stay Put; Eye Expansion, Beacon Hill Backing," *Boston Globe,* Oct. 2, 1997, A1.

130. Ron Borges, "TV Dealer Was at His Most Crafty," *Boston Globe,* Jan. 18, 1998, D9.

131. Tina Cassidy, "Senate President Asks Kraft to Build a New Stadium," *Boston Globe,* Feb. 11, 1998, A1.

132. Derrick Jackson, "Birmingham's Odd Request," *Boston Globe,* Feb. 13, 1998, A27.

133. Ed Hayward, "Citizens Say Pats, Sox Can Beg Elsewhere," *Boston Herald,* Feb. 2, 1998, 14.

134. Anthony Flint, "Fenway Park Backed in Poll; Red Sox Insist Talk of Redesign is Premature," *Boston Globe,* Jan. 22, 1998, B1.

135. Anthony Flint, "Reaction Cool to Idea of a New Ballpark," *Boston Globe,* Apr. 3, 1998, B2.

136. "A New and Better Ballpark" (editorial), *Boston Globe,* Apr. 16, 1998, A26.

137. Tina Cassidy, "Report Shows Slow Profits for Stadium; Conn. Could Lose Money for Years Before Patriots Deal Earns Return," *Boston Globe,* Dec. 2, 1998, A1.

138. Associated Press, "Pats Plan Jumps $25 M; Conn. Officials Add Cost of Inflation," *Boston Globe,* Nov. 30, 1998, B2.

139. The final tally was 97-49 in the House and 27-8 in the Senate.

140. Hillary Chabot, "Finneran Finds Support," *Boston Globe,* Nov. 21, 1998, A12.

141. Dan Shaughnessy, "Kraft Hits Paydirt: Connecticut Legislative Approval of Stadium Deal Is No-Brainer," *Boston Globe,* Dec. 16, 1998, F1. Shaughnessy concluded that an "inferiority complex" propelled the state to overbid for the right host an NFL team.

142. Associated Press, "Poll Conn.-cludes [*sic*] Support Slipping," *Boston Herald,* Apr. 1, 1999, 40. The poll, conducted by the University of Connecticut for the *Hartford Courant,* revealed that project support had slipped from 58 percent in December 1998 to 45 percent in March 1999. Opposition had increased from 35 percent to 48 percent.

143. Cosmo Macero, "Conn. Gov Gains Ground in Effort to Land Pats," *Boston Herald,* Apr. 1, 1999, 40.

144. Tina Cassidy, "Stadium Deal Gives Patriots an Escape," *Boston Globe,* Feb. 13, 1999, B1.

145. Steve Baily, "Save the Pats," *Boston Globe,* Apr. 2, 1999, E1.

146. For detail about issues that complicated the Red Sox sale, see Will McDonough, "Potential Problems Limitless," *Boston Globe,* Oct. 14, 2000, G1.

147. Charges of racism in ballplayer hiring may have been the most difficult-to-defend public relations problem faced by the Red Sox in the 1950s and 1960s.

148. Scott Van Voorhis, "Henry Spends Day in Washington," *Boston Herald,* Feb. 7, 2002, 38.

149. The complex move achieved two goals. It offered John Henry tax benefits (in the neighborhood of $20 to $30 million), and it gave Major League Baseball control of a faltering team, allowing them to determine its future home or, in a worst-case scenario, whether to eliminate the team completely. If owners resold the team, they would divide the profits.

150. Jackie MacMullan, "Final Say in Last Hours as Boss, Harrington Reflects," *Boston Globe,* Feb. 27, 2002, E1.

151. Joan Vennochi, "Red Sox Hire Women Consultants in Push for a New Ballpark," *Boston Globe,* Mar. 30, 1999, A13.

152. Eileen McNamara, "Red Sox Plan Rings a Bell," *Boston Globe,* Nov. 15, 1998, B1.

153. John Harrington, "Why Red Sox Need a New Park," *Boston Globe,* May 15, 1999, A19.

154. For an example of this argument, see Stout and Johnson, *Red Sox Century,* 442–43. The "curse of the Bambino" is a legend that the Red Sox were forever doomed to fall short of a baseball championship because the team sent Babe Ruth to the Yankees in 1919.

155. Gregg Kruppa and Meg Villaincourt, "Fenway: A New Pitch, Proposed $545m Ballpark to Retain Cherished Details," *Boston Globe,* May 16, 1999, A1.

156. Steven Wilmsen, "Proprietor Expresses Dismay with Ballpark Site Proposal," *Boston Globe,* May 16, 1999, A14.

157. "Fenway Pork: What's the Deal with the Red Sox New Stadium Proposal?" *Boston Phoenix,* July 14, 2000, special advertising section.

158. Eileen McNamara, "Bad Vibes for Red Sox," *Boston Globe,* Feb. 16, 2000, B1.

159. Will McDonough, "No Roadblocks in Drive for New Fenway," *Boston Globe,* Feb. 26, 2000, G1.

160. Will McDonough, "Take NY Cash into Account," *Boston Globe,* Mar. 25, 2000, G1.

161. Meg Vaillancourt, "Sox Pitch Change in Ballpark Proposal," *Boston Globe,* Dec. 16, 2000, A1.

162. Dan Shaughnessy, "Lucchino Checks In—and Checks Out Fine: Changeup Is Called for, but Curve Is Thrown," *Boston Globe*, Feb. 20, 2002, D10.

163. Steve Buckley, "The New Course at Fens; Renovation May Keep Park Around," *Boston Herald*, Aug. 19, 2003, 82.

164. Meg Vaillancourt, "It's Official: Henry Owns Sox," *Boston Globe*, Feb. 28, 2002, C1. All quotes in this paragraph were extracted from this article.

165. Scott Greenberger, "Red Sox See Home Field Advantage—Fenway Lore Offers a Lure No New Park Could Match," *Boston Globe*, June 13, 2002, B1.

166. Mike Fine, "Facelift: Fenway Park Construction Ongoing," *Patriot Ledger*, Jan. 30, 2003, 27. The Smith quote in the previous paragraph was extracted from this source. 167. Michael Silverman, "Baseball: A Q&A With Red Sox Chairman Tom Warner," *Boston Herald*, May 26, 2002, B20. The Red Sox own approximately 80 percent of New England Sports Network.

168. Dan Shaughnessy, "Cool Hand Lucchino," *Boston Globe*, Mar. 31, 2002, magazine section, 8.

169. Joan Graham, "Bottom Line: New Ballpark Needed" (letter to the editor), *Boston Globe*, June 6, 2002, A20. A number of additional fan complaints about the moves described here can be found at Steve Buckley, "Baseball: Only the Beginning for Sox," *Boston Herald*, Feb. 27, 2003, 106.

170. Tony Massarotti, "Baseball: Open Wallets at the Door," *Boston Herald*, Oct. 19, 2002, 40.

171. One of the first indications of a desire to transfer the subsidies from new construction to renovation was made before the owners formally took team control. Meg Vaillancourt, "Ticket Price Hikes on Deck at Fenway," *Boston Globe*, Jan. 30, 2002, A1.

172. Andrea Estes, "Red Sox to Seek Fenway Park Facelift," *Boston Globe*, Nov. 23, 2004, B1.

173. "A Celebration for the Ages at Fenway," *New York Times*, Apr. 12, 2005, A1.

174. Frank Phillips and Sasha Talcott, "Menino Rules Out City Funds to Aid Red Sox Plans," *Boston Globe*, Mar. 23, 2005, A1.

175. Michael Silverman, "Baseball: Red Sox Stick to Their Roots at Fenway Park, Unveil Renovations for This Year and Beyond," *Boston Herald*, Mar. 24, 2005, 100.

176. Sasha Talcott, "Sox to Stay, 'No Strings Attached,' Team Rules Out Public Funds for Ball Park Revamp," *Boston Globe*, Mar. 24, 2005, E1.

8. New York, Part One: Stadium Origins to the Modern Era

1. Abbott, *Boosters and Businessmen*, 127.

2. Cindy Adams, "How Can Those Tourists Squawk About Noo Yawk?" *New York Post*, July 8, 2001, 12.

3. Riess, *City Games*, 9.

4. Guschov, *The Red Stockings of Cincinnati*, 4.

5. Benson, *Ballparks of North America*, 52–53.

6. Ibid., 52–62.

7. Ibid., 57–62.

8. Ibid., 253–55.

9. Ibid., 256–58.

10. Ritter, *Lost Ballparks,* 161.

11. David Kaplan, "The Ballpark by the Bay," *Newsweek,* Apr. 4, 2000, 44.

12. "New St. George Grounds," *New York Times,* Apr. 23, 1886, 3. The upscale nature of the facility seemed to be a primary reporting attraction. Manhattan residents needed to travel here by ferry.

13. No one ever uncovered the cause of the blaze, but street-level speculation included a broad range of theories. Most appeared to be focused on the team's dreaded rival, the Cubs. According to "one popular yarn . . . a platoon of hated Cubs fans had put a match to the vendor's stand." Another story was that "Cubs' manager Frank Chance, a bitter enemy of [John] McGraw, had actually lit the match himself." Other theories included a Bolshevik plot and the notion that the fire was set by Ban Johnson, head of the rival American League. Robinson and Jennison, *Yankee Stadium,* 4.

14. "Polo Grounds Go Up in Flames: Only Bleachers and Clubhouse Saved in Fire North of City," *New York Tribune,* Apr. 14, 1911, 1.

15. "Crandall Comes to Giants Rescue," *New York Times,* Apr. 16, 1911, sporting section, 1.

16. "Crowds at Polo Grounds: Mournful Rooters View Ruins and Wonder When Play Will be Resumed," *New York Times,* Apr. 17, 1911, 9.

17. Benson, *Ballparks of North America,* 260–61.

18. "Ebbets Field Opening Day Victory for Superbas," *New York Times,* Apr. 6, 1913, sporting section, 1. A Sunday picture section (Apr. 6, 1913) offered team photos and photos of an empty Ebbets Field with a similar sized photo of an empty Polo Grounds. No photographic coverage of the opening game was provided.

19. "Thirty Thousand Fans Greet Baseball, Open New Home of Brooklyn Club and See Superbas Beat the Yankees," *New York Tribune,* Apr. 6, 1913, 1.

20. "Ebbets Field Opening To-day," *New York Times,* Apr. 5, 1913, 16; "Taste of Baseball for Hungry 'Fans,' " *New York Tribune,* Apr. 5, 1913, 12.

21. "To Inspect Ebbets Field," *New York Times,* Apr. 2, 1913, 9.

22. "74,200 See Yankees Open New Stadium; Ruth Hits Home Run," *New York Times,* Apr. 19, 1923, 1. The *New York Times* did not provide front-page coverage to preview the opening. Only coverage *after* the event received front-page placement.

23. Ruppert's initial partner was Tillinghast Huston, an engineer and millionaire with wealth that came from public works projects. After stadium construction was complete, Ruppert bought out Huston's share of the team.

24. "Ruppert, Owner of Yankees and Leading Brewer, Dies: Rise of Ruppert in Business Rapid," *New York Times,* Jan. 14, 1939, 7.

25. Letter from Robert Moses to Walter O'Malley, Aug. 15, 1955. Robert Wagner Papers, New York City Municipal Archives. Cited in Sullivan, *The Dodgers Move West,* 232.

26. Caro, *Power Broker,* 777. According to urban expert Charles Abrams, as quoted by Caro, Moses's power was so extensive under Title I of the Housing Act of 1949 that "in my opinion. . . . Macy's could condemn Gimbles—if Robert Moses gave the word." W. Kingland Macy stated that "Mr. Moses told me personally that his power was such that he could seize my house, put me out of it, and arrest me for trespassing if I tried to get into it again."

27. For an overview of O'Malley's failed negotiations with New York City officials, see Sullivan, *The Dodgers Move West,* 45–57.

28. Frommer, *New York City Baseball,* 4.

29. Arthur Dailey, "Sports of the Times: Men in Motion," *New York Times,* Aug. 18, 1955, 29.

30. "Fans Are Frantic Over Game Shifts," *New York Times,* Aug. 18, 1955, 26. This was a rare article that included citizen's response to the issue. All quoted were from the Brooklyn area, not New Jersey.

31. For a description of the proposal that included a mass transit terminal, a ballpark, "and several other civic betterment projects" see Joseph Sheehan, "City Officials to Help Dodgers Get New Stadium and Stay Here," *New York Times,* Aug. 18, 1955. 1.

32. "City Is Asked to Name New Stadium for Shea," *New York Times,* Oct. 30, 1962, 39; "Council Studies Proposal to Name Stadium for Shea," *New York Times,* Oct. 31, 1962, 42. For a general description of the project, see *New York Times,* Aug. 15, 1962, 23.

33. "Escalators at Mets Park to Take Toil Out of Grandstand Climbing," *New York Times,* Apr. 13, 1963, 12.

34. Charles Bennett, "2 Links Approved for Queens Road," *New York Times,* June 28, 1963, 59; Charles Bennett, "Building of Queens Ballpark Held Up by Delays Laid to Subcontractors, Work Stoppages, Severe Weather," *New York Times,* July 12, 1963, 17; Peter Kihss, " 'Truth Squad' Put to Use by Lamula," *New York Times,* July 14, 1963, 52; Peter Kihss, "Negroes Push Picketing in City in Drive for Jobs," *New York Times,* July 29, 1963, 20; Leonard Koppett, "Officials Say Mets Opener Will Be Ready for Mets Opener in April," *New York Times,* Dec. 18, 1963, 52.

35. An investigative series of Moses, run by the *New York World-Telegram and Sun,* relegated some of the stories to inside pages, making some available only in the Brooklyn edition. For information of how editors limited the coverage of this rare journalistic investigation into Moses's, see Caro, *Power Broker,* 1005–13.

36. Even though Moses got the parking lot he wanted on Central Park property, the victory was Pyrrhic. Moses was portrayed in this instance as a bully and a sneak. Caro, *Power Broker,* 984–1004.

37. "The 'Unique' Bob Moses" (editorial), *New York Times,* July 29, 1957, 18.

38. Caro, *Power Broker,* 1099.

39. Smith, *The Ballpark Book,* 69.

40. For a comprehensive overview of the Yankee Stadium renovation project from the perspective of the baseball franchise, see Sullivan, *The Diamond in the Bronx,* 117–44.

41. This unusual ownership structure was the result of an estate settlement. Yankee Stadium had been owned by John Cox, a wealthy Texas executive, before this arrangement.

42. Edward Ranzal, "City to Buy Yankee Stadium in Move to Keep 2 Teams," *New York Times,* Mar. 3, 1971, 1.

43. Murray Schumach, "Neighborhoods: The Stadium Is 'Anchor' to South Bronx," *New York Times,* Apr. 12, 1971, 39.

44. *New York Daily News,* Oct. 11, 1971. Quote extracted from Sullivan, *The Diamond in the Bronx,* 154.

45. Maurice Carroll, "Garelik Proposes Yanks and Football Giants Join Mets and Jets at Shea Stadium," *New York Times,* Apr. 11, 1971, 34.

46. Joseph Durso, "Yankees and Mets Oppose Sharing of Shea Stadium," *New York Times,* Aug. 28, 1971, 52; "New Jersey Mets Team of the Future?" *New York Times,* Sept. 1, 1971, 29. In the September article Grant argued against claims that the Mets were unfairly benefitting in their deal. According to Grant, "We put two or three million dollars of our own money into dining rooms and extra toilet facilities. The city will own all of this at the end of 30 years."

47. Thomas Ronan, "Governor Signs Bill Allowing Purchase of Stadium by City," *New York Times,* July 7, 1971, 1.

48. Ronald Sullivan, "Football Giants to Leave City After 1974 Season," *New York Times,* Aug. 27, 1971, 1.

49. Martin Tolchin, "Lindsay Threatens to Evict the Giants," *New York Times,* Aug. 28, 1971, 52.

50. "Two Bidders Said to Seek CFL Franchise Here," *New York Times,* Nov. 8, 1971, 60.

51. "WFL to Revive New York Team," *New York Times,* Oct. 22, 1974, 52.

52. Edward Ranzal, "Stadium Costs Up By $15.8 Million," *New York Times,* Nov. 8, 1973, 50.

53. Edward Ranzal, "$15.9 Million More Is Voted for the Stadium Project," *New York Times,* Nov. 17, 1973, 39.

54. Maurice Carroll, "Demolition Urged of Tweed Court," *New York Times,* Aug. 11, 1974, 60. Ironically, the stadium-related content of this article was hidden in material related to demolition of a building that served as a monument to the 'Boss Tweed' era of New York history.

55. Edward Ranzal, "Cost for Stadium Put at $66 Million," *New York Times,* Oct. 11, 1975, 1, 29.

56. Martin Waldron, "Yanks Get Windfall as City Shifts Plans," *New York Times,* Dec. 1, 1975, 1.

57. Leonard Koppett, "Paul Defends Yanks' Role in Stadium Building Costs," *New York Times,* Dec. 6, 1975, 37.

58. Susan Fainstein and Norman Fainstein, "New York City: The Manhattan Business District, 1945–1988," in Squires, *Unequal Partnerships,* 59–79.

59. John Hess, "Stadium's Cost Now Seen as Loss," *New York Times,* Apr. 15, 1976, 1.

60. Sullivan, *The Diamond in the Bronx,* 143. Raymond Keating, a policy analyst who has published for the CATO Institute and in the *New York Times,* has placed the final renovation expense at $150 million.

61. Ibid., 140.

62. Hess's concern for cleanliness was evident his use of white uniforms for low-level gas station attendants during the 1960s and 1970s.

63. Joseph Sullivan, "Jersey Senate Backs a Referendum on Baseball Stadium Bonds," *New York Times,* Sept. 15, 1987, B2.

64. Robert Hanley, "Jersey Has Ball Park Site; It Needs a Team," *New York Times,* July 16, 1987, B1.

65. Robert Hanley, "Jersey's Emphasis Shifts in Bid for Baseball Team," *New York Times,* July 19, 1987, 24.

66. Robert Torricelli, "No—It's the Wrong Idea at the Wrong Time," *New York Times,* Nov. 1, 1987, New Jersey opinion section, 30; Anton Campanella, "Yes—The Economy Has Much to Gain," *New York Times,* Nov. 1, 1987, New Jersey opinion section, 30.

67. Sam Howe Verhover, "Yankees to Stay in New York City; Agreement Lasts Until 2032, Parking Garage Is Included," *New York Times,* Nov. 1, 1987, A1, A49. Although this may appear to lock the Yankees into the South Bronx location for at least forty years, sports franchise owners often back out of leases with various strategies.

68. The Yankee's lease was extended to 2032 in 1987. In 1973, when Steinbrenner took over the team, the lease was set to expire in 2002.

69. Richard Sandomir, "Made-for-TV Mystery: What, If Anything, Do Yanks Owe the City?" *New York Times,* June 13, 1993, section 8, 6.

70. This would have rekindled Staten Island's link to major league baseball, which was established in 1886 but abandoned before the twentieth century as rapid transportation to population centers became a more important commercial consideration for team owners. The overture to the Yankees may have been part of a more complex series of political moves intended to apply pressure to the city for concessions that would benefit the citizens of Staten Island. The borough was contemplating a move to secede from New York City.

71. Ian Fischer, "Fearing Move by Yankees, Cuomo Explores Idea for a New Stadium," *New York Times,* June 30, 1993, A1.

72. Harvey Araton, "Where Do George's Critics Live?" *New York Times,* Aug. 1, 1993, section 8, 1.

73. "West Side Park Only Answer to Keeping Yanks" (editorial), *Crain's New York Business,* Oct. 11, 1993, 8.

74. Richard Sandomir, "New Proposal from Cuomo to Yankees," *New York Times,* Oct. 21, 1993, B1.

75. Richard Sandomir, "Yankee Stadium's Future: New Players, Same Old Game," *New York Times,* Nov. 6, 1993, section 1, 26.

76. Richard Sandomir, "Stadium Waiting Game Ads a Pair of Players," *New York Times,* Nov. 12, 1993, B13.

77. "Am I a Bad Person. . . ?" (comic illustration), *New Yorker,* May 18, 1998, 36.

78. Lewis Grossberger, "The Lies Must Stop," *Time,* June 29, 1998, 86.

79. Clyde Haberman, "Thanks Boss, for All Your Help," *New York Times,* June 12, 1998, B1.

80. Raymond Keating, "The House That Taxpayers Built," *New York Times,* Apr. 15, 1998, A25.

81. Harvey Araton, "The Flights of Fancy and Reality," *New York Times,* Apr. 16, 1998, C1.

82. Tichenor, Donohue, and Olien, *Community Conflict and the Press,* 114.

83. T. J. Quinn, Michael Saul, and Tracy Connor, "Yanks'll Pay for New Park Next Door—Plan Old-Style, No Dome Sweet Home for 700M," *New York Daily News,* July 30, 2004, 6.

84. Ibid.

85. Charles Bagli, "What the Teams Want and What the City Gets," *New York Times,* Jan. 16, 2005, 31.

86. Winnie Hu and Charles Bagli, "Bloomberg Says the City Will Help the Franchise That Helps Itself," *New York Times,* July 31, 2004, B1-B3.

9. New York, Part Two: The Olympics, the Jets, and Manhattan

1. Neal Travis, "Jets Might Fly If City Won't Play Ball(Park)," May 2, 2001, *New York Post*, 3.

2. Fox News and the *New York Post* are owned by the same parent company, making shared use of this story more likely. MSNBC is not directly affiliated with either organization.

3. Dan Barry, "Giuliani Offers Plan to Put Up Sports Complex," *New York Times*, Jan. 15, 2001, A1.

4. Timothy Williams, "Bloomberg to Have Final Say Over New York Stadium Proposals," Associated Press, Dec. 29, 2001.

5. Robert Hardt and Maggie Habberman, "Mike's the Lone Defender of the West Side Stadium," *New York Post*, May 29, 2001, 4.

6. Jennifer Steinhauer, "Mayor Says There Is no Money to Build Two Baseball Stadiums," *New York Times*, Jan. 8, 2002, B3.

7. Steven Viuker, "Dan Doctoroff; Deputy Mayor for Economic Development," *Crain's New York Business*, Jan. 21, 2002, 12.

8. Matthew Futterman, "Jets' Stadium a Costly Venture." *Star Ledger*, Mar. 7, 2003, 57.

9. Rudolph Giuliani, The State of the City Address. New York City. Mayors Office. January 13, 2000, www.nyc.gov/html/records/rwg/html/2000a/stcity2000.html.

10. The results were skewed by the menu of possible answers. They were "strongly favor/somewhat favor/oppose." When people are *not* deeply concerned about an issue, pollsters understand the tendency to select the middle position. In this instance, the middle position skewed the results to favor the outcome NYC2012 wanted. Note: the 84 percent result was also offered on the NYC2012 Web site. Quinnipiac results are available at www.quinnipiac.edu/x11369.xml. The poll was released November 22, 2002.

11. David Haffenreffer (anchor), *Market Call*, CNN Financial Network, Oct. 31, 2002, 9:30 A.M.

12. Julia Campbell, "Vaulting Costs: Olympic Games Cost Taxpayers More Than Ever," *ABC News*, Sept. 25, 2002. This article was accessed via www.abcnews.go.com. It is no longer available at this location.

13. Lee Cowan (reporter), Olympic Hosting Story, *CBS Evening News*, Nov. 2, 2002.

14. Ann Curry (anchor), Dan Doctoroff interview, *Today, NBC News*, Nov. 4, 2002.

15. Michael Saul, "New York City Mayor Carries Torch for New Stadium on Manhattan's West Side," *New York Daily News*, Oct. 31, 2002.

16. "City to Unveil Redevelopment Plan for Manhattan's West Side," *Associated Press*, Feb. 10, 2003.

17. Gary Myers, "Tisch: No Facelift, No Supe," *New York Daily News*, Nov. 1, 2002, 93.

18. Gary Myers, "New York Makes Super Bid—Wants '08 Game at Giants Stadium," *New York Daily News*, Oct. 31, 2002, 79. The quote is a reporter's paraphrase of Mara.

19. Bob Glauber, "Tags, Overtime Likely to Change," *Newsday*, Jan. 25, 2003, A27.

20. Richard Sandomir, "Giants Reject Stadium Mediator," *New York Times*, Sept. 9, 2003, D4.

21. Randall Smothers and Richard Sandomir, "Seeking Full Control and No Rent, the Giants Offer to Pay for Stadium," *New York Times*, Dec. 22, 2004, B1.

22. Greg Sargent and Tom McGeveran, "After a Huddle, Jets Start a Rush for the West Side," *New York Observer,* Feb. 24, 2003, 1.

23. Tom Topousis, "Stadium Foes Paid Lobby Teams $14M," *New York Post,* Feb. 17, 2005, 2.

24. Charles Bagli, "Grand Vision for Remaking the West Side," *New York Times,* Feb. 10, 2003, B1.

25. Associated Press, "City Unveils Plans to Rebuild Manhattan's West Side," Feb. 11, 2003.

26. Tom Topousis, "Cheers and Jeers: 700 in Fierce W. Side Stadium Debate," *New York Post,* Sept. 24, 2004, 10.

27. Wendy Fried, "An Olympic Mistake," *New York Times,* Oct. 31, 2002, A27.

28. Johnette Howard, "Doctoroff's Rx Perfect for NY," *Newsday,* Nov. 18, 2001, C2.

29. This information was obtained via e-mail contact on March 9, 2003, with John Fisher, the webmaster, via the site's "HK Forum" icon.

30. After writing an article in New York's *Village Voice* about how the 2012 Olympics might affect the average citizen, I was greeted by an angry e-mail from the site's webmaster hours after the article was released.

31. The NYC2012 proposal was posted on www.hellskitchen.net but has since been removed.

32. E. J. Dionne, "Carey Signs Bill Providing Tax Benefits for Madison Square Garden," *New York Times,* July 8, 1982, B7.

33. David Forman, "Olympic Arguing New York's New Sport" (letter to the editor), *New York Post,* Feb. 18, 2005, 38.

34. Timothy Williams, "Mayor: Garden's Real Rival Is Brooklyn Arena, Not Stadium," *Newsday,* Feb. 18, 2005.

35. New York Sports and Convention Center advertisement, *New York Times,* Jan. 25, 2005, A16.

36. Blair Golson, "Last of the Empire Builders," *New York Observer,* Dec. 20, 2004, 19.

37. deMause, Neil, "West Side Stories," *Village Voice,* Jan. 28, 2003, 46.

38. Phillip Lentz, "City Revamps Finance Plan for Far West Side; Seeks $3 Billion for Improvements," *Crain's New York Business,* Feb. 17, 2003, 1.

39. In the WNBC/Pressman interview, Doctoroff indicated that $900 million, or one-third, of the $2.7 billion total would be allocated to parks and recreational facilities. This figure did *not* include the stadium construction project.

40. Gabe Pressman (host), *News Forum,* WNBC-TV, Nov. 10, 2002, 7:30 A.M.

41. Tom Topousis, "We Got Game: Truly Jets Stadium Would Be NFL's Class Act," *New York Post,* Apr. 19, 2004, 20.

42. Charles Bagli, "Grand Vision for Remaking the West Side," *New York Times,* Feb. 10, 2003, B1.

43. John Tierney, "Convention Business: A Warning," *New York Times,* Apr. 6, 2001, B1.

44. Heywood Sanders, "Space Available: The Realities of Convention Centers as Economic Development Strategy," Brookings Institution: Metropolitan Policy Program Report, Jan. 2005, 1–35.

45. Frankie Edozien, "City Claims Games Will Bring 135,000 Jobs," *New York Post,* Jan. 17, 2004, 10.

46. Charles Bagli, "Financing Plan Adds Complexity to Remaking New York's West Side," *New York Times,* Mar. 1, 2003, B3.

47. Paul Moses, "Giving Away the Store," *Village Voice,* Mar. 1, 2005, 20.

48. Steve Cuozzo, "West Side Games: Mayoral Olympic Dreams vs. Downtown Rebuilding," *New York Post,* Mar. 18, 2004, 37.

49. Mike Lupica, "New Owner Clear, Nets' Future Isn't: Sale Has Zilch to do With Sports," *New York Daily News,* Jan. 23, 2004, 72.

50. Memorandum of Understanding: Empire State Development Corporation, Jets Development, LLC, and the Metropolitan Transportation Authority, Mar. 24, 2004, 1–10.

51. Memorandum of Understanding between the City of New York and the State of New York respecting the Javits Convention Center and the New York Sports and Convention Center, Mar. 25, 2004, 1–5.

52. "Bloomberg/Pataki: 'Stadium a Done Deal!'—But There's Still a Long Way to Go. . . ," Clinton Chronicle, Apr. 2004, 1.

53. Richard Gottfried, "A Shameful Disrespect," *Clinton Chronicle,* Apr. 2004, 1.

54. Scott Stringer, "Concerns About Transparency and Shaky Finances," *Clinton Chronicle,* Apr. 2004, 1.

55. Todd Venezia and Angellina Cappiello, "YesterYanks: New Stadium Would Look Like Babe's Park," *New York Post,* July 31, 2004, 7.

56. Jess Wisloski, "Ratner: I Might Keep Nets in New Jersey," Brooklyn Papers, Oct. 30, 2004, http://www.brooklynpapers.com/html/issues/_vol27/27_42/27_42nets1.

57. "Mayor Michael R. Bloomberg and Governor George E. Pataki Announce Memorandum of understanding for Atlantic Yards Project in Brooklyn, City of New York, Office of the Mayor," press release, Mar. 30, 2005.

58. Empire State Development Companies, New York City Economic Development Corporation, the City of New York, and Forest City Ratner Companies, Memorandum of Understanding: Brooklyn Arena\Mixed Use Development Project, Feb. 18, 2005.

59. Letter from Katherine Lapp, executive director, Metropolitan Transportation Association, regarding Brooklyn Arena/Mixed Use Development Project, to James Stuckey, executive vice president of Forest City Ratner Companies, Feb. 24, 2005.

60. Anne Michaud, "Jets Asking City, State to Kick In $600 Million; Stadium Price Could Keep Rising," *Crain's New York Business,* Dec. 8, 2003, 3.

61. Charles Bagli, "Stadium Opponents Criticize City for Adopting Jets Economic Study," *New York Times,* May 23, 2004, 25.

62. Edozien, "City Claims Games Will Bring 135,000 Jobs," 10.

63. George Sweeting, "Inside the Budget—West Side Stadium: Touchdown for the City?" New York City Independent Budget Office, report number 131, July 1, 2004.

64. "Fulfilling the Promise of Manhattan's Far West Side," Regional Plan Association, July 2004.

65. "An Ambitious Start for an Acting Governor," *New York Times,* Nov. 17, 2004, A1.

66. Matthew Futterman, "Codey Wants New Stadium for Giants," *Star Ledger,* Nov. 10, 2004, 1.

67. "Acting Gov. Cody Wants Lions to Join Big East," *Asbury Park Press,* Dec. 2, 2004, C2.

68. "Grid: Giants Eye New Stadium," *New York Post,* Dec. 2, 2004, 57.

69. Ronald Smothers and Richard Sandomir, "Seeking Full Control and No Rent, Giants Offer to Pay for Stadium," *New York Times,* Dec. 22, 2004, B1.

70. Tom Canavan, "Giants Stadium Talks Headed in the Wrong Direction," *Associated Press,* Jan. 26, 2005.

71. Josh Benson, "4th and Goal: Xanadu, an Odd Mix, Blocks a New Stadium," *New York Times,* Mar. 20, 2005, NJ5.

72. Richard Sandomir, "Sports Business: Giants Could Look at New York of All Places," *New York Times,* Mar. 11, 2005, D8.

73. Richard Sandomir, "Stadium Deal Falls Apart for New Jersey and the Giants," *New York Times,* Mar. 10, 2005, B1.

74. "No Free Lunch" (editorial), *New York Daily News,* Mar. 24, 2000, 54.

75. Tom Topousis and David Seifman, "City Will Wine and Dine Olympic Bigs," *New York Post,* Feb. 15, 2005, 8.

76. David Saltonstall, "Mike Feud Means Nix to Knicks," *New York Daily News,* Dec. 10, 2004, 14.

77. The following stories were offered: Paul Tharp and Malcolm Balfour, "Cable Suit Slams Board," *New York Post,* Mar. 8, 2005; "Standard and Poor's Revises Cablevision's Outlook: Cablevision's Chaos Continues," http://www.standardandpoors.com, no date indicated; Jim Rutenberg, "Cablevision Says No to Pro-Stadium Ads, and Jets Say That Isn't Fair." *New York Times,* Mar. 8, 2005. Above each headline was a Sports and Convention Center Logo and a picture of the proposed stadium.

78. Tom Topousis, "Jets on Offensive with Suit vs. Cablevision," *New York Post,* Mar. 17, 2005, 2.

79. Don Banks, "NFL to Move Draft: League Will Not Hold Event at MSG Because of Jets Tiff," SI.com, Feb. 9, 2005, http://sportsillustrated.cnn.com/2005/writers/don_banks/02/09/banks.snap.draft.site/index.html.

80. Tom Topousis, "City Front-Runner to Score 2010 Super Bowl, NFL Says," *New York Post,* Mar. 16, 2005, 2.

81. Jim Rutenberg, "An Olympic-Sized Saturation Is Planned to Impress 2012 Evaluators," *New York Times,* Feb. 3, 2005, B7.

82. Clemente Lisi, "Pataki Could Derail $5 B: Transit Critics," *New York Post,* Feb. 9, 2005, 2.

83. David Seifman, "Mike Pushes Albany on Subway Rehab $$," *New York Post,* Mar. 25, 2005, 2.

84. Frank Lombardi, "Pols Subpoena MTA," *New York Daily News,* Jan. 28, 2005, 38.

85. David Seifman, "Mike: Jets Stadium Loss Would Hurt Mets, Yanks," *New York Post,* Jan. 29, 2005, 2.

86. Graham Rayman, "Jets, MTA Release Stadium Land Values," *Newsday,* Feb. 1, 2005.

87. Charles Bagli, "Builders Wary of Pursuing Site Sought by Jets for West Side Development," *New York Times,* Feb. 17, 2005, B1.

88. Charles Bagli, "Suddenly Developers Yearn for the Gritty Far West Side," *New York Times,* Feb. 14, 2005, B1.

89. Charles Bagli, "Transit Agency Seeks Other Bids on West Side Site," *New York Times,* Feb. 26, 2005, A1.

90. Charles Bagli, "Cablevision Adds Details on Railyard Bid," *New York Times,* Feb. 12, 2005, B3.

91. Charles Bagli, "Cablevision Bid Said to Beat Jets' Offer," *New York Times,* Mar. 25, 2005, B1.

92. David Seifman, "Foes Pan Garden's Rocky W. Side Bid," *New York Post,* Mar. 26, 2005, 2

93. Charles Bagli, "Jets Final Bid Needed Help from Group of Developers," *New York Times,* Mar. 26, 2005, B1.

94. Tom Topousis, David Seifman, and Kenneth Lovett, "Mike's Stadium Flip: I'll Consider Queens," *New York Post,* Mar. 2, 2005, 2.

95. Tom Topousis and Kenneth Lovett, "Jets: We Won't Land in Queens," *New York Post,* Mar. 3, 2005, 2

96. David Seifman, "Stadium Dragging Mike Down in the Polls," *New York Post,* Mar. 3, 2005, 2.

97. Winnie Hu, "Metro Briefing—New York: Manhattan: Stadium Referendum Urged." *New York Times,* Jan. 27, 2005, B1.

98. Marvin Scott (host), *News Close-Up,* WPIX-TV, Apr. 10, 2005, 6:30 A.M.

99. Fernando Ferrer, "Ferrer to Bloomberg: Stop Attacking and Start Explaining $1 Million Donation from Jets Owner" (campaign press release), Mar. 7, 2005, http://www.ferrer2005.com.

100. Fernando Ferrer, "Ferrer Says New MTA Bid Rules Rigged in Favor of Jets" (campaign press release), Feb. 23, 2005, http://www.ferrer2005.com.

101. Winnie Hu, "Mayor Denies Politics Had Role in Stadium Decision," *New York Times,* Apr. 2, 2005, B4.

102. Jim Ruttenberg and Charles Bagli, "In City's Push for Stadium, Silver's District Reaps Benefits," *New York Times,* Apr. 25, 2005, B1.

103. David Seifman and Carl Campanile, "Mayor $pikes Bruno: Stadium Revenge," *New York Post,* June 8, 2005, 3.

104. Charles Bagli, "Garden Sues to Block Jets' Stadium," *New York Times,* Apr. 6, 2005, B5.

105. "Jersey Slams W. Side Plan." *New York Post,* Oct. 6, 2004, 9.

106. Charles Bagli, "2 Groups Sue to Halt Action on Jets Stadium," *New York Times,* Dec. 23, 2004, B1.

107. Charles Bagli, "Jets Unveil a Redesign for a Less Imposing Football Stadium," *New York Times,* Feb. 3, 2005, B7.

108. Laura Mansnerus, "Giants Agree to Remain in Meadowlands: Stadium to Be Built Next to Old One," *New York Times,* Apr. 14, 2005, B1.

109. David Saltonstall, "Mike Sets Deadline for OK on the Stadium," *New York Daily News,* Apr. 16, 2005, 14.

110. Tom Topousis, "OK Stadium Soon or Bye, Bye, Bowl: Jets," *New York Post,* Apr. 12, 2005, 2.

111. David Andreatta, "Jets in School for 'Class' Action," *New York Post*, Apr. 7, 2005, 2.

112. David Seifman, "Mike to Pols: Stadium Now," *New York Post*, Apr. 7, 2005, 2.

113. "Sharpton Tackles Albany," *New York Post*, May 11, 2005, 6.

114. Charles Bagli, "Pataki Agrees to Delay Vote on Stadium for 2nd Time," May 24, 2005, B4.

115. Matthew Futterman, "Cody Puts Jets' Lease Talks on Hold," *Star Ledger*, May 24, 2005, 13.

116. Charles Bagli and Michael Cooper, "Bloomberg's Stadium Bid Fails; Olympic Bid Is Hurt," *New York Times*, June 7, 2005, A1.

117. Jennifer Steinhauer, "Requiem for a West Side Stadium: Overtures Were Made Too Late," *New York Times*, June 8, 2005, A1.

118. Charles Bagli and Mike McIntire, "Taxpayer Expense Is Less in Deal for New Stadium," *New York Times*, June 14, 2005, B4.

119. T. J. Quinn, "It's Back to the Future for the Yanks," *New York Daily News*, Apr. 15, 2005, 3.

120. Neil deMause, "The Evil Empire Strikes Back: Steinbrenner's Plan to Have Other Teams Buy Him a Stadium," *Baseball Prospectus*, Aug. 1, 2004, http://www.baseballprospectus.com/article.php?articleid=3293.

121. Bill Sanderson, "Bat to the Future," *New York Post*, June 15, 2005, 3.

122. Richard Sandomir, "Bronx Is Up as Yanks Unveil Stadium Plan," *New York Times*, June 16, 2005, D1.

123. Charles Bagli, "More Costs to Taxpayers Seen in Stadium Plans," *New York Times*, June 19, 2005, A27.

124. Lynn Zinser, "New York Entering Phase 2 of Its Revised Olympic Bid," *New York Times*, June 14, 2005, D1.

125. Sam Smith and Angela Montefinise, "Playing Toxic Games," *New York Post*, June 19, 2005, 25.

126. Carl Campanile, "Bloomy's Dazzling Olympic Poll Vault," *New York Post*, June 23, 2005, 4.

127. Michael Gormley, "Legislature Works to Put Deals into Law Before Session Ends," Associated Press, June 24, 2005; Kenneth Lovett, "Albany Steps Up to Plate for Yankees," *New York Post*, June 24, 2005, 2.

128. Carl Campanile and Barry Keevins, " 'Looking Good' on Olympic Bid," *New York Post*, July 3, 2005, 22.

129. Mattew Schuerman, "A Frenzied Bid: The Once and Future Queens," *New York Observer*, June 20, 2005, 1.

130. Michael Bloomberg, "How Games Would Polish the Apple," *New York Post*, June 3, 2005, 22.

131. Bill Sanderson, "Yankees' Latest 'Throwback' Pitch," *New York Post*, Nov. 19, 2005, 16.

132. David Lombino, "Carrion to Unveil Plan for Parkland Lost to Yankee Stadium," *New York Sun*, Dec. 12, 2005, 3.

133. Neil deMause, "Bloomberg's Gift Horse," *Village Voice,* Nov. 14, 2005, http://www.villagevoice.com/news/0546,demause,70002,5.html.

134. Saul Michael, "Jets Declare Game Is Over on W. Side Stadium," *New York Daily News,* Aug. 31, 2005, 16.

135. David Saltonstall and Pete Donohue, "New Deal Building Over Railyards," *New York Daily News,* Dec. 6, 2005, 30.

136. Matthew Futterman, "Jets Scout New Sites in Jersey," *Star Ledger,* Nov. 24, 2005, 48.

137. Matthew Futterman, "Stadium Design Agreed On," *Star Ledger,* Nov. 10, 2005, 34.

138. Charles Bagli, "Deal for Meadowlands Stadium Gives Teams Reason to Cheer," *New York Times,* Jan. 20, 2006, B1.

139. Nicholas Confessore, "From Huge Project, A Mighty Anger Grows," *New York Times,* Oct. 20, 2005, B3.

140. Matthew Futterman and Katie Wang, "New Builder Hired for Devils Project, Owner Confident About Latest Move," *Star Ledger,* July 1, 2006, 17.

141. Daniel Eisenberg, "Michael Bloomberg/New York: Reluctant Pol," *Time,* Apr. 25, 2005, 21–22.

142. John Cassidy, "Bloomberg's Game: Why Is the Mayor Risking His First-Term Successes to Build a Football Stadium?" *New Yorker,* Apr. 4, 2004, 56.

143. David Lombino, "New York in Building Boom of Historic Scale," *New York Sun,* Dec. 30, 2005, 1.

144. Barbara DeLollis and Laura Petrecca, "Four Years after 9/11, New York Is Back," *USA Today,* Sept. 9, 2005, 1B.

10. The New Cathedrals as a Reflection of Our Broader Culture

1. Jeff Duncan and Mike Triplett, "Saints Could Play at LSU," *New Orleans Times-Picayune,* Sept. 1, 2005, Web edition, www.nola.com.

2. Brian Allee-Walsh, "Fielkow Is Shown the Door by Benson," *New Orleans Times-Picayune,* Oct. 18, 2005, S1.

3. Gene Maddaus, "Saints Pass on Rose Bowl," *Pasadena Star-News,* Sept. 3, 2005, A3.

4. Sam Farmer, "NFL Reiterates L.A. Not an Option for Saints," *Los Angeles Times,* Sept. 7, 2005, D7.

5. Johannes Schouten, "Move Afoot," *USA Today,* Nov. 11, 2005, 6C.

6. Peter Finney, "For Now, Common Sense Prevails," *New Orleans Times-Picayune,* Dec. 31, 2005, S1.

7. Joe Kollin and Sarah Talalay, "Weston Pair Pitch Stadium with a Twist; Facility Could House Marlins and Evacuees," *South Florida Sun-Sentinel,* Sept. 30, 2005, 1B.

8. Sarah Talalay, "Marlins Get OK to Seek New Home," *South Florida Sun-Sentinel,* Nov. 23, 2005, 1A.

9. Bernie Miklasz, "Owners Cash in, Make Jockety Pinch Pennies," *St. Louis Post-Dispatch,* Dec. 8, 2005, B1.

10. David Nakamura and Thomas Heath. "D.C. to Seek More Money from Baseball Officials," *Washington Post,* Nov. 16, 2005, B4.

11. David Nakamura and Thomas Heath, "Baseball Files for Stadium Arbitration, *Washington Post,* Jan. 5, 2006, B1.

12. Susan Slusser, "A's Park: Dressed Down, Decked Out," *San Francisco Chronicle,* Dec. 22, 2005, D2.

13. Mike Kaszuba, "Pawlenty Steps in for Twins Stadium," *Star-Tribune,* Dec. 28, 2005, 1B.

14. Mike Kaszuba, "Stadium Proposals Jostle for Support," *Star-Tribune,* Sept. 25, 2005, 1B.

15. Sharon Roffers, "Forget the Stadium" (letter to the editor), *Star-Tribune,* Oct. 21, 2005, 22A.

16. Sally Claunch, "Stadium Is Making Progress," *Fort Worth Star-Telegram,* Jan. 1, 2006, B1.

17. "Correction," *Arizona Republic,* Nov. 9, 2005, A2.

18. Anthony Schoettle, "Finally, a New Stadium and Not Just for Football," *Indianapolis Business Journal,* Dec. 26, 2005, 5.

19. Michelle McNeil, "Start the Clock: 3 Years to Goal," *Indianapolis Star,* Sept. 21, 2005, A1.

20. Mark Alesia, "NFL Chief Tackles Colts' Fate," *Indianapolis Star,* Oct. 9, 2002, A1. On March 20, 2006, Tagliabue announced he would step down as league commissioner once his successor was chosen. Roger Goodell took over before the 2006 season began.

21. Nick Wishart, "Arizona Cards Want Super Bowl for Their New Park," *St. Louis Post-Dispatch,* Feb. 9, 2003, C6.

22. Judy Battista, "Kansas City Will Stage the Super Bowl, With One If," *New York Times,* Nov. 17, 2005, D3.

23. "Sports at Lunch, Sept. 13, Jim Steeg," press release, San Diego Chargers Web site, Sept. 6, 2005, www.chargers.com.

24. Ronald Powell, "Time Is Running Out on Chargers, Team Needs Development Partner in Stadium Proposal," *San Diego Union-Tribune,* Jan. 8, 2006, B1.

25. All data come from Heilbrun and Gray, *The Economics of Art and Culture,* 301, 351–52.

26. Eileen McNamara, "This Developer Can't Play Ball," *Boston Globe,* May 19, 1998, B1.

27. Eileen Silberman, "Future of Fenway; Herald Poll—Voters Favor Saving Fenway, Survey Finds Little Support for New Red Sox Ballpark," *Boston Herald,* May 19, 1999, 1.

28. Gary Levin, "World Series Grounds Out," *USA Today,* Nov. 2, 2005, 4D.

29. "The Ratings," *Entertainment Weekly,* Nov. 1, 2002, 61.

30. Barry Horn, "Ratings Are Down 1 Percent," *USA Today,* Feb. 8, 2005, 10C.

31. "CBS Figures Hit Low for NFL Sunday Games," *USA Today,* Nov. 4, 2005, 3C.

32. Jere Longman, "Pro Leagues' Ratings Drop; Nobody Is Quite Sure Why," *New York Times,* July 29, 2001, section 8, 1.

33. Putnam, *Bowling Alone,* 461.

34. Joe Burris, "Baseball Less of a Hit Among Kids in America," *Baltimore Sun,* Apr. 24, 2005, 1A.

35. Ward Harkavy, "Be Like Ike," *Village Voice,* July 25–31, 2001, www.villagevoice.com/news/0130,harkavy,26657,3.html.

36. Mark Hiestand, "NFL Is Pulling Out All the Stops to Ensure Media Put Out Its Extra Points," *USA Today,* Sept. 9, 2004, 7C.

37. Georgett Roberts, "Bronx Kids Get Field of Dreams," *New York Post,* Aug. 9, 2001, 17.

38. Karen DeMasters, "Diamonds Are for Everyone," *New York Times,* Mar. 31, 2002, NJ3. A benefit of this extensive renovation is design oversight to allow for handicapped participation.

39. Kimberly Atkins, "Park Wins State Approval," *Boston Globe,* Aug. 4, 2002, 5.

40. Mitch Frank, "Minor Miracles," *Time,* Aug. 12, 2002, 54–55.

41. Dick Feagler, "More Wrath Than Reason as Modell Explains Move," *Cleveland Plain Dealer,* Aug. 23, 1996, 2A. Modell followed the remark with the statement that "I say that with all due respect to the learning process."

42. Eric Stern, "For the Most Part, Ballpark Plan Isn't a Hit with Legislators," *St. Louis Post-Dispatch,* Sept. 9, 2001, B1.

43. Christopher Carey, "How Much Will This Seat Cost?," *St. Louis Post-Dispatch,* Sept. 29, 2002, A1.

44. Paul White, "Leading Off: What Fans Want in a Ballpark," *USA Today Sports Weekly,* Feb. 12–18, 2003, 14.

45. Michael Steinberger, "Kick a Team When It's Down," *Financial Times,* Feb. 22, 2003, xxii.

46. Craig Timberg, "Business Fee Eyed to Pay for Stadium," *Washington Post,* Feb. 26, 2003, B1.

47. Steve Farinaru, "Portland Expounds on Its Bid for Expos," *Seattle Times,* Jan. 29, 2003, D1.

48. David Nakamura, "Stadium Cost Rises, But Stays Below Cap," *Washington Post,* Mar. 31, 2005, A1.

49. David Nakamura, "D.C. Council Challenges Stadium Report," *Washington Post,* Apr. 7, 2005, A1.

50. Lowe, *The Kid on the Sandlot,* 128–29.

51. Tuchman, *Making News,* 213–14.

52. Richmond, *Ballpark,* 128–43.

53. Pollard, "Evidence of a Reduced Home Field Advantage When a Team Moves Into a New Stadium," 969–73.

54. Richard Sandomir, "Biggest Drop for Attendance in Major Leagues Since the 1995 Season," *New York Times,* Oct. 1, 2002, D3.

55. Chris Jenkins, "Phils May Advance, but Fans in Retreat," *San Diego Union-Tribune,* Sept. 18, 2005, C9.

56. Stepp, "Signs of Progress," 5. The eight-page report was optimistic about the newspaper industry's ability to maintain public trust, with some information that a segment of the public sees levels of accuracy in reporting improving.

57. "High School Stadiums Prove Costly to Fans," *USA Today,* Sept. 15, 2005, 13C.

58. For insight about how those associated with Harvard have worked to affect policy on a grand scale, see Trumpbour, *How Harvard Rules.*

59. President Bush's ballpark campaign was followed by the sale of his $606,000 investment in the Texas Rangers. He was able to secure $14.9 million for this transaction, largely because the new ballpark increased the market value of the team.

BIBLIOGRAPHY

Books and Journal Articles

Abbott, Carl. *Boosters and Businessmen: Popular Economic Thought and Urban Growth in the Antebellum Middle West.* Westport, Conn.: Greenwood Press, 1981.

Bagdikian, Ben. *The Media Monopoly,* 3rd ed. Boston: Beacon Press, 1990.

Bantz, Charles, Suzanne McCorkle, and Roberta Baade. "The News Factory." *Communication Research,* Jan. 1980, 65.

Bederman, Gail. *Manliness and Civilization: A Cultural History of Gender and Race in the United States, 1880–1917.* Chicago: Univ. of Chicago Press, 1995.

Benedict, Jeff, and Don Yeager. *Pros and Cons: The Criminals Who Play in the NFL.* New York: Warner Books, 1998.

Benson, Michael. *Ballparks of North America: A Comprehensive Historical Reference to Baseball Grounds, Yards, and Stadiums, 1845 to Present.* Jefferson, N.C.: McFarland, 1989.

Bercovitch, Sacvan. *The American Jeremiad.* Madison: Univ. of Wisconsin Press, 1978.

Bertagna, Joe. *Crimson in Triumph.* Lexington, Mass.: Stephen Greene Press, 1986.

Boorstin, Daniel. *The Americans.* New York: Vintage Books, 1965.

Bowra, Cecil Maurice. In *The Oxford Classical Dictionary,* 2nd ed. London: Oxford, 1970.

Buege, Bob. *The Milwaukee Braves: A Baseball Eulogy.* Milwaukee: Douglas American Sports Publications, 1988.

Cagan, Joanna, and Neil deMause. *Field of Schemes: How the Great Stadium Swindle Turns Public Money into Private Profit.* Monroe, Maine: Common Courage Press, 1998.

Carlino, Gerald, and N. Edward Coulson. "Compensating Differentials and the Social Benefits of the NFL." *Journal of Urban Economics,* June 2004, 25–50.

Caro, Robert. *Power Broker: Robert Moses and the Fall of New York.* New York: Alfred A. Knopf, 1974.

Carroll, John. *Red Grange and the Rise of Modern Football.* Urbana: Univ. of Illinois Press, 1999.

Cohane, Tim. *The Yale Football Story.* New York: G. P. Putnam, 1951.

Coombs, Samm, and Bob West, eds. *America's National Game: Historic Facts Concerning the Beginning Evoluton, Development, and Popularity of Base Ball, with Personal Reminiscences of Its Vicissitudes, Its Victories, and Its Votaries* by Albert G. Spalding. San Francisco: Halo Books, 1991.

Couvares, Francis. *The Remaking of Pittsburgh: Class and Culture in an Industrializing City.* Albany: State Univ. of New York Press, 1984.

Cressy, David. *Coming Over: Migration and Communication Between England and New England in the Seventeenth Century.* New York: Cambridge Univ. Press, 1987.

Cutlip, Scott. *Fund Raising in the United States: Its Role in America's Philanthropy.* New Brunswick: Rutgers Univ. Press, 1965.

Danielson, Michael. *Home Team: Professional Sports and the American Metropolis.* Princeton: Princeton Univ. Press, 1997.

Delaney, Kevin, and Rick Eckstein. *Public Dollars, Private Stadiums: The Battle Over Building Sports Stadiums.* New Brunswick: Rutgers Univ. Press, 2003.

DeValleria, Dennis, and Jeanne Burke DeValleria. *Honus Wagner.* New York: Henry Holt, 1996.

Duderstadt, James. *Intercollegiate Athletics and the American University: A University President's Perspective.* Ann Arbor: Univ. of Michigan Press, 2000.

Eisinger, Peter. "The Politics of Bread and Circuses: Building a City for the Visitor Class." *Urban Affairs Review,* Jan. 2000, 316–33.

Euchner, Charles. *Playing the Field: Why Sports Teams Move and Cities Fight to Keep Them.* Baltimore: Johns Hopkins Univ. Press, 1993.

Ewen, Stuart. *PR: A Social History of Spin.* New York: Basic Books, 1996.

Fink, Leon. *Major Problems in the Gilded Age and the Progressive Era.* Lexington, Mass.: DC Heath and Company, 1993.

Fowler, Ed. *Loser Takes All: Bud Adams, Bad Football, and Big Business.* Atlanta: Longstreet Press, 1997.

Fox, Larry. *The New England Patriots.* New York: Atheneum, 1979.

Frommer, Harvey. *New York City Baseball: The Last Golden Age, 1947–1957.* Madison: Univ. of Wisconsin Press, 2004.

Gans, Herbert. *The Urban Villagers: Group and Class in the Life of Italian-Americans.* London: Collier Macmillan Publishers, 1982.

Gillette, Gary. *Total Red Sox 2000.* New York: Total Sports Publishing, 2000.

Glasser, Theodore. "Objectivity Precludes Responsibility." *Quill,* Feb. 1984, 16.

Goff, B. L., and R. Tollison. *Sportometrics.* College Station, Tex.: Texas A&M Univ. Press, 1990.

Gorn, Elliott. *The Manly Art of Bare Knuckle Prize Fighting in America.* Ithaca: Cornell Univ. Press, 1986.

Guschov, Stephen. *The Red Stockings of Cincinnati: Base Ball's First All-Professional Team.* Jefferson, N.C.: McFarland and Company, 1998.

Guttmann, Allen. *From Ritual to Record.* New York: Columbia Univ. Press, 1978.

Harris, David. *The League: The Rise and Decline of the NFL.* New York: Bantam, 1986.

Harrison, William B., and Mitchel Peterson. "Alumni Donations and Colleges' Development Expenditures: Does Spending Matter?" *American Journal of Economics and Sociology,* Oct. 1995, 397–413.

Hartel, William. *A Day at the Park: In Celebration of Wrigley Field.* Champaign, Ill.: Sagamore Publishing, 1994.

Heilbrun, James, and Charles M. Gray. *The Economics of Art and Culture,* 2nd ed. New York: Cambridge Univ. Press, 2001.

Hiebert, Ray Eldon, and Sheila Jean Gibbons. *Exploring Mass Media for a Changing World.* Mahwah, N.J.: Lawrence Earlbaum Associates, 1999.

Johnson, William. *Super Spectator and the Electric Lilliputians.* Boston: Sports Illustrated Books, 1971.

Kaese, Harold. *The Boston Braves.* New York: G. P. Putnam's Sons, 1948.

Kimmel, Michael. *Manhood in America.* New York: Free Press, 1996.

Kuklick, Bruce. *To Everything a Season: Shibe Park and Urban Philadelphia.* Princeton: Princeton Univ. Press, 1991.

Laciani, Rudolfo. *The Ruins and Excavations of Ancient Rome.* New York: Benjamin Blom Publishers, 1967.

Lieb, Frederick George. *The Boston Red Sox.* New York: G. P. Putnam, 1947.

Long, Judith Grant. "Full Count: The Real Cost of Public Funding for Major League Sports Facilities." *Journal of Sports Economics* 6, no. 2 (May 2005): 119–43.

Lorant, Stefan. "Rebirth." In *Pittsburgh: The Story of an American City.* Garden City: Doubleday and Company, 1964.

Lowe, Stephen. *The Kid on the Sandlot: Congress and Professional Sports, 1910–1992.* Bowling Green, Ohio: Popular Press, 1995.

Lowry, Philip. *Green Cathedrals.* Reading, Mass.: Addison-Wesley, 1992.

Lubove, Roy. *Twentieth Century Pittsburgh: Government, Business, and Environmental Change.* New York: John Wiley and Sons, 1969.

Lupica, Mike. *Mad as Hell: How Sports Got Away from the Fans and How We Get It Back.* New York: Contemporary Books, 1998.

Maltby, Marc. *The Origins and Early Development of Professional Football.* New York: Garland Publishing, 1997.

Mason, Daniel. "Revenue Sharing and Agency Problems in Professional Team Sport: The Case of the National Football League." *Journal of Sport Management* 11 (1997): 213.

McClellan, Keith. *The Sunday Game: At the Dawn of Professional Football.* Akron: Univ. of Akron Press, 1998.

McKenzie, Michael. *Arrowhead: Home of the Chiefs.* Lexina, Kans.: Addax Publishing, 1997.

Meyer, Stephen. *The Five Dollar Day: Labor Management and Social Control in the Ford Motor Company.* Albany: State Univ. of New York Press, 1981.

Michener, James. *Sports in America.* New York: Random House, 1976.

Molotch, Harvey. "The City as Growth Machine: Toward a Political Economy of Place." *American Journal of Sociology,* 1976, 309–32.

———. "The Political Economy of Growth Machines." *Journal of Urban Affairs* 1 (1993): 29–53.

Montgomery, David. *Worker's Control in America.* New York: Cambridge Univ. Press, 1979.

Morgan, Jon. *Glory for Sale: Fans, Dollars and the New NFL.* Baltimore: Bancroft Press, 1997.

Mrozek, Donald. *Sport and the American Mentality, 1880–1910.* Knoxville: Univ. of Tennessee Press, 1983.

Mumford, Lewis. *The City in History: Its Origins, Its Transformations, and Its Prospects.* New York: Harcourt, Brace and World, 1989.

Murray, Oswyn. *Early Greece.* Stanford: Stanford Univ. Press, 1980.

Noll, Roger, and Andrew Zimbalist, eds. *Sports, Jobs, and Taxes: The Economic Impact of Sports Teams and Stadiums.* Washington, D.C.: Brookings Institution, 1997.

Nowlin, Bill. "The Boston Pilgrims Never Existed." *National Pastime,* Aug. 2003, 71–76.

O'Connor, Thomas. *Building a New Boston: Politics and Urban Renewal, 1950–1970.* Boston: Northeastern Univ. Press, 1993.

Parkins, Helen, ed. *Roman Urbanism: Beyond the Consumer City.* London: Routlege, 1997.

Peterson, Larry, and Liz Barnett, eds. *USA Today: The Complete Four Sport Stadium Guide,* 2nd ed. New York: Random House, 1996.

Peterson, Paul. *City Limits.* Chicago: Univ. of Chicago Press, 1987.

Peterson, Robert. *Pigskin: The Early History of Pro Football.* New York: Oxford Univ. Press, 1997.

Pollard, Richard. "Evidence of a Reduced Home Field Advantage When a Team Moves Into a New Stadium." *Journal of Sports Sciences,* Dec. 2002, 969–73.

Putnam, Robert. *Bowling Alone.* New York: Simon and Schuster, 2000.

Quirk, James, and Rodney Fort. *Hardball: The Abuse of Power in Pro Team Sports.* Princeton: Princeton Univ. Press, 1999.

———. *Pay Dirt: The Business of Professional Team Sports.* Princeton: Princeton Univ. Press, 1992.

Ragin, Charles. *The Comparative Method: Moving Beyond Qualitative and Quantitative Strategies.* Berkeley: Univ. of California Press, 1987.

Rhoads, Thomas, and Shelby Gerking. "Educational Contributions, Academic

Quality, and Athletic Success." *Contemporary Economic Policy,* Apr. 2000, 248–58.

Richmond, Peter. *Ballpark: Camden Yards and the Building of an American Dream.* New York: Simon and Schuster, 1993.

Riess, Steven. *City Games: The Evolution of American Urban Society and the Rise of Sports.* Urbana: Univ. of Illinois Press, 1989.

———. *Touching Base: Professional Baseball and American Culture in the Progressive Era.* Westport, Conn.: Greenwood Press, 1980.

Ritter, Lawrence. *Lost Ballparks: A Celebration of Baseball's Legendary Fields.* New York: Viking Press, 1992.

Roberts, Randy, and James Olson. *Winning Is the Only Thing.* Baltimore: Johns Hopkins Press, 1989.

Robinson, Ray, and Christopher Jennison. *Yankee Stadium: 75 Years of Drama, Glamour, and Glory.* New York: Penguin Putnam, 1998.

Romano, David Gilman. *Athletics and Mathematics in Archaic Corinth: The Origin of the Greek Stadion.* Philadelphia: American Philosophic Society, 1993.

Rosentraub, Mark. *Major League Losers: The Real Cost of Sports and Who's Paying for It.* New York: Basic Books, 1997.

Rosensweig, Daniel. *Retro Ball Parks: Instant History, Baseball, and the New American City.* Knoxville: Univ. of Tennessee Press, 2005.

Sage, George. "Stealing Home: Political, Economic, and Media Power and a Publicly-Funded Baseball Stadium in Denver." *Journal of Sport and Social Issues* 17, no. 2 (1993): 110–24.

Seymour, Harold. *Baseball: The Early Years.* New York: Oxford Univ. Press, 1960.

Shaughnessy, Dan. *At Fenway: Dispatches from Red Sox Nation.* New York: Three Rivers Press, 1996.

Shaughnessy, Dan, and Stan Grossfeld. *Fenway: A Biography in Words and Pictures.* New York: Houghton Mifflin, 1999.

Sheehan, Richard. *Keeping Score: The Economics of Big-Time Sports.* South Bend, Ind.: Diamond Communications, 1996.

Schudson, Michael. "The Culture of News." *Wilson Quarterly,* autumn 1995, 127.

Sigelman, Lee, and Robert Carter. "Win One for the Giver? Alumni Giving and Big-Time College Sports." *Social Science Quarterly* 60, no. 2 (Sept. 1979): 284–93.

Smith, Ronald. *The Ballpark Book: A Journey Through the Fields of Baseball Magic.* St. Louis: Sporting News, 2000.

———.*Sports and Freedom: The Rise of Big-Time College Athletics.* New York: Oxford Univ. Press, 1988.

Smizik,Bob. *The Pittsburgh Pirates: An Illustrated History.* New York: Walker and Company, 1990.

Squires, Gregory, ed. *Unequal Partnerships: The Political Economy of Urban Redevelopment in Urban Postwar America.* New Brunswick: Rutgers Univ. Press, 1989.

Still, Bayrd. *Urban America: A History with Documents.* Boston: Little Brown, 1974.

Stout, Glenn, and Richard Johnson. *Red Sox Century: One Hundred Years of Red Sox Baseball.* New York: Houghton Mifflin Company, 2000.

Strauss, Lawrence. "Does Money Tilt the Playing Field?" *Columbia Journalism Review,* Sept./Oct. 1998, 16–17.

Stupp, Dann. *Opening Day at Great American Ballpark.* Champaign, Ill.: Sports Publishing, 2003.

Sullivan, Neil. *The Diamond in the Bronx: Yankee Stadium and the Politics of New York.* New York: Oxford Univ. Press, 2001.

———. *The Dodgers Move West.* New York: Oxford Univ. Press, 1987.

Tichenor, Phillip, George Donohue, and Clarice Olien. *Community Conflict and the Press.* Beverly Hills: Sage Publications, 1980.

Toma, J. Douglas, and Michael Cross. "Intercollegiate Athletics and Student College Choice: Exploring the Impact of Championship Seasons on Undergraduate Applications." *Research in Higher Education* 39, no. 6 (Dec. 1998): 633–61.

Trumpbour, John, ed. *How Harvard Rules.* Boston: South End Press, 1989.

Tuchman, Gaye. *Making News: A Study in the Construction of Reality.* New York: Free Press, 1978.

Tucker, Louis Leonard. *Cincinnati's Citizen Crusaders: A History of the Cincinnatus Association, 1920–1965.* Cincinnati: Cincinnati Historical Society, 1967.

Veyne, Paul. *A History of Private Life,* vol. 1. *From Pagan Rome to Byzantium.* Cambridge, Mass.: Belknap Press, 1987.

Voigt, David Quentin. *American Baseball: From the Gentleman's Sport to the Commissioner's System,* vol. 1. University Park: Penn State Univ. Press, 1983.

Walker, Robert Harris. *Cincinnati and the Big Red Machine.* Bloomington: Indiana Univ. Press, 1988.

Walvin, James. *Leisure and Society: 1830–1950.* London: Longman, 1978.

Weiner, Jay. *Stadium Games: Fifty Years of Big League Greed and Bush League Boondoggles.* Minneapolis: Univ. of Minnesota Press, 2000.

Wenner, Lawrence, ed. *Media, Sports, and Society.* Newbury Park, Calif.: Sage, 1989.

Westcott, Rich. *Philadelphia's Old Ballparks.* Philadelphia: Temple Univ. Press, 1996.

Wimmer, Roger, and Joseph Dominick. *Mass Media Research,* 4th ed. Belmont, Calif.: Wadsworth Publishing Company, 1994.

Zimbalist, Andrew. *Unpaid Professionals: Commercialism and Conflict in Big Time Sports.* Princeton: Princeton Univ. Press, 1999.

Reports, Public Documents, and Unpublished Materials

Bast, Joseph L. "Sports Stadium Madness: Why It Started, How to Stop It." Heartland Institute Policy Study no. 86, The Heartland Institute, Feb. 23, 1998, executive summary, 3.

Budig, Jeanne. "The Relationship Among Intercollegiate Athletics, Enrollment, and

Voluntary Support for Public Higher Education." Ph.D. diss., Illinois State Univ., 1976.

Chicago Bears. "Lakefron Improvement Plan." Press release, June 11, 2002.

Cincinnati Planning Commission. "The Cincinnati Metropolitan Area Master Plan and the Official Plan." Cincinnati, Nov. 22, 1948.

Committee on the Judiciary, House of Representatives. *Professional Sports Franchise Relocation: Antitrust Implications.* Serial no. 57, publication no. 23-463-CC. Washington, D.C.: U.S. Government Printing Office, Feb. 6, 1996.

Fitch IBCA. "Public Finance—Changing Game of Sports Finance: Economics of Professional Sports and Trends in Sports Finance." New York, internal industry report. Apr. 28, 1999.

Hamilton County Good Government League. *Good Government Bulletin: The Stadium.* 2009 Carew Tower, Cincinnati, vol. 30, no. 1, May 1966, 1–4.

Keating, Raymond. "Sports Pork: The Costly Relationship Between Major League Sports and Government." Washington, D.C.: Cato Institute, Policy Analysis no. 339, Apr. 5, 1999.

Lassiter, Mark. "Little Change in Social Security Solvency: Trustees Recommend Action." Press release. Washington, D.C.: Social Security Administration, 25 Mar. 2005.

Lomax, Michael, and Amy Armond. "The League That Never Was: Politicians, Local Boosters, and the Rise and Fall of the Continental League." Unpublished paper, Twenty-Eighth Annual Convention for the North American Society of Sport History. Banff, Alberta, May 30, 2000.

Los Angeles Memorial Coliseum Commission vs. NFL. 726 F.2d 1381 (9th Cir. 1984); c.d., 105 S. Ct. 397, 1984.

Marichal, Jose Francisco. "Local Politics on the Sports Page: News Assembly and Its Influence on Stadium Development Policy." Master's thesis, Florida Atlantic Univ., 1995.

Pew Research Center for the People and the Press, "Striking the Balance: Audience Interests, Business Pressures and Journalists' Values." Washington, D.C., 1999, 1.

Public Library of Cincinnati and Hamilton County. *America's Love Affair: Baseball, A Bibliography.* Cincinnati: Public Library of Cincinnati and Hamilton County, 1999.

San Diego Chargers. "Sports at Lunch, Sept. 13, Jim Steeg." Press release, Sept 6. 2005.

"Sports Facility Reports." Milwaukee: National Sports Law Institute, Marquette Univ. Law School. Appendixes 1–4, 2000.

Stepp, Carl Sessions. "Signs of Progress." College Park: Md.: American Journalism Review/Ford Foundation, Mar. 2001, 5.

Trumpbour, Robert. "The New Cathedrals: The Sports Stadium and the Media's

Role in Facilitating New Construction." Ph.D. diss., Pennsylvania State Univ., 2001.

Washington Redskins. "Federal Express Announces Stadium Naming Rights in Deal with Washington Redskins." Press release, Nov. 21, 1999.

Newspapers and Periodicals

Altoona Mirror
Asbury Park Press (Neptune, N.J.)
Arizona Republic
Baltimore Sun
Boston Daily Globe
Boston Herald
Boston Phoenix
Boston Sunday Herald
Centre Daily Times (State College, Penn.)
Christian Science Monitor
Cincinnati Enquirer
Cincinnati Magazine
Cincinnati Post
Cincinnati Post and Times Star
Cleveland Plain Dealer
Clinton Chronicle (New York)
Crain's New York Business
Daily Collegian (University Park, Penn.)
Financial Times
Financial World
Forbes
Fort Worth Star-Telegram
Green Bay News-Chronicle
Hartford Courant
Harvard Crimson
Harvard Magazine
Houston Chronicle
Indianapolis Business Journal
Indianapolis Star
Los Angeles Times
Milwaukee Journal-Sentinel
New Orleans Times-Picayune
News Tribune (Tacoma, Wash.)
Newsday
Newsweek

New York Daily News
New Yorker
New York Post
New York Observer
New York Times
New York Tribune
North Hills News Record (Pittsburgh)
Pasadena Star-News
Patriot Ledger (Harrisburg)
Philadelphia Inquirer
Pittsburg Press
Pittsburgh Courier
Pittsburgh Post
Pittsburgh Post-Gazette
Pittsburgh Tribune-Review
Saint Louis Post-Dispatch
San Diego Daily Transcript
San Diego Union-Tribune
San Francisco Chronicle
Seattle Post-Intelligencer
Seattle Times
South Florida Sun-Sentinel
Sporting News
Sports Illustrated
Stadia
Star Tribune (Minneapolis)
Time
USA Today
USA Today Sports Weekly
US News and World Report
Village Voice
Washington Post
Worcester Telegram and Gazette

INDEX